SO-CFA-491

# TEACHING
# THE ART AND SCIENCE
# OF LOGIC

## A MANUAL FOR THE INSTRUCTOR

DANIEL BONEVAC
ANDREW SCHWARTZ

UNIVERSITY OF TEXAS AT AUSTIN

MAYFIELD PUBLISHING COMPANY
MOUNTAIN VIEW, CALIFORNIA
LONDON • TORONTO

Copyright © 1990 by Mayfield Publishing Company

Use of these pages for purposes other than classroom support
of *The Art and Science of Logic,* by Daniel Bonevac, or for
distribution entailing a cost to the instructor or student is
prohibited without the express written permission of Mayfield
Publishing Company.

International Standard Book Number: 87484-966-7

Manufactured in the United States of America

10  9  8  7  6  5  4  3  2  1

Mayfield Publishing Company
1240 Villa Street
Mountain View, California 94041

# CONTENTS

CHAPTER

# 1

# TRUTH AND VALIDITY

This chapter presents the basic notions of logic in the context of a general theory of communication and argument. In particular, it outlines five conditions of good argumentation: evidence, relevance, grounding, truth, and reliability. It then proceeds to discuss the requirements of truth and reliability more extensively. Some instructors may want to postpone treatment of 1.5 and 1.6 until after Chapter 5 or in conjunction with Chapter 6.

## 1. KEY DEFINITIONS

*Extended* arguments contain other arguments; *simple* arguments don't. We'll be so often concerned with simple arguments that we'll drop the adjective 'simple', and speak simply of *arguments*. An *argument* consists of a finite sequence of sentences, called *premises*, together with another sentence, the *conclusion*, which the premises are taken to support.

The *common ground* of a conversation is the set of beliefs, items of knowledge and assumptions that its participants share. There are five conditions that good arguments must fulfill:

1. *Evidence*. The argument's premises must offer evidence in support of the conclusion.
2. *Relevance*. The argument must be relevant to the proper issue.
3. *Grounding*. The argument must employ, as unstated assumptions, only things in the common ground between advocate and audience.
4. *Truth*. The premises and unstated assumptions used in the argument must be true.
5. *Reliability*. The inference from the premises and unstated assumptions to the conclusion must be reliable.

Good arguments meet all five conditions.

An argument is *deductively valid* if and only if it's impossible for its premises all to be true while its conclusion is false. An argument is *sound* if and only if (a) it is valid and (b) all its premises are true. A set of sentences *implies* a sentence if and only if it's impossible for every member of the set to be true while that sentence is false. One sentence *implies* another if and only if it's impossible for the former to be true while the latter is false. One sentence is *equivalent* to another if and only if it's impossible for them to disagree in truth value.

A sentence is *contingent* if and only if it's possible for it to be true and possible for it to be false. A sentence is a *tautology* (or *tautologous*, *valid*, or *logically true*) if and only if it's impossible for it to be false. A sentence is *contradictory* if and only if it's impossible for it to be true. (Otherwise, the sentence is *satisfiable*.)

# 2. ANSWERS TO UNANSWERED EVEN PROBLEMS

## 1.2 RECOGNIZING ARGUMENTS

There is rarely exactly one way to state the premises and conclusion of an argument. Thus the answers given below are not necessarily the only correct ones.

8. Contains a simple argument:
>A man's accusations of himself are always believed.
>A man's praises of himself are never believed.
>∴ A man never speaks of himself without loss.

10. Contains a simple argument:
>There is no happiness that is not idleness.
>Only what is useless is pleasurable.
>∴ Life does not agree with philosophy.

14. Contains a simple argument:
>You can't get eight cats to pull a sled through snow.
>∴ Cats are smarter than dogs.

16. Contains a simple argument:
>No ordinary man could be such a fool as to believe things like that.
>∴ One has to belong to the intelligensia to believe things like that.

20. Contains two simple arguments:
>I'm inside a coffin.
>If I were alive, I would not be inside a coffin.
>∴ I am not alive.
>
>I have to go to the bathroom.
>If I were dead, I would not have to go to the bathroom.
>∴ I am not dead.

22. Contains a simple argument:
>An iron curtain is being drawn down over their (Russia's and Eastern Europe's) front.
>We do not know what lies behind it.
>∴ It is vital that we reach an understanding with Russia now before we have mortally reduced our armies and before we have withdrawn into our zones of occupation.

26. Contains a simple argument:
>Happiness consists in peace of mind.
>Durable peace of mind depends on the confidence we have in the future.
>The confidence we have in the future is based on the science we should have of the nature of God and the soul.
>∴ Science is necessary for true happiness.

28. When you negotiate with people who take hostages you are obliged to give something, maybe just a little or maybe a lot.
Once you have given something, the kidnapper gains from his action.
People who take hostages do so in the belief that it is a way of obtaining what they cannot obtain by other means, and will do it again if they gain from their initial action.

∴ When you negotiate with people who take hostages, they will kidnap again, in the belief that they will gain from their actions.

When you negotiate with people who take hostages, they will kidnap again, in the belief they will gain from their actions.
∴ When you negotiate with people who take hostages, you engage in an extraordinarily dangerous and irresponsible process.

32. Mars' atmosphere, its accessible surface, its probable availability of water and its relatively moderate temperatures make it the most hospitable of all the planets in the solar system other than earth.
∴ Mars will have priority in any manned solar system exploration program.

Mars will have priority in any manned solar system exploration program.
Mars' resources include materials that could be adapted to support human life, including air, fuels, fertilizers, building materials and an environment that could grow food.
∴ Mars would be the next logical niche for human expansion in the universe.

34. Our border patrol apprehends 3,000 illegal immigrants per day, 1.2 million per year.
Two illegal immigrants get in for every one caught.
Those caught just try again.
There has been a 3,000 percent increase in apprehensions since 1965 with only a 50 percent increase in manpower.
∴ Our borders are totally out of control.

Our borders are totally out of control.
400,000 more people fly into the U.S. than fly out every year.
INS believes that 30 percent of the persons granted permanent residence each year on the basis of family ties are making fraudulent claims.
∴ Not just our borders, but our whole immigration apparatus is out of control.

Our borders are totally out of control.
Not just our borders, but our whole immigration apparatus is out of control.
∴ American immigration policies are in a shambles.

38. Current Soviet foreign policy threatens our interests and security.
∴ If we pay for glasnost and perestroika and if Gorbachev's reforms don't irrevocably alter Soviet foreign policy, we will be subsidizing the threat of our own destruction.

If we pay for glasnost and perestroika and if Gorbachev's reforms don't irrevocably alter Soviet foreign policy, we will be subsidizing the threat of our own destruction.
Gorbachev does not want to overturn the Soviet system; he wants to strengthen it.
∴ We should aplaud glasnost and perestroika but not pay for them.

40. If a being, which during its natural lifetime produces several eggs or seeds, did not suffer destruction during some period of its life, and during some season or occasional year, then, on the principle of geometric increase, its numbers would quickly become so inordinately great that no country could support the product.
∴ Every being, which during its natural lifetime produces several eggs or seeds, must suffer destruction during some period of its life, and during some season or occasional year.

3

Every being, which during its natural lifetime produces several eggs or seeds, must suffer destruction during some period of its life, and during some season or occasional year.

∴ There must in the case of beings, which during their natural lifetimes produce several eggs or seeds, be a struggle for existence, either one individual with another of the same species, or with the individuals of distinct species, or with the physical conditions of life.

There must in the case of beings, which during their natural lifetimes produce several eggs or seeds, be a struggle for existence, either one individual with another of the same species, or with the individuals of distinct species, or with the physical conditions of life.

In the case of the animal (humans apart) and vegetable kingdoms, there can be no artificial increase in food and no prudential restraint from marriage.

∴ The doctrine of Malthus applies with manifold force to the whole animal and vegetable kingdoms.

If all species were increasing, more or less rapidly, in numbers, the whole world would not hold them.

∴ All species cannot be increasing in numbers.

We have the preceding sound arguments.

∴ A struggle for existence inevitably follows from the high rate at which all organic beings tend to increase.

44.   The behavior of all bodies obeying natural laws, even when they lack awareness, hardly ever varies, and will practically always turn out well.

∴ All bodies obeying natural laws, even when they lack awareness, truly tend toward a goal, and do not merely hit it by accident.

All bodies obeying natural laws, even when they lack awareness, truly tend toward a goal, and do not merely hit it by accident.

Nothing that lacks awareness tends toward a goal, except under the direction of someone aware and intelligent.

∴ All things in nature are directed toward a goal by someone intelligent, and this we call 'God'.

46.   Some things are found to be more good, true, and noble, and other things less.

'More' and 'less' describe varying degrees of approximating the maximum.

∴ Something is the best and truest and noblest of things.

Something is the best and truest and noblest of things.

The truest things exist to the highest degree.

∴ Something is the best and truest and noblest of things, and exists to the highest degree.

Something is the best and truest and noblest of things, and exists to the highest degree.

When many things have a common property, the one having it most fully causes the others to have it.

∴ Something causes all other things to be, to be good, and to have any other perfections, and this we call 'God'.

## 1.4  RELIABILITY

| 8. | valid | 10. | valid | 14. | valid | 16. | valid |
|----|-------|-----|-------|-----|-------|-----|-------|
| 20. | valid | | | | | | |

## 1.5 Implication and Equivalence

| | | | | | |
|---|---|---|---|---|---|
| 8. | no implications | 10. | (b) implies (a) | 14. | no implications |
| 16. | equivalent | 20. | (a) implies (b) | 22. | (a) implies (b) |
| 26. | equivalent (but this is somewhat controversial) | | 28. | equivalent | |
| 32. | Nothing relevant. | 34. | Ralph won't fail the final exam. | | |
| 38. | The patient will die. | 40. | no | | |
| 44. | both follows from and implies | 46. | both follows from and implies | | |
| 50. | neither follows from nor implies | 52. | neither follows from nor implies | | |
| 56. | You must file a return. | | | | |
| 58. | You did not have gross income of $3, 560 or more for the year. | | | | |

62.   At least two views seem defensible. (1) They are equivalent. Both say that no words are both vain and real. (2) The first says that a typical real word isn't vain; the second, that a typical vain word isn't real. These are not equivalent. The former could be true and the latter false, for example, if the vain words form a very small subset of the real words.

## 1.6 Logical Properties of Sentences

| | | | | | |
|---|---|---|---|---|---|
| 8. | contradictory | 10. | contingent | 14. | contingent |
| 16. | tautologous | 20. | tautologous | 22. | tautologous |
| 26. | contradictory | 28. | tautologous | 32. | tautologous |
| 34. | tautologous | 38. | tautologous | | |

40.   contingent (This might seem to be valid; but suppose that everyone divides the world into two kinds of people.)

44.   true: what follows from something will be true whenever that something is true; thus, what follows from the true must be true.

46.   true: let S be a sentence that follows from the conclusion of some valid argument; we want to show that whenever the premises of the argument are true, S is true. So, suppose the premises are true. Then (by the definition of "valid") the conclusion is true. Hence (by the definition of "follow from") S is true.

50.   true: let C be a contradictory sentence and let S be any sentence whatsoever. Since it is impossible for C to be true, it is impossible for C to be true while S is false--and this is just what it means for S to follow from C.

52.   true: equivalent sentences are sentences that agree in truth value in all circumstances. Two tautologies always agree in truth value, since a tautology is true in all circumstances.

56.   no (insofar as the first sentence of the invitation was part of the request)

58.   yes

62.   Usually, when 'it' is used to refer deicticly (as in pointing), it refers to something distinct from the speaker (simply because 'I' is available for this); in fact, to something that is not a person (simply because 'he' and 'she' are available for this). An instance of 'It is I' in which 'it' occurs deicticly is an exception. In an anaphoric use, agreement with the antecedent may dictate that 'it' is the most natural pronoun to use even when it refers (ultimately) to the speaker: eg., 'An unexpected factor will upset many pundit's predictions about this election, and it is I.'

64.   Because 'lost' and 'missing' mean the same thing, the sentences 'The child is lost' and 'The child is missing' are equivalent (when 'the child' is taken as referring to the same person in both sentences).

68.   Punch is a knight and Judy is a knave.

70.   Punch is a knight and Judy is a knave.

74.   Punch is a knave and Judy is a knight.

76.   Punch is a knave.

80.   Curly and Larry are knights; Moe is a knave.

82.   'Bald' is vague. A man with no hair at all is plainly bald. Add one hair, and he remains bald. Add one more, and he is still bald. But, after enough hairs have been

added, it becomes somewhat unclear whether he should be called 'bald'. Eventually, of course, he becomes plainly not bald.

86.     The paradox plays on an equivocal use of the phrase 'all of Socrates'. When taken in the sense of 'each proper part of Socrates', the sentence (1) 'All of Socrates is smaller than Socrates' is true; but from this it does not follow that Socrates is smaller than himself. The latter does follow from (1) when 'all of Socrates' is understood in the sense of 'Socrates as a whole'. But (1) so understood is false.

88.     Examining the three possibilities: i) The sentence (1) 'This sentence is not true' is true. This means that what it says about itself is right; so it is not true. Thus alternative i) can be ruled out as leading to contradiction. ii) (1) is false. This means that what it says about itself is incorrect. It says it's not true, so it must be true. We already ruled out this alternative; hence we must rule out ii) as well. iii) (1) is neither true nor false. From this it follows that (1) is not true. This is just what (1) says, though. So, it is true. Again, we must rule out iii) as contradictory.

92.     Suppose the barber shaves himself. Then he wouldn't shave only those people who do not shave themselves. So, suppose the barber does not shave himself, but someone else does. Then the barber wouldn't shave all of the villagers who do not shave themselves.

94.     Suppose 'heterological' is heterological. Then it applies to itself. But from the definition of 'heterological' and the fact that 'heterological' is heterological it follows that 'heterological' doesn't apply to itself. Contradiction. So, suppose 'heterological' is not heterological. Then 'heterological' doesn't apply to itself. But, from the definition of 'heterological', if a term doesn't apply to itself, it is heterological. So 'heterological' is heterological. Contradiction.

6

# EVIDENCE AND RELEVANCE

This chapter discusses two conditions on good arguments:
1. *Evidence.* The premises must offer evidence for the conclusion.
2. *Relevance.* The argument must be relevant to the proper issue.
We can think of the common ground as the starting point of an argument, and a new common ground incorporating the argument's conclusion as its endpoint. A successful argument moves the audience from the starting point to the endpoint. It changes the common ground.

Two aspects of the common ground are important in this chapter. First, relative to the common ground, some sentences are more evident--better known--than others. The evidence condition implies that the premises of a successful argument should be more evident than the conclusion. Second, in an argumentative context, the common ground specifies the issue to be addressed. The relevance condition requires that arguments address that issue.

This chapter discusses a variety of traditional fallacies that result from violations of the conditions of evidence and relevance. Such an approach, which has firm roots in treatments of fallacies by such authors as Aristotle, Arnauld, and Whately, has important advantages. As often explained, for example, it is hard to see why question-begging arguments are fallacious; they are, by definition, valid. According to this chapter's account, they violate the evidence condition. Question-begging arguments cannot be good arguments, therefore, even if they are valid. The account of this chapter relies on two ideas developed in contemporary research in pragmatics: presupposition and accommodation.

## 1. KEY DEFINITIONS

A set of sentences S *presupposes* a sentence A if and only if anyone felicitously asserting S must take A for granted. A question *presupposes* a sentence if and only if the question can't be answered unless the sentence is true.

Fallacies of evidence: An argument *begs the question* if and only if the premises include or presuppose the conclusion. A question is *complex* if and only if it has presuppositions.

Fallacies of relevance: An argument is an *abusive ad hominem* argument if and only if it purports to discredit a position by insulting those who hold it; a *circumstantial ad hominem* argument if and only if it purports to discredit a position by appealing to the circumstances or characteristics of those who hold it; and *tu quoque* if and only if it purports to discredit a position by charging those who hold it with inconsistency or hypocrisy.

An argument is a *red herring* if and only if it tries to justify a conclusion irrelevant to the issue at hand. An argument *erects a straw man* if and only if it tries to justify rejecting a position by attacking a different, and usually weaker, position.

# 2. Answers to Unanswered Even Problems

## 2.1 Begging the Question

8. Federico and Del Rio exist; Federico was in Del Rio around midnight.
10. Hank exists and has a female dog.
14. France exists.
16. France exists.
20. We absconded, but Ben didn't realize it; Ben exists.
22. Begs the question; the conclusion restates the premise.
26. Does not beg the question. The premise presupposes that Mindy is married, but not that Nick knows it.
28. Begs the question.

## 2.2 Complex Questions

8. You've been stealing candy from babies.
10. You've had a beer already.
14. Little children are intelligent and men are stupid.
16. (a) Reconstruction was either shamefully harsh or surprisingly lenient.
    (b) Johnson failed.
    (c) Johnson was either a miserable bungler or a heroic victim.
    (d) The freedman had new responsibilities.
    (e) Racial segregation hardened into an elaborate mold.

## 2.3 Relevance: Refutations

8. Although this attacks the opponents' moral character, it's probably not an ad hominem abusive. Beatty is not arguing against aid by calling those who voted for it contemptible; he is saying that it is contemptible to vote for aid for the reasons they did. I think Beatty assumes that aid is bad and argues for the conclusion that the vote was contemptible.
10. Clearly an ad hominem (and, perhaps, an *ad piscem*).
14. This is tu quoque, despite the disavowal. But it may be a good argument that the Tower debate is an exercise in hypocrisy.
16. An ad hominem, probably abusive, although the abuse is not articulated. Smith dismisses what is said because of who said it.

## 2.4 Relevance: Confusing the Issue

8. This appears to be a red herring. What's the relevance of any of these to the others?
10. This seems to involve a straw man. The evidence adduced shows that women occupy few positions of power in the industry, but does not establish that the system locks women out.

# GROUNDING

An argument tries to justify adding its conclusion to the common ground. Ordinarily, arguments rely extensively on the common ground; many assertions needed to derive the conclusion are not stated but assumed. There is no need to say what the advocate and audience both already accept. In fact, there's a strong presumption in favor of not saying it. Statements reiterating what is already in the common ground, under normal circumstances, don't convey any new information.

The condition of grounding requires that, to be successful, an argument must assume only what's available in the common ground. The unstated assumptions required to derive the argument's conclusion must be shared between advocate and audience for the argument to succeed.

This chapter examines some kinds of argument that violate the grounding condition by assuming things similar to, but not equivalent to, frequent common ground inhabitants. Of course, any argument making an assumption that's illegitimate in its context violates the grounding condition. But all the fallacies presented in this chapter have a common structure: They single out a single factor present in the common ground and treat it as the only relevant factor.

## 1. KEY DEFINITIONS

An argument commits a fallacy of *misapplication* if and only if it tries to justify its conclusion about a particular case by appealing to a rule that is generally sound but inapplicable or outweighed by other considerations in that case.

The common ground usually contains a rule like "Follow your emotions, other things being equal." An argument is an *appeal to the people* (or *to the gallery*) if and only if it tries to justify its conclusion by appealing to the audience's emotions.

*Practical reasoning* aims at a conclusion about what ought to be done. Practical arguments always conclude with a sentence evaluating an action or kind of action.

An argument *appeals to common practice* if and only if it tries to justify a kind of action by appealing to the common practice of the community. Appeals to common practice have the form

> X is common practice. (All, or most, or many people do X.)
> ∴ X is acceptable (or obligatory).

An argument *appeals to force* if and only if it tries to justify a kind of action by threatening the audience.

> If A does X, A will suffer.
> ∴ A shouldn't do X.

An argument *appeals to pity* if and only if it tries to justify a kind of action by arousing sympathy or pity in the audience over the consequences of the action. Appeals to pity try to play on our altruism by presenting an argument having one of these forms:

> A's doing X will harm B.
> ∴ A shouldn't do X.
> A's doing Y will help B.

∴ A should do Y.

An argument *appeals to ignorance* if and only if it tries to justify its conclusion by appealing to what is not known.

An argument *appeals to authority* if and only if it tries to justify its conclusion by citing the opinions of authorities. Appeals to authority thus have the form

A says P.
∴ P.

An argument commits the fallacy of *incomplete enumeration* if and only if it presupposes a disjunction that does not include all available possibilities. An argument commits the fallacy of *accident* if and only if it tries to justify its conclusion by treating an accidental feature of something as essential.

# 2. ANSWERS TO UNANSWERED EVEN PROBLEMS

### 3.1 APPEALS TO EMOTION

8.  (a) usurpation, holy, false monk, confusion, curse, honor, blessing, dared, the Lord's anointed, scorned, abused, ignorant servants not fit to know what their master was doing, vulgar crowd. (b) Henry, king, to Hildebrand, pope. You have never held any office in the Church without causing problems. To mention only the most obvious cases out of many, you have seized and insulted the archbishops, bishops, and priests. This you have done to gain popular support. (c) Henry, king, to Hildebrand, pope. You have never held any office in the Church without instituting changes and displaying creativity, rather than paying homage to the powerful. To mention only the most obvious cases out of many, you have dared to take away the corrupted power of the archbishops, bishops, and priests. This you have done to satisfy the demands of the people.

10. (a) idyllic, pitilessly torn asunder, naked self-interest, callous "cash payment" (b) The bourgeoisie, wherever it has got the upper hand, has put an end to all feudal, patriarchal, traditional relations. It has changed the motley feudal ties that bound man to his "natural superiors," and has left remaining no other nexus between man and man than economics. (c) The bourgeoisie, wherever it has got the upper hand, has put an end to all feudal, patriarchal, antiquated, and oppressive relations. It has liberated all from the motley feudal ties that bound man to his "natural superiors," and has left remaining no other nexus between man and man than the pursuit of happiness and prosperity.

### 3.2 PRACTICAL FALLACIES

8.  This argument combines an appeal to pity ("serious heart problems," "has suffered") with a more legitimate argument that she could do more good on the outside than in prison.

10. Here Increase Mather reasonably accuses others of an illegitimate appeal to authority. Probably nobody, even "Good men," can be authoritative in moral questions.

### 3.3 SUPERFICIALITY

8.  This is surely an appeal to ignorance. Because we have no evidence of subversive activity, that is, are ignorant, the argument concludes that there is very carefully concealed subversive activity.

10. A fallacy of accident. An object's physical size is accidental to its cosmic significance.

16.     Proper: Hurrying through a task makes for a sloppy job. Improper: Overnight mail is wasteful.
20.     Proper: People have romantic images of their hometowns. Improper: Divorce strengthens love.
22.     Proper: Eating more can make a meal less enjoyable. Improper: Getting a raise is a bummer.
26.     Proper: Don't pass up a good job offer on just the chance that something better might come along. Improper: The job you have is OK, even if you aren't very happy with it; don't bother trying for something better.
28.     Proper: The most energetic workers are the most productive. Improper: Never get to a restaurant after 6 o'clock.

# CHAPTER
4

# MEANING

This chapter discusses problems of miscommunication arising from confusion over meanings. It also presents the traditional theory of definition as a way of avoiding such problems.

## 1. KEY DEFINITIONS

An argument is guilty of *equivocation* if and only if it tries to justify its conclusion by relying on an ambiguity in a word or phrase. Some sentences are ambiguous, not because they contain ambiguous words or phrases, but because of their grammatical construction. Such sentences are *syntactically ambiguous*; they can be read in two different ways, because they have two different syntactic or grammatical structures. An argument is guilty of *amphiboly* if and only if it tries to justify its conclusion by relying on such an ambiguity in sentence structure. A special kind of ambiguity, *referential ambiguity*, results from the indeterminacy of the reference of pronouns or other anaphoric devices.

An argument is guilty of *accent* if and only if it tries to justify its conclusion by relying on presuppositions arising from a change in stress in a premise. The fallacy of *composition* consists in attributing something to a whole or group because it can be attributed to the parts or members. The fallacy of *division* involves arguing from the properties of a group or whole to the properties of members or parts.

The *goals* of definition:

1. *Description.* Most definitions try to describe the meaning of a term as it is commonly used. Descriptive definitions are called *lexical*, because they are the kind of definition given in dictionaries or lexicons.
2. *Stipulation.* Stipulative definitions introduce new expressions into discourse, assigning meanings to terms without regard to their ordinary use.
3. *Precision.* Clarifying definitions try to remain close to the meaning of a term in natural language, but also to make that meaning more precise, or more useful for a particular purpose. These definitions are helpful in resolving two kinds of problems: vagueness and ambiguity.
4. *Persuasion.* Persuasive definitions explain the meaning of a term, but contentiously; they try to convey not only the meaning but a certain attitude as well.

The *means* of definition:

1. *Ostension.* Ostensive definitions clarify the meaning of a term by pointing to examples of things to which it applies.
2. *Listing.* Some definitions specify the meanings of words by listing things to which the word applies. Definitions by ostension and by listing are *denotative* definitions: they explain the meanings of terms by listing or pointing to part or all of their denotations.

12

3. *Synonymy.* Synonymous definitions give a synonym for the word being defined.
4. *Analysis.* Analytical definitions try to explain the meaning of a term by indicating what the things to which it applies have in common. Aristotelian logicians refer to such definitions as definitions *per genus et differentiae*, definitions "by genus and difference."

Rules of definition:
1. A definition must state the essential attributes of the kind.
2. A definition must not be circular.
3. A definition must not be negative when it can be positive.
4. A definition must not use ambiguous, obscure, or figurative language.

# 2. Answers to Unanswered Even Problems

## 4.1 Equivocation

8. bass: a kind of fish; singer with a low range; fiddle or guitar that plays low notes.
10. dance: *v.* move rhythmically to music; move rapidly (e.g., bees); *n.* rhythmic movement; kind or style of such movement; one round of such movement; a party for such movement; a piece of music to accompany such movement.
14. ham: smoked pork; show-off.
16. jog: run slowly; nudge; revive.
20. narrow: *adj.* small in width; limited in extent; limited in outlook; thorough; with limited margin; *n.* a narrow part or place; a narrow passage.
22. pin: *n.* small piece of metal with pointed end; small peg of wood or metal; an ornament attaching to clothing; bottle-shaped clubs in bowling; pole with flag to mark holes in golf; rod for holding bone together; *v.* pierce or fasten with a pin; hold firmly in place; give fraternity pin to.
26. tip: *n.* pointed end; something attached to the end; tilt; light, sharp blow; suggestion; gratuity; *v.* strike lightly and sharply; give small present of money for service; overturn, tilt; raise slightly.
28. view: *n.* range of sight; mental examination; scene; visual appearance or aspect; opinion; *v.* inspect; behold; consider; regard.

## 4.2 Amphiboly

8. Nothing is better than liberty. Prison life is better than nothing. So, prison life is better than liberty.
10. Not to give to charity is selfish. To pay the rent is not to give to charity. So, to pay the rent is selfish.
14. Food is necessary to life. Sauerkraut is food. So, sauerkraut is necessary to life.
16. The animal is the one type of sentient being. The wolf is an animal. So, the wolf is the one type of sentient being.
20. Amphiboly: 'drunk as usual at midnight' may modify 'toast', 'champagne', or 'the retiring president'.
22. Equivocation: 'seats' as 'chairs' or 'derrieres'.
26. Columbia, Tenn., which calls itself the largest outdoor mule market in the world, held a mule parade yesterday, headed by the governor. (Jefferson City, Missouri, paper)
28. Equivocation: 'The area in which Miss Ford was injured' may mean 'area of the countryside' or 'area of the body'.
32. Amphiboly: "Austria-Hungary soccer match" as the match between Austria and Hungary, or as the match between Austria-Hungary and someone else.

34. Warhol is complaining about miscommunication. His famous statement is ambiguous: in the future, each person will be famous for 15 minutes (which he intended), or, in the future, there will be 15 minutes when everyone in the world is famous.

38. Equivocation: 'Virgins' as 'Virgin Islands' or 'maidens'. To correct: add 'Islands'.

40. Amphiboly: [Jury gets drunk] [(while) driving case here] or [Jury gets [(a) drunk driving case] here] or even [Jury gets [(a) drunk] [(who was) driving case here]]. To correct: supply hyphen (Jury gets drunk-driving case here).

44. This is not ambiguous, but the headline suggests two very different roles, one economic, the other procreative.

46. Amphiboly: "failing to stop" at what? To correct: supply prepositional phrase like 'at stop sign'.

50. Amphiboly: 'wildcat strike' as a kind of strike or as a strike by wildcats. To correct: use synonym for 'wildcat', such as 'unauthorized'.

52. Equivocation: 'dope' as 'information' or 'stupid person'. To correct: substitute 'story', 'rundown', etc.

56. Equivocation: 'printers' as 'printing machines' or 'persons running printing machines'. To correct: substitute 'printing machines'.

58. Amphiboly: as "[First], run if you haven't seen it" or "[First run], if you haven't seen it." The latter is bizarre, for two reasons: (a) this is the movie's first run whether or not you've seen it before, and (b) if this is its first run, how could you have seen it before?

## 4.3 ACCENT

4.  a. Someone else bet on the Seahawks last time.
    b. Larry had some other relation to the Seahawks last time.
    c. Larry bet on someone else last time.
    d. Larry didn't bet on the Seahawks other times.

## 4.4 COMPOSITION AND DIVISION

8. In addition to other problems (e.g., are the Libertarians I know typical?), this exhibits a fallacy of composition. The group might be extreme even though its members aren't.

10. The first premise is ambiguous. If it means that the typical linguist has the property of being usually clever, the argument is good. More likely, however, it speaks of linguists as a group, and means somthing like "most linguists are clever." In that case, the argument exhibits a fallacy of division.

14. Composition.

16. Division.

20. Composition.

22. This is hard to understand because it provides two conflicting orderings to follow: line up alphabetically, and line up by height. Probably, Mr. Berra meant for the players to line up from shortest to tallest, or vice versa.

## 4.5 TRADITIONAL CRITERIA FOR DEFINITIONS

8. (a) description, analysis. (b) changed; now, too narrow. Compliments are no longer assumed to be insincere.

10. (a) description and persuasion, analysis. (b) unchanged.

14. (a) description, analysis. (b) unchanged.

16. (a) description, synonymy. (b) changed; now, too broad. Not all gibberish is jargon, in contemporary English. But jargon is unintelligible talk to most, though it is presumed to be intelligible to the specialist.

20. (a) description, synonymy. (b) unchanged, but now in common use.

22. (a) description, synonymy. (b) unchanged.

26.    (a) description, synonymy and analysis. (b) changed; the scalp is now the skin on the top and back of the head.

28.    (a) description, synonymy. (b) unchanged, in its primary use, though the word has another, broader sense of *untidy* or *ungroomed.*

30.    (a) description, analysis. (b) unchanged.

# CHAPTER
# 5

# SENTENCES

## 1. KEY DEFINITIONS

A *compound* sentence contains other sentences, which are its *components*. Words that link sentences together to form compounds are *sentence connectives*. An n-*ary sentence connective* is a word or phrase that forms a single, compound sentence from *n* component sentences. An *n*-ary sentence connective is *truth-functional* if and only if the truth values of the n component sentences always completely determine the truth value of the compound sentence formed by the connective.

The *syntax* of a language consists of its vocabulary and grammar. The vocabulary consists of the meaningful signs of the language. The grammar of a language specifies how to put the meaningful signs of the language together to form sentences, or, in symbolic languages, *formulas*. The *semantics* of a language is its theory of meaning.

### Vocabulary of SL

| | |
|---|---|
| Sentence letters: | lower case letters, with or without numerical subscripts |
| Connectives: | ¬ & ∨ → ↔ |
| Grouping Indicators: | ( ) |

### Formation Rules of SL:

1. Any sentence letter is a formula.
2. If $\mathcal{A}$ is a formula, then $\neg\mathcal{A}$ is a formula.
3. If $\mathcal{A}$ and $\mathcal{B}$ are formulas, then $(\mathcal{A}\ \&\ \mathcal{B})$, $(\mathcal{A} \lor \mathcal{B})$, $(\mathcal{A} \to \mathcal{B})$, and $(\mathcal{A} \leftrightarrow \mathcal{B})$ are formulas.
4. Every formula can be constructed by a finite number of applications of these rules.

A formula is *atomic* if and only if it contains no connectives. Any formula appearing at any node of a tree charting the construction of a formula is a *subformula* of the formula at the top of the tree. The *scope* of a connective occurrence in a formula is the connective occurrence itself, together with the subformulas (and any grouping indicators) it links. The *main connective* of a formula is the connective occurrence in the formula with the largest scope. The main connective is always the connective occurrence having the entire formula as its scope.

An n-*ary truth function* is a function taking *n* truth values as inputs and producing a truth value as output.

Basic truth functions of SL:

Negation

| $\mathcal{A}$ | $\neg\mathcal{A}$ |
|---|---|
| T | F |
| F | T |

Conjunction

| $\mathcal{A}$ | $\mathcal{B}$ | $(\mathcal{A}\ \&\ \mathcal{B})$ |
|---|---|---|
| T | T | T |
| T | F | F |
| F | T | F |
| F | F | F |

Conditional

| $\mathcal{A}$ | $\mathcal{B}$ | $(\mathcal{A} \to \mathcal{B})$ |
|---|---|---|
| T | T | T |
| T | F | F |
| F | T | T |
| F | F | T |

| Biconditional | $\mathcal{A}$ | $\mathcal{B}$ | $(\mathcal{A} \leftrightarrow \mathcal{B})$ |
|---|---|---|---|
| | T | T | T |
| | T | F | F |
| | F | T | F |
| | F | F | T |

| Disjunction | $\mathcal{A}$ | $\mathcal{B}$ | $(\mathcal{A} \vee \mathcal{B})$ |
|---|---|---|---|
| | T | T | T |
| | T | F | T |
| | F | T | T |
| | F | F | F |

Any set of truth functions that, like $\{\neg, \&\}$, $\{\neg, \vee\}$, and $\{\neg, \rightarrow\}$, allows us to define every other truth function is *functionally complete.*

To symbolize a discourse in SL,

1. Identify sentence connectives; replace them with symbolic connectives.
2. Identify the smallest sentential components of the sentences, and replace each distinct component with a distinct sentence letter. (A record of which sentence letter symbolizes which sentence component is called a *dictionary.*)
3. Use the structure of the sentence to determine grouping.

The goal of symbolization is to devise a formula that is true exactly when the corresponding sentence is true, and false exactly when that sentence is false.

An *argument form* consists of a finite sequence of formulas, called its *premise formulas*, together with another formula, its *conclusion formula.* An *interpretation* of a sentence letter is an assignment of a truth value to it. An *interpretation* of a formula of SL is an assignment of truth values to its sentence letters. An *interpretation* of an argument form or set of formulas in SL is an assignment of truth values to all the sentence letters in the argument form or set.

A formula is
*valid*    if and only if it's true on every interpretation of it.
*contradictory*    if and only if it's false on every interpretation of it
*satisfiable*    if and only if it's true on at least one interpretation of it
*contingent*    if and only if it's neither valid nor contradictory.

An argument form is *valid* if and only if there is no interpretation of it making its premise formulas all true and its conclusion formula false. A set of formulas S *implies* a formula A if and only if there is no interpretation of S together with A making every member of S true but A false. Two formulas are *equivalent* if and only if they agree in truth value on every interpretation of them.

# 2. ANSWERS TO UNANSWERED EVEN PROBLEMS

## 5.1 SENTENCE CONNECTIVES

8. Not truth-functional. 'May' is ambiguous; in one sense, it conveys permission; in another, possibility. They have slightly different characteristics.

| $\mathcal{A}$ | May $\mathcal{A}$ (possibility) |  | $\mathcal{A}$ | May $\mathcal{A}$ (permission) |
|---|---|---|---|---|
| T | T | | T | T or F |
| F | T or F | | F | T or F |

10. Not truth-functional.

| $\mathcal{A}$ | Could $\mathcal{A}$ |
|---|---|
| T | T |
| F | T or F |

14. Not truth-functional.

| $\mathcal{A}$ | Allegedly $\mathcal{A}$ |
|---|---|
| T | T or F |
| F | T or F |

16. Not truth-functional. 'When' seems to have different logical characteristics, depending on the verbs in the sentences in joins. 'John laughed when Mary did her

Amy Carter impersonation' implies that two events occurred at the same time (or, at least, overlapped), while 'John laughs when he feels uncomfortable' implies that, on every occasion in which he feels uncomfortable, John laughs. A table for the former is on the left.

| $\mathcal{A}$ | $\mathcal{B}$ | $\mathcal{A}$ when $\mathcal{B}$ | | $\mathcal{A}$ | $\mathcal{B}$ | $\mathcal{A}$ when $\mathcal{B}$ |
|---|---|---|---|---|---|---|
| T | T | T or F | | T | T | T or F |
| T | F | F | | T | F | T or F |
| F | T | F | | F | T | F |
| F | F | F | | F | F | T or F |

20.   Not truth-functional.

| $\mathcal{A}$ | it's necessarily true that $\mathcal{A}$ |
|---|---|
| T | T or F |
| F | F |

22.   Not truth-functional.

| $\mathcal{A}$ | $\mathcal{B}$ | $\mathcal{A}$ in spite of $\mathcal{B}$ |
|---|---|---|
| T | T | T or F |
| T | F | F |
| F | T | F |
| F | F | F |

## 5.2 A SENTENTIAL LANGUAGE

8.   a; ∨
10.   b; →
14.   c
16.   c
20.   c
22.   c

## 5.3 TRUTH FUNCTIONS

8.   'If a man sits down to think, he is immediately asked if he has a headache.' This sentence contains two occurrences of 'if'. The second is not a sentence connective at all; it is equivalent to 'whether'. The first differs from the conditional truth function in several ways: (a) if it's false that a man sits down to think, the sentence doesn't become automatically true; (b) it seems impossible to assign the consequent an independent truth value-- who is "he"? This sentence requires predicate logic for an adequate symbolization. See Chapters 10 and 11.

10.   'Lajoie chews Red Devil tobacco. Ask him if he don't.' 'If' is not acting as a sentence connective; it's equivalent to 'whether'.

## 5.4 SYMBOLIZATION

| | | | | |
|---|---|---|---|---|
| 8. | ¬(s ∨ f) & p | | 34. | n → d; w → e |
| 10. | p & g | | 38. | ¬m; c |
| 14. | ¬w ∨ k | | 40. | d & (e → s) |
| 16. | ¬a & s | | 44. | ((e & a) & p) → ¬w |
| 20. | ¬(b ∨ f) | | 46. | a & ¬g |
| 22. | c & ¬v | | 50. | ¬k → r |
| 26. | t → (s ∨ l) | | 52. | p & (¬d & c) |
| 28. | ¬g; t & h | | 56. | ¬b → i |
| 32. | f & ¬s | | 58. | ¬s & e |

## 5.5 VALIDITY

8.   True. Suppose $\mathcal{A}$ is valid and implies $\mathcal{B}$. Then $\mathcal{A}$ is true on every interpretation of it. Moreover, $\mathcal{B}$ is true on every interpretation of the two formulas making $\mathcal{A}$ true. So, on every interpretation of $\mathcal{B}$, $\mathcal{B}$ is true. So, any formula that follows from a valid formula is valid.

10.     True. Suppose 𝒜 and 𝐵 are both contradictory. Then all interpretations of them make them false. Thus, on no interpretation is one true while the other is false. So, all contradictory formulas imply one another.
14.     False. Every contradictory formula implies its own negation.
16.     True. Suppose ¬𝒜 implies 𝒜. Then any interpretation of 𝒜 making ¬𝒜 true would make 𝒜 true too. But no interpretation makes both 𝒜 and ¬𝒜 true. So, there are no interpretations making ¬𝒜 true, that is, making 𝒜 false. So, 𝒜 is valid. Therefore, any formula implied by its own negation is valid.
20.     T       22.     T       26.     T       28.     F
32.     (a) tautology; (b) nothing; (c) contradictory; (d) tautology; (e) nothing; (f) nothing.
34.     (a) contradictory; (b) tautology; (c) tautology; (d) tautology; (e) tautology; (f) tautology.
38.     (a) 𝒜 and 𝐵 aren't both contradictory; (b) both 𝒜 and 𝐵 are contradictory; (c) 𝒜 and 𝐵 aren't both contradictory; neither is a tautology.
40.     (a) 𝒜 and 𝐵 have the same logical property; (b) nothing; (c) 𝒜 and 𝐵 aren't both tautologies; nor are they both contradictions.

19

# TRUTH TABLES

## 1. KEY DEFINITIONS

A *truth table* is a computation of the truth value of a formula or set of formulas under each of its possible interpretations. A truth table for a formula consists of four elements:

(1) a list of the formula's sentence letters
(2) the formula itself
(3) a list of the formula's possible interpretations
and (4) a computation of the formula's truth value on each interpretation.

Truth tables have this form:

| Sentence letters | Formula |
|---|---|
| List of Interpretations | Computation |

To compute the truth value of a formula under each interpretation of it,

1. Copy the interpretations of each sentence letter under its occurrences in the formula;
2. Compute the values of negations of single sentence letters;
3. Compute values of subformulas, working from inside parentheses out.

The *main column* of a truth table is the column under the main connective of the formula at the top of the table.

| Main Column | Formula |
|---|---|
| All Ts | Tautologous (Logically true) |
| All Fs | Contradictory |
| Ts and Fs | Contingent |

To evaluate an argument form, set up a single table that computes values for each of the premise formulas, and the conclusion formula, separately:

(1) list the sentence letters appearing in the argument form;
(2) beneath them, list all possible interpretations of them;
(3) list each premise formula, and then the conclusion formula, as column heads;
and (4) compute the value of each formula.

An argument form is valid just in case no interpretation makes the premise formulas all true but the conclusion formula false.

To find out whether a set of formulas $\{\mathcal{A}_1, \ldots, \mathcal{A}_n\}$ implies a formula $\mathcal{B}$, construct a table for the corresponding-argument form. Equivalence is implication in both directions.

Truth tables constitute a *decision procedure* for validity in SL: a mechanical method for determining, within a finite time, whether any given argument form is or isn't valid.

## 2. ANSWERS TO UNANSWERED EVEN PROBLEMS

### 6.1 TRUTH TABLES FOR FORMULAS

8.  
| p q | ¬(¬p → q) |
|---|---|
| T T | F F T T T |

10.  
| p q | q → (q → p) |
|---|---|
| T T | T T T T T |

TF  **F** F T T F         TF  F **T** F T T
FT  **F** T F T T         FT  T **F** T F F
FF  **T** T F F F         FF  F **T** F T F

14.
| p | (¬p → p) ↔ ¬p |
|---|---|
| T | F T T T **F** F T |
| F | T F F F **F** T F |

16.
| p q | ¬p → (q → p) |
|---|---|
| T T | F T **T** T T T |
| T F | F T **T** F T T |
| F T | T F **F** T F F |
| F F | T F **T** F T F |

20.
| p q | (p → q) ∨ (q → p) |
|---|---|
| T T | T T T **T** T T T |
| T F | T F F **T** F T T |
| F T | F T T **T** T F F |
| F F | F T F **T** F T F |

22.
| p q | (p → q) & ¬(q → p) |
|---|---|
| T T | T T T **F** F T T T |
| T F | T F F **F** F F T T |
| F T | F T T **T** T T F F |
| F F | F T F **F** F F T F |

26.
| p q | (p → q) → (p & q) |
|---|---|
| T T | T T T **T** T T T |
| T F | T F F **T** T F F |
| F T | F T T **F** F F T |
| F F | F T F **F** F F F |

28.
| p q | (p & q) → (p ∨ q) |
|---|---|
| T T | T T T **T** T T T |
| T F | T F F **T** T T F |
| F T | F F T **T** F T T |
| F F | F F F **T** F F F |

32.
| p q | ((p & ¬q) → q) → ¬p |
|---|---|
| T T | T F F T T T **F** F T |
| T F | T T T F F F **T** F T |
| F T | F F F T T T **T** T F |
| F F | F F T F T F **T** T F |

34.
| p q | (p ∨ q) ↔ ¬(¬p & ¬q) |
|---|---|
| T T | T T T **T** T F T F F T |
| T F | T T F **T** T F T F T F |
| F T | F T T **T** T T F F F T |
| F F | F F F **T** F T F T T F |

38.
| p q | p ↔ ((p → ¬q) & (p → ¬¬q)) |
|---|---|
| T T | T **F** T F F T F T T T F T |
| T F | T **F** T T T F F T F F T F |
| F T | F **F** F T F T T F T T F T |
| F F | F **F** F T T F T F T F T F |

40.
| p q r | (q ∨ r) → ((p → q) ∨ (p → r)) |
|---|---|
| T T T | T T T **T** T T T T T T T |
| T T F | T T F **T** T T T T T F F |
| T F T | F T T **T** T F F T T T T |
| T F F | F F F **T** T F F F T F F |
| F T T | T T T **T** F T T T F T T |
| F T F | T T F **T** F T T T F T F |
| F F T | F T T **T** F T F T F T T |
| F F F | F F F **T** F T F T F T F |

44.
| p q r | (p & (q ∨ r)) ↔ ((p & q) ∨ (p & r)) |
|---|---|
| T T T | T T T T T **T** T T T T T T T |
| T T F | T T T T F **T** T T T T T F F |
| T F T | T T F T T **T** T F F T T T T |
| T F F | T F F F F **T** T F F F T F F |
| F T T | F F T T T **T** F F T F F T F |
| F T F | F F T T F **T** F F T F F T F |
| F F T | F F F T T **T** F F F F F T F |
| F F F | F F F F F **T** F F F F F F F |

46.
| p q r | (p → (q ∨ r)) ↔ ((p → q) ∨ (p → r)) |
|---|---|
| T T T | T T T T T **T** T T T T T T T |
| T T F | T T T T F **T** T T T T T F F |
| T F T | T T F T T **T** T F F T T T T |
| T F F | T F F F F **T** T F F F T F F |
| F T T | F T T T T **T** F T T T F T T |
| F T F | F T T T F **T** F T T T F T F |
| F F T | F T F T T **T** F T F T F T T |
| F F F | F T F F F **T** F T F T F T F |

50.

| p q r | ¬(p ↔ ¬(q → r)) ↔ ¬(¬(p ↔ q) → ¬(p ↔ r)) |
|---|---|
| T T T | T T F FTTT **F**F FTTT T FTTT |
| T T F | FT T TTFF **T**F FTTT T TTFF |
| T F T | T T F FFTT **T T** TTFF F FTTT |
| T F F | T T F FFTF **F**F TTFF T TTFF |
| F T T | FF T FTTT **T**F TFFT T TFFT |
| F T F | TF F TTFF **T T** TFFT F FFTF |
| F F T | FF T FFTT **T**F FFTF T TFFT |
| F F F | FF T FFTF **T**F FFTF T FFTF |

## 6.2 OTHER USES OF TRUTH TABLES

8.
p → q
¬p
∴ ¬q
invalid

| p q | p → q | ¬p | ¬q |
|---|---|---|---|
| T T | T T T | F T | F T |
| T F | T F F | F T | T F |
| F T | F T T | T F | F T |
| F F | F T F | T F | T F |

10.
p → q
p
∴ q
valid

| p q | p → q | p | q |
|---|---|---|---|
| T T | T T T | T | T |
| T F | T F F | T | F |
| F T | F T T | F | T |
| F F | F T F | F | F |

14.
¬(p & q)
¬q → r
r → ¬p
∴ ¬p

valid

| p q r | ¬(p & q) | ¬q → r | r → ¬p | ¬p |
|---|---|---|---|---|
| T T T | F T T T | F T T T | T F F T | F T |
| T T F | F T T T | F T T F | F T F T | F T |
| T F T | T T F F | T F T T | T F F T | F T |
| T F F | T T F F | T F F F | F T F T | F T |
| F T T | T F F T | F T T T | T T T F | T F |
| F T F | T F F T | F T T F | F T T F | T F |
| F F T | T F F F | T F T T | T T T F | T F |
| F F F | T F F F | T F F F | F T T F | T F |

16.
p
q ↔ ¬r
p → ¬r
∴ s ∨ q

valid

| p q r s | p | q ↔ ¬r | p → ¬r | s ∨ q |
|---|---|---|---|---|
| T T T T | T | T F F T | T F F T | T T T |
| T T T F | T | T F F T | T F F T | F T T |
| T T F T | T | T T T F | T T T F | T T T |
| T T F F | T | T T T F | T T T F | F T T |
| T F T T | T | F T F T | T F F T | T T F |
| T F T F | T | F T F T | T F F T | F F F |
| T F F T | T | F F T F | T T T F | T T F |
| T F F F | T | F F T F | T T T F | F F F |
| F T T T | F | T F F T | F T F T | T T T |
| F T T F | F | T F F T | F T F T | F T T |
| F T F T | F | T T T F | F T T F | T T T |
| F T F F | F | T T T F | F T T F | F T T |
| F F T T | F | F T F T | F T F T | T T F |
| F F T F | F | F T F T | F T F T | F F F |
| F F F T | F | F F T F | F T T F | T T F |
| F F F F | F | F F T F | F T T F | F F F |

20.
p ∨ ¬p
p → p
¬p → p
∴ p

valid

| p | p ∨ ¬p | p → p | ¬p → p | p |
|---|---|---|---|---|
| T | T T F T | T T T | F T T T | T |
| F | F T T F | F T F | T F F F | F |

22.
p → q
¬q
∴ ¬p

valid

| p q | p → q | ¬q | ¬p |
|---|---|---|---|
| T T | T T T | F T | F T |
| T F | T F F | T F | F T |
| F T | F T T | F T | T F |
| F F | F T F | T F | T F |

26.
p q
¬(p & q)
¬p
∴ q

invalid

| p q | ¬(p & q) | ¬p | q |
|---|---|---|---|
| T T | F T T T | F T | T |
| T F | T T F F | F T | F |
| F T | T F F T | T F | T |
| F F | T F F F | T F | F |

22

**28.**

| p q r | (p & q) → r | ¬r | p | ¬q |
|---|---|---|---|---|
| T T T | T T T  T T | F T | T | F T |
| T T F | T T T  F F | T F | T | F T |
| T F T | T F F  T T | F T | T | T F |
| T F F | T F F  T F | T F | T | T F |
| F T T | F F T  T T | F T | F | F T |
| F T F | F F T  T F | T F | F | F T |
| F F T | F F F  T T | F T | F | T F |
| F F F | F F F  T F | T F | F | T F |

valid

**32.**

| p q | ¬(q ∨ p) | ¬q ∨ ¬p |
|---|---|---|
| T T | F T T T | F T F F T |
| T F | F F T T | T F T F T |
| F T | F T T F | F T T T F |
| F F | T F F F | T F T T F |

¬(q ∨ p) implies ¬q ∨ ¬p

**34.**

| p q | ¬(q → p) | ¬q → ¬p |
|---|---|---|
| T T | F T T T | F T T F T |
| T F | F F T T | T F F F T |
| F T | T T F F | F T T T F |
| F F | F F T F | T F T T F |

¬(q → p) implies ¬q → ¬p

**38.**

| p q | ¬(q & p) | ¬q ∨ ¬p |
|---|---|---|
| T T | F T T T | F T F F T |
| T F | T F F T | T F T F T |
| F T | T T F F | F T T T F |
| F F | T F F F | T F T T F |

equivalent

**40.**

| p q | q & p | (q ∨ p) & (q ↔ p) |
|---|---|---|
| T T | T T T | T T T  T  T T T |
| T F | F F T | F T T  F  F F T |
| F T | T F F | T T F  F  T F F |
| F F | F F F | F F F  F  F T F |

equivalent

**44.**

| p q | q ∨ p | ¬p → q |
|---|---|---|
| T T | T T T | F T T T |
| T F | F T T | F T T F |
| F T | T T F | T F T T |
| F F | F F F | T F F F |

equivalent

**46.**

| p q | q → p | p ↔ (q ∨ p) |
|---|---|---|
| T T | T T T | T T  T T T |
| T F | F T T | T T  F T T |
| F T | T F F | F F  T T F |
| F F | F T F | F T  F F F |

equivalent

**50.**

| p q | q ↔ p | (q ↔ p) ↔ q |
|---|---|---|
| T T | T T T | T T T  T T |
| T F | F F T | F F T  T F |
| F T | T F F | T F F  F T |
| F F | F T F | F T F  F F |

neither implies the other

**52.**

| p r | ¬(r → p) | r → ¬p | yes |
|---|---|---|---|
| T T | F T T T | T F F T | |
| T F | F F T T | F T F T | |
| F T | T T F F | T T T F | |
| F F | F F T F | F T T F | |

**56.**

| p q r | p ↔ (r → (p ∨ ¬q)) | ¬(r → (p ∨ q)) | ¬q | yes |
|---|---|---|---|---|
| T T T | T T  T T  T T F T | F T T  T T T | F T | |
| T T F | T T  F T  T T F T | F F T  T T T | F T | |
| T F T | T T  T T  T T T F | F T T  T T F | T F | |
| T F F | T T  F T  T T T F | F F T  T T F | T F | |
| F T T | F T  T F  F F F T | F T T  F T T | F T | |
| F T F | F F  F T  F F F T | F F T  F T T | F T | |
| F F T | F F  T T  F T T F | T T F  F F F | T F | |
| F F F | F F  F T  F T T F | F F T  F F F | T F | |

**58.**

| p q r | ¬(r → (p & ¬q)) | r ∨ (p & ¬q) | q & ¬(r ∨ p) | no |
|---|---|---|---|---|
| T T T | T T F  T F F T | T T  T F F T | T F  F T T T | |
| T T F | F F T  T F F T | F F  T F F T | T F  F F T T | |
| T F T | F T T  T T T F | T T  T T T F | F F  F T T T | |
| T F F | F F T  T T T F | F T  T T T F | F F  F F T T | |

```
FTT   T TF FFFT   TT FFFT   TF FTTF
FTF   F FT FFFT   FF FFFT   TT TFFF
FFT   T TF FFTF   TT FFTF   FF FTTF
FFF   F FT FFTF   FF FFTF   FF TFFF
```

62.

| p q r | p → (r ∨ q) | r → (q & ¬p) | ¬q → ¬(p & r) | yes |
|---|---|---|---|---|
| T T T | T T T T T | T F T F F T | F T T F T T T | |
| T T F | T T F T T | F T T F F T | F T T T T F F | |
| T F T | T T T T F | T F F F F T | T F F F T T T | |
| T F F | T F F F F | F T F F F T | T F T T T F F | |
| F T T | F T T T T | T T T T T F | F T T T F F T | |
| F T F | F T F T T | F T T T T F | F T T T F F F | |
| F F T | F T T T F | T F F F T F | T F T T F F T | |
| F F F | F T F F F | F T F F T F | T F T T F F F | |

64.

| p q r | r ∨ (p ∨ (¬r & q)) | ¬((r & ¬p) → (q ∨ r)) | ¬(¬r ↔ ¬q) | yes |
|---|---|---|---|---|
| T T T | T T T T F T F T | F T F F T T T T T | F F T T F T | |
| T T F | F T T T T F T T | F F F F T T T T F | T T F F F T | |
| T F T | T T T T F T F F | F T F F T T F T T | T F T F T F | |
| T F F | F T T T T F F F | F F F F T T F F F | F T F T T F | |
| F T T | T T F F F T F T | F T T T F T T T T | F F T T F T | |
| F T F | F T F T T F T T | F F F T F T T T F | T T F F F T | |
| F F T | T T F F F T F F | F T T T F T F T T | T F T F T F | |
| F F F | F F F F T F F F | F F F T F T F F F | F T F T T F | |

68.

| p q | p & q | p ↔ q |
|---|---|---|
| T T | T T T | T T T |
| T F | T F F | T F F |
| F T | F F T | F F T |
| F F | F F F | F T F |

70.

| p q | ¬p | p → q |
|---|---|---|
| T T | F T | T T T |
| T F | F T | T F F |
| F T | T F | F T T |
| F F | T F | F T F |

74.

| p q | ¬(p & q) | (p → ¬q) ↔ ¬(p → q) | no |
|---|---|---|---|
| T T | F T T T | T F F T T F T T T | |
| T F | T T F F | T T T F T T T F F | |
| F T | T F F T | F T F T F F F T T | |
| F F | T F F F | F T T F F F F T F | |

# SEMANTIC TABLEAUX

This chapter presents a system of semantic tableaux, tree-like decision procedures for validity and other logical properties in sentential logic. Semantic tableau descend from Gentzen's consecution calculi, by way of Beth's tableau system. They share the virtues of Jeffrey's truth trees and, in addition, have the subformula property: At each stage of tableau construction, a formula is decomposed into its subformulas.

## 1. KEY DEFINITIONS

*Semantic tableaux* are tree-like diagrams that serve as tests for validity, implication, contradictoriness, etc. Tableaux are trees with labels. At the top of each is its *root*, at the bottom are its *tips*, or *leaves*. A path going directly from the root to a leaf is a *branch*. Trees with more than one branch *split* where the paths diverge. A tableau has exactly as many branches as leaves. The portion of a tree above any splitting is its *trunk*.

A *semantic tableau* is a tree with formulas appearing on it. A formula may appear on either the left side or the right side of a branch. Any formula on the trunk of a tableau appears on every branch. Formulas marked with a *dispatch mark*, √, may be ignored, because we've already taken account of the information they provide. Dispatched formulas are *dead*; undispatched formulas are *live*.

Branches that have the same formula appearing live on both sides are *closed*. Tableaux with all their branches closed are also *closed*. A *tableau branch is closed* if and only if the same formula appears live on both sides of it. Otherwise, the branch is *open*. A *tableau is closed* if and only if every branch of it is closed. Otherwise, it is *open*. A tableau is *finished* if and only if (1) it is closed, or (2) only atomic formulas are live on it.

## 2. SUMMARY OF RULES

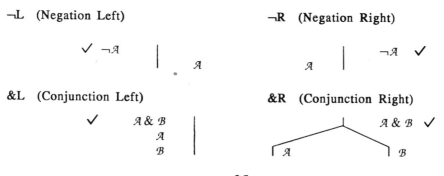

¬L  (Negation Left)

√ ¬𝒜 | 𝒜

¬R  (Negation Right)

𝒜 | ¬𝒜 √

&L  (Conjunction Left)

√ 𝒜 & ℬ
𝒜
ℬ

&R  (Conjunction Right)

𝒜 & ℬ √
𝒜      ℬ

**∨L   (Disjunction Left)**

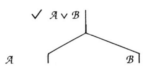

**∨R   (Disjunction Right)**

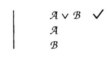

**→L   (Conditional Left)**

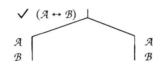

**→R   (Conditional Right)**

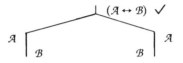

**↔L   (Biconditional Left)**

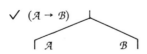

**↔R   (Biconditional Right)**

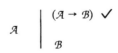

## 3.   STRATEGY

**Policies**

(1)   Always write the new formula at the bottom of the branch, underneath all the formulas already appearing there.

(2)   When applying a rule to a formula, make the entries it calls for on every branch on which that formula appears.

(3)   Apply rules that don't require any splitting before those that do.

(4)   Abandon branches as soon as they close, marking them with the notation 'Cl' to indicate why.

**Test for Argument Form Validity (and Implication)**

Closes: Valid (Argument Form); Implied (Implication)
Open: Invalid (Argument Form); Not Implied (Implication)

**Test for Equivalence**

Closes: 𝒜 implies ℬ       Closes: ℬ implies 𝒜
   Both Close: 𝒜 and ℬ equivalent

**Test for Logical Truth**

| 𝒜

Closes: Tautology
Open: Contingent or
   Contradictory

26

𝓐 |

Closes: Contradictory
Open: Satisfiable

# 4. ANSWERS TO UNANSWERED EVEN PROBLEMS

4.  (1) Left: T: p, r; F: p & r.  Right: T: r; F: r, p & r.  (2) Left: open; Right: closed. Tableau is open.  (3) unfinished.
6.  (1, 2) From the left: a: T: p, q; F: p, r; closed. b: T: q; F: p, q, r; closed. c: T: p, q, r; F: r; closed. d: T: q; F: p, r, q; closed. Tableau is closed. (3) finished.
8.  (1, 2) From the left: a: T: p, r, q; F: s, r, q; closed. b: T: p, r, q, s; F: s, q; closed. c: T: p, r, q; F: r, s; closed. d: T: p, r, q, s; F: s; closed. Tableau is closed. (3) finished.
10.  (1, 2) From the left: a: F: m, p, r, s; open. b: F: m, p; open. c: T: s, q; F: m, r, s; closed. d: T: s, q; F: m, p; open. Tableau is open. (3) finished.

## 7.1 RULES FOR NEGATION, CONJUNCTION AND DISJUNCTION

8.

10.

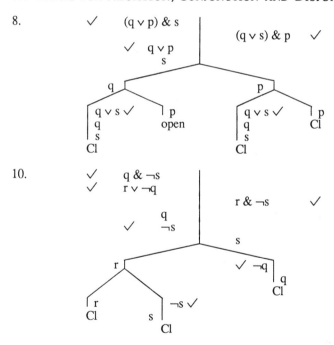

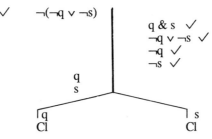

16.

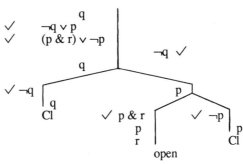

20.

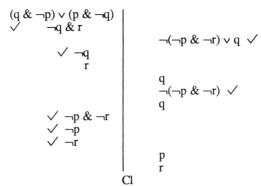

## 7.2 RULES FOR THE CONDITIONAL AND BICONDITIONAL

8.

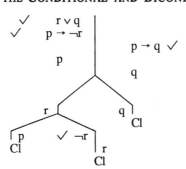

28

10.

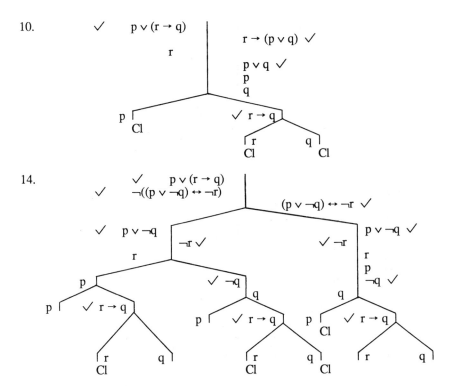

14.

Three interpretations: (1) T: p, r, q; (2) T: p, r, F: q; (3) T: q; F: p, r

20.

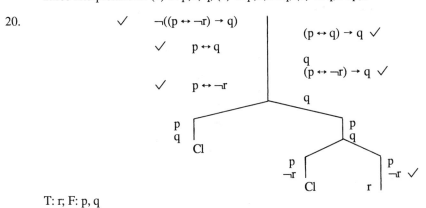

T: r; F: p, q

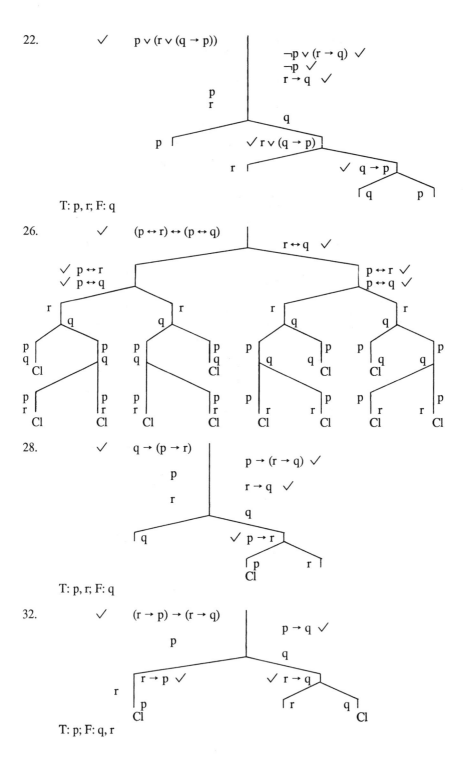

34.           (p → r) ∨ (p → q)

               p

               r

               Cl

                     p → (r ∨ (r → q)) ✓

                     r ∨ (r → q) ✓

                     r

                     r → q ✓

                     q

## 7.3 DECISION PROCEDURES

8.

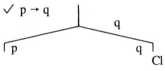

10.

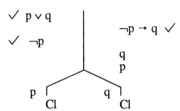

14.

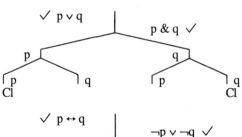

16.

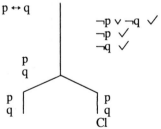

20.

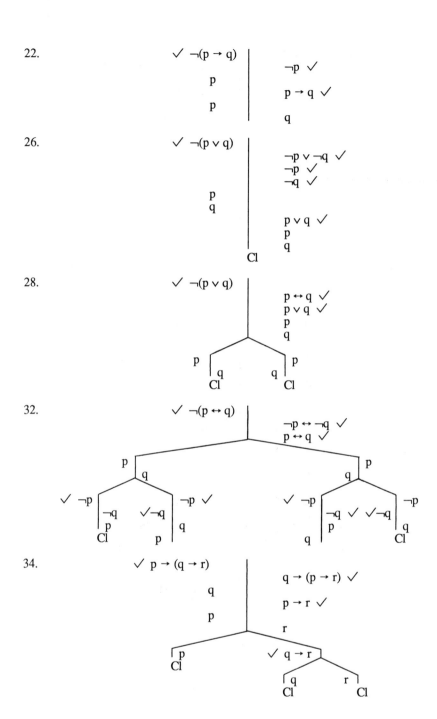

22.

$\checkmark$ ¬(p → q)

p

p

¬p $\checkmark$

p → q $\checkmark$

q

26.

$\checkmark$ ¬(p ∨ q)

p
q

¬p ∨ ¬q $\checkmark$
¬p $\checkmark$
¬q $\checkmark$

p ∨ q $\checkmark$
p
q

Cl

28.

$\checkmark$ ¬(p ∨ q)

p ↔ q $\checkmark$
p ∨ q $\checkmark$
p
q

p
q
Cl

q
p
Cl

32.

$\checkmark$ ¬(p ↔ q)

¬p ↔ ¬q $\checkmark$
p ↔ q $\checkmark$

p
q

¬p $\checkmark$
¬q
p
Cl

$\checkmark$¬q
p

¬p $\checkmark$
q

q
p

$\checkmark$ ¬p
q

¬q $\checkmark$
p

$\checkmark$¬q
q
Cl

¬p
q

34.

$\checkmark$ p → (q → r)

q

p

q → (p → r) $\checkmark$

p → r $\checkmark$

r

p
Cl

$\checkmark$ q → r

q
Cl

r
Cl

38.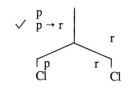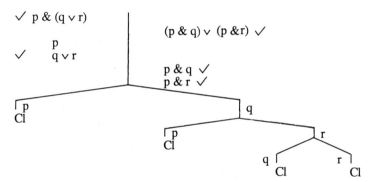

40. Valid

44. Valid

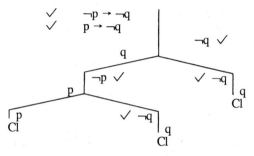

46. Valid

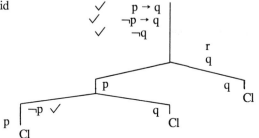

33

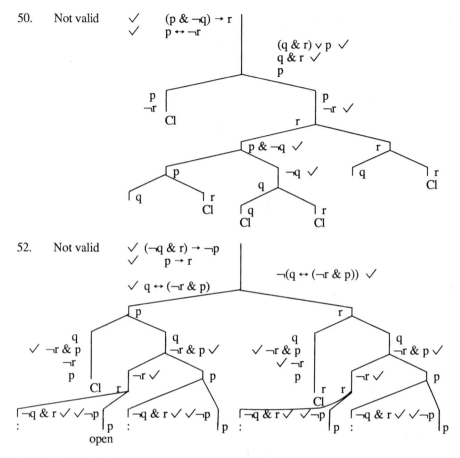

50. Not valid ✓ (p & ¬q) → r
    ✓ p ↔ ¬r

    (q & r) ∨ p ✓
    q & r ✓
    p

52. Not valid ✓ (¬q & r) → ¬p
    ✓ p → r
    ✓ q ↔ (¬r & p)

    ¬(q ↔ (¬r & p)) ✓

54. Not valid, but too long to display here.

34

56. Valid

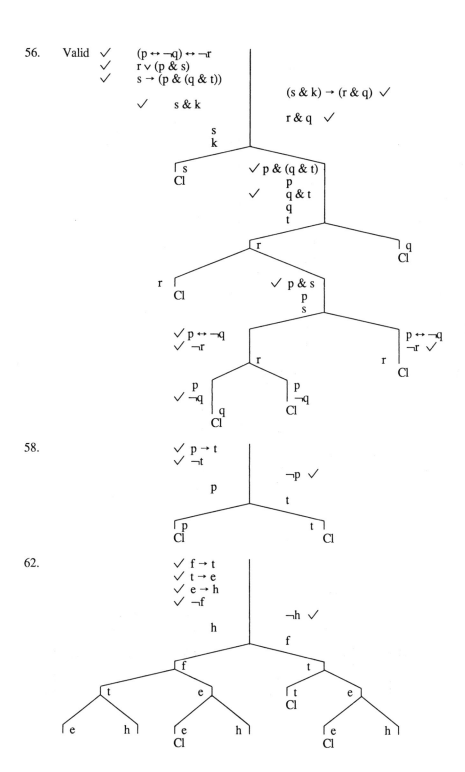

58.

62.

35

64.

68.

70.

74.

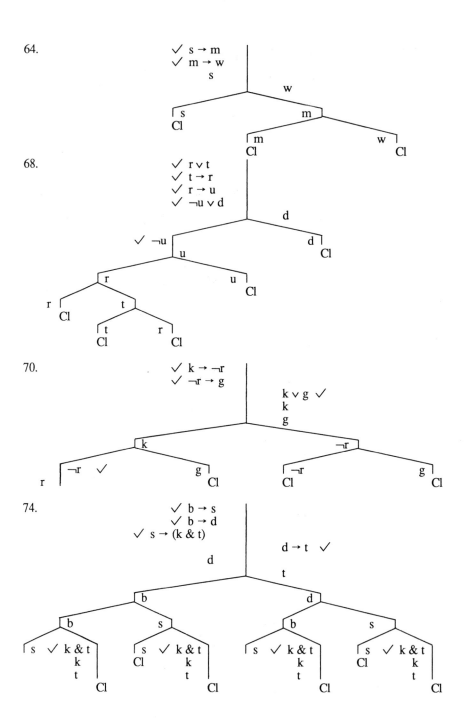

**76.**

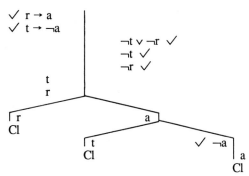

```
✓ r → a
✓ t → ¬a
                    ¬t ∨ ¬r  ✓
                    ¬t  ✓
                    ¬r  ✓
        t
        r
    r                           a
    Cl
            t                        ✓ ¬a      a
            Cl                                 Cl
```

**80.**

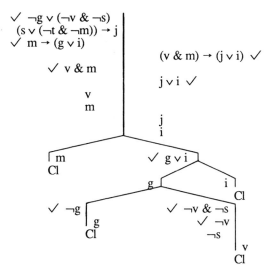

```
✓ ¬g ∨ (¬v & ¬s)
  (s ∨ (¬t & ¬m)) → j
✓ m → (g ∨ i)
                            (v & m) → (j ∨ i)  ✓

    ✓ v & m
                            j ∨ i  ✓
        v
        m
                                j
                                i
        m               ✓ g ∨ i
        Cl
                    g                   i
    ✓ ¬g                                Cl
            g       ✓ ¬v & ¬s
            Cl      ✓ ¬v
                        ¬s
                                v
                                Cl
```

**82.**

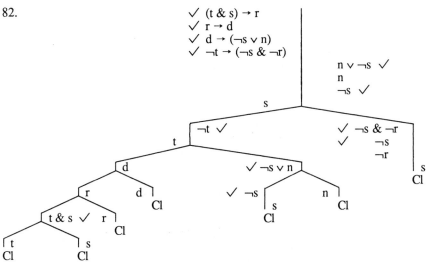

```
✓ (t & s) → r
✓ r → d
✓ d → (¬s ∨ n)
✓ ¬t → (¬s & ¬r)
                            n ∨ ¬s  ✓
                            n
                            ¬s  ✓
                s
        ¬t  ✓                   ✓ ¬s & ¬r
    t                           ✓   ¬s
    d               ✓ ¬s ∨ n        ¬r
    r       d                               s
    Cl      ✓ ¬s         s              Cl
t & s ✓  r   Cl         n   Cl
t      s    Cl
Cl     Cl
```

86.

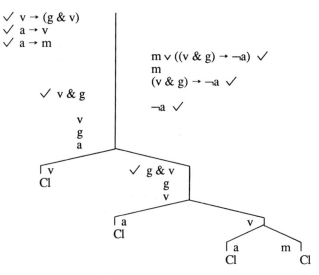

$$\checkmark\ v \to (g \& v)$$
$$\checkmark\ a \to v$$
$$\checkmark\ a \to m$$

$$m \lor ((v \& g) \to \neg a)\ \checkmark$$
$$m$$
$$(v \& g) \to \neg a\ \checkmark$$

$$\checkmark\ v \& g$$

$$\neg a\ \checkmark$$

$$v$$
$$g$$
$$a$$

$$v \qquad\qquad \checkmark\ g \& v$$
$$Cl \qquad\qquad\qquad g$$
$$v$$

$$a \qquad\qquad\qquad\qquad v$$
$$Cl$$

$$a \qquad\qquad m$$
$$Cl \qquad\qquad Cl$$

88.

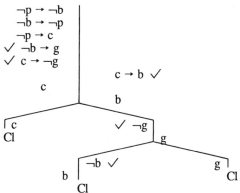

$$\neg p \to \neg b$$
$$\neg b \to \neg p$$
$$\neg p \to c$$
$$\checkmark\ \neg b \to g$$
$$\checkmark\ c \to \neg g$$

$$c \to b\ \checkmark$$
$$c$$
$$b$$

$$c \qquad\qquad \checkmark\ \neg g$$
$$Cl \qquad\qquad\qquad\qquad g$$

$$\neg b\ \checkmark \qquad\qquad g$$
$$b \qquad\qquad\qquad\qquad\qquad Cl$$
$$Cl$$

90.  (i) (d): no

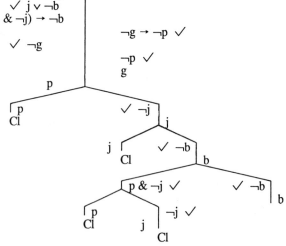

$$\checkmark\ p \to \neg j$$
$$\checkmark\ j \lor \neg b$$
$$\checkmark\ (p \& \neg j) \to \neg b$$

$$\neg g \to \neg p\ \checkmark$$

$$\checkmark\ \neg g$$

$$\neg p\ \checkmark$$
$$g$$

$$p$$

$$p \qquad\qquad \checkmark\ \neg j$$
$$Cl \qquad\qquad\qquad\qquad j$$

$$j \qquad \checkmark\ \neg b$$
$$Cl \qquad\qquad\qquad b$$

$$p \& \neg j\ \checkmark \qquad\qquad \checkmark\ \neg b$$
$$\qquad\qquad\qquad\qquad b$$

$$p \qquad \neg j\ \checkmark$$
$$Cl \qquad j$$
$$\qquad\quad Cl$$

38

(i)    (c): yes

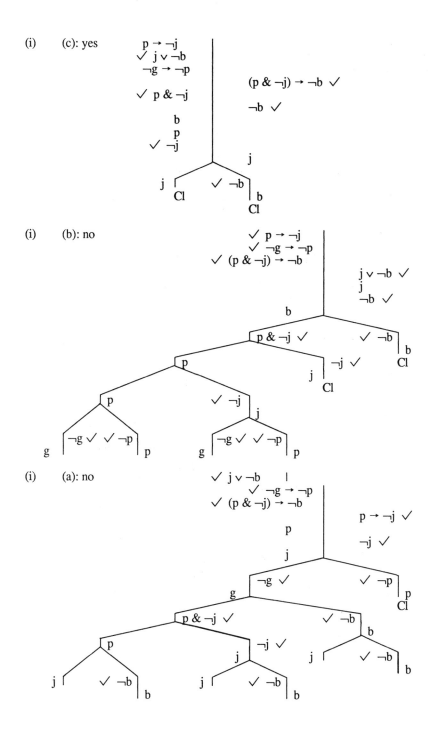

(i)    (b): no

(i)    (a): no

39

(ii) It does not imply his innocence.

$\checkmark\ p \to \neg j$
$\checkmark\ j \vee \neg b$
$\checkmark\ (p \mathbin{\&} \neg j) \to \neg b$
$\checkmark\ \neg g \to \neg p$

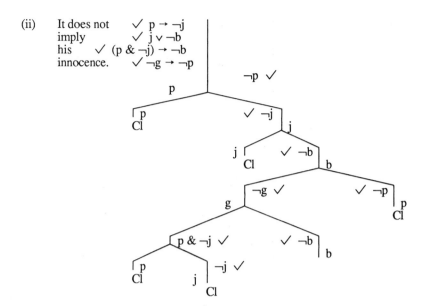

It does not imply his guilt; the tableau, beginning like the last, but with 'p' on the right, remains open, but is too long to present here.

(iii) It does not imply her innocence.

$\checkmark\ p \to \neg j$
$\checkmark\ j \vee \neg b$
$\checkmark\ (p \mathbin{\&} \neg j) \to \neg b$
$\checkmark\ \neg g \to \neg p$

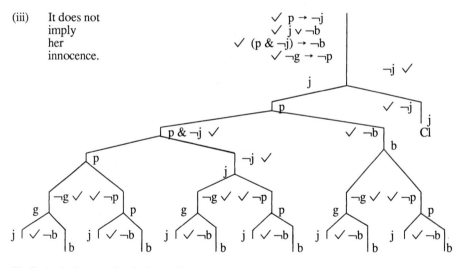

Similarly, it does not imply her guilt.

**92.** $\checkmark$ $a \leftrightarrow ((n \vee r) \vee ((\neg(n \vee r) \& \neg f) \to (c \vee e)))$

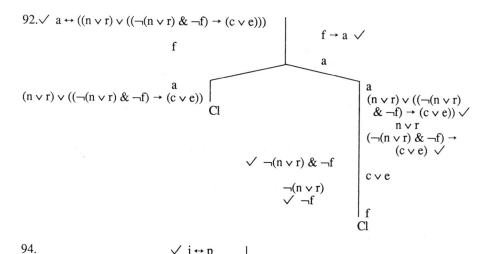

**94.**

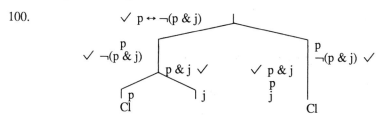

They're both knights or both knaves.

**98.**

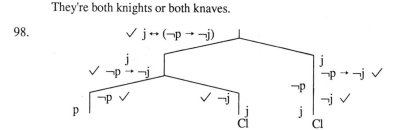

They're both knights.

**100.**

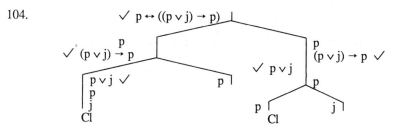

Punch is a knight and Judy's a knave.

**104.**

Either Punch is a knight, or he's a knave and Judy's a knight.

106.

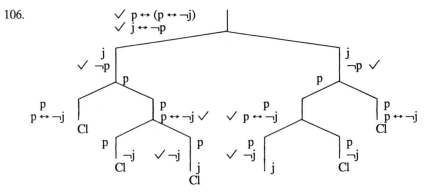

Punch is a knight and Judy's a knave.

110.

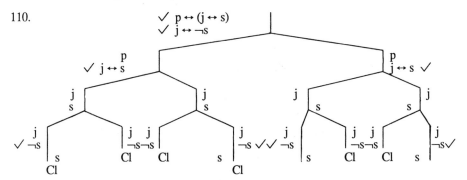

Punch is a knave. Either Judy or her sister is a knave, while the other is a knight.

112.　The tableau begins:　　　✓ c ↔ ¬l |
　　　　　　　　　　✓ m ↔ (¬c ∨ ¬l) |
　　　　　　　✓ l ↔ (¬l → (¬c & ¬m)) |
　　and is too large to reproduce here.　Moe is a knight.

116.　The tableau begins:　✓ c ↔ (m → l) |
　　　　　　　　　✓ m ↔ (¬c → ¬l) |
　　　　　　　　　✓ l ↔ ¬(¬c & ¬m) |
　　and is too large to reproduce here.　Curly, Moe, and Larry are all knights.

118.　The tableau begins:　✓ c ↔ (¬m → ¬l) |
　　　　　　　　　✓ m ↔ (¬l → ¬c) |
　　　　　　✓ l ↔ (m → (c & l & m)) |
　　and is too large to reproduce here.　Curly, Moe, and Larry are all knights.

42

# DEDUCTION

The deduction system of this chapter is conceptually very simple. It uses no complex rules or subordinate proofs. Every formula in a proof is either an assumption or follows from previously given lines by a rule of inference. In these respects, and in many of its rules, it's similar to the system of Irving Copi's *Introduction to Logic*. The system of this chapter, however, allows categorical as well as hypothetical proofs. It thus allows students to prove tautologies as well as to demonstrate the validity of argument forms.

This system differs from Copi's in its rules as well. The two most important differences were inspired by systems of Gentzen and Hilbert and Bernays. First, this system contains a rule of self-implication, allowing us to set down $\mathcal{A} \to \mathcal{A}$ on any line. Second, it contains a rule of consequent conjunction, allowing us to infer $\mathcal{A} \to (\mathcal{B} \& C)$ from $\mathcal{A} \to \mathcal{B}$ and $\mathcal{A} \to C$. The chapter presents basic rules first, followed by derived rules. Proofs from basic rules alone are, in some cases, very difficult. But the basic system is complete. Derived rules make proofs much easier.

Most of the derived rules are familiar and very useful. Some instructors may be tempted to omit the somewhat less familiar weakening rule; don't. In this system, it's invaluable. Others may want to add exportation, which appears in the text only in a problem on page 223; this does make certain proofs easier.

The last section of the chapter presents a simple indirect proof method, inspired by the "main method" of Quine's *Methods of Logic*. It is easy to use, and especially helpful to have in predicate logic.

## 1. KEY DEFINITIONS

A *natural deduction system* is a set of rules: specifically, *rules of inference*, which allow us to deduce formulas from other formulas.

A *proof* in a natural deduction system is a series of *lines*. On each line appears a formula. Each formula in a proof (a) is an assumption or (b) derives from formulas on previously established lines by a rule of inference. The last line of a proof is its *conclusion*; the proof *proves* that formula *from* the assumptions. Conclusions proved from no assumptions at all are *theorems* of the system.

*Hypothetical* proofs begin with *assumptions* (or *hypotheses*).
*Categorical* proofs use no assumptions.

| *Hypothetical Proof* | *Categorical Proof* |
|---|---|
| Assumptions | . |
| . | . |
| . | . |
| . | . |
| Conclusion | Conclusion (Theorem) |

A rule is *invertible* if and only if it works in both directions: We may infer the formula below the double line from the formula above, or vice versa.

The principle of *Replacement* allows us to apply invertible rules to subformulas as well as entire formulas.

# 2. Summary of Rules

## Basic Rules:

*Rules Applying Only to Entire Formulas*

| | Assumption (A) | | | Simplification (S) | |
|---|---|---|---|---|---|
| n. | $\mathcal{A}$ | A | n. | $\underline{\mathcal{A}\ \&\ \mathcal{B}}$ | |
| | | | n+m. | $\mathcal{A}$ (or $\mathcal{B}$) | S, n |

| | Conjunction (C) | | | Consequent Conjunction (CC) | |
|---|---|---|---|---|---|
| n. | $\mathcal{A}$ | | n. | $\mathcal{A} \rightarrow \mathcal{B}$ | |
| m. | $\underline{\mathcal{B}}$ | | m. | $\underline{\mathcal{A} \rightarrow \mathcal{C}}$ | |
| p. | $\mathcal{A}\ \&\ \mathcal{B}$ | C, n, m | p. | $\mathcal{A} \rightarrow (\mathcal{B}\ \&\ \mathcal{C})$ | CC, n, m |

| | Modus Ponens (MP) | | | Addition (Ad) | |
|---|---|---|---|---|---|
| n. | $\mathcal{A} \rightarrow \mathcal{B}$ | | n. | $\underline{\mathcal{A}}$ (or $\mathcal{B}$) | |
| m. | $\underline{\mathcal{A}}$ | | n+p. | $\mathcal{A} \vee \mathcal{B}$ | Ad, n |
| p. | $\mathcal{B}$ | MP, n, m | | | |

| | Self Implication (SI) | | | Constructive Dilemma (CD) | |
|---|---|---|---|---|---|
| n. | $\mathcal{A} \rightarrow \mathcal{A}$ | SI | n. | $\mathcal{A} \vee \mathcal{B}$ | |
| | | | m. | $\mathcal{A} \rightarrow \mathcal{C}$ | |
| | | | p. | $\underline{\mathcal{B} \rightarrow \mathcal{D}}$ | |
| | | | q. | $\mathcal{C} \vee \mathcal{D}$ | CD, n, m, p |

*Invertible Rules*

| | Double Negation (DN) | | | Biconditional (B) | |
|---|---|---|---|---|---|
| n. | $\underline{\mathcal{A}}$ | DN, m | n. | $\underline{\mathcal{A} \leftrightarrow \mathcal{B}}$ | B, m |
| m. | $\neg\neg\mathcal{A}$ | DN, n | m. | $(\mathcal{A} \rightarrow \mathcal{B})\ \&\ (\mathcal{B} \rightarrow \mathcal{A})$ | B, n |

| | Commutativity of Disjunction (Cm) | | | Associativity of Disjunction (As) | |
|---|---|---|---|---|---|
| n. | $\underline{\mathcal{A} \vee \mathcal{B}}$ | Cm, n | n. | $\underline{(\mathcal{A} \vee \mathcal{B}) \vee \mathcal{C}}$ | As, m |
| m. | $\mathcal{B} \vee \mathcal{A}$ | Cm, n | m. | $\mathcal{A} \vee (\mathcal{B} \vee \mathcal{C})$ | As, n |

44

| DeMorgan's Law #1 (DM) | | | DeMorgan's Law #2 (DM) | | |
|---|---|---|---|---|---|
| n. | $\neg(\mathcal{A}\ \&\ \mathcal{B})$ | DM, m | n. | $\neg(\mathcal{A} \vee \mathcal{B})$ | DM, m |
| m. | $\neg\mathcal{A} \vee \neg\mathcal{B}$ | DM, n | m. | $\neg\mathcal{A}\ \&\ \neg\mathcal{B}$ | DM, n |

### Material Conditional (MC)

| n. | $\mathcal{A} \rightarrow \mathcal{B}$ | MC, m |
|---|---|---|
| m. | $\neg\mathcal{A} \vee \mathcal{B}$ | MC, n |

## Derived Rules:

### Rules Applying Only to Entire Formulas

**Modus Tollens (MT)**

| n. | $\mathcal{A} \rightarrow \mathcal{B}$ | |
|---|---|---|
| m. | $\neg\mathcal{B}$ | |
| p. | $\neg\mathcal{A}$ | MT, n, m |

**Hypothetical Syllogism (HS)**

| n. | $\mathcal{A} \rightarrow \mathcal{B}$ | |
|---|---|---|
| m. | $\mathcal{B} \rightarrow C$ | |
| p. | $\mathcal{A} \rightarrow C$ | HS, n, m |

**Biconditional Exploitation (BE)**

| n. | $\mathcal{A} \leftrightarrow \mathcal{B}$ | | |
|---|---|---|---|
| m. | $\mathcal{A}$ | (or $\mathcal{B}$) | |
| p. | $\mathcal{B}$ | (or $\mathcal{A}$) | BE, n, m |

**Contradiction (!)**

| n. | $\mathcal{A}$ | |
|---|---|---|
| m. | $\neg\mathcal{A}$ | |
| p. | $\mathcal{B}$ | !, n, m |

| n. | $\mathcal{A} \leftrightarrow \mathcal{B}$ | | |
|---|---|---|---|
| m. | $\neg\mathcal{A}$ | (or $\neg\mathcal{B}$) | |
| p. | $\neg\mathcal{B}$ | (or $\neg\mathcal{A}$) | BE, n, m |

**Weakening (W)**

| n. | $(\mathcal{A}\ \&\ \mathcal{B}) \rightarrow \mathcal{A}$ (or $(\mathcal{A}\ \&\ \mathcal{B}) \rightarrow \mathcal{B}$) | W |
|---|---|---|
| n. | $\mathcal{A} \rightarrow (\mathcal{A} \vee \mathcal{B})$ (or $\mathcal{B} \rightarrow (\mathcal{A} \vee \mathcal{B})$) | W |

**Disjunctive Syllogism (DS)**

| n. | $\mathcal{A} \vee \mathcal{B}$ | | |
|---|---|---|---|
| m. | $\neg\mathcal{A}$ | (or $\neg\mathcal{B}$) | |
| p. | $\mathcal{B}$ | (or $\mathcal{A}$) | DS, n, m |

### Invertible Rules

**Negated Conditional (NC)**

| n. | $\neg(\mathcal{A} \rightarrow \mathcal{B})$ | NC, m |
|---|---|---|
| m. | $\mathcal{A}\ \&\ \neg\mathcal{B}$ | NC, n |

**Negated Biconditional (NB)**

| n. | $\neg(\mathcal{A} \leftrightarrow \mathcal{B})$ | NB, m |
|---|---|---|
| m. | $\neg\mathcal{A} \leftrightarrow \mathcal{B}$ (or $\mathcal{A} \leftrightarrow \neg\mathcal{B}$) | NB, n |

**Commutativity of Conjunction (Cm)**

| n. | $\mathcal{A}\ \&\ \mathcal{B}$ | Cm, m |
|---|---|---|
| m. | $\mathcal{B}\ \&\ \mathcal{A}$ | Cm, n |

**Associativity of Conjunction (As)**

| n. | $(\mathcal{A}\ \&\ \mathcal{B})\ \&\ C$ | As, m |
|---|---|---|
| m. | $\mathcal{A}\ \&\ (\mathcal{B}\ \&\ C)$ | As, n |

**Idempotence (I)**

| n. | $\mathcal{A} \vee \mathcal{A}$ | I, m |
|---|---|---|
| m. | $\mathcal{A}$ | I, n |

**Transposition (Tr)**

| n. | $\mathcal{A} \rightarrow \mathcal{B}$ | Tr, m |
|---|---|---|
| m. | $\neg\mathcal{B} \rightarrow \neg\mathcal{A}$ | Tr, n |

45

Distribution  (D)

| n. | $\underline{\mathcal{A}\ \&\ (\mathcal{B} \vee C)}$ | D, m | n. | $\underline{\mathcal{A} \vee (\mathcal{B}\ \&\ C)}$ | D, m |
|----|----|----|----|----|----|
| m. | $(\mathcal{A}\ \&\ \mathcal{B}) \vee (\mathcal{A}\ \&\ C)$ | D, n | m. | $(\mathcal{A} \vee \mathcal{B})\ \&\ (\mathcal{A} \vee C)$ | D, n |

Indirect Proof (Hypothetical)                    Indirect Proof (Categorical)

| 1. | $\mathcal{A}_1$ | A | 1. | $\neg\mathcal{B}$ | AIP |
|----|----|----|----|----|----|
| | . | | | . | |
| | . | | | . | |
| | . | | | . | |
| n. | $\mathcal{A}_n$ | A | m. | $C\ \&\ \neg C$ | |
| n+1. | $\neg\mathcal{B}$ | AIP | | | |
| | . | | | | |
| | . | | | | |
| | . | | | | |
| m. | $C\ \&\ \neg C$ | | | | |

# 3.  STRATEGY

| To get | Try to |
|----|----|
| $\neg\mathcal{A}$ | use double negation, DeMorgan's laws or modus tollens. |
| $\mathcal{A}\ \&\ \mathcal{B}$ | prove $\mathcal{A}$ and $\mathcal{B}$ separately. |
| $\mathcal{A} \vee \mathcal{B}$ | use constructive dilemma, or material implication, or prove $\mathcal{A}$ or $\mathcal{B}$ separately. |
| $\mathcal{A} \to \mathcal{B}$ | use material implication, consequent conjunction, hypothetical syllogism, self-implication, weakening or transposition. |
| $\mathcal{A} \leftrightarrow \mathcal{B}$ | prove the two conditionals $\mathcal{A} \to \mathcal{B}$ and $\mathcal{B} \to \mathcal{A}$. |

| To exploit | Try to |
|----|----|
| $\neg\mathcal{A}$ | use it with other lines that have $\mathcal{A}$ as a part, or use DeMorgan's laws or negated (bi)conditional. |
| $\mathcal{A}\ \&\ \mathcal{B}$ | use S to get $\mathcal{A}$ and $\mathcal{B}$ individually. |
| $\mathcal{A} \vee \mathcal{B}$ | get the negation of one disjunct, and use disjunctive syllogism to get the other, or use constructive dilemma by taking each case separately, or use material implication. |
| $\mathcal{A} \to \mathcal{B}$ | get $\mathcal{A}$ and then reach $\mathcal{B}$ by modus ponens, or use hypothetical syllogism, consequent conjunction or material implication, or get $\neg\mathcal{B}$ and then reach $\neg\mathcal{A}$ by modus tollens. |
| $\mathcal{A} \leftrightarrow \mathcal{B}$ | use biconditional to obtain a conjunction of conditionals. |

# 4. ANSWERS TO UNANSWERED EVEN PROBLEMS

## 8.2 Conjunction and Negation Rules

8.
| 1. | ¬p & ¬q | A |
| 2. | r & ¬s | A |
| 3. | ¬¬r & ¬s | DN, 2 |

10.
| 1. | ¬p → ¬q | A |
| 2. | ¬p → q | A |
| 3. | ¬p → (q & ¬q) | CC, 2, 1 |

14.
| 1. | (p ↔ ¬r) & (q & ¬s) | A |
| 2. | p ↔ ¬r | S, 1 |
| 3. | q & ¬s | S, 1 |
| 4. | ¬s | S, 3 |
| 5. | q | S, 3 |
| 6. | q & (p ↔ ¬r) | C, 5, 2 |
| 7. | ¬s & (q & (p ↔ ¬r)) | C, 4, 6 |

16.
| 1. | p | A |
| 2. | q → r | A |
| 3. | ¬r | A |
| 4. | ¬¬q → s | A |
| 5. | q → s | DN, 4 |
| 6. | q → (r & s) | CC, 2, 5 |
| 7. | ¬r & p | C, 3, 1 |
| 8. | (q → (r & s)) & (¬r & p) | C, 6, 7 |

20.
| 1. | (¬p → q) & (q → ¬¬r) | A |
| 2. | (¬p → s) & (q → ¬t) | A |
| 3. | ¬p → q | S, 1 |
| 4. | q → ¬¬r | S, 1 |
| 5. | ¬p → s | S, 2 |
| 6. | q → ¬t | S, 2 |
| 7. | ¬p → (q & s) | CC, 3, 5 |
| 8. | q → r | DN, 4 |
| 9. | q → (r & ¬t) | CC, 8, 6 |
| 10. | (¬p → (q & s)) & (q → (r & ¬t)) | C, 7, 9 |

## 8.3 Conditional and Biconditional Rules

8.
| 1. | p → q | A |
| 2. | p → r | A |
| 3. | p | A |
| 4. | q | MP, 1, 3 |
| 5. | r | MP, 2, 3 |
| 6. | q & r | C, 4, 5 |

10.
| 1. | p ↔ q | A |
| 2. | p → r | A |
| 3. | (p → q) & (q → p) | B, 1 |
| 4. | p → q | S, 3 |
| 5. | p → (q & r) | CC, 4, 2 |

14.
| | | | |
|---|---|---|---|
| | 1. | p & ¬t | A |
| | 2. | p → (r & q) | A |
| | 3. | r → s | A |
| | 4. | p | S, 1 |
| | 5. | r & q | MP, 2, 4 |
| | 6. | r | S, 5 |
| | 7. | q | S, 5 |
| | 8. | s | MP, 3, 6 |
| | 9. | s & q | C, 8, 7 |

16.
| | | | |
|---|---|---|---|
| | 1. | p & q | A |
| | 2. | ¬¬p → r | A |
| | 3. | q → s | A |
| | 4. | p → t | A |
| | 5. | p | S, 1 |
| | 6. | q | S, 1 |
| | 7. | s | MP, 3, 6 |
| | 8. | t | MP, 4, 5 |
| | 9. | ¬¬p | DN, 5 |
| | 10. | r | MP, 2, 9 |
| | 11. | r & t | C, 10, 8 |
| | 12. | (r & t) & s | C, 11, 7 |

20.
| | | | |
|---|---|---|---|
| | 1. | p ↔ q | A |
| | 2. | p ↔ r | A |
| | 3. | r → q | A |
| | 4. | (p → q) & (q → p) | B, 1 |
| | 5. | p → q | S, 4 |
| | 6. | (p → r) & (r → p) | B, 2 |
| | 7. | p → r | S, 6 |
| | 8. | r → p | S, 6 |
| | 9. | p → (q & r) | CC, 5, 7 |
| | 10. | r → (p & q) | CC, 8, 3 |
| | 11. | (p → (q & r)) & (r → (p & q)) | C, 9, 10 |

22.
| | | | |
|---|---|---|---|
| | 1. | s → (q & t) | A |
| | 2. | ¬m → p | A |
| | 3. | (p → r) & ¬k | A |
| | 4. | p & s | A |
| | 5. | (q & r) → ¬m | A |
| | 6. | p | S, 4 |
| | 7. | s | S, 4 |
| | 8. | q & t | MP, 1, 7 |
| | 9. | q | S, 8 |
| | 10. | p → r | S, 3 |
| | 11. | r | MP, 10, 6 |
| | 12. | q & r | C, 9, 11 |
| | 13. | ¬m | MP, 5, 12 |
| | 14. | ¬m & (q & r) | C, 13, 12 |

26.   d: The Democrats obstruct the President's legislative program; m: The market will lose confidence; p: The Democrats can gain politically by obstructing.

| | | |
|---|---|---|
| 1. | d → m | A |
| 2. | d → p | A |
| 3. | d | A |
| 4. | p | MP, 2, 3 |
| 5. | m | MP, 1, 3 |
| 6. | p & m | C, 4, 5 |

28.   g: Georgia will lose the case; d: The Court decides to base its decision on *Davis*; c: The composition of the Court is more conservative than it was a few years ago.

| | | |
|---|---|---|
| 1. | g ↔ d | A |
| 2. | c & d | A |
| 3. | d | S, 2 |
| 4. | (g → d) & (d → g) | B, 1 |
| 5. | d → g | S, 4 |
| 6. | g | MP, 5, 3 |

## 8.4   Disjunction Rules

8.
| | | |
|---|---|---|
| 1. | p ↔ ¬q | A |
| 2. | ¬p ∨ q | A |
| 3. | r | A |
| 4. | (p → ¬q) & (¬q → p) | B, 1 |
| 5. | p → ¬q | S, 4 |
| 6. | ¬p → ¬p | SI |
| 7. | ¬p ∨ ¬q | MC, 5 |
| 8. | ¬q ∨ ¬p | Cm, 7 |
| 9. | (¬q ∨ ¬p) ∨ s | Ad, 8 |
| 10. | ¬q ∨ (¬p ∨ s) | As, 9 |
| 11. | q → (¬p ∨ s) | MC, 10 |
| 12. | q → (p → s) | MC, 11 |
| 13. | ¬p ∨ (p → s) | CD, 2, 6, 12 |

10.
| | | |
|---|---|---|
| 1. | p ↔ s | A |
| 2. | q ∨ p | A |
| 3. | q → r | A |
| 4. | (p → s) & (s → p) | B, 1 |
| 5. | p → s | S, 4 |
| 6. | r ∨ s | CD, 2, 3, 5 |
| 7. | s ∨ r | Cm, 6 |

14.
| | | |
|---|---|---|
| 1. | p ∨ r | A |
| 2. | ¬p ∨ ¬q | A |
| 3. | p | A |
| 4. | ¬r ∨ q | A |
| 5. | p → ¬q | MC, 2 |
| 6. | ¬q | MP, 5, 3 |
| 7. | q ∨ ¬r | Cm, 4 |
| 8. | ¬¬q ∨ ¬r | DN, 7 |
| 9. | ¬q → ¬r | MC, 8 |
| 10. | ¬r | MP, 9, 6 |

49

| | | | |
|---|---|---|---|
| 16. | 1. | p ∨ q | A |
| | 2. | r ∨ s | A |
| | 3. | ¬q & ¬s | A |
| | 4. | ¬q | S, 3 |
| | 5. | ¬s | S, 3 |
| | 6. | q ∨ p | Cm, 1 |
| | 7. | ¬¬q ∨ p | DN, 6 |
| | 8. | ¬q → p | MC, 7 |
| | 9. | p | MP, 8, 4 |
| | 10. | s ∨ r | Cm, 2 |
| | 11. | ¬¬s ∨ r | DN, 10 |
| | 12. | ¬s → r | MC, 11 |
| | 13. | r | MP, 12, 5 |
| | 14. | p & r | C, 9, 13 |
| | 15. | (p & r) ∨ t | Ad, 14 |
| | | | |
| 20. | 1. | p & s | A |
| | 2. | p → (¬s ∨ r) | A |
| | 3. | p | S, 1 |
| | 4. | s | S, 1 |
| | 5. | ¬s ∨ r | MP, 2, 3 |
| | 6. | s → r | MC, 5 |
| | 7. | r | MP, 6, 4 |
| | | | |
| 22. | 1. | p & q | A |
| | 2. | r & ¬s | A |
| | 3. | q → (p → k) | A |
| | 4. | k → (r → (s ∨ m)) | A |
| | 5. | p | S, 1 |
| | 6. | q | S, 1 |
| | 7. | r | S, 2 |
| | 8. | ¬s | S, 2 |
| | 9. | p → k | MP, 3, 6 |
| | 10. | k | MP, 9, 5 |
| | 11. | r → (s ∨ m) | MP, 4, 10 |
| | 12. | s ∨ m | MP, 11, 7 |
| | 13. | ¬¬s ∨ m | DN, 12 |
| | 14. | ¬s → m | MC, 13 |
| | 15. | m | MP, 14, 8 |
| | | | |
| 26. | 1. | p & q | A |
| | 2. | p → ¬¬r | A |
| | 3. | q → s | A |
| | 4. | ¬r ∨ m | A |
| | 5. | p → t | A |
| | 6. | p | S, 1 |
| | 7. | q | S, 1 |
| | 8. | ¬¬r | MP, 2, 6 |
| | 9. | s | MP, 3, 7 |
| | 10. | r | DN, 8 |
| | 11. | r → m | MC, 4 |
| | 12. | m | MP, 11, 10 |
| | 13. | t | MP, 5, 6 |
| | 14. | m & s | C, 12, 9 |
| | 15. | (m & s) & t | C, 14, 13 |

28. 
|  |  |  |  |
|---|---|---|---|
| 1. | $(p \lor (q \lor r)) \to (p \lor (q \lor r))$ | SI |
| 2. | $(p \lor (q \lor r)) \to ((p \lor q) \lor r)$ | As, 1 |

32. d: The dollar will fall; s: Foreign banks sterilize their intervention in the currency markets; f: The Fed does nothing to defend it; g: Germany and Japan are eager to keep their currencies strong; i: They'll intervene in the markets.

|  |  |  |
|---|---|---|
| 1. | $(s \lor f) \to d$ | A |
| 2. | $g \& (d \to i)$ | A |
| 3. | $g \to s$ | A |
| 4. | $g$ | S, 2 |
| 5. | $s$ | MP, 3, 4 |
| 6. | $s \lor f$ | Ad, 5 |
| 7. | $d$ | MP, 1, 6 |
| 8. | $d \to i$ | S, 2 |
| 9. | $i$ | MP, 8, 7 |

34. c: Patricia is clever, but won't w: Patricia will work very hard. If she's clever, b: the boss will like her and either p: promote her or g: give her a bonus. If Patricia is promoted, she'll work hard. Therefore, the boss will give Patricia a bonus.

|  |  |  |
|---|---|---|
| 1. | $c \& \neg w$ | A |
| 2. | $c \to (b \& (p \lor g))$ | A |
| 3. | $p \to w$ | A |
| 4. | $c$ | S, 1 |
| 5. | $\neg w$ | S, 1 |
| 6. | $b \& (p \lor g)$ | MP, 2, 4 |
| 7. | $p \lor g$ | S, 6 |
| 8. | $\neg p \lor w$ | MC, 3 |
| 9. | $\neg p \lor \neg\neg w$ | DN, 8 |
| 10. | $\neg\neg w \lor \neg p$ | Cm, 9 |
| 11. | $\neg w \to \neg p$ | MC, 10 |
| 12. | $\neg p$ | MP, 11, 5 |
| 13. | $\neg\neg p \lor g$ | DN, 7 |
| 14. | $\neg p \to g$ | MC, 13 |
| 15. | $g$ | MP, 14, 12 |

## 8.5   Rules of Definition

14. 
|  |  |  |
|---|---|---|
| 1. | $r \to (p \lor q)$ | A |
| 2. | $\neg r \lor (p \lor q)$ | MC, 1 |
| 3. | $(\neg r \lor p) \lor q$ | As, 2 |
| 4. | $(r \to p) \lor q$ | MC, 3 |

16. 
|  |  |  |
|---|---|---|
| 1. | $\neg s \lor (s \& r)$ | A |
| 2. | $(s \to r) \to q$ | A |
| 3. | $r \to r$ | SI |
| 4. | $\neg r \lor r$ | MC, 3 |
| 5. | $\neg s \lor (\neg r \lor r)$ | Ad, 4 |
| 6. | $(\neg s \lor \neg r) \lor r$ | As, 5 |
| 7. | $\neg\neg(\neg s \lor \neg r) \lor r$ | DN, 6 |
| 8. | $\neg(\neg s \lor \neg r) \to r$ | MC, 7 |
| 9. | $(\neg\neg s \& \neg\neg r) \to r$ | DM, 8 |
| 10. | $(s \& r) \to r$ | DN, 9 |
| 11. | $\neg s \to \neg s$ | SI |
| 12. | $\neg s \lor r$ | CD, 1, 11, 10 |
| 13. | $s \to r$ | MC, 12 |
| 14. | $q$ | MP, 2, 13 |

| 20. | 1. | $r \to \neg p$ | A |
| | 2. | $q$ | A |
| | 3. | $q \to (p \lor \neg s)$ | A |
| | 4. | $p \lor \neg s$ | MP, 3, 2 |
| | 5. | $\neg r \lor \neg p$ | MC, 1 |
| | 6. | $\neg p \lor \neg r$ | Cm, 5 |
| | 7. | $p \to \neg r$ | MC, 6 |
| | 8. | $\neg s \to \neg s$ | SI |
| | 9. | $\neg r \lor \neg s$ | CD, 4, 7, 8 |
| | 10. | $\neg s \lor \neg r$ | Cm, 9 |
| | 11. | $s \to \neg r$ | MC, 10 |

| 22. | 1. | $r \to \neg p$ | A |
| | 2. | $\neg r \to \neg q$ | A |
| | 3. | $q \lor \neg s$ | A |
| | 4. | $\neg s \to \neg s$ | SI |
| | 5. | $r \to r$ | SI |
| | 6. | $\neg r \lor r$ | MC, 5 |
| | 7. | $\neg q \lor \neg p$ | CD, 6, 2, 1 |
| | 8. | $q \to \neg p$ | MC, 7 |
| | 9. | $\neg p \lor \neg s$ | CD, 3, 8, 4 |

| 26. | 1. | $r \,\&\, p$ | A |
| | 2. | $r \to (s \lor q)$ | A |
| | 3. | $\neg(q \,\&\, p)$ | A |
| | 4. | $r$ | S, 1 |
| | 5. | $p$ | S, 1 |
| | 6. | $\neg q \lor \neg p$ | DM, 3 |
| | 7. | $s \lor q$ | MP, 2, 4 |
| | 8. | $\neg p \lor \neg q$ | Cm, 6 |
| | 9. | $p \to \neg q$ | MC, 8 |
| | 10. | $\neg q$ | MP, 9, 5 |
| | 11. | $q \lor s$ | Cm, 7 |
| | 12. | $\neg\neg q \lor s$ | DN, 11 |
| | 13. | $\neg q \to s$ | MC, 12 |
| | 14. | $s$ | MP, 13, 10 |

| 28. | 1. | $s \to r$ | A |
| | 2. | $(s \,\&\, r) \to p$ | A |
| | 3. | $q \to t$ | A |
| | 4. | $q \lor s$ | A |
| | 5. | $s \lor q$ | Cm, 4 |
| | 6. | $\neg s \to \neg s$ | SI |
| | 7. | $s \to s$ | SI |
| | 8. | $s \to (s \,\&\, r)$ | CC, 7, 1 |
| | 9. | $\neg s \lor (s \,\&\, r)$ | MC, 8 |
| | 10. | $\neg s \lor p$ | CD, 9, 6, 2 |
| | 11. | $s \to p$ | MC, 10 |
| | 12. | $p \lor t$ | CD, 5, 11, 3 |

| 32. | 1. | r & (¬p & ¬t) | A |
|---|---|---|---|
| | 2. | r → (s → q) | A |
| | 3. | s → (q ↔ (t ∨ p)) | A |
| | 4. | r | S, 1 |
| | 5. | ¬p & ¬t | S, 1 |
| | 6. | ¬(p ∨ t) | DM, 5 |
| | 7. | s → q | MP, 2, 4 |
| | 8. | ¬(t ∨ p) | Cm, 6 |
| | 9. | ¬s ∨ (q ↔ (t ∨ p)) | MC, 3 |
| | 10. | ¬s ∨ ((q → (t ∨ p)) & ((t ∨ p) → q)) | B, 9 |
| | 11. | ¬s → ¬s | SI |
| | 12. | (q → (t ∨ p)) → (q → (t ∨ p)) | SI |
| | 13. | ¬(q → (t ∨ p)) ∨ (q → (t ∨ p)) | MC, 12 |
| | 14. | ¬((t ∨ p) → q) ∨ (¬(q → (t ∨ p)) ∨ (q → (t ∨ p))) | Ad, 13 |
| | 15. | (¬((t ∨ p) → q) ∨ ¬(q → (t ∨ p))) ∨ (q → (t ∨ p)) | As, 14 |
| | 16. | (¬(q → (t ∨ p)) ∨ ¬((t ∨ p) → q)) ∨ (q → (t ∨ p)) | Cm, 15 |
| | 17. | ¬((q → (t ∨ p)) & ((t ∨ p) → q)) ∨ (q → (t ∨ p)) | DM, 16 |
| | 18. | ((q → (t ∨ p)) & ((t ∨ p) → q)) → (q → (t ∨ p)) | MC, 17 |
| | 19. | ¬s ∨ (q → (t ∨ p)) | CD, 10, 11, 18 |
| | 20. | ¬s ∨ (¬q ∨ (t ∨ p)) | MC, 19 |
| | 21. | (¬s ∨ ¬q) ∨ (t ∨ p) | As, 20 |
| | 22. | ¬(s & q) ∨ (t ∨ p) | DM, 21 |
| | 23. | (t ∨ p) ∨ ¬(s & q) | Cm, 22 |
| | 24. | ¬¬(t ∨ p) ∨ ¬(s & q) | DN, 23 |
| | 25. | ¬(t ∨ p) → ¬(s & q) | MC, 24 |
| | 26. | ¬(s & q) | MP, 25, 8 |
| | 27. | ¬s ∨ ¬q | DM, 26 |
| | 28. | s → ¬q | MC, 27 |
| | 29. | s → (q & ¬q) | CC, 7, 28 |
| | 30. | q → q | SI |
| | 31. | ¬q ∨ q | MC, 30 |
| | 32. | ¬q ∨ ¬¬q | DN, 31 |
| | 33. | ¬(q & ¬q) | DM, 32 |
| | 34. | ¬s ∨ (q & ¬q) | MC, 29 |
| | 35. | ¬s ∨ ¬¬(q & ¬q) | DN, 34 |
| | 36. | ¬¬(q & ¬q) ∨ ¬s | Cm, 35 |
| | 37. | ¬(q & ¬q) → ¬s | MC, 36 |
| | 38. | ¬s | MP, 37, 33 |

| 34. | 1. | ¬(p ∨ ¬s) | A |
|---|---|---|---|
| | 2. | ¬p → (q ∨ r) | A |
| | 3. | ¬r ∨ ¬s | A |
| | 4. | ((q ∨ t) → (m & (k → ¬s)) | A |
| | 5. | ¬p & ¬¬s | DM, 1 |
| | 6. | ¬p | S, 5 |
| | 7. | q ∨ r | MP, 2, 6 |
| | 8. | ¬¬s | S, 5 |
| | 9. | s | DN, 8 |
| | 10. | ¬s ∨ ¬r | Cm, 3 |
| | 11. | s → ¬r | MC, 10 |
| | 12. | ¬r | MP, 11, 9 |
| | 13. | r ∨ q | Cm, 7 |
| | 14. | ¬¬r ∨ q | DN, 13 |
| | 15. | ¬r → q | MC, 14 |
| | 16. | q | MP, 15, 12 |
| | 17. | q ∨ t | Ad, 16 |
| | 18. | m & (k → ¬s) | MP, 4, 17 |

|     |     |     |
| --- | --- | --- |
| 19. | m | S, 18 |
| 20. | k → ¬s | S, 18 |
| 21. | ¬k ∨ ¬s | MC, 20 |
| 22. | ¬s ∨ ¬k | Cm, 21 |
| 23. | s → ¬k | MC, 22 |
| 24. | ¬k | MP, 23, 9 |
| 25. | m & ¬k | C, 19, 24 |
| 26. | ¬¬m & ¬k | DN, 25 |
| 27. | ¬(¬m ∨ k) | DM, 26 |
| 28. | ¬(m → k) | MC, 27 |

| 38. |     |     |     |
| --- | --- | --- | --- |
|     | 1. | p | A |
|     | 2. | ¬p | A |
|     | 3. | ¬p ∨ q | Ad, 2 |
|     | 4. | p → q | MC, 3 |
|     | 5. | q | MP, 4, 1 |

| 40. |     |     |     |
| --- | --- | --- | --- |
|     | 1. | p & (q ∨ r) | A |
|     | 2. | p | S, 1 |
|     | 3. | q ∨ r | S, 1 |
|     | 4. | ¬q ∨ p | Ad, 2 |
|     | 5. | q → p | MC, 4 |
|     | 6. | q → q | SI |
|     | 7. | q → (p & q) | CC, 5, 6 |
|     | 8. | ¬r ∨ p | Ad, 2 |
|     | 9. | r → p | MC, 8 |
|     | 10. | r → r | SI |
|     | 11. | r → (p & r) | CC, 9, 10 |
|     | 12. | (p & q) ∨ (p & r) | CD, 3, 7, 11 |

| 44. |     |     |     |
| --- | --- | --- | --- |
|     | 1. | p ↔ ¬q | A |
|     | 2. | (p → ¬q) & (¬q → p) | B, 1 |
|     | 3. | p → ¬q | S, 2 |
|     | 4. | ¬q → p | S, 2 |
|     | 5. | p → p | SI |
|     | 6. | p → (p & ¬q) | CC, 5, 3 |
|     | 7. | ¬¬q ∨ p | MC, 4 |
|     | 8. | p ∨ ¬¬q | Cm, 7 |
|     | 9. | ¬¬p ∨ ¬¬q | DN, 8 |
|     | 10. | ¬p → ¬¬q | MC, 9 |
|     | 11. | ¬p → ¬p | SI |
|     | 12. | ¬p → (¬¬q & ¬p) | CC, 10, 11 |
|     | 13. | ¬¬p ∨ ¬p | MC, 11 |
|     | 14. | p ∨ ¬p | DN, 13 |
|     | 15. | (p & ¬q) ∨ (¬¬q & ¬p) | CD, 14, 6, 12 |
|     | 16. | (¬¬p & ¬q) ∨ (¬¬q & ¬p) | DN, 15 |
|     | 17. | ¬(¬p ∨ q) ∨ ¬(¬q ∨ p) | DM, 16 |
|     | 18. | ¬((¬p ∨ q) & (¬q ∨ p)) | DM, 17 |
|     | 19. | ¬((p → q) & (q → p)) | MC, 18 |
|     | 20. | ¬(p ↔ q) | B, 19 |

46.
| | | | |
|---|---|---|---|
| | 1. | (p & q) ∨ (p & r) | A |
| | 2. | p → p | SI |
| | 3. | ¬p ∨ p | MC, 2 |
| | 4. | ¬q ∨ (¬p ∨ p) | Ad, 3 |
| | 5. | (¬q ∨ ¬p) ∨ p | As, 4 |
| | 6. | (¬p ∨ ¬q) ∨ p | Cm, 5 |
| | 7. | ¬(p & q) ∨ p | DM, 6 |
| | 8. | (p & q) → p | MC, 7 |
| | 9. | ¬r ∨ (¬p ∨ p) | Ad, 3 |
| | 10. | (¬r ∨ ¬p) ∨ p | As, 9 |
| | 11. | (¬p ∨ ¬r) ∨ p | Cm, 10 |
| | 12. | ¬(p & r) ∨ p | DM, 11 |
| | 13. | (p & r) → p | MC, 12 |
| | 14. | q → q | SI |
| | 15. | ¬q ∨ q | MC, 14 |
| | 16. | ¬p ∨ (¬q ∨ q) | Ad, 15 |
| | 17. | (¬p ∨ ¬q) ∨ q | As, 16 |
| | 18. | ¬(p & q) ∨ q | DM, 17 |
| | 19. | (p & q) → q | MC, 18 |
| | 20. | r → r | SI |
| | 21. | ¬r ∨ r | MC, 20 |
| | 22. | ¬p ∨ (¬r ∨ r) | Ad, 21 |
| | 23. | (¬p ∨ ¬r) ∨ r | As, 22 |
| | 24. | ¬(p & r) ∨ r | DM, 23 |
| | 25. | (p & r) → r | MC, 24 |
| | 26. | q ∨ r | CD, 1, 19, 25 |
| | 27. | p ∨ p | CD, 1, 8, 13 |
| | 28. | ¬p ∨ ¬¬p | DN, 3 |
| | 29. | ¬(p & ¬p) | DM, 28 |
| | 30. | ¬¬p ∨ p | DN, 27 |
| | 31. | ¬p → p | MC, 30 |
| | 32. | ¬p → ¬p | SI |
| | 33. | ¬p → (p & ¬p) | CC, 31, 32 |
| | 34. | ¬¬p ∨ (p & ¬p) | MC, 33 |
| | 35. | ¬¬p ∨ ¬¬(p & ¬p) | DN, 34 |
| | 36. | ¬¬(p & ¬p) ∨ ¬¬p | Cm, 35 |
| | 37. | ¬(p & ¬p) → ¬¬p | MC, 36 |
| | 38. | ¬¬p | MP, 37, 29 |
| | 39. | p | DN, 38 |
| | 40. | p & (q ∨ r) | C, 39, 26 |

50. r: I'm right; f: I'm a fool.

| | | | |
|---|---|---|---|
| | 1. | r → f | A |
| | 2. | f → ¬r | A |
| | 3. | ¬f ∨ ¬r | MC, 2 |
| | 4. | ¬r ∨ ¬f | Cm, 3 |
| | 5. | r → ¬f | MC, 4 |
| | 6. | r → (f & ¬f) | CC, 1, 5 |
| | 7. | f → f | SI |
| | 8. | ¬f ∨ f | MC, 7 |
| | 9. | ¬f ∨ ¬¬f | DN, 8 |
| | 10. | ¬(f & ¬f) | DM, 9 |
| | 11. | ¬r ∨ (f & ¬f) | MC, 6 |
| | 12. | (f & ¬f) ∨ ¬r | Cm, 11 |
| | 13. | ¬¬(f & ¬f) ∨ ¬r | DN, 12 |
| | 14. | ¬(f & ¬f) → ¬r | MC, 13 |
| | 15. | ¬r | MP, 14, 10 |

52.  s: Socrates died; l: He died while he was living; d: He died while he was dead.

| | | |
|---|---|---|
| 1. | s → (l ∨ d) | A |
| 2. | ¬l | A |
| 3. | ¬d | A |
| 4. | ¬s ∨ (l ∨ d) | MC, 1 |
| 5. | (l ∨ d) ∨ ¬s | Cm, 4 |
| 6. | ¬¬(l ∨ d) ∨ ¬s | DN, 5 |
| 7. | ¬(l ∨ d) → ¬s | MC, 6 |
| 8. | ¬l & ¬d | C, 2, 3 |
| 9. | ¬(l ∨ d) | DM, 8 |
| 10. | ¬s | MP, 7, 9 |

56.  u: The United States agrees to arms limitation talks; t: Tensions with the Soviets will remain high.

| | | |
|---|---|---|
| 1. | ¬u → t | A |
| 2. | u → t | A |
| 3. | ¬u ∨ t | MC, 2 |
| 4. | t → t | SI |
| 5. | t ∨ t | CD, 3, 1, 4 |
| 6. | ¬¬t ∨ t | DN, 5 |
| 7. | ¬t → t | MC, 6 |
| 8. | ¬t → ¬t | SI |
| 9. | ¬t → (t & ¬t) | CC, 7, 8 |
| 10. | ¬t ∨ t | MC, 4 |
| 11. | ¬t ∨ ¬¬t | DN, 10 |
| 12. | ¬(t & ¬t) | DM, 11 |
| 13. | ¬¬t ∨ (t & ¬t) | MC, 9 |
| 14. | (t & ¬t) ∨ ¬¬t | Cm, 13 |
| 15. | ¬¬(t & ¬t) ∨ t | DN, 14 |
| 16. | ¬(t & ¬t) → t | MC, 15 |
| 17. | t | MP, 16, 12 |

58.  p: God is all powerful; a: He is able to prevent evil; g: He is all good; w: He is willing to prevent evil; e: Evil exists; x: God exists.

| | | |
|---|---|---|
| 1. | p → a | A |
| 2. | g → w | A |
| 3. | ¬e ∨ (¬w ∨ ¬a) | A |
| 4. | x → (g & p) | A |
| 5. | p → p | SI |
| 6. | ¬p ∨ p | MC, 5 |
| 7. | ¬g ∨ (¬p ∨ p) | Ad, 6 |
| 8. | (¬g ∨ ¬p) ∨ p | As, 7 |
| 9. | ¬(g & p) ∨ p | DM, 8 |
| 10. | g → g | SI |
| 11. | ¬g ∨ g | MC, 10 |
| 12. | ¬p ∨ (¬g ∨ g) | Ad, 11 |
| 13. | (¬p ∨ ¬g) ∨ g | As, 12 |
| 14. | (¬g ∨ ¬p) ∨ g | Cm, 13 |
| 15. | ¬(g & p) ∨ g | DM, 14 |
| 16. | ¬(g & p) → ¬(g & p) | SI |
| 17. | ¬(g & p) ∨ a | CD, 9, 16, 1 |
| 18. | ¬(g & p) ∨ w | CD, 15, 16, 2 |
| 19. | (g & p) → a | MC, 17 |
| 20. | (g & p) → w | MC, 18 |
| 21. | (g & p) → (a & w) | CC, 19, 20 |
| 22. | ¬x ∨ (g & p) | MC, 4 |
| 23. | ¬x → ¬x | SI |

| 24. | $\neg x \lor (a \mathrel{\&} w)$ | CD, 22, 23, 21 |
| 25. | $\neg e \lor (\neg a \lor \neg w)$ | Cm, 3 |
| 26. | $\neg e \lor \neg(a \mathrel{\&} w)$ | DM, 25 |
| 27. | $\neg(a \mathrel{\&} w) \lor \neg e$ | Cm, 26 |
| 28. | $(a \mathrel{\&} w) \to \neg e$ | MC, 27 |
| 29. | $\neg x \lor \neg e$ | CD, 24, 23, 28 |
| 30. | $\neg e \lor \neg x$ | Cm, 29 |
| 31. | $e \to \neg x$ | MC, 30 |

## 8.6 Derived Rules

8.  c: My cat sings opera; l: All the lights are out; i: I am very insistent; h: I howl at the moon.

| 1. | $\neg c \lor l$ | A |
| 2. | $i \to c$ | A |
| 3. | $(l \lor h) \to i$ | A |
| 4. | $\neg i \to h$ | A |
| 5. | $h \to (l \lor h)$ | W |
| 6. | $\neg i \to (l \lor h)$ | HS, 4, 5 |
| 7. | $\neg i \to i$ | HS, 6, 3 |
| 8. | $\neg\neg i \lor i$ | MC, 7 |
| 9. | $i \lor i$ | DN, 8 |
| 10. | $i$ | I, 9 |
| 11. | $c$ | MP, 2, 10 |
| 12. | $c \to l$ | MC, 1 |
| 13. | $l$ | MP, 12, 11 |
| 14. | $l \mathrel{\&} i$ | C, 13, 10 |
| 15. | $(l \mathrel{\&} i) \mathrel{\&} c$ | C, 14, 11 |

10. s: Money serves you; d: Money dominates you; w: You handle it wisely; h: It can help you to attain happiness; g: You will gain much of it; l: You'll be satisfied with your lot.

| 1. | $(s \lor d) \mathrel{\&} \neg(s \mathrel{\&} d)$ | A |
| 2. | $(s \mathrel{\&} w) \to h$ | A |
| 3. | $d \to (g \mathrel{\&} \neg l)$ | A |
| 4. | $l \leftrightarrow \neg h$ | A |
| 5. | $s \lor d$ | S, 1 |
| 6. | $\neg(s \mathrel{\&} w) \lor h$ | MC, 2 |
| 7. | $(\neg s \lor \neg w) \lor h$ | DM, 6 |
| 8. | $\neg s \lor (\neg w \lor h)$ | As, 7 |
| 9. | $s \to (w \to h)$ | MC, 8 |
| 10. | $(g \mathrel{\&} \neg l) \to \neg l$ | W |
| 11. | $d \to \neg l$ | HS, 3, 10 |
| 12. | $(l \to \neg h) \mathrel{\&} (\neg h \to l)$ | B, 4 |
| 13. | $\neg h \to l$ | S, 12 |
| 14. | $\neg l \to \neg\neg h$ | Tr, 13 |
| 15. | $\neg l \to h$ | DN, 14 |
| 16. | $d \to h$ | HS, 11, 15 |
| 17. | $\neg d \lor h$ | MC, 16 |
| 18. | $(\neg d \lor h) \lor \neg w$ | Ad, 17 |
| 19. | $\neg d \lor (h \lor \neg w)$ | As, 18 |
| 20. | $d \to (h \lor \neg w)$ | MC, 19 |
| 21. | $d \to (\neg w \lor h)$ | Cm, 20 |
| 22. | $d \to (w \to h)$ | MC, 21 |
| 23. | $w \to h$ | CD, 5, 9, 22 |

14.     d: Happiness can be defined; m: There's a way to measure it; s: We can say whether someone is happy; w: We take that person's word for it.; t: We can test the psychological effects of jobs of various kinds.

| | | |
|---|---|---|
| 1. | ¬d → ¬m | A |
| 2. | ¬m → (s → w) | A |
| 3. | t → s | A |
| 4. | ¬w | A |
| 5. | ¬d → (s → w) | HS, 1, 2 |
| 6. | ¬t ∨ ¬w | Ad, 4 |
| 7. | t → ¬w | MC, 6 |
| 8. | t → (s & ¬w) | CC, 3, 7 |
| 9. | ¬(s → w) → ¬¬d | Tr, 5 |
| 10. | (s & ¬w) → ¬¬d | NC, 9 |
| 11. | t → ¬¬d | HS, 8, 10 |
| 12. | t → d | DN, 11 |
| 13. | ¬d → ¬t | Tr, 12 |

16.     s: We maintain high educational standards; a: We accept almost every high school graduate; f: We fail large numbers of students; p: Many students do poorly; l: We will placate the legislature.

| | | |
|---|---|---|
| 1. | ¬(s & a) ∨ (f ↔ p) | A |
| 2. | s | A |
| 3. | l & a | A |
| 4. | ¬(l & f) | A |
| 5. | l | S, 3 |
| 6. | a | S, 3 |
| 7. | s & a | C, 2, 6 |
| 8. | ¬¬(s & a) | DN, 7 |
| 9. | f ↔ p | DS, 1, 8 |
| 10. | ¬l ∨ ¬f | DM, 4 |
| 11. | ¬¬l | DN, 5 |
| 12. | ¬f | DS, 10, 11 |
| 13. | ¬p | BE, 9, 12 |

20.     r: The Soviet economy is restructured; d: Decision-making will have to be decentralized; s: Bureaucracies in charge of economic planning will have to become smaller; p: Bureaucracies in charge of economic planning will have to become less powerful; b: Bureaucrats can help it; w: The party hierarchy is willing to cede power to a wide group it can't easily control; c: Central planning will continue to dominate the economy.

| | | |
|---|---|---|
| 1. | r → (d & (s & p)) | A |
| 2. | b → ¬s | A |
| 3. | d → w | A |
| 4. | p ∨ (¬d & c) | A |
| 5. | (d & (s & p)) → d | W |
| 6. | (d & (s & p)) → w | HS, 5, 3 |
| 7. | r → w | HS, 1, 6 |
| 8. | (d & (s & p)) → (s & p) | W |
| 9. | (s & p) → s | W |
| 10. | r → (s & p) | HS, 1, 8 |
| 11. | r → s | HS, 10, 9 |
| 12. | s → ¬b | Tr, 2 |
| 13. | r → ¬b | HS, 11, 12 |
| 14. | r → (w & ¬b) | CC, 7, 13 |
| 15. | ¬(w & ¬b) → ¬r | Tr, 14 |
| 16. | (¬w ∨ ¬¬b) → ¬r | DM, 15 |
| 17. | (¬w ∨ b) → ¬r | DN, 16 |

22.　p: The party maintains its current economic policy; f: There will be a flight of capital to other countries; i: The party improves its image abroad; t: It tightens its control over the economy; h: The nation will have to pay large amounts of foreign debt in hard currency.

| | | |
|---|---|---|
| 1. | $p \rightarrow f$ | A |
| 2. | $t \rightarrow \neg i$ | A |
| 3. | $(p \ \& \ f) \rightarrow t$ | A |
| 4. | $(\neg i \rightarrow h) \ \& \ \neg h$ | A |
| 5. | $\neg i \rightarrow h$ | S, 4 |
| 6. | $\neg h$ | S, 4 |
| 7. | $\neg\neg i$ | MT, 5, 6 |
| 8. | $\neg t$ | MT, 2, 7 |
| 9. | $\neg(p \ \& \ f)$ | MT, 3, 8 |
| 10. | $p \rightarrow p$ | SI |
| 11. | $p \rightarrow (p \ \& \ f)$ | CC, 10, 1 |
| 12. | $\neg p$ | MT, 11, 9 |

26.

| | | |
|---|---|---|
| 1. | $p \leftrightarrow q$ | A |
| 2. | $\neg(m \rightarrow q)$ | A |
| 3. | $m \ \& \ \neg q$ | NC, 2 |
| 4. | $\neg q$ | S, 3 |
| 5. | $\neg p$ | BE, 1, 4 |

28.

| | | |
|---|---|---|
| 1. | $p \ \& \ q$ | A |
| 2. | $p$ | S, 1 |
| 3. | $q$ | S, 1 |
| 4. | $q \vee r$ | Ad, 3 |
| 5. | $\neg(\neg q \ \& \ \neg r)$ | DM, 4 |
| 6. | $\neg(\neg q \ \& \ \neg r) \ \& \ p$ | C, 5, 2 |

32.

| | | |
|---|---|---|
| 1. | $(p \ \& \ q) \rightarrow r$ | A |
| 2. | $\neg(p \ \& \ q) \vee r$ | MC, 1 |
| 3. | $(\neg p \vee \neg q) \vee r$ | DM, 2 |
| 4. | $\neg p \vee (\neg q \vee r)$ | As, 3 |
| 5. | $p \rightarrow (\neg q \vee r)$ | MC, 4 |
| 6. | $p \rightarrow (q \rightarrow r)$ | MC, 5 |

34.

| | | |
|---|---|---|
| 1. | $p \leftrightarrow q$ | A |
| 2. | $(p \rightarrow q) \ \& \ (q \rightarrow p)$ | B, 1 |
| 3. | $(\neg p \vee q) \ \& \ (\neg q \vee p)$ | MC, 2 |
| 4. | $(\neg p \ \& \ (\neg q \vee p)) \vee (q \ \& \ (\neg q \vee p))$ | D, 3 |
| 5. | $((\neg p \ \& \ \neg q) \vee (\neg p \ \& \ p)) \vee ((q \ \& \ \neg q) \vee (q \ \& \ p))$ | D, 4 |
| 6. | $q \rightarrow q$ | SI |
| 7. | $\neg q \vee q$ | MC, 6 |
| 8. | $\neg q \vee \neg\neg q$ | DN, 7 |
| 9. | $\neg(q \ \& \ \neg q)$ | DM, 8 |
| 10. | $\neg p \rightarrow \neg p$ | SI |
| 11. | $\neg\neg p \vee \neg p$ | MC, 10 |
| 12. | $\neg(\neg p \ \& \ p)$ | DM, 11 |
| 13. | $(((\neg p \ \& \ \neg q) \vee (\neg p \ \& \ p)) \vee (q \ \& \ \neg q)) \vee (q \ \& \ p)$ | As, 5 |
| 14. | $(q \ \& \ p) \vee (((\neg p \ \& \ \neg q) \vee (\neg p \ \& \ p)) \vee (q \ \& \ \neg q))$ | Cm, 13 |
| 15. | $(q \ \& \ p) \vee ((\neg p \ \& \ \neg q) \vee ((\neg p \ \& \ p) \vee (q \ \& \ \neg q)))$ | As, 14 |
| 16. | $((q \ \& \ p) \vee (\neg p \ \& \ \neg q)) \vee ((\neg p \ \& \ p) \vee (q \ \& \ \neg q))$ | As, 15 |
| 17. | $\neg(\neg p \ \& \ p) \ \& \ \neg(q \ \& \ \neg q)$ | C, 12, 9 |
| 18. | $\neg((\neg p \ \& \ p) \vee (q \ \& \ \neg q))$ | DM, 17 |
| 19. | $(q \ \& \ p) \vee (\neg p \ \& \ \neg q)$ | DS, 16, 18 |
| 20. | $(p \ \& \ q) \vee (\neg p \ \& \ \neg q)$ | Cm, 19 |

| 38. | 1. | $p \leftrightarrow q$ | A |
|---|---|---|---|
| | 2. | $(p \rightarrow q) \ \& \ (q \rightarrow p)$ | B, 1 |
| | 3. | $(q \rightarrow p) \ \& \ (p \rightarrow q)$ | Cm, 2 |
| | 4. | $q \leftrightarrow p$ | B, 3 |

| 40. | 1. | $p \rightarrow q$ | A |
|---|---|---|---|
| | 2. | $p \rightarrow r$ | A |
| | 3. | $\neg q \lor \neg r$ | A |
| | 4. | $\neg q \rightarrow \neg p$ | Tr, 1 |
| | 5. | $\neg r \rightarrow \neg p$ | Tr, 2 |
| | 6. | $\neg p \lor \neg p$ | CD, 3, 4, 5 |
| | 7. | $\neg p$ | I, 6 |

44. (a)

| | 1. | $a \rightarrow b$ | A |
|---|---|---|---|
| | 2. | $c \rightarrow (a \rightarrow \neg b)$ | A |
| | 3. | $c \rightarrow (\neg a \lor \neg b)$ | MC, 2 |
| | 4. | $\neg c \lor (\neg a \lor \neg b)$ | MC, 3 |
| | 5. | $\neg (c \ \& \ \neg(\neg a \lor \neg b))$ | DM, 4 |
| | 6. | $\neg (c \ \& \ (a \ \& \ b))$ | DM, 5 |

(b)

| | 1. | $a \rightarrow b$ | A |
|---|---|---|---|
| | 2. | $c \rightarrow (a \rightarrow \neg b)$ | A |
| | 3. | $c \rightarrow (\neg a \lor \neg b)$ | MC, 2 |
| | 4. | $\neg c \lor (\neg a \lor \neg b)$ | MC, 3 |
| | 5. | $(\neg c \lor \neg a) \lor \neg b$ | As, 4 |
| | 6. | $\neg b \lor (\neg c \lor \neg a)$ | Cm, 5 |
| | 7. | $b \rightarrow (\neg c \lor \neg a)$ | MC, 6 |
| | 8. | $a \rightarrow (\neg c \lor \neg a)$ | HS, 1, 7 |
| | 9. | $\neg a \lor (\neg c \lor \neg a)$ | MC, 8 |
| | 10. | $\neg a \lor (\neg a \lor \neg c)$ | Cm, 9 |
| | 11. | $(\neg a \lor \neg a) \lor \neg c$ | As, 10 |
| | 12. | $\neg a \lor \neg c$ | I, 11 |

(c)

| | 1. | $a \rightarrow b$ | A |
|---|---|---|---|
| | 2. | $c \rightarrow (a \rightarrow \neg b)$ | A |
| | 3. | $b \rightarrow (b \lor c)$ | W |
| | 4. | $a \rightarrow (b \lor c)$ | HS, 1, 3 |
| | 5. | $\neg(b \lor c) \rightarrow \neg a$ | Tr, 4 |
| | 6. | $(\neg b \ \& \ \neg c) \rightarrow \neg a$ | DM, 5 |

| 46. | 1. | $p \rightarrow (q \lor r)$ | A |
|---|---|---|---|
| | 2. | $(\neg q \ \& \ m) \lor (s \rightarrow \neg p)$ | A |
| | 3. | $\neg(\neg r \rightarrow \neg p)$ | A |
| | 4. | $\neg r \ \& \ \neg\neg p$ | NC, 3 |
| | 5. | $\neg\neg p$ | S, 4 |
| | 6. | $p$ | DN, 5 |
| | 7. | $\neg r$ | S, 4 |
| | 8. | $q \lor r$ | MP, 1, 6 |
| | 9. | $q$ | DS, 8, 7 |
| | 10. | $q \lor \neg m$ | Ad, 9 |
| | 11. | $\neg\neg q \lor \neg m$ | DN, 10 |
| | 12. | $\neg(\neg q \ \& \ m)$ | DM, 11 |
| | 13. | $s \rightarrow \neg p$ | DS, 2, 12 |
| | 14. | $\neg s$ | MT, 13, 5 |
| | 15. | $\neg s \ \& \ q$ | C, 14, 9 |

| 50. | 1. | $(p \ \& \ \neg r) \leftrightarrow (s \lor \neg q)$ | A |
|---|---|---|---|
| | 2. | $t \ \& \ ((\neg s \ \& \ \neg r) \rightarrow p)$ | A |
| | 3. | $(t \rightarrow q) \lor (t \rightarrow r)$ | A |
| | 4. | $(p \ \& \ s) \rightarrow r$ | A |
| | 5. | $t$ | S, 2 |
| | 6. | $(\neg s \ \& \ \neg r) \rightarrow p$ | S, 2 |
| | 7. | $(\neg t \lor q) \lor (\neg t \lor r)$ | MC, 3 |
| | 8. | $\neg t \lor (q \lor (\neg t \lor r))$ | As, 7 |
| | 9. | $\neg t \lor ((\neg t \lor r) \lor q)$ | Cm, 8 |
| | 10. | $\neg t \lor (\neg t \lor (r \lor q))$ | As, 9 |
| | 11. | $(\neg t \lor \neg t) \lor (r \lor q)$ | As, 10 |
| | 12. | $\neg t \lor (r \lor q)$ | I, 11 |
| | 13. | $\neg\neg t$ | DN, 5 |
| | 14. | $r \lor q$ | DS, 12, 13 |

|     |     |                                                                                      |                 |
|-----|-----|--------------------------------------------------------------------------------------|-----------------|
|     | 15. | $r \to (\neg p \lor r)$                                                              | W               |
|     | 16. | $r \to (\neg p \lor \neg\neg r)$                                                     | DN, 15          |
|     | 17. | $r \to \neg(p \And \neg r)$                                                          | DM, 16          |
|     | 18. | $((p \And \neg r) \to (s \lor \neg q)) \And ((s \lor \neg q) \to (p \And \neg r))$   | B, 1            |
|     | 19. | $(s \lor \neg q) \to (p \And \neg r)$                                                | S, 18           |
|     | 20. | $\neg(p \And \neg r) \to \neg(s \lor \neg q)$                                        | Tr, 19          |
|     | 21. | $r \to \neg(s \lor \neg q)$                                                          | HS, 17, 20      |
|     | 22. | $r \to (\neg s \And \neg\neg q)$                                                     | DM, 21          |
|     | 23. | $r \to (\neg s \And q)$                                                              | DN, 22          |
|     | 24. | $(\neg s \And q) \to q$                                                              | W               |
|     | 25. | $r \to q$                                                                            | HS, 23, 24      |
|     | 26. | $r \to r$                                                                            | SI              |
|     | 27. | $r \to (q \And r)$                                                                   | CC, 25, 26      |
|     | 28. | $q \And r$                                                                           |                 |

52.
|     |     |                                      |          |
|-----|-----|--------------------------------------|----------|
|     | 1.  | $p \to (p \lor q)$                   | W        |
|     | 2.  | $p \to (\neg\neg p \lor q)$          | DN, 1    |
|     | 3.  | $p \to (\neg p \to q)$               | MC, 2    |

56.
|     |     |                                                                                                                 |                  |
|-----|-----|-----------------------------------------------------------------------------------------------------------------|------------------|
|     | 1.  | $((\neg p \lor q) \And (p \And \neg r)) \to ((\neg p \lor q) \And (p \And \neg r))$                             | SI               |
|     | 2.  | $((\neg p \lor q) \And (p \And \neg r)) \to ((\neg p \And (p \And \neg r)) \lor (q \And (p \And \neg r)))$      | D, 1             |
|     | 3.  | $\neg p \to \neg p$                                                                                             | SI               |
|     | 4.  | $\neg\neg p \lor \neg p$                                                                                        | MC, 3            |
|     | 5.  | $p \lor \neg p$                                                                                                 | DN, 4            |
|     | 6.  | $(p \lor \neg p) \lor r$                                                                                        | Ad, 5            |
|     | 7.  | $\neg\neg(p \lor \neg p) \lor \neg\neg r$                                                                       | DN, 6            |
|     | 8.  | $\neg(\neg(p \lor \neg p) \And \neg r)$                                                                         | DM, 7            |
|     | 9.  | $\neg((\neg p \And \neg\neg p) \And \neg r)$                                                                    | DM, 8            |
|     | 10. | $\neg((\neg p \And p) \And \neg r)$                                                                             | DN, 9            |
|     | 11. | $\neg(\neg p \And (p \And \neg r))$                                                                             | As, 10           |
|     | 12. | $\neg((\neg p \lor q) \And (p \And \neg r)) \lor ((\neg p \And (p \And \neg r)) \lor (q \And (p \And \neg r)))$ | MC, 2            |
|     | 13. | $\neg((\neg p \lor q) \And (p \And \neg r)) \lor ((q \And (p \And \neg r)) \lor (\neg p \And (p \And \neg r)))$ | Cm, 12           |
|     | 14. | $(\neg((\neg p \lor q) \And (p \And \neg r)) \lor (q \And (p \And \neg r))) \lor (\neg p \And (p \And \neg r))$ | As, 13           |
|     | 15. | $\neg((\neg p \lor q) \And (p \And \neg r)) \lor (q \And (p \And \neg r))$                                      | DS, 14, 11       |
|     | 16. | $((\neg p \lor q) \And (p \And \neg r)) \to (q \And (p \And \neg r))$                                           | MC, 15           |
|     | 17. | $\neg(q \And (p \And \neg r)) \to \neg((\neg p \lor q) \And (p \And \neg r))$                                   | Tr, 16           |
|     | 18. | $\neg((q \And p) \And \neg r) \to \neg((\neg p \lor q) \And (p \And \neg r))$                                   | As, 17           |
|     | 19. | $\neg((p \And q) \And \neg r) \to \neg((\neg p \lor q) \And (p \And \neg r))$                                   | Cm, 18           |
|     | 20. | $\neg(p \And (q \And \neg r)) \to \neg((\neg p \lor q) \And (p \And \neg r))$                                   | As, 19           |
|     | 21. | $(p \to \neg(q \And \neg r)) \to \neg((\neg p \lor q) \And (p \And \neg r))$                                    | NC, 20           |
|     | 22. | $(p \to (q \to r)) \to \neg((\neg p \lor q) \And (p \And \neg r))$                                              | NC, 21           |
|     | 23. | $(p \to (q \to r)) \to ((\neg p \lor q) \to \neg(p \And \neg r))$                                               | NC, 22           |
|     | 24. | $(p \to (q \to r)) \to ((\neg p \lor q) \to (p \to r))$                                                         | NC, 23           |
|     | 25. | $(p \to (q \to r)) \to ((p \to q) \to (p \to r))$                                                               | MC, 24           |

58.
|     |     |                                    |          |
|-----|-----|------------------------------------|----------|
|     | 1.  | $\neg p \to \neg p$                | SI       |
|     | 2.  | $\neg p \to (\neg p \And \neg p)$  | CC, 1, 1 |
|     | 3.  | $\neg(\neg p \And \neg p) \to \neg\neg p$ | Tr, 2    |
|     | 4.  | $(p \lor p) \to \neg\neg p$        | DM, 3    |
|     | 5.  | $(p \lor p) \to p$                 | DN, 4    |

62.
1. $(q \rightarrow r) \rightarrow (q \rightarrow r)$      SI
2. $\neg p \rightarrow \neg p$      SI
3. $\neg\neg\neg p \vee \neg p$      MC, 2
4. $p \vee \neg p$      DN, 3
5. $\neg(q \rightarrow r) \vee (p \vee \neg p)$      Ad, 4
6. $(q \rightarrow r) \rightarrow (p \vee \neg p)$      MC, 5
7. $(q \rightarrow r) \rightarrow ((q \rightarrow r) \,\&\, (p \vee \neg p))$      CC, 1, 6
8. $(q \rightarrow r) \rightarrow ((\neg q \vee r) \,\&\, (p \vee \neg p))$      MC, 7
9. $(q \rightarrow r) \rightarrow ((\neg q \,\&\, (p \vee \neg p)) \vee (r \,\&\, (p \vee \neg p)))$      D, 8
10. $(q \rightarrow r) \rightarrow (((\neg q \,\&\, p) \vee (\neg q \,\&\, \neg p)) \vee (r \,\&\, (p \vee \neg p)))$      D, 9
11. $(q \rightarrow r) \rightarrow (((\neg q \,\&\, \neg p) \vee (\neg q \,\&\, p)) \vee (r \,\&\, (p \vee \neg p)))$      Cm, 10
12. $(q \rightarrow r) \rightarrow (((\neg p \,\&\, \neg q) \vee (\neg q \,\&\, p)) \vee (r \,\&\, (p \vee \neg p)))$      Cm, 11
13. $\neg(q \rightarrow r) \vee (((\neg p \,\&\, \neg q) \vee (\neg q \,\&\, p)) \vee (r \,\&\, (p \vee \neg p)))$      MC, 12
14. $(\neg(q \rightarrow r) \vee ((\neg p \,\&\, \neg q) \vee (\neg q \,\&\, p))) \vee (r \,\&\, (p \vee \neg p))$      As, 13
15. $(\neg(q \rightarrow r) \vee ((\neg p \,\&\, \neg q) \vee (\neg q \,\&\, p))) \rightarrow$
$(\neg(q \rightarrow r) \vee ((\neg p \,\&\, \neg q) \vee (\neg q \,\&\, p)))$      SI
16. $(r \,\&\, (p \vee \neg p)) \rightarrow r$      W
17. $(\neg(q \rightarrow r) \vee ((\neg p \,\&\, \neg q) \vee (\neg q \,\&\, p))) \vee r$      CD, 14, 15, 16
18. $((\neg(q \rightarrow r) \vee (\neg p \,\&\, \neg q)) \vee (\neg q \,\&\, p)) \vee r$      As, 17
19. $(\neg(q \rightarrow r) \vee (\neg p \,\&\, \neg q)) \vee ((\neg q \,\&\, p) \vee r)$      As, 18
20. $(\neg(q \rightarrow r) \vee (\neg p \,\&\, \neg q)) \vee (r \vee (\neg q \,\&\, p))$      Cm, 19
21. $((\neg(q \rightarrow r) \vee (\neg p \,\&\, \neg q)) \vee r) \vee (\neg q \,\&\, p)$      As, 20
22. $((\neg(q \rightarrow r) \vee (\neg p \,\&\, \neg q)) \vee r) \rightarrow ((\neg(q \rightarrow r) \vee (\neg p \,\&\, \neg q)) \vee r)$      SI
23. $(\neg q \,\&\, p) \rightarrow p$      W
24. $((\neg(q \rightarrow r) \vee (\neg p \,\&\, \neg q)) \vee r) \vee p$      CD, 21, 22, 23
25. $(\neg(q \rightarrow r) \vee (\neg p \,\&\, \neg q)) \vee (r \vee p)$      As, 24
26. $\neg(q \rightarrow r) \vee ((\neg p \,\&\, \neg q) \vee (r \vee p))$      As, 25
27. $\neg(q \rightarrow r) \vee ((\neg p \,\&\, \neg q) \vee (p \vee r))$      Cm, 26
28. $(q \rightarrow r) \rightarrow ((\neg p \,\&\, \neg q) \vee (p \vee r))$      MC, 27
29. $(q \rightarrow r) \rightarrow (\neg(p \vee q) \vee (p \vee r))$      DM, 28
30. $(q \rightarrow r) \rightarrow ((p \vee q) \rightarrow (p \vee r))$      MC, 29

64.
1. $((\neg p \vee r) \,\&\, (p \,\&\, (\neg q \vee \neg r))) \rightarrow ((\neg p \vee r) \,\&\, (p \,\&\, (\neg q \vee \neg r)))$      SI
2. $((\neg p \vee r) \,\&\, (p \,\&\, (\neg q \vee \neg r))) \rightarrow (((\neg p \vee r) \,\&\, p) \,\&\, (\neg q \vee \neg r))$      As, 1
3. $((\neg p \vee r) \,\&\, (p \,\&\, (\neg q \vee \neg r))) \rightarrow (((\neg p \,\&\, p) \vee (r \,\&\, p)) \,\&\, (\neg q \vee \neg r))$      D, 2
4. $((\neg p \vee r) \,\&\, (p \,\&\, (\neg q \vee \neg r))) \rightarrow$
$(((\neg p \,\&\, p) \,\&\, (\neg q \vee \neg r)) \vee ((r \,\&\, p) \,\&\, (\neg q \vee \neg r)))$      D, 3
5. $\neg p \rightarrow \neg p$      SI
6. $\neg\neg\neg p \vee \neg p$      MC, 5
7. $(\neg\neg p \vee \neg p) \vee \neg(\neg q \vee \neg r)$      Ad, 6
8. $\neg(\neg p \,\&\, p) \vee \neg(\neg q \vee \neg r)$      DM, 7
9. $\neg((\neg p \,\&\, p) \,\&\, (\neg q \vee \neg r))$      DM, 8
10. $\neg((\neg p \vee r) \,\&\, (p \,\&\, (\neg q \vee \neg r))) \vee$
$(((\neg p \,\&\, p) \,\&\, (\neg q \vee \neg r)) \vee ((r \,\&\, p) \,\&\, (\neg q \vee \neg r)))$      MC, 4
11. $\neg((\neg p \vee r) \,\&\, (p \,\&\, (\neg q \vee \neg r))) \vee$
$(((r \,\&\, p) \,\&\, (\neg q \vee \neg r)) \vee ((\neg p \,\&\, p) \,\&\, (\neg q \vee \neg r)))$      Cm, 10
12. $(\neg((\neg p \vee r) \,\&\, (p \,\&\, (\neg q \vee \neg r))) \vee$
$((r \,\&\, p) \,\&\, (\neg q \vee \neg r))) \vee ((\neg p \,\&\, p) \,\&\, (\neg q \vee \neg r))$      As, 11
13. $\neg((\neg p \vee r) \,\&\, (p \,\&\, (\neg q \vee \neg r))) \vee ((r \,\&\, p) \,\&\, (\neg q \vee \neg r))$      DS, 12, 9
14. $\neg((\neg p \vee r) \,\&\, (p \,\&\, (\neg q \vee \neg r))) \vee (((r \,\&\, p) \,\&\, \neg q) \vee ((r \,\&\, p) \,\&\, \neg r))$      D, 13
15. $(\neg((\neg p \vee r) \,\&\, (p \,\&\, (\neg q \vee \neg r))) \vee ((r \,\&\, p) \,\&\, \neg q)) \vee ((r \,\&\, p) \,\&\, \neg r)$      As, 14
16. $r \rightarrow r$      SI
17. $\neg r \vee r$      MC, 16
18. $(\neg r \vee r) \vee \neg p$      Ad, 17
19. $\neg r \vee (r \vee \neg p)$      As, 18
20. $\neg r \vee (\neg p \vee r)$      Cm, 19
21. $(\neg r \vee \neg p) \vee r$      As, 20

| | | | |
|---|---|---|---|
| 22. | ¬(r & p) ∨ r | | DM, 21 |
| 23. | ¬(r & p) ∨ ¬¬r | | DN, 22 |
| 24. | ¬((r & p) & ¬r) | | DM, 23 |
| 25. | ¬((¬p ∨ r) & (p & (¬q ∨ ¬r))) ∨ ((r & p) & ¬q) | | DS, 15, 24 |
| 26. | ((¬p ∨ r) & (p & (¬q ∨ ¬r))) → ((r & p) & ¬q) | | MC, 25 |
| 27. | ((¬p ∨ r) & (p & (¬q ∨ ¬r))) → (r & (p & ¬q)) | | As, 26 |
| 28. | (r & (p & ¬q)) → (p & ¬q) | | W |
| 29. | ((¬p ∨ r) & (p & (¬q ∨ ¬r))) → (p & ¬q) | | HS, 27, 28 |
| 30. | ¬(p & ¬q) → ¬((¬p ∨ r) & (p & (¬q ∨ ¬r))) | | Tr, 29 |
| 31. | (p → q) → ¬((¬p ∨ r) & (p & (¬q ∨ ¬r))) | | NC, 30 |
| 32. | (p → q) → ((¬p ∨ r) → ¬(p & (¬q ∨ ¬r))) | | NC, 31 |
| 33. | (p → q) → ((p → r) → ¬(p & (¬q ∨ ¬r))) | | MC, 32 |
| 34. | (p → q) → ((p → r) → (p → ¬(¬q ∨ ¬r))) | | NC, 33 |
| 35. | (p → q) → ((p → r) → (p → ¬¬(q & r))) | | DM, 34 |
| 36. | (p → q) → ((p → r) → (p → (q & r))) | | DN, 35 |

## 8.7  Indirect Proof

from 8.5:

| | | | |
|---|---|---|---|
| 14. | 1. | r → (p ∨ q) | A |
| | 2. | ¬((r → p) ∨ q) | AIP |
| | 3. | ¬(r → p) & ¬q | DM, 2 |
| | 4. | (r & ¬p) & ¬q | NC, 3 |
| | 5. | r & (¬p & ¬q) | As, 4 |
| | 6. | r | S, 5 |
| | 7. | p ∨ q | MP, 1, 6 |
| | 8. | ¬p & ¬q | S, 5 |
| | 9. | ¬(p ∨ q) | DM, 8 |
| | 10. | (p ∨ q) & ¬(p ∨ q) | C, 7, 9 |

| | | | |
|---|---|---|---|
| 16. | 1. | ¬s ∨ (s & r) | A |
| | 2. | (s → r) → q | A |
| | 3. | ¬q | AIP |
| | 4. | ¬(s → r) | MT, 2, 3 |
| | 5. | s & ¬r | NC, 4 |
| | 6. | s | S, 5 |
| | 7. | ¬r | S, 5 |
| | 8. | ¬¬s | DN, 6 |
| | 9. | s & r | DS, 1, 8 |
| | 10. | r | S, 9 |
| | 11. | r & ¬r | C, 10, 7 |

| | | | |
|---|---|---|---|
| 20. | 1. | r → ¬p | A |
| | 2. | q | A |
| | 3. | q → (p ∨ ¬s) | A |
| | 4. | ¬(s → ¬r) | AIP |
| | 5. | s & ¬¬r | NC, 4 |
| | 6. | ¬¬r | S, 5 |
| | 7. | r | DN, 6 |
| | 8. | ¬p | MP, 1, 7 |
| | 9. | s | S, 5 |
| | 10. | p ∨ ¬s | MP, 3, 2 |
| | 11. | ¬s | DS, 10, 8 |
| | 12. | s & ¬s | C, 9, 11 |

| 22. | 1. | $r \to \neg p$ | A |
| | 2. | $\neg r \to \neg q$ | A |
| | 3. | $q \lor \neg s$ | A |
| | 4. | $\neg(\neg p \lor \neg s)$ | AIP |
| | 5. | $\neg\neg p \,\&\, \neg\neg s$ | DM, 4 |
| | 6. | $\neg\neg p$ | S, 5 |
| | 7. | $\neg\neg s$ | S, 5 |
| | 8. | $\neg r$ | MT, 1, 6 |
| | 9. | $\neg q$ | MP, 2, 8 |
| | 10. | $\neg s$ | DS, 3, 9 |
| | 11. | $\neg s \,\&\, \neg\neg s$ | C, 10, 7 |

| 26. | 1. | $r \,\&\, p$ | A |
| | 2. | $r \to (s \lor q)$ | A |
| | 3. | $\neg(q \,\&\, p)$ | A |
| | 4. | $\neg s$ | AIP |
| | 5. | $r$ | S, 1 |
| | 6. | $p$ | S, 1 |
| | 7. | $\neg q \lor \neg p$ | DM, 3 |
| | 8. | $s \lor q$ | MP, 2, 4 |
| | 9. | $q$ | DS, 8, 4 |
| | 10. | $\neg\neg q$ | DN, 9 |
| | 11. | $\neg p$ | DS, 7, 10 |
| | 12. | $p \,\&\, \neg p$ | C, 6, 11 |

| 28. | 1. | $s \to r$ | A |
| | 2. | $(s \,\&\, r) \to p$ | A |
| | 3. | $q \to t$ | A |
| | 4. | $q \lor s$ | A |
| | 5. | $\neg(p \lor t)$ | AIP |
| | 6. | $\neg p \,\&\, \neg t$ | DM, 5 |
| | 7. | $\neg p$ | S, 6 |
| | 8. | $\neg t$ | S, 6 |
| | 9. | $\neg q$ | MT, 3, 8 |
| | 10. | $s$ | DS, 4, 9 |
| | 11. | $r$ | MP, 1, 10 |
| | 12. | $s \,\&\, r$ | C, 10, 11 |
| | 13. | $p$ | MP, 2, 12 |
| | 14. | $p \,\&\, \neg p$ | C, 13, 7 |

| 32. | 1. | $r \,\&\, (\neg p \,\&\, \neg t)$ | A |
| | 2. | $r \to (s \to q)$ | A |
| | 3. | $s \to (q \leftrightarrow (t \lor p))$ | A |
| | 4. | $\neg\neg s$ | AIP |
| | 5. | $s$ | DN, 4 |
| | 6. | $q \leftrightarrow (t \lor p)$ | MP, 3, 5 |
| | 7. | $r$ | S, 1 |
| | 8. | $\neg p \,\&\, \neg t$ | S, 1 |
| | 9. | $\neg(p \lor t)$ | DM, 5 |
| | 10. | $s \to q$ | MP, 2, 7 |
| | 11. | $\neg(t \lor p)$ | Cm, 9 |
| | 12. | $q$ | MP, 10, 5 |
| | 13. | $t \lor p$ | BE, 6, 12 |
| | 14. | $(t \lor p) \,\&\, \neg(t \lor p)$ | C, 13, 11 |

34.
| | | |
|---|---|---|
| 1. | ¬(p ∨ ¬s) | A |
| 2. | ¬p → (q ∨ r) | A |
| 3. | ¬r ∨ ¬s | A |
| 4. | (q ∨ t) → (m & (k → ¬s)) | A |
| 5. | ¬¬(m → k) | AIP |
| 6. | m → k | DN, 5 |
| 7. | ¬p & ¬¬s | DM, 1 |
| 8. | ¬p | S, 7 |
| 9. | q ∨ r | MP, 2, 8 |
| 10. | ¬¬s | S, 7 |
| 11. | ¬r | DS, 3, 10 |
| 12. | q | DS, 9, 11 |
| 13. | q ∨ t | Ad, 12 |
| 14. | m & (k → ¬s) | MP, 4, 13 |
| 15. | m | S, 14 |
| 16. | k → ¬s | S, 14 |
| 17. | k | MP, 6, 15 |
| 18. | ¬s | MP, 16, 17 |
| 19. | ¬s & ¬¬s | C, 18, 10 |

38.
| | | |
|---|---|---|
| 1. | p | A |
| 2. | ¬p | A |
| 3. | ¬q | AIP |
| 4. | p & ¬p | C, 1, 2 |

40.
| | | |
|---|---|---|
| 1. | p & (q ∨ r) | A |
| 2. | ¬((p & q) ∨ (p & r)) | AIP |
| 3. | p | S, 1 |
| 4. | q ∨ r | S, 1 |
| 5. | ¬(p & q) & ¬(p & r) | DM, 2 |
| 6. | ¬(p & q) | S, 5 |
| 7. | ¬(p & r) | S, 5 |
| 8. | ¬p ∨ ¬q | DM, 6 |
| 9. | ¬¬p | DN, 3 |
| 10. | ¬q | DS, 8, 9 |
| 11. | r | DS, 4, 10 |
| 12. | p & r | C, 3, 11 |
| 13. | (p & r) & ¬(p & r) | C, 12, 7 |

44.
| | | |
|---|---|---|
| 1. | p ↔ ¬q | A |
| 2. | ¬¬(p ↔ q) | AIP |
| 3. | p ↔ q | DN, 2 |
| 4. | (p → ¬q) & (¬q → p) | B, 1 |
| 5. | p → ¬q | S, 4 |
| 6. | (p → q) & (q → p) | B, 3 |
| 7. | p → q | S, 6 |
| 8. | p → (q & ¬q) | CC, 7, 5 |
| 9. | q → q | SI |
| 10. | ¬q ∨ q | MC, 9 |
| 11. | ¬q ∨ ¬¬q | DN, 10 |
| 12. | ¬(q & ¬q) | DM, 11 |
| 13. | ¬p | MT, 8, 12 |
| 14. | ¬¬q | BE, 1, 13 |
| 15. | ¬q | BE, 3, 13 |
| 16. | ¬q & ¬¬q | C, 15, 14 |

| 46. | 1. | (p & q) ∨ (p & r) | A |
|-----|-----|------------------|----|
| | 2. | ¬(p & (q ∨ r)) | AIP |
| | 3. | ¬p ∨ ¬(q ∨ r) | DM, 2 |
| | 4. | (p & q) → p | W |
| | 5. | (p & r) → p | W |
| | 6. | p ∨ p | CD, 1, 4, 5 |
| | 7. | p | I, 6 |
| | 8. | ¬¬p | DN, 7 |
| | 9. | ¬(q ∨ r) | DS, 3, 8 |
| | 10. | (p & q) → q | W |
| | 11. | (p & r) → r | W |
| | 12. | q ∨ r | CD, 1, 10, 11 |
| | 13. | (q ∨ r) & ¬(q ∨ r) | C, 12, 9 |

| 50. | 1. | r → f | A |
|-----|-----|-------|----|
| | 2. | f → ¬r | A |
| | 3. | ¬¬r | AIP |
| | 4. | ¬f | MT, 2, 3 |
| | 5. | ¬r | MT, 1, 4 |
| | 6. | ¬r & ¬¬r | C, 5, 3 |

| 52. | 1. | s → (l ∨ d) | A |
|-----|-----|-------------|----|
| | 2. | ¬l | A |
| | 3. | ¬d | A |
| | 4. | ¬¬s | AIP |
| | 5. | s | DN, 4 |
| | 6. | l ∨ d | MP, 1, 5 |
| | 7. | d | DS, 6, 2 |
| | 8. | d & ¬d | C, 7, 3 |

| 56. | 1. | ¬u → t | A |
|-----|-----|--------|----|
| | 2. | u → t | A |
| | 3. | ¬t | AIP |
| | 4. | ¬u | MT, 2, 3 |
| | 5. | t | MP, 1, 4 |
| | 6. | t & ¬t | C, 5, 3 |

| 58. | 1. | p → a | A |
|-----|-----|-------|----|
| | 2. | g → w | A |
| | 3. | ¬e ∨ (¬w ∨ ¬a) | A |
| | 4. | x → (g & p) | A |
| | 5. | ¬(e → ¬x) | AIP |
| | 6. | e & ¬¬x | NC, 5 |
| | 7. | e | S, 6 |
| | 8. | ¬¬x | S, 6 |
| | 9. | x | DN, 8 |
| | 10. | ¬¬e | DN, 7 |
| | 11. | ¬w ∨ ¬a | DS, 3, 10 |
| | 12. | g & p | MP, 4, 9 |
| | 13. | g | S, 12 |
| | 14. | p | S, 12 |
| | 15. | a | MP, 1, 14 |
| | 16. | w | MP, 2, 13 |
| | 17. | w & a | C, 16, 15 |
| | 18. | ¬(w & a) | DM, 11 |
| | 19. | (w & a) & ¬(w & a) | C, 17, 18 |

**from 8.6:**

Problems for which indirect proof makes little difference are omitted.

| 10. | 1. | (s ∨ d) & ¬(s & d) | A |
|---|---|---|---|
| | 2. | (s & w) → h | A |
| | 3. | d → (g & ¬l) | A |
| | 4. | l ↔ ¬h | A |
| | 5. | ¬(w → h) | AIP |
| | 6. | w & ¬h | NC, 5 |
| | 7. | s ∨ d | S, 1 |
| | 8. | ¬h | S, 6 |
| | 9. | ¬(s & w) | MT, 2, 8 |
| | 10. | ¬s ∨ ¬w | DM, 9 |
| | 11. | w | S, 6 |
| | 12. | ¬¬w | DN, 11 |
| | 13. | ¬s | DS, 10, 12 |
| | 14. | d | DS, 7, 13 |
| | 15. | g & ¬l | MP, 3, 14 |
| | 16. | l | BE, 4, 8 |
| | 17. | ¬l | S, 15 |
| | 18. | l & ¬l | C, 16, 17 |

| 14. | 1. | ¬d → ¬m | A |
|---|---|---|---|
| | 2. | ¬m → (s → w) | A |
| | 3. | t → s | A |
| | 4. | ¬w | A |
| | 5. | ¬(¬d → ¬t) | AIP |
| | 6. | ¬d & ¬¬t | NC, 5 |
| | 7. | ¬d | S, 6 |
| | 8. | ¬¬t | S, 6 |
| | 9. | t | DN, 8 |
| | 10. | s | MP, 3, 9 |
| | 11. | ¬m | MP, 1, 7 |
| | 12. | s → w | MP, 2, 11 |
| | 13. | w | MP, 12, 10 |
| | 14. | w & ¬w | C, 13, 4 |

| 16. | 1. | ¬(s & a) ∨ (f ↔ p) | A |
|---|---|---|---|
| | 2. | s | A |
| | 3. | l & a | A |
| | 4. | ¬(l & f) | A |
| | 5. | ¬¬p | AIP |
| | 6. | p | DN, 5 |
| | 7. | l | S, 3 |
| | 8. | a | S, 3 |
| | 9. | s & a | C, 2, 8 |
| | 10. | ¬¬(s & a) | DN, 9 |
| | 11. | f ↔ p | DS, 1, 10 |
| | 12. | f | BE, 11, 6 |
| | 13. | l & f | C, 7, 12 |
| | 14. | (l & f) & ¬(l & f) | C, 13, 4 |

| 20. | 1.  | r → (d & (s & p))              | A            |
|     | 2.  | b → ¬s                         | A            |
|     | 3.  | d → w                          | A            |
|     | 4.  | p ∨ (¬d & c)                   | A            |
|     | 5.  | ¬((¬w ∨ b) → ¬r)               | AIP          |
|     | 6.  | (¬w ∨ b) & ¬¬r                 | NC, 5        |
|     | 7.  | ¬¬r                            | S, 6         |
|     | 8.  | ¬w ∨ b                         | S, 6         |
|     | 9.  | r                              | DN, 7        |
|     | 10. | d & (s & p)                    | MP, 1, 9     |
|     | 11. | d                              | S, 10        |
|     | 12. | s & p                          | S, 10        |
|     | 13. | s                              | S, 12        |
|     | 14. | w                              | MP, 3, 11    |
|     | 15. | ¬¬w                            | DN, 14       |
|     | 16. | b                              | DS, 8, 15    |
|     | 17. | ¬s                             | MP, 2, 16    |
|     | 18. | s & ¬s                         | C, 13, 17    |

| 22. | 1.  | p → f                          | A            |
|     | 2.  | t → ¬i                         | A            |
|     | 3.  | (p & f) → t                    | A            |
|     | 4.  | (¬i → h) & ¬h                  | A            |
|     | 5.  | ¬¬p                            | AIP          |
|     | 6.  | p                              | DN, 5        |
|     | 7.  | ¬i → h                         | S, 4         |
|     | 8.  | ¬h                             | S, 4         |
|     | 9.  | ¬¬i                            | MT, 7, 8     |
|     | 10. | ¬t                             | MT, 2, 9     |
|     | 11. | f                              | MP, 1, 6     |
|     | 12. | p & f                          | C, 6, 11     |
|     | 13. | t                              | MP, 3, 12    |
|     | 14. | t & ¬t                         | C, 13, 10    |

| 26. | 1.  | p ↔ q                          | A            |
|     | 2.  | ¬(m → q)                       | A            |
|     | 3.  | ¬¬p                            | AIP          |
|     | 4.  | p                              | DN, 3        |
|     | 5.  | q                              | BE, 1, 4     |
|     | 6.  | m & ¬q                         | NC, 2        |
|     | 7.  | ¬q                             | S, 6         |
|     | 8.  | q & ¬q                         | C, 5, 7      |

| 32. | 1.  | (p & q) → r                    | A            |
|     | 2.  | ¬(p → (q → r))                 | AIP          |
|     | 3.  | p & ¬(q → r)                   | NC, 2        |
|     | 4.  | p & (q & ¬r)                   | NC, 3        |
|     | 5.  | p                              | S, 4         |
|     | 6.  | q & ¬r                         | S, 4         |
|     | 7.  | q                              | S, 6         |
|     | 8.  | ¬r                             | S, 6         |
|     | 9.  | p & q                          | C, 5, 7      |
|     | 10. | r                              | MP, 1, 9     |
|     | 11. | r & ¬r                         | C, 10, 8     |

| 34. | 1. | $p \leftrightarrow q$ | A |
|---|---|---|---|
| | 2. | $\neg((p \mathbin{\&} q) \vee (\neg p \mathbin{\&} \neg q))$ | AIP |
| | 3. | $\neg(p \mathbin{\&} q) \mathbin{\&} \neg(\neg p \mathbin{\&} \neg q)$ | DM, 2 |
| | 4. | $\neg(p \mathbin{\&} q)$ | S, 3 |
| | 5. | $\neg(\neg p \mathbin{\&} \neg q)$ | S, 3 |
| | 6. | $p \vee q$ | DM, 5 |
| | 7. | $(p \rightarrow q) \mathbin{\&} (q \rightarrow p)$ | B, 1 |
| | 8. | $p \rightarrow q$ | S, 7 |
| | 9. | $q \rightarrow p$ | S, 7 |
| | 10. | $p \rightarrow p$ | SI |
| | 11. | $q \rightarrow q$ | SI |
| | 12. | $p \rightarrow (p \mathbin{\&} q)$ | CC, 10, 8 |
| | 13. | $q \rightarrow (p \mathbin{\&} q)$ | CC, 9, 11 |
| | 14. | $(p \mathbin{\&} q) \vee (p \mathbin{\&} q)$ | CD, 6, 12, 13 |
| | 15. | $p \mathbin{\&} q$ | I, 14 |
| | 16. | $(p \mathbin{\&} q) \mathbin{\&} \neg(p \mathbin{\&} q)$ | C, 15, 4 |

| 40. | 1. | $p \rightarrow q$ | A |
|---|---|---|---|
| | 2. | $p \rightarrow r$ | A |
| | 3. | $\neg q \vee \neg r$ | A |
| | 4. | $\neg\neg p$ | AIP |
| | 5. | $p$ | DN, 4 |
| | 6. | $q$ | MP, 1, 5 |
| | 7. | $r$ | MP, 2, 5 |
| | 8. | $\neg\neg r$ | DN, 7 |
| | 9. | $\neg q$ | DS, 3, 8 |
| | 10. | $q \mathbin{\&} \neg q$ | C, 6, 9 |

| 44. (a) | 1. | $a \rightarrow b$ | A | (b) | 1. | $a \rightarrow b$ | A |
|---|---|---|---|---|---|---|---|
| | 2. | $c \rightarrow (a \rightarrow \neg b)$ | A | | 2. | $c \rightarrow (a \rightarrow \neg b)$ | A |
| | 3. | $\neg\neg(c \mathbin{\&} (a \mathbin{\&} b))$ | AIP | | 3. | $\neg(\neg a \vee \neg c)$ | AIP |
| | 4. | $c \mathbin{\&} (a \mathbin{\&} b)$ | DN, 3 | | 4. | $\neg\neg a \mathbin{\&} \neg\neg c$ | DM, 3 |
| | 5. | $c$ | S, 4 | | 5. | $a \mathbin{\&} c$ | DN, 4 |
| | 6. | $a \mathbin{\&} b$ | S, 4 | | 6. | $a$ | S, 5 |
| | 7. | $a$ | S, 6 | | 7. | $c$ | S, 5 |
| | 8. | $a \rightarrow \neg b$ | MP, 2, 5 | | 8. | $b$ | MP, 1, 6 |
| | 9. | $\neg b$ | MP, 8, 7 | | 9. | $a \rightarrow \neg b$ | MP, 2, 7 |
| | 10. | $b$ | S, 6 | | 10. | $\neg b$ | MP, 9, 6 |
| | 11. | $b \mathbin{\&} \neg b$ | C, 10, 9 | | 11. | $b \mathbin{\&} \neg b$ | C, 8, 10 |

| 50. | 1. | $(p \mathbin{\&} \neg r) \leftrightarrow (s \vee \neg q)$ | A |
|---|---|---|---|
| | 2. | $t \mathbin{\&} ((\neg s \mathbin{\&} \neg r) \rightarrow p)$ | A |
| | 3. | $(t \rightarrow q) \vee (t \rightarrow r)$ | A |
| | 4. | $(p \mathbin{\&} s) \rightarrow r$ | A |
| | 5. | $\neg(q \mathbin{\&} r)$ | AIP |
| | 6. | $\neg q \vee \neg r$ | DM, 5 |
| | 7. | $t$ | S, 2 |
| | 8. | $(\neg s \mathbin{\&} \neg r) \rightarrow p$ | S, 2 |
| | 9. | $\neg q \rightarrow (s \vee \neg q)$ | W |
| | 10. | $((p \mathbin{\&} \neg r) \rightarrow (s \vee \neg q)) \mathbin{\&} ((s \vee \neg q) \rightarrow (p \mathbin{\&} \neg r))$ | B, 1 |
| | 11. | $(s \vee \neg q) \rightarrow (p \mathbin{\&} \neg r)$ | S, 10 |
| | 12. | $(p \mathbin{\&} \neg r) \rightarrow (s \vee \neg q)$ | S, 10 |
| | 13. | $\neg q \rightarrow (p \mathbin{\&} \neg r)$ | HS, 9, 11 |
| | 14. | $(p \mathbin{\&} \neg r) \rightarrow \neg r$ | W |
| | 15. | $\neg q \rightarrow \neg r$ | HS, 13, 14 |
| | 16. | $\neg r \rightarrow \neg r$ | SI |
| | 17. | $\neg r \vee \neg r$ | CD, 6, 15, 16 |

| | | |
|---|---|---|
| 18. | ¬r | I, 17 |
| 19. | ¬(p & s) | MT, 4, 18 |
| 20. | ¬p ∨ ¬s | DM, 19 |
| 21. | ¬p → ¬(¬s & ¬r) | Tr, 8 |
| 22. | ¬p → (¬¬s ∨ ¬¬r) | DM, 21 |
| 23. | ¬p → (s ∨ r) | DN, 22 |
| 24. | t & ¬r | C, 7, 18 |
| 25. | ¬(t → r) | NC, 24 |
| 26. | t → q | DS, 3, 25 |
| 27. | q | MP, 26, 7 |
| 28. | ¬¬s ∨ q | Ad, 27 |
| 29. | ¬s → q | MC, 28 |
| 30. | ¬s → ¬s | SI |
| 31. | ¬s → (¬s & q) | CC, 30, 29 |
| 32. | ¬s → (¬s & ¬¬q) | DN, 31 |
| 33. | ¬s → ¬(s ∨ ¬q) | DM, 32 |
| 34. | ¬(s ∨ ¬q) → ¬(p & ¬r) | Tr, 12 |
| 35. | ¬s → ¬(p & ¬r) | HS, 33, 34 |
| 36. | ¬s → (¬p ∨ ¬¬r) | DM, 35 |
| 37. | ¬¬s ∨ (¬p ∨ ¬¬r) | MC, 36 |
| 38. | (¬¬s ∨ ¬p) ∨ ¬¬r | As, 37 |
| 39. | (¬¬s ∨ ¬p) ∨ r | DN, 38 |
| 40. | ¬¬s ∨ ¬p | DS, 39, 18 |
| 41. | ¬s → ¬p | MC, 40 |
| 42. | ¬¬p ∨ (s ∨ r) | MC, 23 |
| 43. | (¬¬p ∨ s) ∨ r | As, 42 |
| 44. | ¬¬p ∨ s | DS, 43, 18 |
| 45. | ¬p → s | MC, 44 |
| 46. | p → s | Tr, 41 |
| 47. | p → p | SI |
| 48. | ¬p ∨ p | MC, 47 |
| 49. | s ∨ s | CD, 48, 45, 46 |
| 50. | s | I, 49 |
| 51. | s ∨ ¬q | Ad, 50 |
| 52. | p & ¬r | MP, 11, 51 |
| 53. | p | S, 52 |
| 54. | ¬¬p | DN, 53 |
| 55. | ¬s | DS, 20, 54 |
| 56. | s & ¬s | C, 50, 55 |

| | | | |
|---|---|---|---|
| 56. | 1. | ¬((p → (q → r)) → ((p → q) → (p → r))) | AIP |
| | 2. | (p → (q → r)) & ¬((p → q) → (p → r)) | NC, 1 |
| | 3. | p → (q → r) | S, 2 |
| | 4. | ¬((p → q) → (p → r)) | S, 2 |
| | 5. | (p → q) & ¬(p → r) | NC, 4 |
| | 6. | p → q | S, 5 |
| | 7. | ¬(p → r) | S, 5 |
| | 8. | p & ¬r | NC, 7 |
| | 9. | p | S, 8 |
| | 10. | ¬r | S, 8 |
| | 11. | q | MP, 6, 9 |
| | 12. | q → r | MP, 3, 9 |
| | 13. | r | MP, 12, 11 |
| | 14. | r & ¬r | C, 13, 10 |

58.  1.  ¬((p ∨ p) → p)                          AIP
     2.  (p ∨ p) & ¬p                             NC, 1
     3.  p & ¬p                                   I, 2

62.  1.  ¬((q → r) → ((p ∨ q) → (p ∨ r)))        AIP
     2.  (q → r) & ¬((p ∨ q) → (p ∨ r))          NC, 1
     3.  q → r                                    S, 2
     4.  ¬((p ∨ q) → (p ∨ r))                     S, 2
     5.  (p ∨ q) & ¬(p ∨ r)                       NC, 4
     6.  p ∨ q                                    S, 5
     7.  ¬(p ∨ r)                                 S, 5
     8.  ¬p & ¬r                                  DM, 7
     9.  ¬p                                       S, 8
    10.  ¬r                                       S, 8
    11.  q                                        DS, 6, 9
    12.  r                                        MP, 3, 11
    13.  r & ¬r                                   C, 12, 10

64.  1.  ¬((p → q) → ((p → r) → (p → (q & r))))  AIP
     2.  (p → q) & ¬((p → r) → (p → (q & r)))     NC, 1
     3.  p → q                                    S, 2
     4.  ¬((p → r) → (p → (q & r)))               S, 2
     5.  (p → r) & ¬(p → (q & r))                 NC, 4
     6.  p → r                                    S, 5
     7.  ¬(p → (q & r))                           S, 5
     8.  p & ¬(q & r)                             NC, 7
     9.  p                                        S, 8
    10.  ¬(q & r)                                 S, 8
    11.  q                                        MP, 3, 9
    12.  r                                        MP, 6, 9
    13.  q & r                                    C, 11, 12
    14.  (q & r) & ¬(q & r)                       C, 13, 10

71

# CHAPTER
# 9

# Sᴎʟʟᴏɢɪsᴍs

This chapter discusses Aristotelian logic. It presents two methods for evaluating the validity of syllogisms: Venn diagrams and rules. (The reduction method and rules reflecting existential import are developed in exercises.) The final section of the chapter expands the usual syllogistic language and Venn diagram method to incorporate sentence negations and predicate complements.

## 1.  Kᴇʏ Dᴇғɪɴɪᴛɪᴏɴs

A *general term* is an expression that is true or false of individual objects. It yields a truth value when combined with the name of an object. Objects of which a general term are true *satisfy* it; the general term *applies to* them.

Each general term sorts objects into two groups: those of which it's true, and those of which it's false. The set of objects of which a general term is true is the *extension* of the term.

A *determiner* such as 'all', 'every', 'any', 'each', 'most', 'many', 'few', 'no', 'some', 'several', 'a' or 'an' may relate two general terms. Sentences combining a determiner with a pair of general terms are *general* sentences. The determiner that forms a sentence by linking two general terms is the sentence's *main determiner*. Singular and general sentences together comprise the class of *categorical sentences* (so-called because they contain no sentential connectives except, perhaps, negation).

Aristotelian logic treats a limited class of general sentences:

|           | Affirmative        | Negative               |
|-----------|--------------------|------------------------|
| Universal | A:  All F are G     | E:  No F are G          |
| Particular| I:  Some F are G    | O:  Some F are not G    |

The language AL:

*Vocabulary*
Predicates:  upper-case letters, with or without numerical subscripts
Determiners:  All, No, Some
Particle:  not

*Formation Rules*
1.    If X and Y are predicates, then All X are Y, No X are Y, Some X are Y and Some X are not Y are formulas.
2.    There are no other formulas.

The *converse* of a sentence form results from switching its terms. E and I sentence forms are equivalent to their converses. Two sentences (or sentence forms) are *contradictories* if and only if they always disagree in truth value. I and E forms are contradictories. So are A and O forms.

Two sentences (or sentence forms) are contraries if and only if they can never both be true, but can both be false. Two sentences (or sentence forms) are subcontraries if and only if they can never both be false, but can both be true.

The *complement* nonF of a predicate F is true of exactly those things of which F is false. The *contrapositive* of a categorical sentence form is the form that results from (1) switching the order of the terms and (2) replacing each term with its complement. A and O sentence forms are equivalent to their contrapositives. The *obverse* of a categorical sentence form is the sentence form that results from (1) changing its quality (from affirmative to negative, or *vice versa*) and (2) replacing its predicate term with its complement. Any categorical sentence form is equivalent to its obverse.

A syllogism is an argument form containing three categorical sentence forms and three predicates, where each predicate appears in two sentence forms.

To summarize the Venn diagram method:
1. Construct a diagram consisting of three intersecting circles.
2. Label each circle with a predicate.
3. Diagram the first premise.
4. Diagram the second premise.
5. Check to see whether the diagram guarantees the truth of the conclusion. If it does, the syllogism is valid. If not, it is not valid.

The conclusion's grammatical predicate is the *major term* of the syllogism. The conclusion's grammatical subject is the *minor term*. The term appearing in both premises is the *middle term*. The *major premise* contains the major term; the *minor premise* contains the minor term. A syllogism is in *standard form* if and only if it's stated in this form:

Major premise
Minor premise
∴ Conclusion

A syllogism's *mood* is a list of three letters signifying the form of the major premise, minor premise and conclusion. This chart summarizes the figures according to the position of the middle term, M, in standard form (where J is the major, and N the minor, term):

|  | First figure | | Second figure | | Third figure | | Fourth figure | |
|---|---|---|---|---|---|---|---|---|
| Major premise | M | J | J | M | M | J | J | M |
| Minor premise | N | M | N | M | M | N | M | N |
| Conclusion | N | J | N | J | N | J | N | J |

Distribution:

| | | | | |
|---|---|---|---|---|
| Universal affirmative: | All | FDistributed | are | GUndistributed |
| Particular Affirmative: | Some | FUndistributed | are | GUndistributed |
| Universal Negative: | No | FDistributed | are | GDistributed |
| Particular Negative: | Some | FUndistributed | are not | GDistributed |

There are three rules for validity that any valid syllogism must satisfy:
1. The occurrences of the middle term must disagree in distribution.
2. a. The occurrences of the major term must agree in distribution.
   b. The occurrences of the minor term must also agree.
3. a. If the conclusion is affirmative, both premises must be affirmative.
   b. If the conclusion is negative, exactly one premise must be negative.

The expanded language AL*:

*Vocabulary*

Predicates: upper-case letters, with or without numerical subscripts
Determiners: All, No, Some
Particles: ¬, non

*Formation Rules*

1. If X is a predicate, then nonX is a predicate.
2. If X and Y are predicates, then All X are Y, No X are Y, and Some X are Y are formulas.
3. If $\mathcal{A}$ is a formula, then $\neg\mathcal{A}$ is a formula.
4. There are no other formulas.

73

A *syllogism* within AL* is an argument form containing three AL*-formulas and three predicates (with, perhaps, their complements, complements of their complements, etc.), where each predicate appears in two formulas. To summarize the Venn diagram method for these syllogisms:

1. Construct a diagram consisting of three intersecting circles inside a box (representing the universe of discourse).
2. Label each circle with a predicate.
3. Convert negations of sentence forms into equivalent, "positive" sentence forms.
4. Delete two adjacent negation signs ($\neg\neg$) or two adjacent *nons* (*nonnon*).
5. Diagram the premises.
6. Check to see whether the diagram guarantees the truth of the conclusion. If it does, the syllogism is valid. If not, it is not valid.

This adds only two things to the usual Venn diagram method: we must "cancel" double negations and complements and convert negated sentence forms into equivalents that aren't negated.

# 2. ANSWERS TO UNANSWERED EVEN PROBLEMS

## 9.1 CATEGORICAL SENTENCES

| | | | | | |
|---|---|---|---|---|---|
| 8. | not a general term | 10. | general term | 14. | not a general term |
| 16. | not a general term | 20. | general term | 22. | particular negative |

26. neither universal nor particular; affirmative
28. neither universal nor particular (not general); negative
32. particular affirmative
34. neither universal nor particular; affirmative
38. neither universal nor particular; affirmative
40. neither universal nor particular (not general); affirmative

## 9.2 DIAGRAMMING CATEGORICAL SENTENCE FORMS

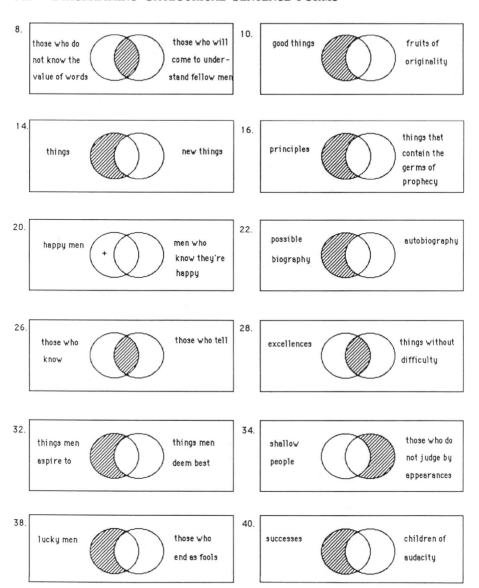

75

## 9.3    IMMEDIATE INFERENCE

8.    (a)    Only those who die young are good.     not equivalent
      (b)    No one who dies young is not good.     equivalent
      (c)    Only those who do not die young are not good.     equivalent
      (d)    Some who die young are not good.     not equivalent

10.    (a)    None but those who deserve the fair are brave.     not equivalent
      (b)    No one who deserves the fair is not brave.     equivalent
      (c)    None but those who do not deserve the fair are not brave.     equivalent
      (d)    Some who deserve the fair are not brave.     not equivalent

14.    (a)    Nothing that expresses something other than itself is art.     equivalent
      (b)    All art fails to express something other than itself.     equivalent
      (c)    Nothing that does not express something other than itself is not art.     not equivalent
      (d)    Some art expresses something other than itself.     not equivalent

16.    (a)    All who doubt, remember.     not equivalent
      (b)    No one who remembers does not doubt.     equivalent
      (c)    All who do not doubt, do not remember.     equivalent
      (d)    Someone who remembers does not doubt.     not equivalent

20.    (a)    Nothing that will be restrained from them is such that they have imagined to do it.     equivalent
      (b)    Everything which they have imagined to do is such that it will not be restrained from them.     equivalent
      (c)    Nothing which is not such that they have imagined to do it will not be restrained from them.     not equivalent
      (d)    Something which they have imagined to do will be restrained from them.     not equivalent

22.    (a)    Jesse is not sick today.
      (b)    Jesse is extremely healthy today.
      (c)    Jesse is not extremely sick today.

26.    (a)    Albania or Bulgaria is not a Balkan country.
      (b)    Albania is not a Balkan country.
      (c)    It's raining or it's not raining.

28.    (a)    You argue with me, and I listen to you.
      (b)    It's raining and it's not raining.
      (c)    You argue with me.

32.    (a) nothing; (b) nothing; (c) true; (d) nothing; (e) nothing; (f) false; (g) false; (h) nothing; (i) nothing

34.    (a) nothing; (b) true; (c) nothing; (d) false

38.    (a) true; (b) nothing; (c) nothing; (d) false; (e) true; (f) nothing; (g) nothing; (h) true; (i) nothing; (j) nothing

76

## 9.4 SYLLOGISMS

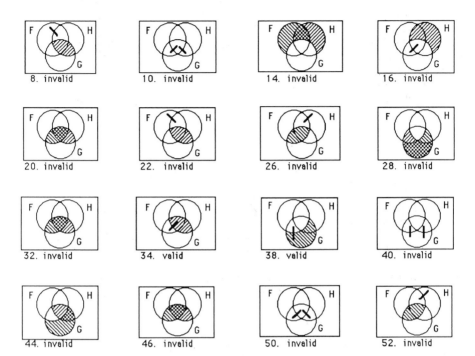

8. invalid
10. invalid
14. invalid
16. invalid

20. invalid
22. invalid
26. invalid
28. invalid

32. invalid
34. valid
38. valid
40. invalid

44. invalid
46. invalid
50. invalid
52. invalid

77

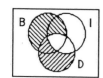

56. All D are I
    All B are D
    ∴ All B are I
    valid

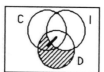

58. All D are I
    Some D are C
    ∴ Some C are I
    valid

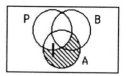

62. Some A are not B
    All A are P
    ∴ Some P are not B
    valid

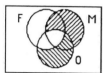

64. All M are O
    All O are F
    ∴ Some F are M
    invalid

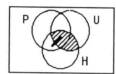

68. No U are H
    Some H are P
    ∴ Some P are not U
    valid

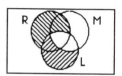

70. All L are M
    All R are L
    ∴ All R are M
    valid

## 9.5  RULES FOR VALIDITY

| | | | |
|---|---|---|---|
| 8. | invalid: violates rules 1, 3b | 10. | invalid: 1, 3b |
| 14. | invalid: 1 | 16. | invalid: 1, 2a, 2b |
| 20. | valid | 22. | invalid: 1, 3b |
| 26. | invalid: 2a | 28. | invalid: 2a |
| 32. | valid | 34. | invalid: 1 |
| 38. | valid | 40. | invalid: 1, 2a, 2b |
| 44. | invalid: 1, 2a, 2b, 3a | 46. | valid |
| 50. | invalid: 1, 3b | 52. | invalid: 2b, 3b |
| 56. | valid | 58. | invalid: 1, 2b |
| 62. | invalid: 1, 2a | 64. | invalid: 2a |
| 68. | valid | 70. | invalid: 2a, 2b |
| 74. | valid | 76. | invalid: 1 |
| 80. | valid | | |

82. according to the rules in 9.5, invalid: 1; according to the Aristotelian rules, valid. The Aristotelian rules assume that the occurrence of every term in every kind of categorical sentence carries existential import. The rules in section 9.5 attribute no existential import to the predicate of a sentence of type O nor to any term in a universal sentence.

86. according to the rules in 9.5, valid; according to the Aristotelian rules, valid.

88. according to the rules in 9.5, valid; according to the Aristotelian rules, valid.

92. according to the rules in 9.5, valid; according to the Aristotelian rules, valid.

94. according to the rules in 9.5, valid; according to the Aristotelian rules, valid.

98. according to the rules in 9.5, valid; according to the Aristotelian rules, valid.

100. according to the rules in 9.5, invalid: 1, 2a, 3a; according to the Aristotelian rules, invalid: 3a.

104. enthymeme. missing premise: No sensible man proves nothing.

106. conclusion: Children like cookies (All cookies are liked by children).

110. conclusion: None of my friends has a neat kitchen.

112. no syllogistic conclusion follows; (rule 1 violated).

116. Suppose there were a valid syllogism having two particular premises. Rule 3 means that at least one of them must be affirmative. If both were affirmative, the middle term would be undistributed in both, violating rule 1; so, one of the premises must be negative. According to rule 3, this entails that the conclusion is negative, and thus contains at least one distributed term--which, by rule 2, must also be distributed in the premises. However, there is only one distributed term in the pair of premises, and we have already specified this as the middle term.

118. Suppose we have a valid second figure syllogism. The middle term of a second figure syllogism occurs in the predicate of both premises. Rule 1 means that exactly one of these occurrences must be distributed. It follows that exactly one of the premises must be negative (since the predicate of a categorical sentence is distributed if and only if its quality is negative). Rule 3 then dictates that the conclusion must be negative.

122. Distribution in an AOO syllogism conforms to the following pattern:  d u
Since rule 1 requires one distributed and one undistributed occurrence of  u d
the middle term, the diagram makes clear that figures one and four are  u d
not options for validity. Since the major term is distributed in the conclusion, it must be distributed in the major premise (by rule 2a), and will thus be that premise's subject. This forces the middle term to be the predicate, and rules out figure three as an option for validity. However, none of the rules are violated if we suppose an AOO syllogism to have figure two.

124. Suppose we have a valid fourth figure syllogism with an affirmative conclusion. Rule 3 guarantees that both premises are affirmative, and thus that their predicates, as well as that of the conclusion, are undistributed. Since in a fourth figure syllogism the major term is the subject of the major premise and the minor term is the predicate of the major premise, we know by rule 2 that the major premise and conclusion have undistributed subjects, and therefore are particular sentences. Being in addition affirmative, they are of type I. Since the middle term is undistributed in the major premise, it follows from rule 1 that its occurrence as the subject of the minor premise is distrubuted. The minor premise is thus universal affirmative--type A. We have, in effect, examined the consequences of the assumption that the rules hold in the case of our syllogism, and have seen that no contradiction results; so, a fourth figure IAI syllogism is valid.

128. Suppose we have a valid syllogism with a particular affirmative conclusion. Rule 3 guarantees that both premises are affirmative. Assume that both are universal. Then there are exactly two occurrences of undistributed terms in the premises (namely, the subjects). By rule 2, these positions must be occupied by the terms in the conclusion, both of which are undistributed. This leaves only distributed positions open to the middle term, forcing a rule 1 violation. Thus at least one premise must be particular. If both were, then all terms in the premises would be undistributed, and rule 1 would be violated.

130. Suppose there were a valid first figure syllogism having a negative minor premise. Rule 3 would then entail that the conclusion is negative, making its predicate (the major term) distributed. By rule 2, the position occupied by the major term must be distributed in the major premise; and in a first figure syllogism this position is the predicate. Thus, the major premise would be negative in addition to the minor one, violating rule 3.

134. Suppose we have two syllogisms with contradictory minor premises and the same major premise. Then, whatever their respective moods and figures, the positions occupied by the major, minor, and middle terms will be the same in both. Since the minor premises are contradictory, one of them is negative and the other affirmative.

Consider first the syllogism with the negative minor premise. Rule 3 allows us to infer that the major premise is affirmative and the conclusion is negative, and thus that the predicate of the latter--the major term--is distributed. Applying this information now to the syllogism with the affirmative minor premise: since both its premises are affirmative, rule 3 implies that its conclusion is affirmative. It follows that its major term is undistributed. Rule 2 tells us that in the case of each of the syllogisms the occurrence of the major term in the conclusion agrees in distribution with its occurrence in the major premise. Since the occurrences of the major term in the major premises of both syllogisms agree in distribution, the major term (it is the same in both syllogisms) must be both distributed and undistributed, an impossibility.

136.  No G are H           All G are nonH              All G are H
      All F are G   ⇒     All F are G        ⇒       All F are G
      ∴ No F are H         ∴ All F are nonH            ∴ All F are H

138.  All H are G          All nonG are nonH           All G are H
      No F are G    ⇒     All F are nonG     ⇒       All F are G
      ∴ No F are H         ∴ All F are nonH            ∴ All F are H

140.  No H are G           No G are H
      All F are G   ⇒     All F are G        ⇒       (See 136. above.)
      ∴ No F are H         ∴ No F are H

142.  All G are H          All G are H
      Some G are F ⇒      Some F are G
      ∴ Some F are H       ∴ Some F are H

144.  Some G are H         All G are F            All G are F            All G are H
      All G are F   ⇒     Some G are H    ⇒      Some H are G    ⇒      Some F are G
      ∴ Some F are H       ∴ Some F are H          ∴ Some H are F         ∴ Some F are

146.  All H are G          All H are G
      No G are F    ⇒     No F are G         ⇒       (See 138. above.)
      ∴ No F are H         ∴ No F are H

148.  Some H are G         Some G are H
      All G are F   ⇒     All G are F        ⇒       (See 144. above.)
      ∴ Some F are H       ∴ Some F are H

## 9.6  EXPANDING THE ARISTOTELIAN LANGUAGE

8.  Valid

10.  Valid

14.  Invalid

16.  Invalid

80

20. Valid

22. Invalid

26. Invalid

28. Invalid

32. Some H are F
No nonH are S
∴ Some F are nonS
Invalid

34. All L are J
No nonJ are H
∴ All L are H
Invalid

38. No nonP are B
No S are P
∴ No S are B
Valid

40. No M are W
All P are nonW
∴ All M are P
Invalid

44. No B are C
No nonB are G
∴ No C are G
Valid

46. No B are L
Some B are nonC
∴ Some nonL are nonC
Valid

50. All nonS are L
Some nonR are nonL
∴ Some nonR are S
Valid

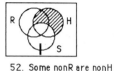

52. Some nonR are nonH
All H are S
∴ Some nonR are nonS
Invalid

56. All nonF are B
Some O are nonB
∴ Some O are F
Valid

58. All nonO are P
¬All A are O
∴ ¬No P are A
Valid

62. All L are P
No P are D
∴ No L are D

No L are D
All nonC are L
∴ All D are C

All D are C
All C are S
∴ No nonS are D

81

64. All E are V
No S are V
∴ No S are E

No S are E
All R are S
∴ No R are E

No R are E
No nonR are H
∴ No E are H

68. No K are S
All G are S
∴ No K are G

No K are G
All P are G
∴ No K are P

No K are P
No nonP are N
∴ No K are N

No K are N
No nonN are M
∴ No K are M

No K are M
No C are nonM
∴ No K are C

No K are C
All H are C
∴ No K are H

No K are H
No nonH are T
∴ No K are T

No K are T
All nonT are D
∴ All K are D

All K are D
All D are A
∴ All K are A

82

# QUANTIFIERS

## 1. KEY DEFINITIONS

All verb phrases are *general terms* in the sense that they are true or false of individual objects. Objects of which the verb phrase or general term are true *satisfy* it; the verb phrase or general term *applies to* them. Verb phrases and other general terms classify objects into two categories: those of which they are true, and those of which they are false. The set of objects of which a general term is true is called its *extension*.

*Universal affirmative* sentences:   All F are G        $\forall x(Fx \rightarrow Gx)$
*Particular affirmative* sentences:   Some F are G      $\exists x(Fx \,\&\, Gx)$
*Universal negative* sentences:       No F are G        $\neg\exists x(Fx \,\&\, Gx)$ or $\forall x(Fx \rightarrow \neg Gx)$

Vocabulary of QL (* with or without numerical subscripts):
Sentence Letter Constants: p, q, r, s *
n-ary Predicate Constants: $A^n$, $B^n$, . . ., $Z^n$ *
Individual Constants: a, b, c, . . ., o *
Individual Variables: t, u, v, w, x, y, z *
Sentential Connectives: $\neg$, $\rightarrow$, &, $\vee$, $\leftrightarrow$
Quantifiers: $\forall$, $\exists$
Grouping Indicators: (, )

Form $\mathcal{A}[c/d]$ ($\mathcal{A}$, with $c$ substituted for $d$) by replacing every occurrence of the constant $d$ with an occurrence of the constant $c$.

Formation rules for QL:
1.    Any sentence letter constant is a formula. (Specifically, an *atomic* formula.)
2.    An n-ary predicate followed by n constants is a formula. (Again, an *atomic* formula.)
3.    If $\mathcal{A}$ is a formula, $\neg\mathcal{A}$ is a formula.
4.    If $\mathcal{A}$ and $\mathcal{B}$ are formulas, then $(\mathcal{A} \rightarrow \mathcal{B})$, $(\mathcal{A} \,\&\, \mathcal{B})$, $(\mathcal{A} \vee \mathcal{B})$, and $(\mathcal{A} \leftrightarrow \mathcal{B})$ are formulas.
5.    If $\mathcal{A}$ is a formula with a constant $c$, and $v$ is a variable that does not appear in $\mathcal{A}$, then $\exists v\mathcal{A}[v/c]$ and $\forall v\mathcal{A}[v/c]$ are formulas.
6.    Every formula can be constructed by a finite number of applications of these rules.

When we form $\forall v\mathcal{A}[v/c]$ or $\exists v\mathcal{A}[v/c]$ in accordance with these rules, we'll say that the *scope* of $\forall v$ or $\exists v$ is all of $\forall v\mathcal{A}[v/c]$ or $\exists v\mathcal{A}[v/c]$.

An *interpretation* M of a set S of formulas of QL consists of a nonempty set D (M's *domain*, or *universe of discourse*) and a function $\varphi$ assigning (1) truth values to sentence letters in S, (2) elements of D to constants in S, and (3) sets of n-tuples of elements of D to n-ary predicates in S. This table summarizes how the interpretation function works.

| *Symbol* | $\varphi$ | *Interpretation* |
|---|---|---|
| sentence letter | $\Rightarrow$ | truth value |
| constant | $\Rightarrow$ | object in the domain |
| n-ary predicate | $\Rightarrow$ | set of n-tuples of objects in domain |

Truth definition:

(1) $p$ is true on M if and only if $\varphi(p) = T$.

(2) $Ra_1 \ldots a_n$ is true on M if and only if $<\varphi(a_1), \ldots, \varphi(a_n)>$ belongs to $\varphi(R)$.

(3) $\neg \mathcal{A}$ is true on M if and only if $\mathcal{A}$ is false on M.

(4) $(\mathcal{A} \& \mathcal{B})$ is true on M if and only if $\mathcal{A}$ and $\mathcal{B}$ are both true on M.

(5) $(\mathcal{A} \vee \mathcal{B})$ is true on M if and only if either $\mathcal{A}$ or $\mathcal{B}$ is true on M.

(6) $(\mathcal{A} \to \mathcal{B})$ is true on M if and only if $\mathcal{A}$ is false on M or $\mathcal{B}$ is true on M.

(7) $(\mathcal{A} \leftrightarrow \mathcal{B})$ is true on M if and only if $\mathcal{A}$ and $\mathcal{B}$ have the same truth value on M.

(8) $\exists v \mathcal{A}$ is true on M iff $\mathcal{A}[c/v]$ is true on a $c$-variant of M.

(9) $\forall v \mathcal{A}$ is true on M iff $\mathcal{A}[c/v]$ is true on every $c$-variant of M.

where M′ is a *c-variant* of M iff M and M′ (1) have the same domain and (2) have interpretation functions agreeing on the interpretation of every item in the language except c.

# 2. ANSWERS TO UNANSWERED EVEN PROBLEMS

## 10.2 CATEGORICAL SENTENCE FORMS

Many English sentences have alternative symbolizations of equal merit. The answers below are not the only ones possible.

| | | | | | |
|---|---|---|---|---|---|
| 8. | $\forall x(Ix \to Lx)$ | | | | |
| 10. | $\neg \exists x(Px \& Ex)$, where "P" corresponds to "is a person". | | | | |
| 14. | $\forall x(H_1 x \to H_2 x)$ | 16. | $\forall x(Fx \to Sx)$ | 20. | $\forall x(Wx \to Ox)$ |
| 22. | $\forall x(Px \to Ix)$ | 26. | $\forall x(Ax \to Dx)$ | 28. | $\forall x(\neg Jx \to Sx)$ |

## 10.3 POLYADIC PREDICATES

8.   $\exists x Ahx$          10.   $\exists x(Fx \& Ahx)$

14.   $\forall x(Gx \to \exists y(Ry \& Fxy))$

16.   $\forall x(Cx \to \exists y(Sy \& Hxy))$

20.   $\neg \exists x \forall y(Py \to Gxy)$, where 'P' symbolizes 'is a person'.

22.   $\neg \forall x(Mx \to \exists y(Sy \& Axy))$

26.   $\forall x(Mx \to \forall y(Ay \to Pxy))$, where 'A' symbolizes 'is an action' and 'P' symbolizes 'has the power not to do...'. Or, $\forall x(Mx \to Nx)$, where 'Nx' symbolizes 'x has the power to do nothing'.

28.   $\forall x(Px \to \exists y(Cy \& \forall z(Pz \to Hxyz)))$, where 'P' symbolizes 'is a person'.

32.   $\forall x(Px \to \forall y(Fyx \to \exists z((Ez \& Oyzx) \& Axzy)))$, where 'P' symbolizes 'is a person','F', 'is a fresh experience for', 'E', 'is a form of error', 'O', 'points out ... to', and 'A', 'will carefully avoid ... after'.

34.   $\exists x(Ahx \& Abx)$      38.   $\forall x(Axb \to \neg Ahx)$   40.   $\forall x(Axh \to \forall yAxy)$

## 10.4 THE LANGUAGE QL

| | | | | | | | | | | |
|---|---|---|---|---|---|---|---|---|---|---|
| 8. | (a) | 10. | (a) | 14. | (a) | 16. | (a) | 20. | (b) | 22. | (b) |
| 26. | (b) | 28. | (b) | 32. | (a) | 34. | (b) | 38. | (b) | 40. | (b) |

| | | | |
|---|---|---|---|
| 44. | (a) | Hxy | not a formula |
| | (b) | Hxy | not a formula |
| | (c) | Hxy | not a formula |
| | (d) | Hxy | not a formula |
| | (e) | Hyy | not a formula |

84

| 46. | (a) | ∀xFxc ↔ ∃xFcx | formula |
| | (b) | ∀xFxd ↔ ∃xFdx | formula |
| | (c) | ∀xFxx ↔ ∃xFdx | formula |
| | (d) | ∀xFxc ↔ ∃xFyx | not a formula |
| | (e) | ∀yFyc ↔ ∃yFdy | formula |
| 50. | (a) | Fxc & ∀xFxc | not a formula |
| | (b) | Fxd & ∀xFxd | not a formula |
| | (c) | Fxx & ∀xFxd | not a formula |
| | (d) | Fxc & ∀xFxy | not a formula |
| | (e) | Fyc & ∀yFyd | not a formula |

| 52. | false | 56. | true | 58. | true | 62. | true | 64. | false | 68. | true |
| 70. | true | 74. | true | 76. | true | 80. | true | 82. | true | 86. | true |
| 88. | true | 92. | false | 94. | false | 98. | false | 100. | false | 104. | true |
| 106. | true | 110. | true | 112. | false | 116. | true | 118. | false | | |

# CHAPTER
# 11

# Symbolization

This chapter discusses detailed strategies for symbolizing natural language sentences in predicate logic. Some issues arise primarily in connection with polyadic predicates. Instructors who wish to restrict their attention to monadic predicates or singly quantified sentences may use this chapter, but should warn their students that some examples go beyond the fragment of predicate logic they know.

## 1. KEY DEFINITIONS

Some verbs are *intransitive*; they cannot take objects. 'Fall', 'walk', 'expire', 'come', 'go', 'smile' and 'die' are all intransitive. *Transitive* verbs take noun phrases as direct objects. Examples are 'throw', 'win' and 'examine'. Some of these, such as 'give' and 'send', also take noun phrases as indirect objects. Other verbs take sentences, or grammatical constructions closely related to sentences, as objects. 'Believe', 'know' and 'persuade' are such *clausally complemented* verbs.

        Modern requirements of definition:
1.     *Eliminability.* A defined term must be eliminable, without ambiguity, from any sentence in which it occurs.
2.     *Noncreativity.* A definition must imply nothing that does not contain the term it defines.

To define an n-ary predicate F: devise a formula of the form $\forall x_1 \ldots \forall x_n (Fx_1 \ldots x_n \leftrightarrow \mathcal{A})$, where $\mathcal{A}$ contains only primitive and previously defined expressions as nonlogical symbols.

        To define an individual constant $c$: devise a formula of the form $\forall x(x \text{ is } c \leftrightarrow \mathcal{A})$, where $\mathcal{A}$ contains only primitive and previously defined expressions as nonlogical symbols, and where it is possible to prove that one and only one thing satisfies $\mathcal{A}$.

## 2. ANSWERS TO UNANSWERED EVEN PROBLEMS

### 11.1 NOUN PHRASES

8.     nonintersective:eg., the same person may be a bad director and a good actor.
10.     nonintersective:eg., a little whale might be a big animal.
14.     nonintersective:eg., the same person might be an experienced parachutist and an inexperienced pilot.
16.     $\forall x((Dx \, \& \, Mx) \rightarrow \neg \exists y(T_1 y \, \& \, T_2 xy))$
20.     $\neg \exists x(T_1 x \, \& \, T_2 xx)$
22.     $\forall x((C_1 x \, \& \, T_1 x) \rightarrow (Bx \lor \exists y((C_2 y \, \& \, Py) \, \& \, T_2 yx)))$, where '$C_2$' symbolizes 'clever for a person'.
26.     $\forall x(Px \rightarrow \neg \exists y((Ty \, \& \, \neg \exists z((Iz \, \& \, Cz) \, \& \, Hyz)) \, \& \, Lxy))$
28.     $\forall x((Tx \, \& \, Axa) \rightarrow \exists y((P_1 y \, \& \, Rya) \, \& \, P_2 xy))$

32. $\forall x((Mx \;\&\; \exists y(Ny \;\&\; Oyx)) \to Lx)$, where 'L' symbolizes 'large for a manor'.
34. $\forall x(Mx \to (\exists y(Ny \;\&\; Oyx) \;\&\; Lx))$, where 'L' symbolizes 'large for a manor'.
38. $\exists x(Px \;\&\; Fxj)$
40. $\forall x(C_1 x \to (Nx \;\&\; \exists y(Ty \;\&\; C_2 xy)))$, where '$C_1$' symbolizes 'can have an army'.
44. $\forall x(Nx \to (\neg \exists y((P_1 y \;\&\; Wyx) \;\&\; \forall z((Tz \;\&\; Ozx) \to Cxzy)) \;\&\; \exists y((Ty \;\&\; Oyx) \;\&\; P_2 xyj)))$, where 'O' symbolizes 'is of'.
46. $\forall x((Bx \;\&\; Wx) \to Gx)$, where 'G' symbolizes 'grows light for a burden'.
50. $\forall x(P_1 x \to (\forall y((T_1 y \;\&\; H_1 xy) \to H_2 y) \to \forall z(P_2 zx \to T_2 xz)))$, where '$P_1$' symbolizes 'is a person', '$P_2$', 'is a problem for', and '$T_2$', 'tends to see...as a nail'.
52. $\forall x((Px \;\&\; (\forall y \forall z(Gxyz \to \neg Rxyz) \;\&\; \forall y \forall z(Txyz \to \neg Fxyz))) \to Bx)$, where 'G' symbolizes 'gives ... to', 'R', 'remembers giving ... to', 'T', 'takes ... from', and 'F', 'forgets taking ... from'.
56. $\forall x((Ixb \;\&\; \neg Sxa) \to \neg Vxa)$, where 'V' symbolizes 'is as valuable as' and 'S' symbolizes 'is the same as'.
58. $\forall x(Sx \to \forall y((Byx \;\&\; ((Ly \;\&\; Cy) \vee (Dy \;\&\; Ty))) \to Hxy))$, where 'B' symbolizes 'belongs to'.
62. $\forall x \forall y((Px \;\&\; \exists z Rxyz) \to \exists z Gxyz)$
64. $\forall x \forall y(((Fxy \;\&\; Pxy) \;\&\; My) \to Exx)$
68. $\forall x \forall y(((Px \;\&\; Cy) \;\&\; \forall z(Mzy \to \neg Kxz)) \to \neg Cxy)$, where 'M' symbolizes 'is the mechanical side of', and 'C', 'can judge'.
70. $Gm \;\&\; \forall x(P_1 xm \to ((Ux \;\&\; P_2 x) \vee Cx))$, where '$P_1$' symbolizes 'possesses', and 'U', 'unknown as a philosopher'.
74. $\forall x(Px \to (Kxa \to Sxc))$
76. $\forall x(Tx \to \forall y(Ixy \to \neg Ryx))$, where 'Ixy' symbolizes 'x imagines to do y'.
80. $\forall x \forall y((Px \;\&\; (Fy \;\&\; Dxy)) \to \exists z(Pz \;\&\; (Sz \;\&\; Fxyz)))$, where 'S' symbolizes 'strong as a principle' and 'F' symbolizes 'x did y from z'.
82. $\forall x(((Mx \;\&\; Hxa) \;\&\; (Gx \;\&\; Cx)) \to \exists y(Ey \;\&\; Txy))$

## 11.2 VERB PHRASES

| 8. | transitive | 10. | transitive and intransitive | 14. | transitive |
|----|-----------|-----|-----------------------------|-----|-----------|
| 16. | transitive | 20. | transitive | 22. | transitive |

26. $\neg \exists x(E_1 x \;\&\; Nlx) \;\&\; E_2 ll$
28. $\forall x \forall y((A_1 x \;\&\; Ty) \to ((P_1 xy \to \forall z(O_1 zxy \to \exists w((Tw \;\&\; P_2 wy) \;\&\; O_2 zw))) \to \neg \exists v(Tv \;\&\; A_2 xv)))$, where '$A_1$' symbolizes 'is an action', 'T', 'is a time','$P_1$', 'it is permissible to attempt ... at', '$O_1$', 'is an objection to attempting ... at', '$P_2$', 'precedes', '$O_2$', 'is overcome at', and '$A_2$', 'is attempted at'.
32. $(\exists x Lxi \to Si) \;\&\; \forall x(Lix \to Iix)$, where 'S' symbolizes 'has all needs satisfied', and 'I', 'loves ... indeed'. Or, $\forall x(Nix \to Sxb) \;\&\; \forall x(Lix \to Iix)$, where 'S' symbolizes 'is the same as' and 'b' symbolizes 'to be beloved'.
34. $\forall x((Ex \;\&\; \exists y(Py \;\&\; H_1 xy)) \to \exists z(Jz \;\&\; H_2 xz))$, where '$H_1$' symbolizes 'has' and '$H_2$' symbolizes 'will have'.
38. $\forall x((Mx \;\&\; (Wx \;\&\; \neg Axx)) \to Gx)$, where 'A' symbolizes 'admits that ... is wrong'.
40. $\neg \exists x Ccx \;\&\; \forall x Bcx$
44. $\forall x \forall y((Px \;\&\; Ryx) \to (\neg Wx \to \neg Wy))$, where 'R' symbolizes 'is a rule for ...'s success'; or, $\forall x \forall y((Px \;\&\; Ry) \to (\neg W_1 x \to \neg W_2 yx))$, where '$W_2$' symbolizes 'y will work for x'.
46. $\forall x((Px \;\&\; \exists z(Mz \;\&\; Hxz)) \to \exists w Fwx)$, or, making 'always' explicit, $\forall x \forall y(((Px \;\&\; Ty) \;\&\; \exists z(Mz \;\&\; Hxzy)) \to \exists w Fwxt)$, where 'T' symbolizes 'is a time'.
50. This appears to be ambiguous. One reading: $\forall x \forall y(\neg Syx \to (Eyx \vee Dyx))$, or, making 'never' explicit, $\forall x \forall y(((Px \;\&\; Py) \;\&\; \neg \exists z(Tz \;\&\; Syxz)) \to (Eyx \vee Dyx))$; the other, $\forall x(\forall y \neg Syx \to (Ex \vee Dx))$.
52. $\forall x(\neg \forall y(Gxy \to Lyx) \;\&\; \neg \forall y(Exy \to Hyx))$
56. $\forall x(Wx \to (R_1 x \vee R_2 x))$

58. Literally, $\neg$Sif & $\neg\forall$x(Px $\rightarrow$ Tiax); to express what 'speak falsehood' and tell the truth' mean, one could try $\neg\exists$x(Fx & Six) & $\exists$y$\exists$z($P_1$y & (($T_1$z & $P_2$iz) & Wizy)), where '$P_1$' symbolizes 'is a person', '$T_1$', 'is a truth', 'W', 'withholds',and '$P_2$', 'is in possession of'.

62. $\forall$x(Lx $\rightarrow$ $\exists$yMyx) & $\forall$yLy; or $\forall$x(Px $\rightarrow$ ($\forall$y((Ly & Hxy) $\rightarrow$ Mxy) & $\forall$y(Hxy $\rightarrow$ Ly))), where 'H' symbolizes 'has' and 'M', 'must pay for'.

64. $\forall$x$\forall$y((Px & Ty) $\rightarrow$ (($\exists$z(Pz & Mxzy) $\vee$ Wxy) & $\neg$($\exists$z(Pz & Mxzy) & Wxy))), where 'P' symbolizes 'is a person' and 'T', 'is a time'. An alternative translation would omit the disjunction; is the $\vee$ part really being asserted?

68. Ambiguous: $\forall$x(($S_1$x & Mx) $\rightarrow$ Bxl) & $\forall$x(((Wx & $S_2$x) & Mx) $\rightarrow$ Bxc), where '$S_1$' symbolizes 'shallow for a man', 'W', 'wise for a man', '$S_2$', 'strong for a man', and 'c', 'cause and effect'; or $\forall$x(($S_1$x & Mx) $\rightarrow$ Bxl) & $\forall$x(((Wx $\vee$ $S_2$x) & Mx) $\rightarrow$ Bxc).

70. $\forall$x((Ax & Pxa) $\rightarrow$ $\exists$y((Qy & My) & Ixy)), where 'A' symbolizes 'adequate as perception of the world', 'P', 'is perception of', 'a', 'the world', and 'Q', 'quiet for a mind'.

74. $\forall$x$\forall$y(($P_1$x & (Ty & Gyx)) $\rightarrow$ $P_2$yx), where '$P_1$' symbolizes 'is a person', 'T', 'true(genuine) as a gift', and 'G', 'is a gift from'.

76. $\forall$x$\forall$y((Mx & My) $\rightarrow$ ($T_1$xy $\rightarrow$ $T_2$xy)), where '$T_1$' symbolizes 'thinks less than' and '$T_2$', 'talks more than'.

80. $\neg\exists$x(($T_1$x & $\exists$y(($T_2$y & By) & $T_3$xy)) & $\neg$Cx), where '$T_2$' symbolizes 'is a time', 'B', 'belongs to the interval spanning the past 100 years', and 'C', 'guilty of cheating'.

82. $\forall$x(Px $\rightarrow$ ($\neg$Sax $\rightarrow$ $\neg\exists$yLyax)), where 'P' symbolizes 'is a person', 'S', 'is on ...'s side', 'a', 'reason', and 'L', 'has an uglier look than ... to'.

86. $\exists$x(Cx & ((Oxi & Six) & Pxa)), where 'C' symbolizes 'is a conviction', 'O', 'is of', 'S', 'is saddened by', 'P', 'has as propositional content', and 'a', 'the proposition that people can only agree about what they're not really interested in'. (Russell's sentence translates with difficulty, in that QL lacks the means to describe the content of Russell's conviction using the same symbols and syntax with which QL expresses propositions.)

88. $\forall$x$\forall$y((Px & (Oxy & Cxy) $\rightarrow$ Ecy), where 'P' symbolizes 'is a person', 'O', 'obtains', 'C', 'obtains ... too cheaply', and 'E', 'esteems ... too lightly'.

92. $\forall$x$\forall$y((Px & My) $\rightarrow$ ($\neg$Ayx & Fyy))

94. $\forall$x$\forall$y((Px & My) $\rightarrow$ (Txya $\rightarrow$ (Byb & Byc))), where 'P' symbolizes 'is a person', 'M', 'is a man', 'T', 'thinks that ... has the attribute', 'a', 'having a clear brain', 'B', 'believes', 'b', 'the proposition that everything is wrong', and 'c', 'the proposition that everything will get worse'. (The English translates with difficulty for the same reason as #86 does. In addition, #94 brings out that, not only in the case of propositions but also in that of predicates, QL lacks the resources to describe them using the same symbols and syntax with which QL expresses them.)

98. $\forall$x((Wx & Mx) $\rightarrow$ Cxaa), where 'W' symbolizes 'wise for a man'.

100. $\forall$x$\forall$y$\forall$z((((Px & $C_1$y) & (Tz &Mxyz)) $\rightarrow$ $\exists$w((Dw & Iwx) & (Awy & $\neg$ $C_2$xwz))), where 'P' symbolizes 'is a person', 'T', 'is a time', 'I', 'is interior to', and '$C_2$', 'is conscious of ... at'.

104. $\forall$x((($M_1$x & Sxx) $\rightarrow$ Lx) & ($\forall$y((Ay & ($M_2$xy & Oyx)) $\rightarrow$ $\forall$z(($P_1$z & Hzy) $\rightarrow$ Bzy)) & $\forall$y(($P_2$y & ($M_2$xy & Oyx)) $\rightarrow$ $\forall$z(($P_1$x & Hzy) $\rightarrow$ $\neg$Bzy)))), where '$M_2$' symbolizes 'makes', 'O', 'is of', '$P_1$', 'is a person' and 'H', 'hears about'.

106. $\forall$x$\forall$y((My & Hyx) $\rightarrow$ $\neg\exists$z((Wz & Tz) & Ozy)), where 'H' symbolizes 'has ... to do', 'W', 'is a work week', 'T', 'thirty hours long', and 'O', 'is of'.

## 11. 3 DEFINITIONS

8. formally adequate
10. not formally adequate (Violates noncreativity: uniqueness fails.)
14. formally adequate

16.   not formally adequate (Even reading 'one' as 'fool' and assuming the latter to be either primitive or previously defined, uniqueness fails, and so the definition violates noncreativity.)

20.   formally adequate    22.    formally adequate    26.    formally adequate

28.   formally adequate

32.   not formally adequate (The proposed definition would be formally adequate as a definition of the predicate 'x has political power'; if we expressed this definition in (hybrid) QL, we would have something like '$\forall x$(x has political power $\leftrightarrow \exists y(\neg y$ is x & x has the power to oppress y))'. However, when the proposed definition is taken as a definition of the 'constant' 'political power' and expressed in QL, the result is not a formula, since 'others' introduces a variable that remains unbound; thus the eliminability criterion is violated.)

34.   formally adequate           38.    formally adequate

40.   not formally adequate (Violates noncreativity: uniqueness fails.)

44.   not formally adequate (Violates noncreativity: uniqueness fails.)

46.   formally adequate (Assuming there is a unique content of all small men in high places.)

50.   not formally adequate (Violates eliminability: when the proposed definition is expressed in (hybrid) QL, the result is not a formula, since 'your' symbolizes an expression containing an unbound variable.)

52.   formally adequate

56.   not formally adequate (Violates eliminability:when the proposed definition is expressed in (hybrid) QL, the result is not a formula, since 'you' symbolizes an unbound variable.)

58.   not formally adequate (Violates noncreativity: uniqueness fails.)

# QUANTIFIED TABLEAUX

## 1. KEY DEFINITIONS AND RULES

$\mathcal{A}[c/v]$ is the result of substituting $c$ for every occurrence of $v$ throughout the formula $\mathcal{A}$. If $\forall v \mathcal{A}$ and $\exists v \mathcal{A}$ are formulas, then $\mathcal{A}[c/v]$ is an *instance* of them. Conversely, $\forall v \mathcal{A}$ and $\exists v \mathcal{A}$ are *generics* of $\mathcal{A}[c/v]$.

Rules for quantifiers:

Existential Left (∃L)

Existential Right (∃R)

$$\checkmark \; \exists v \mathcal{A} \quad \Big| \qquad \qquad \Big| \quad \exists v \mathcal{A} *$$
$$\mathcal{A}[c/v] \qquad \qquad \qquad \qquad \mathcal{A}[c/v]$$

Here $c$ must be a constant new to the tableau.      Here $c$ may be any constant.

Universal Left (∀L)

Universal Right (∀R)

$$* \; \forall v \mathcal{A} \quad \Big| \qquad \qquad \Big| \quad \forall v \mathcal{A} \; \checkmark$$
$$\mathcal{A}[c/v] \qquad \qquad \qquad \qquad \mathcal{A}[c/v]$$

Here $c$ may be any constant.      Here $c$ must be a constant new to the tableau.

## 2. STRATEGY

In addition to the strategies for sentential logic:
1.  Introduce constants as quickly as possible by applying ∃L and ∀R before applying ∃R and ∀L. That is, apply the quantifier rules introducing new constants as soon as possible.
2.  Use constants already on the tableau whenever possible.
3.  Continue instantiating as far as possible using the constants on the branch.

# 3. ANSWERS TO UNANSWERED EVEN PROBLEMS

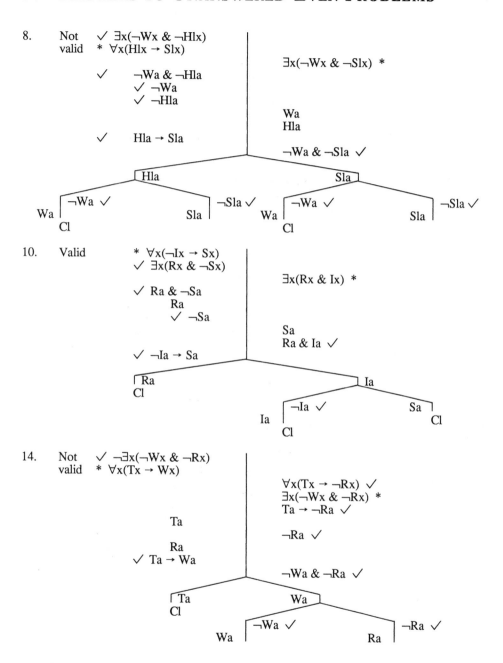

8.  Not valid

    Not    ✓ ∃x(¬Wx & ¬Hlx)
    valid    * ∀x(Hlx → Slx)

    ✓      ¬Wa & ¬Hla
         ✓ ¬Wa
         ✓ ¬Hla

    ✓      Hla → Sla

    ∃x(¬Wx & ¬Slx) *

    Wa
    Hla

    ¬Wa & ¬Sla ✓

    |‾Hla‾|           |‾Sla‾|

    Wa   ¬Wa ✓      ¬Sla ✓    Wa   ¬Wa ✓      ¬Sla ✓
            Sla                   Sla
    Cl                           Cl

10. Valid

    * ∀x(¬Ix → Sx)
    ✓ ∃x(Rx & ¬Sx)

    ✓ Ra & ¬Sa
       Ra
       ✓ ¬Sa

    ∃x(Rx & Ix) *

    Sa
    Ra & Ia ✓

    ✓ ¬Ia → Sa

    |‾Ra
    Cl                          Ia‾|

                    Ia   ¬Ia ✓      Sa‾|
                          Cl              Cl

14. Not valid

    Not    ✓ ¬∃x(¬Wx & ¬Rx)
    valid    * ∀x(Tx → Wx)

    ∀x(Tx → ¬Rx) ✓
    ∃x(¬Wx & ¬Rx) *
    Ta → ¬Ra ✓

    Ta

    ¬Ra ✓

    Ra
    ✓ Ta → Wa

    ¬Wa & ¬Ra ✓

    |‾Ta                    Wa‾|
    Cl

                    ¬Wa ✓         ¬Ra ✓
            Wa                     Ra

16.  Not      * ∀x(¬Ex → Sx)
     valid    * ∀x(Tx → Ex)

                                              ¬∃x(Tx & Sx) ✓

              ✓ ∃x(Tx & Sx)
              ✓ Ta & Sa
                  Ta
                  Sa
              ✓ ¬Ea → Sa
              ✓ Ta → Ea

              ⌈ Ta                              Ea
              Cl
                                      ⌈ ¬Ea ✓                Sa ⌉
                              Ea ⌊

20.  Not      ✓ ¬∃x(Mx & Wx)
     valid    * ∀x(Px → ¬Wx)

                                          ∀x(Mx → Px) ✓
                                          ∃x(Mx & Wx) *
                                          Ma → Pa ✓

                                          Pa
                         Ma               Ma & Wa ✓

              ✓ Pa → ¬Wa
                      ⌈ Ma                      Wa
                      Cl
                              ⌈ Pa              ✓ ¬Wa ⌉
                                                        Wa

22.  Valid    ✓ ¬∃x(Bx & Lx)
              ✓ ∃x(Bx & ¬Cx)

                                          ∃x(¬Lx & ¬Cx) *
                                          ∃x(Bx & Lx) *

              ✓      Ba & ¬Ca
                     Ba
              ✓ ¬Ca
                                          Ca
                                          Ba & La ✓
                                          ¬La & ¬Ca ✓

                      ⌈ Ba                      La
                      Cl
                              ⌈ ¬La ✓                    ¬Ca ✓
                      La ⌊     Cl              Ca ⌉      Cl

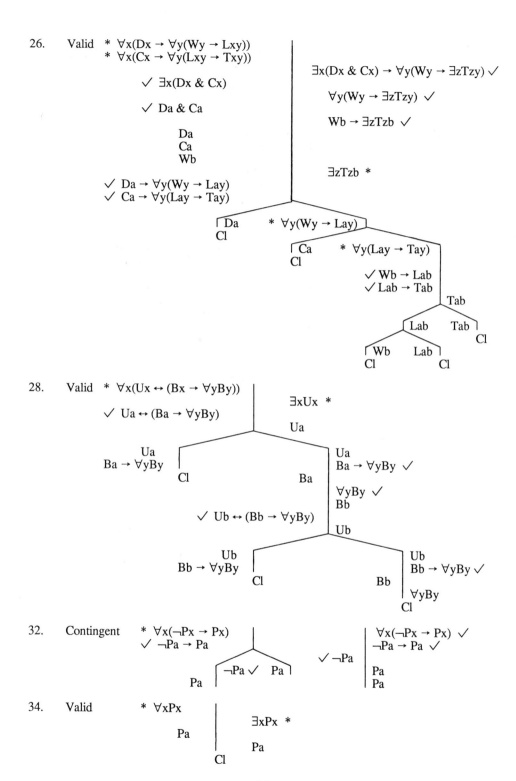

26. Valid
* ∀x(Dx → ∀y(Wy → Lxy))
* ∀x(Cx → ∀y(Lxy → Txy))

✓ ∃x(Dx & Cx)

✓ Da & Ca

Da
Ca
Wb

∃x(Dx & Cx) → ∀y(Wy → ∃zTzy) ✓

∀y(Wy → ∃zTzy) ✓

Wb → ∃zTzb ✓

∃zTzb *

✓ Da → ∀y(Wy → Lay)
✓ Ca → ∀y(Lay → Tay)

```
         ⌐ Da        * ∀y(Wy → Lay)
           Cl
                    ⌐ Ca        * ∀y(Lay → Tay)
                      Cl
                            ✓ Wb → Lab
                            ✓ Lab → Tab
                                        ⌐ Tab
                                  ⌐ Lab      Tab ⌐
                                              Cl
                              ⌐ Wb    Lab ⌐
                                Cl        Cl
```

28. Valid
* ∀x(Ux ↔ (Bx → ∀yBy))

✓ Ua ↔ (Ba → ∀yBy)

∃xUx *

Ua

```
    Ua                            Ua
Ba → ∀yBy                    Ba → ∀yBy ✓
         Cl        Ba         ∀yBy ✓
                              Bb
          ✓ Ub ↔ (Bb → ∀yBy)
                              Ub
        Ub                            Ub
   Bb → ∀yBy                    Bb → ∀yBy ✓
          Cl        Bb         ∀yBy
                               Cl
```

32. Contingent
* ∀x(¬Px → Px)
✓ ¬Pa → Pa

```
                    ⌐ ¬Pa ✓    Pa ⌐
          Pa                        ∀x(¬Px → Px) ✓
                        ✓ ¬Pa       ¬Pa → Pa ✓
                                    Pa
                                    Pa
```

34. Valid
* ∀xPx

Pa

∃xPx *

Pa

Cl

**93**

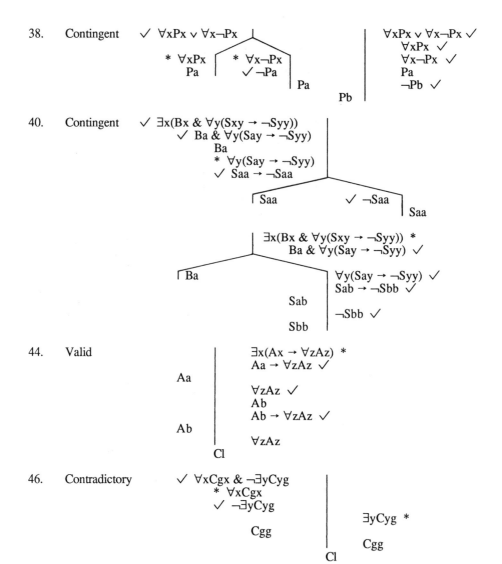

38.  Contingent  ✓ ∀xPx ∨ ∀x¬Px

\*  ∀xPx          \*  ∀x¬Px
    Pa              ✓ ¬Pa
                          Pa

                    Pb

∀xPx ∨ ∀x¬Px ✓
∀xPx ✓
∀x¬Px ✓
Pa
¬Pb ✓

40.  Contingent  ✓ ∃x(Bx & ∀y(Sxy → ¬Syy))
                 ✓ Ba & ∀y(Say → ¬Syy)
                    Ba
                 \* ∀y(Say → ¬Syy)
                 ✓ Saa → ¬Saa

                    Saa               ✓ ¬Saa
                                               Saa

∃x(Bx & ∀y(Sxy → ¬Syy)) \*
Ba & ∀y(Say → ¬Syy) ✓

                    Ba          ∀y(Say → ¬Syy) ✓
                                Sab → ¬Sbb ✓
                    Sab
                                ¬Sbb ✓
                    Sbb

44.  Valid       ∃x(Ax → ∀zAz) \*
                 Aa → ∀zAz ✓
        Aa
                 ∀zAz ✓
                 Ab
                 Ab → ∀zAz ✓
        Ab
                 ∀zAz
        Cl

46.  Contradictory  ✓ ∀xCgx & ¬∃yCyg
                    \* ∀xCgx
                    ✓ ¬∃yCyg

                       Cgg
                                    ∃yCyg \*

                                    Cgg
                       Cl

**94**

50.　Contingent　　　✓ ∀x∃yFyx → ¬∃xFxx

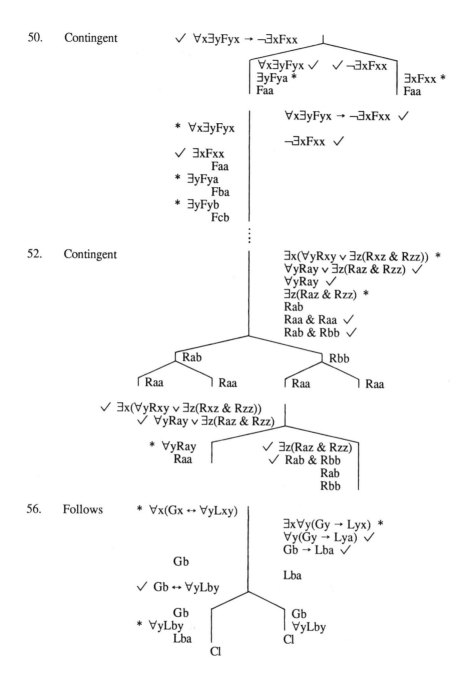

∀x∃yFyx ✓　　✓ ¬∃xFxx
∃yFya *　　　　　　　　　∃xFxx *
Faa　　　　　　　　　　　Faa

\* ∀x∃yFyx

∀x∃yFyx → ¬∃xFxx ✓

✓ ∃xFxx
Faa　　　　¬∃xFxx ✓
\* ∃yFya
Fba
\* ∃yFyb
Fcb

52.　Contingent

∃x(∀yRxy ∨ ∃z(Rxz & Rzz)) *
∀yRay ∨ ∃z(Raz & Rzz) ✓
∀yRay ✓
∃z(Raz & Rzz) *
Rab
Raa & Raa ✓
Rab & Rbb ✓

Rab　　　　　　　　　Rbb
Raa　　Raa　　　Raa　　Raa

✓ ∃x(∀yRxy ∨ ∃z(Rxz & Rzz))
✓ ∀yRay ∨ ∃z(Raz & Rzz)

\* ∀yRay　　　✓ ∃z(Raz & Rzz)
Raa　　　　　✓ Rab & Rbb
　　　　　　　Rab
　　　　　　　Rbb

56.　Follows　　\* ∀x(Gx ↔ ∀yLxy)

∃x∀y(Gy → Lyx) *
∀y(Gy → Lya) ✓
Gb → Lba ✓

Gb

Lba

✓ Gb ↔ ∀yLby

Gb　　　　　　　　Gb
\* ∀yLby　　　　　∀yLby
Lba　　　　　　　Cl
　　　　Cl

95

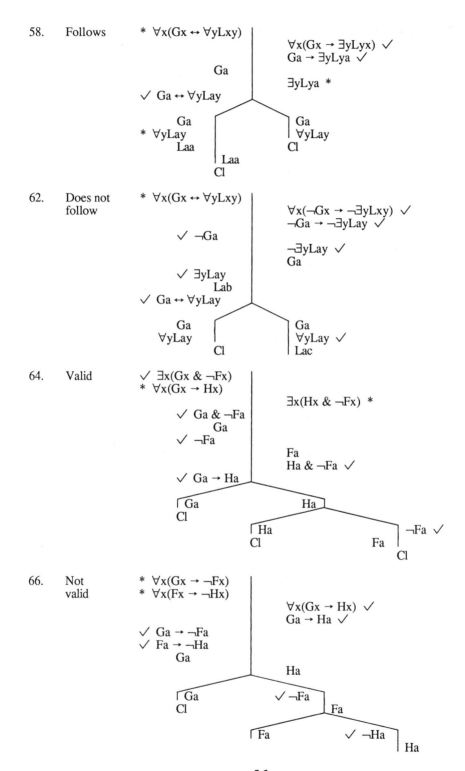

58. Follows

62. Does not follow

64. Valid

66. Not valid

68.    Valid   *  ∀x(Gx → (Hx & Jx))
            *  ∀x((Fx ∨ ¬Jx) → Gx)

                                              ∀x(Fx → Hx) ✓
                                              Fa → Ha ✓

                        Fa                    Ha

            ✓ Ga → (Ha & Ja)
            ✓ (Fa ∨ ¬Ja) → Ga

                Fa ∨ ¬Ja ✓                              Ga
                Fa                          Ga              ✓ Ha & Ja
                ¬Ja                         Cl                 Ha
                Cl                                             Ja
                                                                  Cl

70.    Valid      *  ∀x(Gx → Hx)
            ✓ ∃x(Fx & Gx & Mx)
                                              ∃x(Fx & Hx & Mx) *

            ✓ Fa & Ga & Ma
                ✓ Ga → Ha                    Fa & Ha & Ma ✓

                    Fa
                    Ga
                    Ma

                Ga                    Ha
                Cl
                        Fa                          Ha & Ma ✓
                        Cl
                                        Ha              Ma
                                        Cl              Cl

72.    Not valid    ✓ ¬∃x(Gx & ¬Hx)
                *  ∀x(Fx → ¬Gx)

                                              ∀x((Fx & ¬Gx) → ¬Hx) ✓
                                              ∃x(Gx & ¬Hx) *
                                              (Fa & ¬Ga) → ¬Ha ✓

                ✓ Fa & ¬Ga                    ¬Ha ✓

                    Ha
                ✓ Fa → ¬Ga
                    Fa
                    ✓ ¬Ga

                                              Ga
                                              Ga & ¬Ha ✓

                        Fa                  ✓ ¬Ga
                        Cl                          Ga

                                                Ga              ¬Ha ✓
                                                    Ha

97

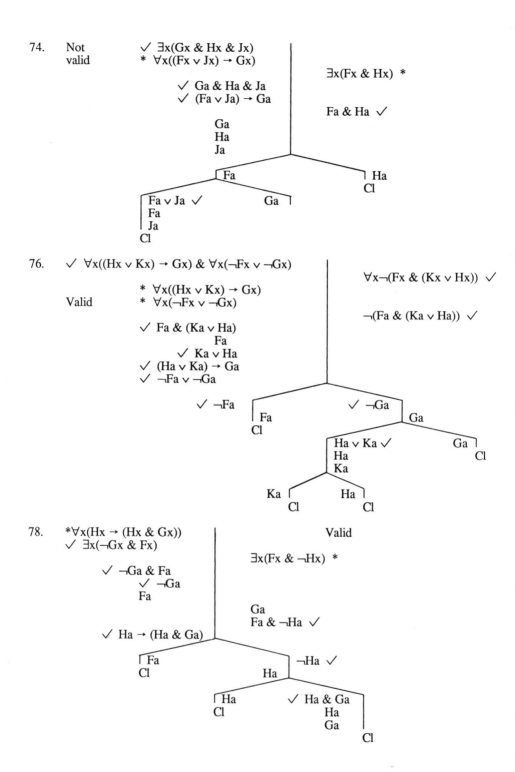

74.  Not        ✓ ∃x(Gx & Hx & Jx)
     valid      * ∀x((Fx ∨ Jx) → Gx)

                        ✓ Ga & Ha & Ja
                        ✓ (Fa ∨ Ja) → Ga

                                              ∃x(Fx & Hx)  *

                            Ga
                            Ha                Fa & Ha  ✓
                            Ja

                                Fa                      Ha
                                                        Cl

                    Fa ∨ Ja ✓          Ga
                    Fa
                    Ja
                    Cl

76.  ✓ ∀x((Hx ∨ Kx) → Gx) & ∀x(¬Fx ∨ ¬Gx)

                                                  ∀x¬(Fx & (Kx ∨ Hx))  ✓
                    * ∀x((Hx ∨ Kx) → Gx)
     Valid          * ∀x(¬Fx ∨ ¬Gx)
                                                  ¬(Fa & (Ka ∨ Ha))  ✓
                    ✓ Fa & (Ka ∨ Ha)
                        Fa
                        ✓ Ka ∨ Ha
                    ✓ (Ha ∨ Ka) → Ga
                    ✓ ¬Fa ∨ ¬Ga

                        ✓ ¬Fa                        ✓ ¬Ga
                            Fa                                Ga
                            Cl
                                        Ha ∨ Ka ✓                Ga
                                        Ha                       Cl
                                        Ka

                                    Ka            Ha
                                    Cl            Cl

78.  *∀x(Hx → (Hx & Gx))                          Valid
     ✓ ∃x(¬Gx & Fx)
                                      ∃x(Fx & ¬Hx)  *

                ✓ ¬Ga & Fa
                    ✓ ¬Ga
                    Fa
                                        Ga
                                        Fa & ¬Ha  ✓
            ✓ Ha → (Ha & Ga)

                    Fa                      ¬Ha  ✓
                    Cl
                                    Ha
                            Ha              ✓ Ha & Ga
                            Cl              Ha
                                            Ga
                                                Cl

98

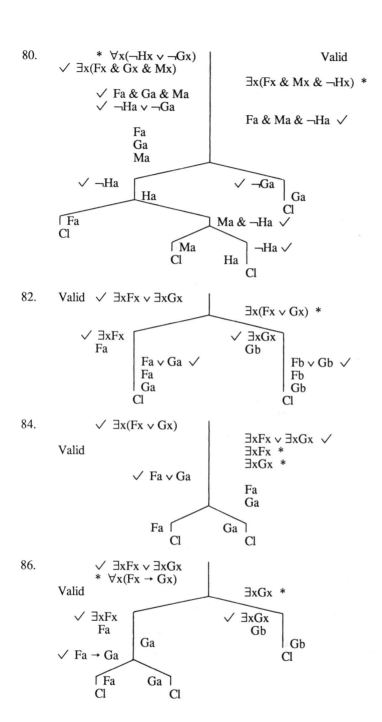

80.　　　　　\* ∀x(¬Hx ∨ ¬Gx)　　　　　　　　Valid
　　✓ ∃x(Fx & Gx & Mx)
　　　　　　　　　　　　　　　　　∃x(Fx & Mx & ¬Hx) \*
　　　　✓ Fa & Ga & Ma
　　　　✓ ¬Ha ∨ ¬Ga　　　　　　　　Fa & Ma & ¬Ha ✓
　　　　　　Fa
　　　　　　Ga
　　　　　　Ma
　　✓ ¬Ha　　　　　　　　　✓ ¬Ga　　Ga
　　　　　　Ha　　　　　　　　　　　　Cl
　　Fa　　　　　　　　Ma & ¬Ha ✓
　　Cl
　　　　　　　Ma　　　　　　¬Ha ✓
　　　　　　　Cl　　　Ha
　　　　　　　　　　　　　Cl

82.　　Valid　✓ ∃xFx ∨ ∃xGx
　　　　　　　　　　　　　　∃x(Fx ∨ Gx) \*
　　✓ ∃xFx　　　　　　　　✓ ∃xGx
　　　　Fa　　　　　　　　　　Gb
　　　　　　Fa ∨ Ga ✓　　　　　　Fb ∨ Gb ✓
　　　　　　Fa　　　　　　　　　　Fb
　　　　　　Ga　　　　　　　　　　Gb
　　　　　　Cl　　　　　　　　　　Cl

84.　　　　✓ ∃x(Fx ∨ Gx)
　　　　　　　　　　　　　　∃xFx ∨ ∃xGx ✓
　　Valid　　　　　　　　　∃xFx \*
　　　　　　　　　　　　　　∃xGx \*
　　　　　　✓ Fa ∨ Ga
　　　　　　　　　　　　　　Fa
　　　　　　　　　　　　　　Ga
　　　　　Fa　　　　Ga
　　　　　　Cl　　　　Cl

86.　　　　✓ ∃xFx ∨ ∃xGx
　　　　　　\* ∀x(Fx → Gx)
　　Valid　　　　　　　　　∃xGx \*
　　　　✓ ∃xFx　　　　　　　✓ ∃xGx
　　　　　　Fa　　　　　　　　Gb
　　　　　　　　Ga　　　　　　　　Gb
　　✓ Fa → Ga　　　　　　　Cl
　　　　Fa　　　Ga
　　　　Cl　　　Cl

**99**

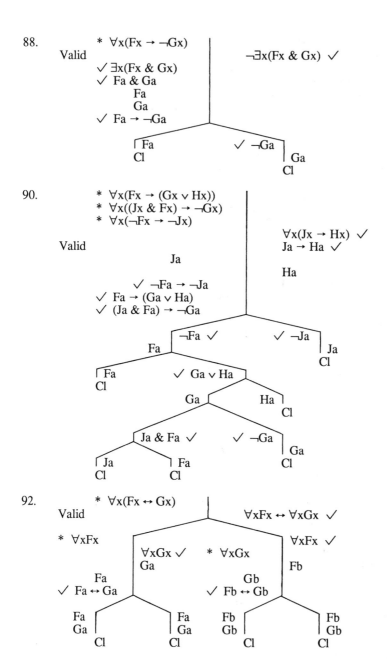

88.  Valid

\* ∀x(Fx → ¬Gx)                    ¬∃x(Fx & Gx) ✓

✓ ∃x(Fx & Gx)
✓ Fa & Ga
   Fa
   Ga
✓ Fa → ¬Ga

⌐ Fa          ✓ ¬Ga
   Cl                      Ga
                            Cl

90.

\* ∀x(Fx → (Gx ∨ Hx))
\* ∀x((Jx & Fx) → ¬Gx)
\* ∀x(¬Fx → ¬Jx)

Valid                                      ∀x(Jx → Hx) ✓
                                           Ja → Ha ✓
              Ja
                                              Ha
         ✓ ¬Fa → ¬Ja
    ✓ Fa → (Ga ∨ Ha)
    ✓ (Ja & Fa) → ¬Ga

                    ¬Fa ✓          ✓ ¬Ja
              Fa                            Ja
                                            Cl
    ⌐ Fa        ✓ Ga ∨ Ha
       Cl
              Ga        Ha
                         Cl

         Ja & Fa ✓      ✓ ¬Ga
                         Ga
    ⌐ Ja      ⌐ Fa       Cl
    Cl        Cl

92.  Valid

\* ∀x(Fx ↔ Gx)                    ∀xFx ↔ ∀xGx ✓

\* ∀xFx                            ∀xFx ✓

         ∀xGx ✓     \* ∀xGx
         Ga                        Fb
    Fa
✓ Fa ↔ Ga              Gb
                  ✓ Fb ↔ Gb

Fa        Fa     Fb        Fb
Ga        Ga     Gb        Gb
   Cl        Cl     Cl        Cl

94.

$\checkmark\ \exists x(Fx \leftrightarrow Gx)$

$\forall xFx \leftrightarrow \exists xGx\ \checkmark$

Not valid     $\checkmark\ Fa \leftrightarrow Ga$

* $\forall xFx$

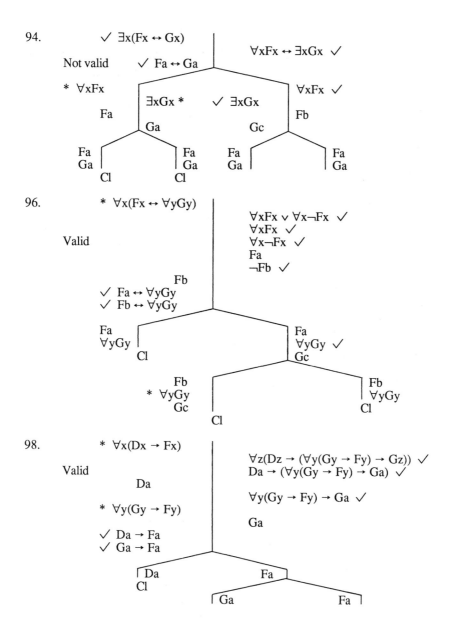

$\exists xGx$ *

$\checkmark\ \exists xGx$

$\forall xFx\ \checkmark$

Fa

Ga

Gc

Fb

Fa
Ga
Cl

Fa
Ga
Cl

Fa
Ga

Fa
Ga

96.

* $\forall x(Fx \leftrightarrow \forall yGy)$

$\forall xFx \lor \forall x\neg Fx\ \checkmark$
$\forall xFx\ \checkmark$
$\forall x\neg Fx\ \checkmark$
Fa
$\neg Fb\ \checkmark$

Valid

Fb
$\checkmark\ Fa \leftrightarrow \forall yGy$
$\checkmark\ Fb \leftrightarrow \forall yGy$

Fa
$\forall yGy$
Cl

Fa
$\forall yGy\ \checkmark$
Gc

Fb
* $\forall yGy$
Gc
Cl

Fb
$\forall yGy$
Cl

98.

* $\forall x(Dx \to Fx)$

$\forall z(Dz \to (\forall y(Gy \to Fy) \to Gz))\ \checkmark$
$Da \to (\forall y(Gy \to Fy) \to Ga)\ \checkmark$

Valid

Da

$\forall y(Gy \to Fy) \to Ga\ \checkmark$

* $\forall y(Gy \to Fy)$

Ga

$\checkmark\ Da \to Fa$
$\checkmark\ Ga \to Fa$

Da
Cl

Fa

Ga

Fa

101

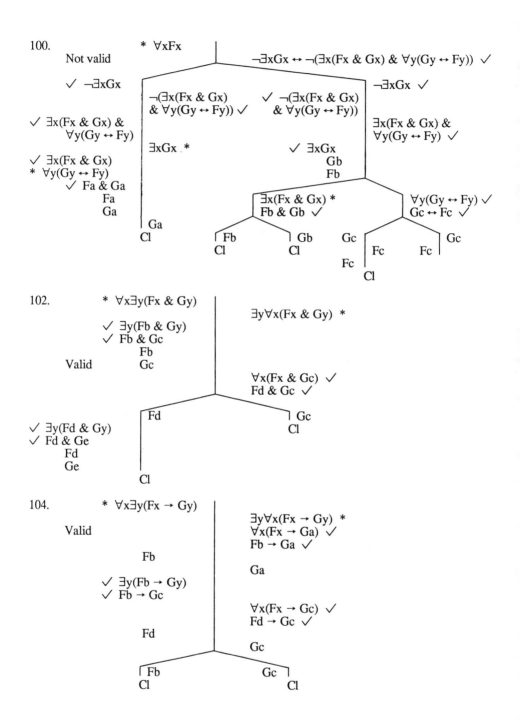

100.
Not valid

* ∀xFx
                                ¬∃xGx ↔ ¬(∃x(Fx & Gx) & ∀y(Gy ↔ Fy)) ✓

✓ ¬∃xGx

                                                                    ¬∃xGx ✓

                ¬(∃x(Fx & Gx)        ✓ ¬(∃x(Fx & Gx)
                & ∀y(Gy ↔ Fy)) ✓     & ∀y(Gy ↔ Fy))
✓ ∃x(Fx & Gx) &                                                    ∃x(Fx & Gx) &
    ∀y(Gy ↔ Fy)                                                     ∀y(Gy ↔ Fy) ✓
                ∃xGx . *              ✓ ∃xGx
✓ ∃x(Fx & Gx)                          Gb
* ∀y(Gy ↔ Fy)                          Fb
    ✓ Fa & Ga
    Fa                    ∃x(Fx & Gx) *              ∀y(Gy ↔ Fy) ✓
    Ga                    Fb & Gb ✓                  Gc ↔ Fc ✓
            Ga                                                Gc              Gc
    Cl       ⌐ Fb      ⌐ Gb      Gc  ⌐        ⌐  Fc
            Cl         Cl             Fc      Fc
                                     Fc
                                     Cl

102.        * ∀x∃y(Fx & Gy)
                                    ∃y∀x(Fx & Gy)  *
            ✓ ∃y(Fb & Gy)
            ✓ Fb & Gc
                Fb
Valid           Gc
                                    ∀x(Fx & Gc) ✓
                                    Fd & Gc ✓
                        ⌐ Fd                      ⌐ Gc
✓ ∃y(Fd & Gy)                                     Cl
✓ Fd & Ge
    Fd
    Ge
            Cl

104.        * ∀x∃y(Fx → Gy)
                                    ∃y∀x(Fx → Gy)  *
Valid                               ∀x(Fx → Ga) ✓
                                    Fb → Ga ✓
                Fb
                                    Ga
    ✓ ∃y(Fb → Gy)
    ✓ Fb → Gc
                                    ∀x(Fx → Gc) ✓
                                    Fd → Gc ✓
                Fd
                                    Gc
            ⌐ Fb              Gc ⌐
            Cl                     Cl

**102**

106.    * ∀x(∃yFyx → ∀zFxz)

|                                  |                                  |
|                                  | ∀y∀x(Fyx → Fxy) ✓                |
| Valid                            | ∀x(Fax → Fxa) ✓                  |
|                                  | Fab → Fba ✓                      |
|                                  |                                  |
|              Fab                 | Fba                              |
|                                  |                                  |
|   ✓ ∃yFyb → ∀zFbz                |                                  |

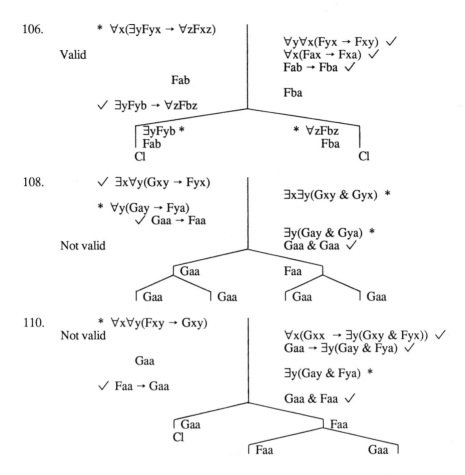

```
              ⌐∃yFyb *              * ∀zFbz ⌐
              | Fab                   Fba   |
               Cl                           Cl
```

108.    ✓ ∃x∀y(Gxy → Fyx)

```
        * ∀y(Gay → Fya)             ∃x∃y(Gxy & Gyx) *
           ✓ Gaa → Faa
                                     ∃y(Gay & Gya) *
   Not valid                         Gaa & Gaa ✓


              ⌐ Gaa              Faa
          ⌐ Gaa    ⌐ Gaa    ⌐ Gaa    ⌐ Gaa
```

110.    * ∀x∀y(Fxy → Gxy)
        Not valid

```
              Gaa                    ∀x(Gxx → ∃y(Gxy & Fyx)) ✓
                                     Gaa → ∃y(Gay & Fya) ✓
          ✓ Faa → Gaa
                                     ∃y(Gay & Fya) *

                                     Gaa & Faa ✓

              ⌐ Gaa               Faa
               Cl          ⌐ Faa          Gaa ⌐
```

112.

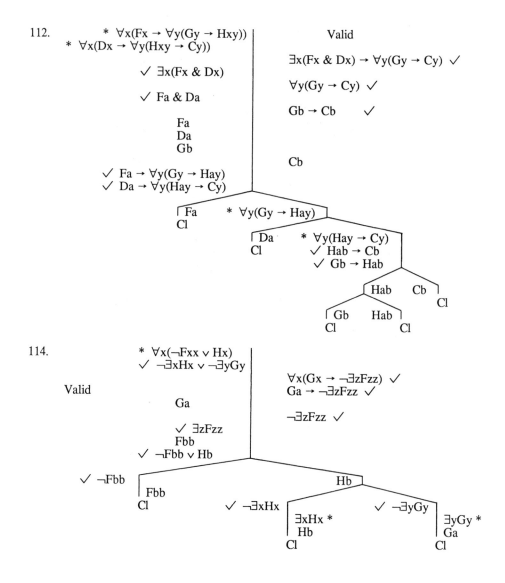

114.

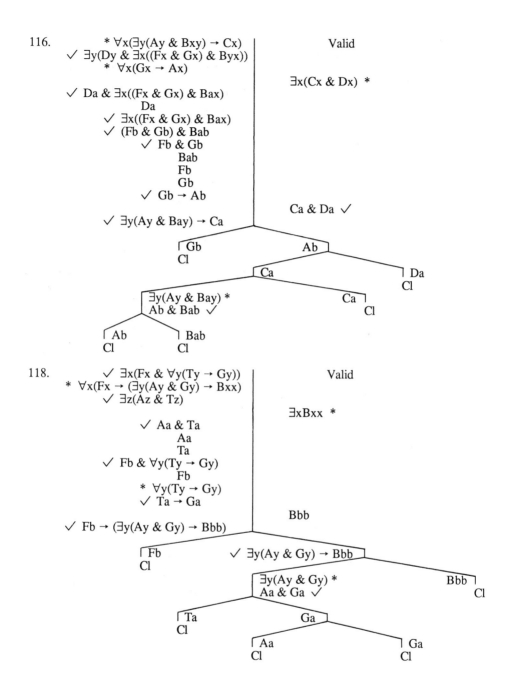

116.

        * ∀x(∃y(Ay & Bxy) → Cx)           Valid
    ✓ ∃y(Dy & ∃x((Fx & Gx) & Byx))
        * ∀x(Gx → Ax)

                    ∃x(Cx & Dx) *

  ✓ Da & ∃x((Fx & Gx) & Bax)
           Da
    ✓ ∃x((Fx & Gx) & Bax)
    ✓ (Fb & Gb) & Bab
      ✓ Fb & Gb
        Bab
        Fb
        Gb
      ✓ Gb → Ab

118.

      ✓ ∃x(Fx & ∀y(Ty → Gy))        Valid
 * ∀x(Fx → (∃y(Ay & Gy) → Bxx)
      ✓ ∃z(Az & Tz)

                  ∃xBxx *

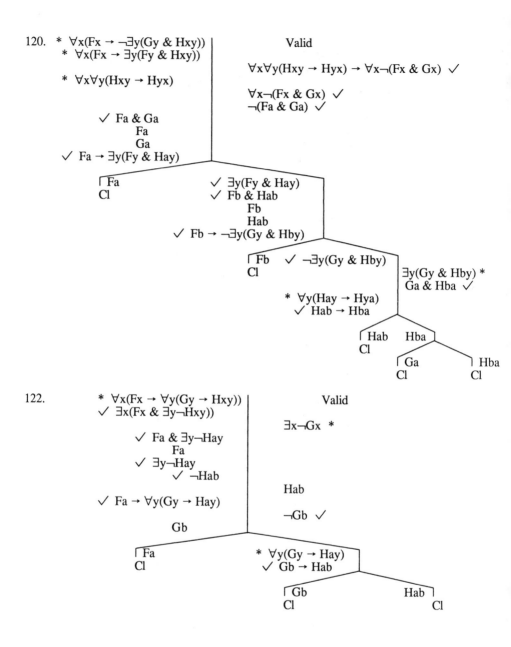

120.  * ∀x(Fx → ¬∃y(Gy & Hxy))                      Valid
      * ∀x(Fx → ∃y(Fy & Hxy))
                                          ∀x∀y(Hxy → Hyx) → ∀x¬(Fx & Gx)  ✓
      * ∀x∀y(Hxy → Hyx)
                                          ∀x¬(Fx & Gx)  ✓
                                          ¬(Fa & Ga)  ✓

          ✓ Fa & Ga
            Fa
            Ga
        ✓ Fa → ∃y(Fy & Hay)

            ⌈ Fa              ✓ ∃y(Fy & Hay)
            Cl               ✓ Fb & Hab
                               Fb
                               Hab
                     ✓ Fb → ¬∃y(Gy & Hby)

                         ⌈ Fb    ✓ ¬∃y(Gy & Hby)
                         Cl
                                                    ∃y(Gy & Hby) *
                                                    Ga & Hba  ✓
                              * ∀y(Hay → Hya)
                                ✓ Hab → Hba

                                   ⌈ Hab    Hba ⌉
                                   Cl
                                         ⌈ Ga      Hba ⌉
                                         Cl        Cl

122.        * ∀x(Fx → ∀y(Gy → Hxy))                  Valid
            ✓ ∃x(Fx & ∃y¬Hxy))
                                              ∃x¬Gx  *
                ✓ Fa & ∃y¬Hay
                  Fa
                ✓ ∃y¬Hay
                     ✓ ¬Hab
                                              Hab
            ✓ Fa → ∀y(Gy → Hay)
                                              ¬Gb  ✓
                Gb

            ⌈ Fa              * ∀y(Gy → Hay)
            Cl                ✓ Gb → Hab

                                 ⌈ Gb            Hab ⌉
                                 Cl              Cl

106

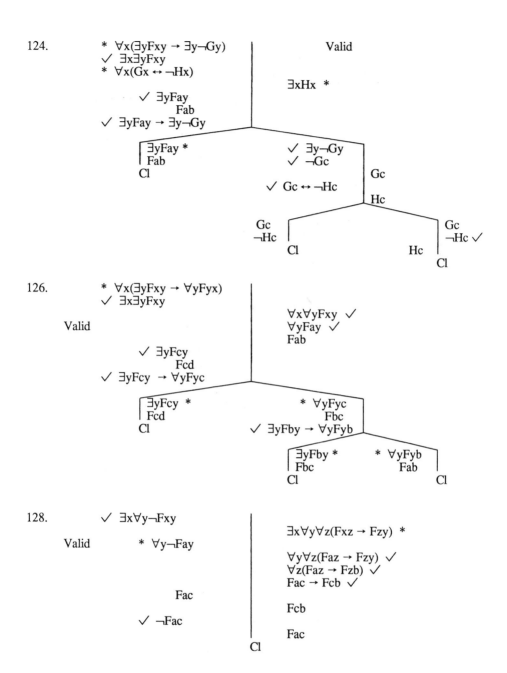

124.
* ∀x(∃yFxy → ∃y¬Gy)          Valid
✓ ∃x∃yFxy
* ∀x(Gx ↔ ¬Hx)
                             ∃xHx *
      ✓ ∃yFay
          Fab
✓ ∃yFay → ∃y¬Gy

    ┌─────────────────────────┐
    │ ∃yFay *          ✓ ∃y¬Gy
    │ Fab              ✓ ¬Gc
    │ Cl                          Gc
                    ✓ Gc ↔ ¬Hc
                                  Hc
              ┌──────────────────────────────┐
              Gc              │          Gc
              ¬Hc             │          ¬Hc ✓
                            Cl      Hc       Cl

126.
* ∀x(∃yFxy → ∀yFyx)
✓ ∃x∃yFxy
                             ∀x∀yFxy ✓
  Valid                      ∀yFay ✓
                             Fab
      ✓ ∃yFcy
          Fcd
✓ ∃yFcy → ∀yFyc

    ┌─────────────────────────┐
    │ ∃yFcy *          * ∀yFyc
    │ Fcd              Fbc
    │ Cl          ✓ ∃yFby → ∀yFyb

                   ┌──────────────────────────┐
                   ∃yFby *       * ∀yFyb
                   Fbc           Fab
                   Cl                      Cl

128.
✓ ∃x∀y¬Fxy
                             ∃x∀y∀z(Fxz → Fzy) *
  Valid       * ∀y¬Fay
                             ∀y∀z(Faz → Fzy) ✓
                             ∀z(Faz → Fzb) ✓
                             Fac → Fcb ✓

              Fac
                             Fcb
          ✓ ¬Fac
                             Fac
                      Cl

130.

$* \ \forall x \forall y((Ax \ \& \ By) \to Cxy)$
$\checkmark \ \exists y(Fy \ \& \ \forall z(Hz \to Cyz))$
$* \ \forall x \forall y \forall z((Cxy \ \& \ Cyz) \to Cxz)$
$* \ \forall x(Fx \to Bx)$

$\checkmark \ Fa \ \& \ \forall z(Hz \to Caz)$

$\checkmark \ Ab \ \& \ Hc$

Fa
$* \ \forall z(Hz \to Caz)$
Ab
Hc
$* \ \forall y((Ab \ \& \ By) \to Cby)$
$\checkmark \ Fa \to Ba$
$\checkmark \ Hc \to Cac$
$\checkmark \ (Ab \ \& \ Ba) \to Cba$
$* \ \forall y \forall z((Cby \ \& \ Cyz) \to Cbz)$
$* \ \forall z((Cba \ \& \ Caz) \to Cbz)$
$\checkmark \ (Cba \ \& \ Cac) \to Cbc$

Valid

$\forall z \forall y((Az \ \& \ Hy) \to Czy) \ \checkmark$

$\forall y((Ab \ \& \ Hy) \to Cby) \ \checkmark$
$(Ab \ \& \ Hc) \to Cbc \ \checkmark$

Cbc

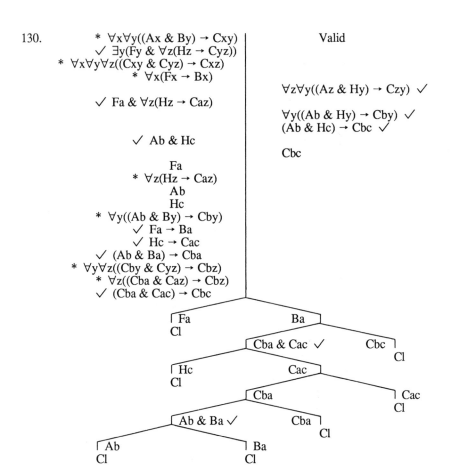

108

# QUANTIFIED DEDUCTION

This chapter extends the deduction system of Chapter 8 to predicate logic. The first two sections present the basic rules for quantifiers. Instances of quantified formulas always involve constants; indeed, in this language, formulas never contain free variables. This simplifies quantifier rules. The last two sections extend the system to multiply quantified formulas; instructors who wish to restrict themselves to singly quantified formulas should omit those sections, with the exception, perhaps, of the quantifier negation rule, discussed near the beginning of 13.4. The rules for full predicate logic derive from the system of the first edition of Copi's *Symbolic Logic*, by way of revisions by Kalish and Prawitz. To make the restrictions on rules easy to apply, the method uses Fine's dependency diagrams.

## 1. KEY DEFINITIONS

The deduction rules needed for quantificational logic are very straightforward. Say that $\mathcal{A}[c/v]$ is the result of substituting $c$ for every occurrence of $v$ throughout the formula $\mathcal{A}$. If $\forall v \mathcal{A}$ and $\exists v \mathcal{A}$ are formulas, then $\mathcal{A}[c/v]$ is an *instance* of them. Conversely, $\forall v \mathcal{A}$ and $\exists v \mathcal{A}$ are *generics* of $\mathcal{A}[c/v]$. If $\mathcal{A}[c/v]$ is an instance of $\forall v \mathcal{A}$ and $\exists v \mathcal{A}$, and those formulas do not contain $c$, then $\mathcal{A}[c/v]$ is a *conservative instance* of $\forall v \mathcal{A}$ and $\exists v \mathcal{A}$.

A constant $c$ *immediately depends on* a constant $d$ in a proof if and only if $c$ is introduced into the proof by applying ES to a formula containing $d$. A constant $c$ *depends on* a constant $d$ if and only if there is a chain of constants $c_1, ..., c_n$ such that $c$ immediately depends on $c_1$, $c_1$ immediately depends on $c_2$, ..., and $c_n$ immediately depends on $d$. (The chain may be empty; immediate dependence is a kind of dependence.)

*Dependency diagrams* change only when we apply ES. When we do apply existential specification, moving from $\exists v \mathcal{A}$ to $\mathcal{A}[c/v]$, we (1) write, horizontally, the constants in $\exists v \mathcal{A}$ not already in the diagram; and (2) add the new constant $c$ below the constants in $\exists v \mathcal{A}$, circling it and drawing lines linking it to them. We can use these diagrams to check the fulfillment of the third and fourth restrictions on UG. The third bans the use of the same constant in ES and UG. So, applying UG to a constant circled in the diagram is prohibited. The fourth restriction requires that, in moving from $\mathcal{A}[c/v]$ to $\forall v \mathcal{A}$, no constant in $\forall v \mathcal{A}$ depend on $c$. It is satisfied so long as no constant in $\mathcal{A}[c/v]$ is linked upward to $c$.

A *proto-formula* of QL is a string of symbols that results from deleting one or more quantifiers from a formula of QL. If a deleted quantifier was on a variable $v$, then $v$ is *free* in the proto-formula.

# 2. SUMMARY OF RULES

Existential Generalization (EG)

n.　　$A[c/v]$
n+p.　　$\exists vA$　　　EG, n
Here $c$ may be any constant.

Existential Specification (ES)

n.　　$\exists vA$
n+p.　　$A[c/v]$　　　ES, n
Here $c$ must be a constant new to the proof,
and must not appear in the proof's conclusion.

Universal Specification (US)

n.　　　$\forall vA$
n+p.　　$A[c/v]$　　　US, n
Here $c$ may be any constant.

Quantifier Negation (QN)

n.　　$\neg\exists vA$　　　QN, m
m.　　$\forall v\neg A$　　　QN, n

n.　　$\neg\forall vA$　　　QN, m
m.　　$\exists v\neg A$　　　QN, n

Universal Generalization (UG)

n.　　　$A[c/v]$
n+p.　　$\forall vA$　　　UG, n
Here　(1) $c$ must not occur in $\forall vA$;
(2) $c$ must not occur in the assumptions or conclusion
of the proof;
(3) $c$ must not have been introduced by ES;
(4) no term remaining in $\forall vA$ may depend on $c$.

Rule of Passage-- Disjunction (RP∨)

Existential:

n.　$\exists vA \vee B$　(or $B \vee \exists vA$)　RP∨, m
m.　$\exists v(A \vee B)$　(or $\exists v(B \vee A)$)　RP∨, n
where $v$ is in $A$ but not $B$.

Universal:

n.　$\forall vA \vee B$　(or $B \vee \forall vA$)　RP∨, m
m.　$\forall v(A \vee B)$　(or $\forall v(B \vee A)$)　RP∨, n
where $v$ is in $A$ but not $B$.

Rule of Passage-- Conditional (Consequents) (RP→)

Existential:

n.　　$A \to \exists vB$　　　RP→, m
m.　　$\exists v(A \to B)$　　　RP→, n
Here $v$ is in $B$ but not $A$.

Universal:

n.　　$A \to \forall vB$　　　RP→, m
m.　　$\forall v(A \to B)$　　　RP→, n
Here $v$ is in $B$ but not $A$.

Rule of Passage-- Conditional (Antecedents) (RP→)

Existential:

n.　　$\exists vA \to B$　　　RP→, m
m.　　$\forall v(A \to B)$　　　RP→, n
Here $v$ is in $A$ but not $B$.

Universal:

n.　　$\forall vA \to B$　　　RP→, m
m.　　$\exists v(A \to B)$　　　RP→, n
Here $v$ is in $A$ but not $B$.

Rules of Passage-- Conjunction (RP&)

Existential:

n. $\underline{\exists v \mathcal{A} \ \& \ \mathcal{B}}$   (or $\mathcal{B} \ \& \ \exists v \mathcal{A}$) RP&, m

m. $\exists v(\mathcal{A} \ \& \ \mathcal{B})$   (or $\exists v(\mathcal{B} \ \& \ \mathcal{A})$ RP&, n

where $v$ is in $\mathcal{A}$ but not $\mathcal{B}$.

Universal:

n. $\underline{\forall v \mathcal{A} \ \& \ \mathcal{B}}$   (or $\mathcal{B} \ \& \ \forall v \mathcal{A}$)  RP&, m

m. $\forall v(\mathcal{A} \ \& \ \mathcal{B})$ (or $\forall v(\mathcal{B} \ \& \ \mathcal{A})$  RP&, n

where $v$ is in $\mathcal{A}$ but not $\mathcal{B}$.

Variable Rewrite (VR)

n. $\underset{=}{\mathcal{A}}$        VR, m

m. $\mathcal{A}[v/u]$     VR, n

where $u$ is in $\mathcal{A}$ but $v$ is not.


# 3. ANSWERS TO UNANSWERED EVEN PROBLEMS

## 13.1 DEDUCTION RULES FOR QUANTIFIERS

The policy that guided symbolization for this chapter was to introduce (more or less) only as much complexity as is needed to enable the proofs to go through. In those cases in which the meaning of the English is intended to be captured not only through appropriate interpretation of constants but also by circumscribing the universe of discourse, this is indicated.

8.    1.   $\forall x(H_1 x \rightarrow (Lx \ \& \ H_2 x))$    A     (universe: insects)
     2.   $\exists x(H_1 x \ \& \ Px)$          A
     3.   $H_1 a \ \& \ Pa$            ES, 2
     4.      $H_1 a \rightarrow (La \ \& \ H_2 a)$        US, 1
     5.   $H_1 a$               S, 3
     6.   $La \ \& \ H_2 a$           MP, 4, 5
     7.   $Pa$                S, 3
     8.   $(La \ \& \ H_2 a) \ \& \ Pa$      C, 6, 7
     9.   $\exists x((Lx \ \& \ H_2 x) \ \& \ Px)$    EG, 8

10.   1.   $\forall x Axd$            A     (universe: people)
     2.   $\forall x(Adx \rightarrow Cxd)$     A
     3.   $Add \rightarrow Cdd$        US, 2
     4.   $Add$              US, 1
     5.   $Cdd$             MP, 3, 4

14.   1.   $\exists x(Bx \ \& \ Sx)$      A     (universe: people)
     2.   $\forall x(Sx \rightarrow \neg Dx)$     A
     3.   $Ba \ \& \ Sa$           ES, 1
     4.   $Sa \rightarrow \neg Da$         US, 2
     5.   $Sa$                S, 3
     6.   $\neg Da$             MP, 4, 5
     7.   $Ba$               S, 3
     8.   $Ba \ \& \ \neg Da$         C, 7, 6
     9.   $\exists x(Bx \ \& \ \neg Dx)$     EG, 8

16. 
1.  ∃x(Ax & Bx) & ∃x(Ax & Cx)    A    (universe: people)
2.  ∀x(Cx → Rx)    A
3.  ∀x(Mx → ¬Bx)    A
4.  ∃x(Ax & Cx)    S, 1
5.  Aa & Ca    ES, 4
6.  Ca → Ra    US, 2
7.  Ca    S, 5
8.  Ra    MP, 6, 7
9.  Aa    S, 5
10. Aa & Ra    C, 9, 8
11. ∃x(Ax & Rx)    EG, 10
12. ∃x(Ax & Bx)    S, 1
13. Ab & Bb    ES, 12
14. Bb    S, 13
15. Mb → ¬Bb    US, 3
16. ¬¬Bb    DN, 14
17. ¬Mb    MT, 15, 16
18. Ab    S, 13
19. Ab & ¬Mb    C, 18, 17
20. ∃x(Ax & ¬Mx)    EG, 19
21. ∃x(Ax & Rx) & ∃x(Ax & ¬Mx)    C, 11, 20

20. 
1.  ∀x(Mx → ¬Lx)    A
2.  ∃x(Sx & Mx)    A
3.  Sa & Ma    ES, 2
4.  Ma → ¬La    US, 1
5.  Ma    S, 3
6.  ¬La    MP, 4, 5
7.  Sa    S, 3
8.  Sa & ¬La    C, 7, 6
9.  ∃x(Sx & ¬Lx)    EG, 8

22. 
1.  ∀x(Lx → Mx)    A
2.  ∃x(Sx & ¬Mx)    A
3.  Sa & ¬Ma    ES, 2
4.  La → Ma    US, 1
5.  ¬Ma    S, 3
6.  ¬La    MT, 4, 5
7.  Sa    S, 3
8.  Sa & ¬La    C, 7, 6
9.  ∃x(Sx & ¬Lx)    EG, 8

26. 
1.  ∀x(Mx → Lx)    A
2.  ∃x(Mx & Sx)    A
3.  Ma & Sa    ES, 2
4.  Ma → La    US, 1
5.  Ma    S, 3
6.  La    MP, 4, 5
7.  Sa    S, 3
8.  Sa & La    C, 7, 6
9.  ∃x(Sx & Lx)    EG, 8

| 28. | 1. | $\forall x(Mx \rightarrow \neg Lx)$ | A |
| | 2. | $\exists x(Mx \;\&\; Sx)$ | A |
| | 3. | Ma & Sa | ES, 2 |
| | 4. | Ma $\rightarrow$ ¬La | US, 1 |
| | 5. | Ma | S, 3 |
| | 6. | ¬La | MP, 4, 5 |
| | 7. | Sa | S, 3 |
| | 8. | Sa & ¬La | C, 7, 6 |
| | 9. | $\exists x(Sx \;\&\; \neg Lx)$ | EG, 8 |

| 32. | 1. | $\forall x(Lx \rightarrow Mx)$ | A |
| | 2. | $\forall x(Sx \rightarrow \neg Mx)$ | A |
| | 3. | $\exists x Sx$ | A |
| | 4. | Sa | ES, 3 |
| | 5. | Sa $\rightarrow$ ¬Ma | US, 2 |
| | 6. | ¬Ma | MP, 5, 4 |
| | 7. | La $\rightarrow$ Ma | US, 1 |
| | 8. | ¬La | MT, 7, 6 |
| | 9. | Sa & ¬La | C, 4, 8 |
| | 10. | $\exists x(Sx \;\&\; \neg Lx)$ | EG, 9 |

| 34. | 1. | $\forall x(Mx \rightarrow Lx)$ | A |
| | 2. | $\exists x(Sx \;\&\; Mx)$ | A |
| | 3. | Sa & Ma | ES, 2 |
| | 4. | Ma $\rightarrow$ La | US, 1 |
| | 5. | Ma | S, 3 |
| | 6. | La | MP, 4, 5 |
| | 7. | Sa | S, 3 |
| | 8. | La & Sa | C, 6, 7 |
| | 9. | $\exists x(Lx \;\&\; Sx)$ | EG, 8 |

| 38. | 1. | $\exists x Fx$ | A |
| | 2. | $\forall x Gx$ | A |
| | 3. | Fa | ES, 1 |
| | 4. | Ga | US, 2 |
| | 5. | Fa & Ga | C, 3, 4 |
| | 6. | $\exists x(Fx \;\&\; Gx)$ | EG, 5 |

| 40. | 1. | $\forall x(Gx \rightarrow Hx)$ | A |
| | 2. | $\exists x(Fx \;\&\; Gx)$ | A |
| | 3. | Fa & Ga | ES, 2 |
| | 4. | Ga $\rightarrow$ Ha | US, 1 |
| | 5. | Ga | S, 3 |
| | 6. | Ha | MP, 4, 5 |
| | 7. | Fa | S, 3 |
| | 8. | Fa & Ha | C, 7, 6 |
| | 9. | $\exists x(Fx \;\&\; Hx)$ | EG, 8 |

| 44. | 1. | $\forall x(Gx \rightarrow Hx)$ | A |
| | 2. | $\exists x(Gx \;\&\; Fx)$ | A |
| | 3. | Ga & Fa | ES, 2 |
| | 4. | Ga $\rightarrow$ Ha | US, 1 |
| | 5. | Ga | S, 3 |
| | 6. | Ha | MP, 4, 5 |
| | 7. | Fa | S, 3 |
| | 8. | Fa & Ha | C, 7, 6 |
| | 9. | $\exists x(Fx \;\&\; Hx)$ | EG, 8 |

113

| 46. | 1. | ∃x(Gx & Hx) | A |
| | 2. | ∀x(Gx →Fx) | A |
| | 3. | Ga & Ha | ES, 1 |
| | 4. | Ga → Fa | US, 2 |
| | 5. | Ga | S, 3 |
| | 6. | Fa | MP, 4, 5 |
| | 7. | Ha | S, 3 |
| | 8. | Fa & Ha | C, 6, 7 |
| | 9. | ∃x(Fx & Hx) | EG, 8 |

| 50. | 1. | ∃x(¬Fx & ¬Gx) | A |
| | 2. | ∀x(¬Gx → ¬Hx) | A |
| | 3. | ¬Fa & ¬Ga | ES, 1 |
| | 4. | ¬Ga → ¬Ha | US, 2 |
| | 5. | ¬Ga | S, 3 |
| | 6. | ¬Ha | MP, 4, 5 |
| | 7. | ¬Fa | S, 3 |
| | 8. | ¬Ha & ¬Fa | C, 6, 7 |
| | 9. | ∃x(¬Hx & ¬Fx) | EG, 8 |

| 52. | 1. | ∀x(Fx ↔ Gx) | A |
| | 2. | ∀x(Fx ↔ Hx) | A |
| | 3. | ∃x(¬Hx ∨ Gx) | A |
| | 4. | Fa ↔ Ha | US, 2 |
| | 5. | (Fa → Ha) & (Ha → Fa) | B, 4 |
| | 6. | Ha → Fa | S, 5 |
| | 7. | Fa ↔ Ga | US, 1 |
| | 8. | (Fa → Ga) & (Ga → Fa) | B, 7 |
| | 9. | Fa → Ga | S, 8 |
| | 10. | Ha → Ga | HS, 6, 9 |
| | 11. | Ha → (Ga & Fa) | CC, 10, 6 |
| | 12. | ¬Ha ∨ (Ga & Fa) | MC, 11 |
| | 13. | ∃x(¬Hx ∨ (Gx & Fx)) | EG, 12 |

| 56. | 1. | ∃yFyy | A |
| | 2. | ∃x∀zGxz | A |
| | 3. | Faa | ES, 1 |
| | 4. | ∀zGbz | ES, 2 |
| | 5. | Gba | US, 4 |
| | 6. | Gba & Faa | C, 5, 3 |
| | 7. | ∃y(Gya & Faa) | EG, 6 |
| | 8. | ∃x∃y(Gyx & Fxx) | EG, 7 |

| 58. | 1. | ∃xGx & ∃x¬Gx | A |
| | 2. | ∀x∀y(Fxy ↔ (Gx & ¬Gy)) | A |
| | 3. | ∃xGx | S, 1 |
| | 4. | Ga | ES, 3 |
| | 5. | ∃x¬Gx | S, 1 |
| | 6. | ¬Gb | ES, 5 |
| | 7. | ∀y(Fay ↔ (Ga & ¬Gy)) | US, 2 |
| | 8. | Fab ↔ (Ga & ¬Gb) | US, 7 |
| | 9. | Ga & ¬Gb | C, 4, 6 |
| | 10. | Fab | BE, 8, 9 |
| | 11. | ∃yFay | EG, 10 |
| | 12. | ∃x∃yFxy | EG, 11 |

| | | | |
|---|---|---|---|
| 62. | 1. | ∃x∃y(Fx & Gyx) | A |
| | 2. | ∀x∀y((Fx & Hy) → ¬Jxy) | A |
| | 3. | ∃y(Fa & Gya) | ES, 1 |
| | 4. | Fa & Gba | ES, 3 |
| | 5. | ∀y((Fa & Hy) → ¬Jay) | US, 2 |
| | 6. | (Fa & Hb) → ¬Jab | US, 5 |
| | 7. | Fa | S, 4 |
| | 8. | ¬Hb ∨ Fa | Ad, 7 |
| | 9. | Hb → Hb | SI |
| | 10. | ¬Hb ∨ Hb | MC, 9 |
| | 11. | (¬Hb ∨ Fa) & (¬Hb ∨ Hb) | C, 8, 10 |
| | 12. | ¬Hb ∨ (Fa & Hb) | D, 11 |
| | 13. | Hb → (Fa & Hb) | MC, 12 |
| | 14. | Hb → ¬Jab | HS, 13, 6 |
| | 15. | ¬Hb ∨ ¬Jab | MC, 14 |
| | 16. | ¬(Hb & Jab) | DM, 15 |
| | 17. | Gba | S, 4 |
| | 18. | Gba & ¬(Hb & Jab) | C, 17, 16 |
| | 19. | ∃y(Gby & ¬(Hb & Jyb)) | EG, 18 |
| | 20. | ∃x∃y(Gxy & ¬(Hx & Jyx)) | EG, 19 |
| 64. | 1. | ∀z∀x(¬Hz ↔ (Fx & Gz)) | A |
| | 2. | ∀x∃y(Gy & Fx) | A |
| | 3. | ∃y(Gy & Fa) | US, 2 |
| | 4. | Gb & Fa | ES, 3 |
| | 5. | ∀x(¬Hb ↔ (Fx & Gb)) | US, 1 |
| | 6. | ¬Hb ↔ (Fa & Gb) | US, 5 |
| | 7. | Fa | S, 4 |
| | 8. | Gb | S, 4 |
| | 9. | Fa & Gb | C, 7, 8 |
| | 10. | ¬Hb | BE, 6, 9 |
| | 11. | ∃x¬Hx | EG, 10 |

## 13.2 UNIVERSAL GENERALIZATION

| | | | |
|---|---|---|---|
| 8. | 1. | ∀x(Gx → Hx) | A |
| | 2. | ∀x(¬Gx → ¬Sx) | A |
| | 3. | Ga → Ha | US, 1 |
| | 4. | ¬Ha → ¬Ga | Tr, 3 |
| | 5. | ¬Ga → ¬Sa | US, 2 |
| | 6. | ¬Ha → ¬Sa | HS, 4, 5 |
| | 7. | ∀x(¬Hx → ¬Sx) | UG, 6 |
| 10. | 1. | ∀x(Ix → ¬Px) | A (universe: businesses) |
| | 2. | ∀x(Ux → Ix) | A |
| | 3. | Ua → Ia | US, 2 |
| | 4. | Ia → ¬Pa | US, 1 |
| | 5. | Ua → ¬Pa | HS, 3, 4 |
| | 6. | ∀x(Ux → ¬Px) | UG, 5 |
| 14. | 1. | ∀x(Sx → ¬¬Hx) | A (universe: men) |
| | 2. | ∀x(Hx → Rx) | A |
| | 3. | Sa → ¬¬Ha | US, 1 |
| | 4. | Ha → Ra | US, 2 |
| | 5. | ¬¬Ha → ¬¬Ra | DN, 4 |
| | 6. | Sa → ¬¬Ra | HS, 3, 5 |
| | 7. | ∀x(Sx → ¬¬Rx) | UG, 6 |

16. 1. $\forall x((Yx \,\&\, Lx) \to Jx)$    A    (universe: animals)
    2. $\forall x((Yx \,\&\, Jx) \to \neg\neg Hx)$    A
    3. $(Ya \,\&\, La) \to Ya$    W
    4. $(Ya \,\&\, La) \to Ja$    US, 1
    5. $(Ya \,\&\, La) \to (Ya \,\&\, Ja)$    CC, 3, 4
    6. $(Ya \,\&\, Ja) \to \neg\neg Ha$    US, 2
    7. $(Ya \,\&\, La) \to \neg\neg Ha$    HS, 5, 6
    8. $(Ya \,\&\, La) \to Ha$    DN, 7
    9. $\forall x((Yx \,\&\, Lx) \to Hx)$    UG, 8

20. 1. $\forall x(Wx \to Fx)$    A    (universe: men)
    2. $\forall x(\neg Wx \to Hx)$    A
    3. $Wa \to Wa$    SI
    4. $\neg Wa \lor Wa$    MC, 3
    5. $\neg Wa \to Ha$    US, 2
    6. $Wa \to Fa$    US, 1
    7. $Ha \lor Fa$    CD, 4, 5, 6
    8. $\forall x(Hx \lor Fx)$    UG, 7

22. 1. $\forall x(Jx \to \neg Ox)$    A
    2. $\forall x(Px \to \neg\neg Ox)$    A
    3. $\neg Oa \to \neg Oa$    SI
    4. $\neg\neg Oa \lor \neg Oa$    MC, 3
    5. $Ja \to \neg Oa$    US, 1
    6. $\neg\neg Oa \to \neg Ja$    Tr, 5
    7. $Pa \to \neg\neg Oa$    US, 2
    8. $Pa \to Oa$    DN, 7
    9. $\neg Oa \to \neg Pa$    Tr, 8
    10. $\neg Ja \lor \neg Pa$    CD, 4, 6, 9
    11. $\neg(Ja \,\&\, Pa)$    DM, 10
    12. $\forall x\neg(Jx \,\&\, Px)$    UG, 11

26. 1. $\forall x(Tx \to \neg Wx)$    A
    2. $\forall x(\neg Wx \to \neg Cx)$    A
    3. $\forall x(\neg Tx \to \neg Hx)$    A
    4. $Ta \to \neg Wa$    US, 1
    5. $\neg Wa \to \neg Ca$    US, 2
    6. $Ta \to \neg Ca$    HS, 4, 5
    7. $\neg\neg Ca \to \neg Ta$    Tr, 6
    8. $Ca \to \neg Ta$    DN, 7
    9. $\neg Ta \to \neg Ha$    US, 3
    10. $Ca \to \neg Ha$    HS, 8, 9
    11. $\forall x(Cx \to \neg Hx)$    UG, 10

28. 1. $\forall x(Sx \to Tx)$    A    (universe: people)
    2. $\forall x(Wx \to \neg\neg Gx)$    A
    3. $\forall x(Tx \to \neg Gx)$    A
    4. $Sa \to Ta$    US, 1
    5. $Ta \to \neg Ga$    US, 3
    6. $Sa \to \neg Ga$    HS, 4, 5
    7. $Wa \to \neg\neg Ga$    US, 2
    8. $Wa \to Ga$    DN, 7
    9. $\neg Ga \to \neg Wa$    Tr, 8
    10. $Sa \to \neg Wa$    HS, 6, 9
    11. $\forall x(Sx \to \neg Wx)$    UG, 10

| 32. | 1. | $\forall x(\neg Sx \rightarrow Rx)$ | A | (universe: my ideas) |
|---|---|---|---|---|
| | 2. | $\forall x(Bx \rightarrow \neg Wx)$ | A | |
| | 3. | $\forall x(\neg Tx \rightarrow \neg Sx)$ | A | |
| | 4. | $\forall x(Rx \rightarrow \neg\neg Lx)$ | A | |
| | 5. | $\forall x(Dx \rightarrow Bx)$ | A | |
| | 6. | $\forall x(\neg Lx \lor Wx)$ | A | |
| | 7. | $Da \rightarrow Ba$ | US, 5 | |
| | 8. | $Ba \rightarrow \neg Wa$ | US, 2 | |
| | 9. | $Da \rightarrow \neg Wa$ | HS, 7, 8 | |
| | 10. | $\neg La \lor Wa$ | US, 6 | |
| | 11. | $Wa \lor \neg La$ | Cm, 10 | |
| | 12. | $\neg\neg Wa \lor \neg La$ | DN, 11 | |
| | 13. | $\neg Wa \rightarrow \neg La$ | MC, 12 | |
| | 14. | $Da \rightarrow \neg La$ | HS, 9, 13 | |
| | 15. | $Ra \rightarrow \neg\neg La$ | US, 4 | |
| | 16. | $Ra \rightarrow La$ | DN, 15 | |
| | 17. | $\neg La \rightarrow \neg Ra$ | Tr, 16 | |
| | 18. | $Da \rightarrow \neg Ra$ | HS, 14, 17 | |
| | 19. | $\neg Sa \rightarrow Ra$ | US, 1 | |
| | 20. | $\neg Ra \rightarrow \neg\neg Sa$ | Tr, 19 | |
| | 21. | $Da \rightarrow \neg\neg Sa$ | HS, 18, 20 | |
| | 22. | $\neg Ta \rightarrow \neg Sa$ | US, 3 | |
| | 23. | $\neg\neg Sa \rightarrow \neg\neg Ta$ | Tr, 22 | |
| | 24. | $Da \rightarrow \neg\neg Ta$ | HS, 21, 23 | |
| | 25. | $Da \rightarrow Ta$ | DN, 24 | |
| | 26. | $\forall x(Dx \rightarrow Tx)$ | UG, 25 | |

| 34. | 1. | $\forall x(Sx \rightarrow Cx)$ | A | (universe: students) |
|---|---|---|---|---|
| | 2. | $\forall x(Cx \rightarrow Lx)$ | A | |
| | 3. | $Sa \rightarrow Ca$ | US, 1 | |
| | 4. | $Ca \rightarrow La$ | US, 2 | |
| | 5. | $Sa \rightarrow La$ | HS, 3, 4 | |
| | 6. | $\forall x(Sx \rightarrow Lx)$ | UG, 5 | |

| 38. | 1. | $\forall x(\neg Fx \rightarrow Cx)$ | A | (universe: people) |
|---|---|---|---|---|
| | 2. | $\forall x(Cx \rightarrow Dx)$ | A | |
| | 3. | $\neg Fa \rightarrow Ca$ | US, 1 | |
| | 4. | $Ca \rightarrow Da$ | US, 2 | |
| | 5. | $\neg Fa \rightarrow Da$ | HS, 3, 4 | |
| | 6. | $\neg Da \rightarrow \neg\neg Fa$ | Tr, 5 | |
| | 7. | $\neg Da \rightarrow Fa$ | DN, 6 | |
| | 8. | $\forall x(\neg Dx \rightarrow Fx)$ | UG, 7 | |

| 40. | 1. | $\forall x((Ix \lor Fx) \rightarrow Dx)$ | A | (universe: people) |
|---|---|---|---|---|
| | 2. | $\forall x(Dx \rightarrow (Bx \ \& \ \neg Ox))$ | A | |
| | 3. | $\forall x(Tx \rightarrow Fx)$ | A | |
| | 4. | $\forall x(\neg Cx \rightarrow Ix)$ | A | |
| | 5. | $(Ia \lor Fa) \rightarrow Da$ | US, 1 | |
| | 6. | $Da \rightarrow (Ba \ \& \ \neg Oa)$ | US, 2 | |
| | 7. | $(Ia \lor Fa) \rightarrow (Ba \ \& \ \neg Oa)$ | HS, 5, 6 | |
| | 8. | $\neg(Ba \ \& \ \neg Oa) \rightarrow \neg(Ia \lor Fa)$ | Tr, 7 | |
| | 9. | $(\neg Ba \lor \neg\neg Oa) \rightarrow (\neg Ia \ \& \ \neg Fa)$ | DM, 8 | |
| | 10. | $(\neg Ba \lor Oa) \rightarrow (\neg Ia \ \& \ \neg Fa)$ | DN, 9 | |
| | 11. | $(\neg Ia \ \& \ \neg Fa) \rightarrow \neg Ia$ | W | |
| | 12. | $(\neg Ba \lor Oa) \rightarrow \neg Ia$ | HS, 10, 11 | |
| | 13. | $\neg Ca \rightarrow Ia$ | US, 4 | |
| | 14. | $\neg Ia \rightarrow \neg\neg Ca$ | Tr, 13 | |

117

|     |     |                                                  |            |
|-----|-----|--------------------------------------------------|------------|
|     | 15. | ¬Ia → Ca                                         | DN, 14     |
|     | 16. | (¬Ba ∨ Oa) → Ca                                  | HS, 12, 15 |
|     | 17. | (¬Ia & ¬Fa) → ¬Fa                                | W          |
|     | 18. | (¬Ba ∨ Oa) → ¬Fa                                 | HS, 10, 17 |
|     | 19. | Ta → Fa                                          | US, 3      |
|     | 20. | ¬Fa → ¬Ta                                        | Tr, 19     |
|     | 21. | (¬Ba ∨ Oa) → ¬Ta                                 | HS, 18, 20 |
|     | 22. | (¬Ba ∨ Oa) → (Ca & ¬Ta)                          | CC, 16, 21 |
|     | 23. | ∀x((¬Bx ∨ Ox) → (Cx & ¬Tx))                      | UG, 22     |

| 44. | 1.  | ∀x(Fx ↔ (Gx & Hx))                               | A          |
|-----|-----|--------------------------------------------------|------------|
|     | 2.  | Fa ↔ (Ga & Ha)                                   | US, 1      |
|     | 3.  | (Fa → (Ga & Ha)) & ((Ga & Ha) → Fa)             | B, 2       |
|     | 4.  | Fa → (Ga & Ha)                                   | S, 3       |
|     | 5.  | (Ga & Ha) → Ga                                   | W          |
|     | 6.  | Fa → Ga                                          | HS, 4, 5   |
|     | 7.  | ∀x(Fx → Gx)                                      | UG, 6      |
|     | 8.  | (Ga & Ha) → Ha                                   | W          |
|     | 9.  | Fa → Ha                                          | HS, 4, 8   |
|     | 10. | ∀x(Fx → Hx)                                      | UG, 9      |
|     | 11. | ∀x(Fx → Gx) & ∀x(Fx → Hx)                        | C, 7, 10   |

| 46. | 1.  | ∀x(Fx → Hx)                                      | A          |
|-----|-----|--------------------------------------------------|------------|
|     | 2.  | ∀x(Gx → Hx)                                      | A          |
|     | 3.  | Fa → Ha                                          | US, 1      |
|     | 4.  | Ga → Ha                                          | US, 2      |
|     | 5.  | ¬Fa ∨ Ha                                         | MC, 3      |
|     | 6.  | ¬Ga ∨ Ha                                         | MC, 4      |
|     | 7.  | (¬Fa ∨ Ha) & (¬Ga ∨ Ha)                          | C, 5, 6    |
|     | 8.  | (Ha ∨ ¬Fa) & (Ha ∨ ¬Ga)                          | Cm, 7      |
|     | 9.  | Ha ∨ (¬Fa & ¬Ga)                                 | D, 8       |
|     | 10. | (¬Fa & ¬Ga) ∨ Ha                                 | Cm, 9      |
|     | 11. | ¬(Fa ∨ Ga) ∨ Ha                                  | DM, 10     |
|     | 12. | (Fa ∨ Ga) → Ha                                   | MC, 11     |
|     | 13. | ∀x((Fx ∨ Gx) → Hx)                               | UG, 12     |

| 50. | 1.  | ∀x(Fx ↔ (¬Gx ↔ ¬Fx))                             | A          |
|-----|-----|--------------------------------------------------|------------|
|     | 2.  | Fa ↔ (¬Ga ↔ ¬Fa)                                 | US, 1      |
|     | 3.  | (Fa → (¬Ga ↔ ¬Fa)) & ((¬Ga ↔ ¬Fa) → Fa)        | B, 2       |
|     | 4.  | Fa → Fa                                          | SI         |
|     | 5.  | ¬Fa ∨ Fa                                         | MC, 4      |
|     | 6.  | (¬Ga ↔ ¬Fa) → Fa                                 | S, 3       |
|     | 7.  | ¬(¬Ga ↔ ¬Fa) ∨ Fa                                | MC, 6      |
|     | 8.  | (¬¬Ga ↔ ¬Fa) ∨ Fa                                | NB, 7      |
|     | 9.  | (Ga ↔ ¬Fa) ∨ Fa                                  | DN, 8      |
|     | 10. | Fa ∨ (Ga ↔ ¬Fa)                                  | Cm, 9      |
|     | 11. | Fa ∨ ((Ga → ¬Fa) & (¬Fa → Ga))                  | B, 10      |
|     | 12. | (Fa ∨ (Ga → ¬Fa)) & (Fa ∨ (¬Fa → Ga))           | D, 11      |
|     | 13. | Fa ∨ (¬Fa → Ga)                                  | S, 12      |
|     | 14. | Fa ∨ (¬¬Fa ∨ Ga)                                 | MC, 13     |
|     | 15. | ¬¬Fa ∨ (¬¬Fa ∨ Ga)                               | DN, 14     |
|     | 16. | (¬¬Fa ∨ ¬¬Fa) ∨ Ga                               | As, 15     |
|     | 17. | ¬¬Fa ∨ Ga                                        | I, 16      |
|     | 18. | ¬Fa → Ga                                         | MC, 17     |
|     | 19. | Fa → (¬Ga ↔ ¬Fa)                                 | S, 3       |
|     | 20. | ¬Fa ∨ (¬Ga ↔ ¬Fa)                                | MC, 19     |
|     | 21. | ¬Fa ∨ ((¬Ga → ¬Fa) & (¬Fa → ¬Ga))              | B, 20      |

| | | | |
|---|---|---|---|
| | 22. | $(\neg Fa \lor (\neg Ga \rightarrow \neg Fa))\ \&\ (\neg Fa \lor (\neg Fa \rightarrow \neg Ga))$ | D, 21 |
| | 23. | $\neg Fa \lor (\neg Ga \rightarrow \neg Fa)$ | S, 22 |
| | 24. | $\neg Fa \lor (\neg\neg Ga \lor \neg Fa)$ | MC, 23 |
| | 25. | $\neg Fa \lor (Ga \lor \neg Fa)$ | DN, 24 |
| | 26. | $\neg Fa \lor (\neg Fa \lor Ga)$ | Cm, 25 |
| | 27. | $(\neg Fa \lor \neg Fa) \lor Ga$ | As, 26 |
| | 28. | $\neg Fa \lor Ga$ | I, 27 |
| | 29. | $Fa \rightarrow Ga$ | MC, 28 |
| | 30. | $Ga \lor Ga$ | CD, 5, 18, 29 |
| | 31. | $Ga$ | I, 30 |
| | 32. | $\forall x Gx$ | UG, 31 |

| | | | |
|---|---|---|---|
| 52. | 1. | $\forall x((Fx\ \&\ Gx) \rightarrow Hx)$ | A |
| | 2. | $\forall x Gx\ \&\ \forall x Fx$ | A |
| | 3. | $\forall x Fx$ | S, 2 |
| | 4. | $Fa$ | US, 3 |
| | 5. | $\forall x Gx$ | S, 2 |
| | 6. | $Ga$ | US, 5 |
| | 7. | $(Fa\ \&\ Ga) \rightarrow Ha$ | US, 1 |
| | 8. | $Fa\ \&\ Ga$ | C, 4, 6 |
| | 9. | $Ha$ | MP, 7, 8 |
| | 10. | $Fa\ \&\ Ha$ | C, 4, 9 |
| | 11. | $\forall x(Fx\ \&\ Hx)$ | UG, 10 |

| | | | |
|---|---|---|---|
| 56. | 1. | $\forall x \forall y (Fxy \rightarrow Fyx)$ | A |
| | 2. | $\forall y (Fay \rightarrow Fya)$ | US, 1 |
| | 3. | $Fab \rightarrow Fba$ | US, 2 |
| | 4. | $\forall y (Fby \rightarrow Fyb)$ | US, 1 |
| | 5. | $Fba \rightarrow Fab$ | US, 4 |
| | 6. | $(Fab \rightarrow Fba)\ \&\ (Fba \rightarrow Fab)$ | C, 3, 5 |
| | 7. | $Fab \leftrightarrow Fba$ | B, 6 |
| | 8. | $\forall y (Fay \leftrightarrow Fya)$ | UG, 7 |
| | 9. | $\forall x \forall y (Fxy \leftrightarrow Fyx)$ | UG, 8 |

| | | | |
|---|---|---|---|
| 58. | 1. | $\forall x \forall y (Fxy \lor Fyx)$ | A |
| | 2. | $\forall x \forall y (Fxy \rightarrow Fyx)$ | A |
| | 3. | $\forall y (Fay \lor Fya)$ | US, 1 |
| | 4. | $Fab \lor Fba$ | US, 3 |
| | 5. | $\forall y (Fay \rightarrow Fya)$ | US, 2 |
| | 6. | $Fab \rightarrow Fba$ | US, 5 |
| | 7. | $Fba \rightarrow Fba$ | SI |
| | 8. | $Fba \lor Fba$ | CD, 4, 6, 7 |
| | 9. | $Fba$ | I, 8 |
| | 10. | $\forall y Fby$ | UG, 9 |
| | 11. | $\forall x \forall y Fxy$ | UG, 10 |

| | | | |
|---|---|---|---|
| 62. | 1. | $\forall x \forall y \forall z((Fxy\ \&\ Fyz) \rightarrow Fxz)$ | A |
| | 2. | $\forall x \forall y (Fxy \rightarrow Fyx)$ | A |
| | 3. | $\exists x \exists y Fxy$ | A |
| | 4. | $\exists y Fay$ | ES, 3 |
| | 5. | $Fab$ | ES, 4 |
| | 6. | $\forall y (Fay \rightarrow Fya)$ | US, 2 |
| | 7. | $Fab \rightarrow Fba$ | US, 6 |
| | 8. | $Fba$ | MP, 7, 5 |
| | 9. | $\forall y \forall z((Fay\ \&\ Fyz) \rightarrow Faz)$ | US, 1 |
| | 10. | $\forall z((Fab\ \&\ Fbz) \rightarrow Faz)$ | US, 9 |
| | 11. | $(Fab\ \&\ Fba) \rightarrow Faa$ | US, 10 |

| 12. | Fab & Fba | C, 5, 8 |
| 13. | Faa | MP, 11, 12 |
| 14. | ∃xFxx | EG, 13 |

| 64. | 1. | ∀x∀y∀z((Fxy & Fxz) → Fyz) | A |
| | 2. | ∀x∀y(Fxy → Fyx) | A |
| | 3. | ∀xFxx | A |
| | 4. | (Fab & Fbc) → Fab | W |
| | 5. | ∀y(Fay → Fya) | US, 2 |
| | 6. | Fab → Fba | US, 5 |
| | 7. | (Fab & Fbc) → Fba | HS, 4, 6 |
| | 8. | (Fab & Fbc) → Fbc | W |
| | 9. | (Fab & Fbc) → (Fba & Fbc) | CC, 7, 8 |
| | 10. | ∀y∀z((Fby & Fbz) → Fyz) | US, 1 |
| | 11. | ∀z((Fba & Fbz) → Faz) | US, 10 |
| | 12. | (Fba & Fbc) → Fac | US, 11 |
| | 13. | (Fab & Fbc) → Fac | HS, 9, 12 |
| | 14. | ∀z((Fab & Fbz) → Faz) | UG, 13 |
| | 15. | ∀y∀z((Fay & Fyz) → Faz) | UG, 14 |
| | 16. | ∀x∀y∀z((Fxy & Fyz) → Fxz) | UG, 15 |

## 13.3 FORMULAS WITH OVERLAPPING QUANTIFIERS

| 6. | 1. | ∀x∀y∃z(Fxz & Fzy) | A |
| | 2. | ∀x∀y(Fxy → Gyx) | A |
| | 3. | ∀y∃z(Faz & Fzy) | US, 1 |
| | 4. | ∃z(Faz & Fzb) | US, 3 |
| | 5. | Fac & Fcb | ES, 4 |
| | 6. | ∀y(Fay → Gya) | US, 2 |
| | 7. | Fac → Gca | US, 6 |
| | 8. | Fac | S, 5 |
| | 9. | Gca | MP, 7, 8 |
| | 10. | ∀y(Fcy → Gyc) | US, 2 |
| | 11. | Fcb → Gbc | US, 10 |
| | 12. | Fcb | S, 5 |
| | 13. | Gbc | MP, 11, 12 |
| | 14. | Gca & Gbc | C, 9, 13 |
| | 15. | ∀z(Gca & Gzc) | UG, 14 (Wrong!) |
| | 16. | ∀y∀z(Gcy & Gzc) | UG, 15 (Wrong!) |
| | 17. | ∃x∀y∀z(Gxy & Gzx) | EG, 16 |

| 8. | 1. | ∀x(Fx → ∀y(Gy → Hxy)) | A |
| | 2. | ∃x(Fx & ∃y¬Hxy) | A |
| | 3. | Fa & ∃y¬Hay | ES, 2 |
| | 4. | ∃y¬Hay | S, 3 |
| | 5. | ¬Hab | ES, 4 |
| | 6. | Fa → ∀y(Gy → Hay) | US, 1 |
| | 7. | Fa | S, 3 |
| | 8. | ∀y(Gy → Hay) | MP, 6, 7 |
| | 9. | Gb → Hab | US, 8 |
| | 10. | ¬Gb | MT, 9, 5 |
| | 11. | ∃x¬Gx | EG, 10 |

10.
| | | | |
|---|---|---|---|
| 1. | $\forall x(\exists yFxy \rightarrow \exists y\neg Gy)$ | A | |
| 2. | $\exists x\exists yFxy$ | A | |
| 3. | $\forall x(Gx \leftrightarrow \neg Hx)$ | A | |
| 4. | $\exists yFay$ | ES, 2 | |
| 5. | $\exists yFay \rightarrow \exists y\neg Gy$ | US, 1 | |
| 6. | $\exists y\neg Gy$ | MP, 5, 4 | |
| 7. | $\neg Gb$ | ES, 6 | |
| 8. | $Gb \leftrightarrow \neg Hb$ | US, 3 | |
| 9. | $\neg\neg Hb$ | BE, 8, 7 | |
| 10. | $Hb$ | DN, 9 | |
| 11. | $\exists xHx$ | EG, 10 | |

14.
| | | | |
|---|---|---|---|
| 1. | $\exists x\forall y\neg Fxy$ | A | |
| 2. | $\forall y\neg Fay$ | ES, 1 | |
| 3. | $\neg Fab$ | US, 2 | |
| 4. | $\neg Fab \lor Fbc$ | Ad, 3 | |
| 5. | $Fab \rightarrow Fbc$ | MC, 4 | |
| 6. | $\forall z(Faz \rightarrow Fzc)$ | UG, 5 | |
| 7. | $\forall y\forall z(Faz \rightarrow Fzy)$ | UG, 6 | |
| 8. | $\exists x\forall y\forall z(Fxz \rightarrow Fzy)$ | EG, 7 | |

16.
| | | |
|---|---|---|
| 1. | $\forall x(\exists y(Ay \& Bxy) \rightarrow Cx)$ | A |
| 2. | $\exists y(Dy \& \exists x((Fx \& Gx) \& Byx))$ | A |
| 3. | $\forall x(Fx \rightarrow Ax)$ | A |
| 4. | $\exists x(Cx \& Dx) \rightarrow (\exists y(Dy \& \exists zByz) \rightarrow \forall xFx)$ | A |
| 5. | $Da \& \exists x((Fx \& Gx) \& Bax)$ | ES, 2 |
| 6. | $\exists x((Fx \& Gx) \& Bax)$ | S, 5 |
| 7. | $(Fb \& Gb) \& Bab$ | ES, 6 |
| 8. | $Fb \& Gb$ | S, 7 |
| 9. | $Fb \rightarrow Ab$ | US, 3 |
| 10. | $Fb$ | S, 8 |
| 11. | $Ab$ | MP, 9, 10 |
| 12. | $Bab$ | S, 7 |
| 13. | $Ab \& Bab$ | C, 11, 12 |
| 14. | $\exists y(Ay \& Bay) \rightarrow Ca$ | US, 1 |
| 15. | $\exists y(Ay \& Bay)$ | EG, 13 |
| 16. | $Ca$ | MP, 14, 15 |
| 17. | $Da$ | S, 5 |
| 18. | $Ca \& Da$ | C, 16, 17 |
| 19. | $\exists x(Cx \& Dx)$ | EG, 18 |
| 20. | $\exists y(Dy \& \exists zByz) \rightarrow \forall xFx$ | MP, 4, 19 |
| 21. | $\exists zBaz$ | EG, 12 |
| 22. | $Da \& \exists zBaz$ | C, 17, 21 |
| 23. | $\exists y(Dy \& \exists zByz)$ | EG, 22 |
| 24. | $\forall xFx$ | MP, 20, 23 |
| 25. | $Fc \rightarrow Ac$ | US, 3 |
| 26. | $Fc$ | US, 24 |
| 27. | $Ac$ | MP, 25, 26 |
| 28. | $\forall xAx$ | UG, 27 |

## 13.4 QUANTIFIERS AND CONNECTIVES

8.
| | | | |
|---|---|---|---|
| 1. | $\forall x(Ax \rightarrow \forall y(Ty \rightarrow Oxy))$ | A | (universe: people) |
| 2. | $\neg\exists x(Tx \& Oxx)$ | A | |
| 3. | $\neg\neg\exists x(Tx \& Ax)$ | AIP | |
| 4. | $\exists x(Tx \& Ax)$ | DN, 3 | |

|     |     |                              |              |
|-----|-----|------------------------------|--------------|
|     | 5.  | Ta & Aa                      | ES, 4        |
|     | 6.  | ∀x¬(Tx & Oxx)                | QN, 2        |
|     | 7.  | ¬(Ta & Oaa)                  | US, 6        |
|     | 8.  | Aa → ∀y(Ty → Oay)            | US, 1        |
|     | 9.  | Aa                           | S, 5         |
|     | 10. | ∀y(Ty → Oay)                 | MP, 8, 9     |
|     | 11. | Ta → Oaa                     | US, 10       |
|     | 12. | Ta                           | S, 5         |
|     | 13. | Oaa                          | MP, 11, 12   |
|     | 14. | Ta & Oaa                     | C, 12, 13    |
|     | 15. | (Ta & Oaa) & ¬(Ta & Oaa)     | C, 14, 7     |
| 10. | 1.  | ∀x(Ax ↔ (∃yPy → Px)          | A            |
|     | 2.  | ¬∃xAx                        | AIP          |
|     | 3.  | ∀x¬Ax                        | QN, 2        |
|     | 4.  | Aa ↔ (∃yPy → Pa)             | US, 1        |
|     | 5.  | ¬Aa                          | US, 3        |
|     | 6.  | ¬(∃yPy → Pa)                 | BE, 4, 5     |
|     | 7.  | ∃yPy & ¬Pa                   | NC, 6        |
|     | 8.  | ∃yPy                         | S, 7         |
|     | 9.  | Pb                           | ES, 8        |
|     | 10. | ¬∃yPy ∨ Pb                   | Ad, 9        |
|     | 11. | Ab ↔ (∃yPy → Pb)             | US, 1        |
|     | 12. | ∃yPy → Pb                    | MC, 10       |
|     | 13. | Ab                           | BE, 11, 12   |
|     | 14. | ¬Ab                          | US, 3        |
|     | 15. | Ab & ¬Ab                     | C, 13, 14    |
| 14. | 1.  | ∀x∃y(Fx → Gy)                | A            |
|     | 2.  | ¬∃y∀x(Fx → Gy)               | AIP          |
|     | 3.  | ∀y∃x¬(Fx → Gy)               | $QN^2$, 2    |
|     | 4.  | ∃x¬(Fx → Ga)                 | US, 3        |
|     | 5.  | ¬(Fb → Ga)                   | ES, 4        |
|     | 6.  | Fb & ¬Ga                     | NC, 5        |
|     | 7.  | ∃y(Fb → Gy)                  | US, 1        |
|     | 8.  | Fb → Gc                      | ES, 7        |
|     | 9.  | Fb                           | S, 6         |
|     | 10. | Gc                           | MP, 8, 9     |
|     | 11. | ∃x¬(Fx → Gc)                 | US, 3        |
|     | 12. | ¬(Fd → Gc)                   | ES, 11       |
|     | 13. | Fd & ¬Gc                     | NC, 12       |
|     | 14. | ¬Gc                          | S, 13        |
|     | 15. | Gc & ¬Gc                     | C, 10, 14    |
| 16. | 1.  | ∃xFx → ∃xGx                  | A            |
|     | 2.  | ∃xFx → ∃yGy                  | VR, 1        |
|     | 3.  | ∃y(∃xFx → Gy)                | RP→, 2       |
|     | 4.  | ∃xFx → Ga                    | ES, 3        |
|     | 5.  | ∀x(Fx → Ga)                  | RP→, 4       |
|     | 6.  | Fa → Ga                      | US, 5        |
|     | 7.  | ∃x(Fx → Gx)                  | EG, 6        |
| 20. | 1.  | ∃xFx → ∀y(Gy → Hy)           | A            |
|     | 2.  | ∃xJx → ∃xGx                  | A            |
|     | 3.  | ¬(∃x(Fx & Jx) → ∃zHz)        | AIP          |
|     | 4.  | ∃x(Fx & Jx) & ¬∃zHz          | NC, 3        |
|     | 5.  | ∃x(Fx & Jx)                  | S, 4         |

|  |  |  |  |
|---|---|---|---|
| 6. | Fa & Ja | ES, 5 | |
| 7. | Ja | S, 6 | |
| 8. | ∃xJx | EG, 7 | |
| 9. | ∃xGx | MP, 2, 8 | |
| 10. | Gb | ES, 9 | |
| 11. | Fa | S, 6 | |
| 12. | ∃xFx | EG, 11 | |
| 13. | ∀y(Gy → Hy) | MP, 1, 12 | |
| 14. | Gb → Hb | US, 13 | |
| 15. | Hb | MP, 14, 10 | |
| 16. | ∃zHz | EG, 15 | |
| 17. | ¬EzHz | S, 4 | |
| 18. | ∃zHz & ¬∃zHz | C, 16, 17 | |

| | | | |
|---|---|---|---|
| 22. | 1. | ∀x(∃yFyx → ∀zFxz) | A |
| | 2. | ∃yFya → ∀zFaz | US, 1 |
| | 3. | ∀y(Fya → ∀zFaz) | RP→, 2 |
| | 4. | Fba → ∀zFaz | US, 3 |
| | 5. | ∀z(Fba → Faz) | RP→, 4 |
| | 6. | Fba → Fab | US, 5 |
| | 7. | ∀x(Fbx → Fxb) | UG, 6 |
| | 8. | ∀y∀x(Fyx → Fxy) | UG, 7 |

| | | | |
|---|---|---|---|
| 26. | 1. | ∀x(Fx → ∀y(Gy → Hxy)) | A |
| | 2. | ∀x(Dx → ∀y(Hxy → Cy)) | A |
| | 3. | ¬(∃x(Fx & Dx) → ∀y(Gy → Cy)) | AIP |
| | 4. | ∃x(Fx & Dx) & ¬∀y(Gy → Cy) | NC, 3 |
| | 5. | ∃x(Fx & Dx) | S, 4 |
| | 6. | Fa & Da | ES, 5 |
| | 7. | Fa → ∀y(Gy → Hay) | US, 1 |
| | 8. | Fa | S, 6 |
| | 9. | ∀y(Gy → Hay) | MP, 7, 8 |
| | 10. | Da → ∀y(Hay → Cy) | US, 2 |
| | 11. | Da | S, 6 |
| | 12. | ∀y(Hay → Cy) | MP, 10, 11 |
| | 13. | Gb → Hab | US, 9 |
| | 14. | Hab → Cb | US, 12 |
| | 15. | Gb → Cb | HS, 13, 14 |
| | 16. | ∀y(Gy → Cy) | UG, 15 |
| | 17. | ¬∀y(Gy → Cy) | S, 4 |
| | 18. | ∀y(Gy → Cy) & ¬∀y(Gy → Cy) | C, 16, 17 |

| | | | |
|---|---|---|---|
| 28. | 1. | ∀x∀y(Gxy ↔ (Fy → Hx)) | A |
| | 2. | ∀zGaz | A |
| | 3. | ∀y(Gay ↔ (Fy → Ha)) | US, 1 |
| | 4. | Gab ↔ (Fb → Ha) | US, 3 |
| | 5. | Gab | US, 2 |
| | 6. | Fb → Ha | BE, 4, 5 |
| | 7. | ∃x(Fb → Hx) | EG, 6 |
| | 8. | Fb → ∃xHx | RP→, 7 |
| | 9. | ∀y(Fy → ∃xHx) | UG, 8 |
| | 10. | ∃yFy → ∃xHx | RP→, 9 |
| | 11. | ∃xFx → ∃xHx | VR, 10 |

| | | | |
|---|---|---|---|
| 32. | 1. | ∃x(Fx & ∀y(Gy → Hy)) | A |
| | 2. | ∀x(Fx → (¬Lx → ¬∃z(Kz & Hz))) | A |
| | 3. | Fa & ∀y(Gy → Hy) | ES, 1 |

| | | | |
|---|---|---|---|
| | 4. | Fa → (¬La → ¬∃z(Kz & Hz)) | US, 2 |
| | 5. | Fa | S, 3 |
| | 6. | ¬La → ¬∃z(Kz & Hz) | MP, 4, 5 |
| | 7. | ∃z(Kz & Hz) → La | Tr, 6 |
| | 8. | ∀z((Kz & Hz) → La) | RP→, 7 |
| | 9. | (Kb & Gb) → Gb | W |
| | 10. | ∀y(Gy → Hy) | S, 3 |
| | 11. | Gb → Hb | US, 10 |
| | 12. | (Kb & Gb) → Hb | HS, 9, 11 |
| | 13. | (Kb & Gb) → Kb | W |
| | 14. | (Kb & Gb) → (Kb & Hb) | CC, 13, 12 |
| | 15. | (Kb & Hb) → La | US, 8 |
| | 16. | (Kb & Gb) → La | HS, 14, 15 |
| | 17. | ∃x((Kb & Gb) → Lx) | EG, 16 |
| | 18. | (Kb & Gb) → ∃xLx | RP→, 17 |
| | 19. | ∀y((Ky & Gy) → ∃xLx) | UG, 18 |
| | 20. | ∃y(Ky & Gy) → ∃xLx | RP→, 19 |
| | 21. | ∃x(Kx & Gx) → ∃xLx | VR, 20 |
| 34. | 1. | ¬∀x(Hx ∨ Kx) | A |
| | 2. | ∀x((Fx ∨ ¬Kx) → Gxx) | A |
| | 3. | ∃x¬(Hx ∨ Kx) | QN, 1 |
| | 4. | ¬(Ha ∨ Ka) | ES, 3 |
| | 5. | ¬Ha & ¬Ka | DM, 4 |
| | 6. | ¬Ka | S, 5 |
| | 7. | (Fa ∨ ¬Ka) → Gaa | US, 2 |
| | 8. | Fa ∨ ¬Ka | Ad, 6 |
| | 9. | Gaa | MP, 7, 8 |
| | 10. | ∃xGxx | EG, 9 |
| 38. | 1. | ∀x∀y∀z((Fxy & Fyz) → Fxz) | A |
| | 2. | ¬∃xFxx | A |
| | 3. | ∀y∀z((Fay & Fyz) → Faz) | US, 1 |
| | 4. | ∀z((Fab & Fbz) → Faz) | US, 3 |
| | 5. | (Fab & Fba) → Faa | US, 4 |
| | 6. | ∀x¬Fxx | QN, 2 |
| | 7. | ¬Faa | US, 6 |
| | 8. | ¬(Fab & Fba) | MT, 5, 7 |
| | 9. | ¬Fab ∨ ¬Fba | DM, 8 |
| | 10. | Fab → ¬Fba | MC, 9 |
| | 11. | ∀y(Fay → ¬Fya) | UG, 10 |
| | 12. | ∀x∀y(Fxy → ¬Fyx) | UG, 11 |
| 40. | 1. | Fa → (∃xGx → Gb) | A |
| | 2. | ∀x(Gx → Hx) | A |
| | 3. | ∀x(¬Jx → ¬Hx) | A |
| | 4. | ¬Fa ∨ (¬∃xGx ∨ Gb) | MC, 1 |
| | 5. | ¬Fa ∨ (∀x¬Gx ∨ Gb) | QN, 4 |
| | 6. | (¬Fa ∨ ∀x¬Gx) ∨ Gb | As, 5 |
| | 7. | Gb ∨ (¬Fa ∨ ∀x¬Gx) | Cm, 6 |
| | 8. | ¬¬Gb ∨ (¬Fa ∨ ∀x¬Gx) | DN, 7 |
| | 9. | ¬Gb → (¬Fa ∨ ∀x¬Gx) | MC, 8 |
| | 10. | Gb → Hb | US, 2 |
| | 11. | ¬Hb → ¬Gb | Tr, 10 |
| | 12. | ¬Hb → (¬Fa ∨ ∀x¬Gx) | HS, 11, 9 |
| | 13. | ¬Jb → ¬Hb | US, 3 |
| | 14. | ¬Jb → (¬Fa ∨ ∀x¬Gx) | HS, 13, 12 |

124

| 44. | 1. | $\forall x \neg Fxc \rightarrow \exists x Gxb$ | A |
|---|---|---|---|
| | 2. | $\neg \exists x(\neg Fxc \rightarrow Gxb)$ | AIP |
| | 3. | $\forall x \neg(\neg Fxc \rightarrow Gxb)$ | QN, 2 |
| | 4. | $\neg(\neg Fac \rightarrow Gab)$ | US, 3 |
| | 5. | $\neg Fac \& \neg Gab$ | NC, 4 |
| | 6. | $\neg Fac$ | S, 5 |
| | 7. | $\forall x \neg Fxc$ | UG, 6 |
| | 8. | $\exists x Gxb$ | MP, 1, 7 |
| | 9. | $\neg Gab$ | S, 5 |
| | 10. | $\forall x \neg Gxb$ | UG, 9 |
| | 11. | $\neg \exists x Gxb$ | QN, 10 |
| | 12. | $\exists x Gxb \& \neg \exists x Gxb$ | C, 8, 11 |

| 46. | 1. | $\exists x(Px \& \neg Mx) \rightarrow \forall y(Py \rightarrow Ly)$ | A |
|---|---|---|---|
| | 2. | $\exists x(Px \& Nx)$ | A |
| | 3. | $\forall x(Px \rightarrow \neg Lx)$ | A |
| | 4. | $Pa \& Na$ | ES, 2 |
| | 5. | $Pa \rightarrow \neg La$ | US, 3 |
| | 6. | $Pa$ | S, 4 |
| | 7. | $\neg La$ | MP, 5, 6 |
| | 8. | $Pa \& \neg La$ | C, 6, 7 |
| | 9. | $\neg(Pa \rightarrow La)$ | NC, 8 |
| | 10. | $\exists y \neg(Py \rightarrow Ly)$ | EG, 9 |
| | 11. | $\neg \forall y(Py \rightarrow Ly)$ | QN, 10 |
| | 12. | $\neg \exists x(Px \& \neg Mx)$ | MT, 1, 11 |
| | 13. | $\forall x \neg(Px \& \neg Mx)$ | QN, 12 |
| | 14. | $\neg(Pa \& \neg Ma)$ | US, 13 |
| | 15. | $\neg Pa \lor \neg \neg Ma$ | DM, 14 |
| | 16. | $\neg Pa \lor Ma$ | DN, 15 |
| | 17. | $\neg \neg Pa$ | DN, 6 |
| | 18. | $Ma$ | DS, 16, 17 |
| | 19. | $Na$ | S, 4 |
| | 20. | $Na \& Ma$ | C, 19, 18 |
| | 21. | $\exists x(Nx \& Mx)$ | EG, 20 |

| 50. | 1. | $\forall x(Cx \rightarrow Fx)$ | A |
|---|---|---|---|
| | 2. | $(Cb \& Dab) \rightarrow Cb$ | W |
| | 3. | $Cb \rightarrow Fb$ | US, 1 |
| | 4. | $(Cb \& Dab) \rightarrow Fb$ | HS, 2, 3 |
| | 5. | $(Cb \& Dab) \rightarrow Dab$ | W |
| | 6. | $(Cb \& Dab) \rightarrow (Fb \& Dab)$ | CC, 4, 5 |
| | 7. | $(Pa \& (Cb \& Dab)) \rightarrow (Cb \& Dab)$ | W |
| | 8. | $(Pa \& (Cb \& Dab)) \rightarrow (Fb \& Dab)$ | HS, 7, 6 |
| | 9. | $\exists z((Pa \& (Cb \& Dab)) \rightarrow (Fz \& Daz))$ | EG, 8 |
| | 10. | $(Pa \& (Cb \& Dab)) \rightarrow \exists z(Fz \& Daz)$ | RP$\rightarrow$, 9 |
| | 11. | $\forall y((Pa \& (Cy \& Day)) \rightarrow \exists z(Fz \& Daz))$ | UG, 10 |
| | 12. | $\exists y(Pa \& (Cy \& Day)) \rightarrow \exists z(Fz \& Daz)$ | RP$\rightarrow$, 11 |
| | 13. | $(Pa \& \exists y(Cy \& Day)) \rightarrow \exists z(Fz \& Daz)$ | RP&, 12 |
| | 14. | $\forall x((Px \& \exists y(Cy \& Dxy)) \rightarrow \exists z(Fz \& Dxz))$ | UG, 13 |

| 52. | 1. | $Pmj$ | A | (universe: people) |
|---|---|---|---|---|
| | 2. | $\exists x(Pxm \& Tx)$ | A | |
| | 3. | $\neg Tj$ | A | |
| | 4. | $\neg \neg \forall x(\exists y(Pyx \& Ty) \rightarrow Tx)$ | AIP | |
| | 5. | $\forall x(\exists y(Pyx \& Ty) \rightarrow Tx)$ | DN, 4 | |
| | 6. | $\exists y(Pym \& Ty) \rightarrow Tm$ | US, 5 | |
| | 7. | $\exists y(Pym \& Ty)$ | VR, 2 | |

| | 8. | Tm | MP, 6, 7 |
|---|---|---|---|
| | 9. | Pmj & Tm | C, 1, 8 |
| | 10. | ∃y(Pyj & Ty) → Tj | US, 5 |
| | 11. | ∃y(Pyj & Ty) | EG, 9 |
| | 12. | Tj | MP, 10, 11 |
| | 13. | Tj & ¬Tj | C, 12, 3 |

54.
| | 1. | ∀x(∀y(Oay → Oxy) → Oax) | A    (universe: people) |
|---|---|---|---|
| | 2. | ∀y(Oay → Oay) → Oaa | US, 1 |
| | 3. | Oab → Oab | SI |
| | 4. | ∀y(Oay → Oay) | UG, 3 |
| | 5. | Oaa | MP, 2, 4 |

56.
| | 1. | ∀x(Fx → ∀y(Sy → Axy)) | A    (universe: people) |
|---|---|---|---|
| | 2. | ∀x∀y((Sx & Axy) → Cy) | A |
| | 3. | ¬∀x((Fx & Sx) → Cx) | AIP |
| | 4. | ∃x¬((Fx & Sx) → Cx) | QN, 3 |
| | 5. | ¬((Fa & Sa) → Ca) | ES, 4 |
| | 6. | (Fa & Sa) & ¬Ca | NC, 5 |
| | 7. | Fa & Sa | S, 6 |
| | 8. | Fa → ∀y(Sy → Aay) | US, 1 |
| | 9. | Fa | S, 7 |
| | 10. | ∀y(Sy → Aay) | MP, 8, 9 |
| | 11. | Sa → Aaa | US, 10 |
| | 12. | Sa | S, 7 |
| | 13. | Aaa | MP, 11, 12 |
| | 14. | ∀y((Sa & Aay) → Cy) | US, 2 |
| | 15. | (Sa & Aaa) → Ca | US, 14 |
| | 16. | Sa & Aaa | C, 12, 13 |
| | 17. | Ca | MP, 15, 16 |
| | 18. | ¬Ca | S, 6 |
| | 19. | Ca & ¬Ca | C, 17, 18 |

58.
| | 1. | ∀x∀y(Lyx → Lxy) | A    (universe: people) |
|---|---|---|---|
| | 2. | ∀x(Wx ↔ ∀yLxy) | A |
| | 3. | ∀x(Wx → ∃yTyx) | A |
| | 4. | ∃x∀y¬Tyx | A |
| | 5. | ∀y¬Tya | ES, 4 |
| | 6. | Wa → ∃yTya | US, 3 |
| | 7. | ¬∃yTya | QN, 5 |
| | 8. | ¬Wa | MT, 6, 7 |
| | 9. | Wa ↔ ∀yLay | US, 2 |
| | 10. | ¬∀yLay | BE, 9, 8 |
| | 11. | ∃y¬Lay | QN, 10 |
| | 12. | ∃x∃y¬Lxy | EG, 11 |

60.
| | 1. | ∀xKax | A    (universe: people) |
|---|---|---|---|
| | 2. | ∀x(Dxl ↔ Cx) | A |
| | 3. | ∀x(¬Cx → ¬Kxx) | A |
| | 4. | Kaa | US, 1 |
| | 5. | ¬Ca → ¬Kaa | US, 3 |
| | 6. | ¬¬Kaa | DN, 4 |
| | 7. | ¬¬Ca | MT, 5, 6 |
| | 8. | Dal ↔ Ca | US, 2 |
| | 9. | Ca | DN, 7 |
| | 10. | Dal | BE, 8, 9 |

# CHAPTER
## 14

# GENERALIZATIONS

## 1. KEY DEFINITIONS

An argument is *reliable* if and only if the truth of the premises makes the truth of the conclusion probable. An argument is *inductively reliable* if and only if it is reliable but not valid.

Argument by enumeration: Supporting instances: $a_1$ is both F and G
$a_2$ is both F and G
.
.
.
$a_n$ is both F and G

Generalization: ∴ All Fs are Gs

To evaluate such arguments, consider:
1. *Sample Size.* How many objects of the appropriate kind have been observed? In general, the more objects that have been observed, the more reliable the argument from them to the conclusion. Generalizations obtained from inadequate enumeration are called *hasty.*
2. *Sample Variation.* How varied are the observed instances? How homogeneous is the sample? In general, the more varied the sample, the more reliable the argument. Ideally, we want a sample to be *representative*-- to mirror the total population in its relevant characteristics. Unrepresentative samples are *biased.* The more varied the sample, the greater its chances of being representative.

Statistical Generalization: n% of observed Fs are G
∴ n% of Fs are G

To determine an appropriate sample size, we need to specify two things: the *confidence interval*, or *margin of error*, or *accuracy* we want, and the *degree of confidence* or *reliability* we want. The confidence interval is so-called because it is the range into which n% of the actual values for the population will fall, where n% is the confidence level.

To represent these concepts visually:

Margin of error: e%
Accuracy: 1 - e%
Confidence interval: n-e% to n+e%

Level of confidence: m% (m% of values for population fall within confidence interval)
More precisely, the form of a statistical generalization is:

n% of the sample are F
∴ n%, $\pm$ e%, of the population are F                Confidence: m%

where e is the margin of error; n-e to n+e is the confidence interval; and m is the confidence limit, the measure of the reliability of the inference.

A sample of a population is *random* if and only if every member of the population has an equal chance of being included in it. With populations that divide into quite distinct subgroups, with different characteristics, we can do better with *stratified random sampling*: applying random sampling techniques separately to each subgroup.

An *analogy* is a similarity, in certain respects, between distinct things. And an *argument by analogy* is an argument inferring a similarity from other similarities:

$a_1, ..., a_n$ and b are all $F_1, F_2, ...$ and $F_k$.              All H and all J are $F_1, F_2, ...$ and $F_k$.
$a_1 ... a_n$ are G.                                                   All H are G.
∴ b is G.                                                             ∴ All J are G

To evaluate analogical arguments, consider:

1. *The number and relevance of similarities.* The more relevant similarities the premises offer, the more reliable the analogical inference.
2. *The number and relevance of dissimilarities.* In general, the more relevant dissimilarities there are, the weaker the argument.
3. *The variety and number of analogous objects or circumstances.* The more cases we observe with similar characteristics, the more reliable the argument. Also, the more varied a group we observe with similar characteristics, the stronger the argument.
4. *The strength of premises and conclusion.* The stronger a conclusion we try to derive-- the more informative and detailed we wish it to be-- the weaker the argument becomes.

# 2. ANSWERS TO UNANSWERED EVEN PROBLEMS

## 14.1 INDUCTIVE RELIABILITY

The following judgments about reliability are not the only defensible answers.

| | | | |
|---|---|---|---|
| 8. | Deductively reliable. | 10. | Deductively reliable. |
| 14. | Inductively reliable, if at all. | 16. | Deductively reliable. |
| 20. | The implicit arguments are deductively reliable. | 22. | Inductively reliable. |
| 26. | Deductively reliable. | 28. | Deductively reliable. |
| 32. | Inductively reliable. | 34. | Deductively reliable. |
| 38. | Inductively reliable. | 40. | Deductively reliable. |
| 44. | Deductively reliable, if at all. | 46. | Deductively reliable, if at all. |

## 14.3 EVALUATING ENUMERATIONS

1.  a.  Less reliable. While Orlando's sample is varied to some degree, all its members are highly educated professionals.
    b.  Neither. (But see Chapter 15 on the method of difference.)
    c.  Neither.
    d.  Neither.
    e.  More reliable; the sample size and variation are increased.

## 14.4 STATISTICAL GENERALIZATIONS

4. a.  This sample is likely to be biased. Some people are much more likely to be at a shopping center and, so, be part of the sample than others. In particular, the high and low ends of the economic spectrum will probably be underrepresented, and, in the middle, the upper end may be overrepresented. Moreover, some shoppers may be much more likely to vote than others; some may not even be registered. So, nonvoters will have substantial representation in the sample; their opinions, however, may differ significantly from those of voters.
   b.  This sample can be fairly representative, though it will exclude those without telephones. This could be a serious problem if a substantial portion of the

population does not have a phone. Also, unless numbers are screened to eliminate all but residential phones, people with a phone at work will be overrepresented, while those who do not work, or work far from a telephone, will be underrepresented. To maintain the randomness of the sample, callers must be persistent in trying to reach people at the numbers selected, calling at different times of day, on different days, and so on. Some who answer may be much more likely to vote than others; some may not even be registered. So, nonvoters will have substantial representation in the sample; their opinions, however, may differ significantly from those of voters. Finally, the survey may be biased by sociological factors: who in a family is more likely to be at home at various times of the day? Who, if several family members are present, is most likely to answer the phone?

c.     This sample should be fairly representative. The voter registration lists may exclude some people who will vote, through error or last-minute registration, but these should be minor. Much more serious is the problem that the lists will include many people who will not vote. Since nonvoters' views may differ significantly from the views of voters, this may bias the sample. Many surveys prior to an election try to judge how likely people are to vote to compensate for this factor.

d.     This is a self-selected sample, highly likely to be biased.

e.     This is a stratified random sample, which is likely to be representative of the surveyed population. That population, however, will exclude those who were not counted in the census (for example, some illegal aliens), and will include many people who will not vote. Since nonvoters' views may differ significantly from the views of voters, this may bias the sample. Many surveys prior to an election try to judge how likely people are to vote to compensate for this factor.

8.     This is notoriously difficult to determine. The Census Bureau has itself devised several alternate methods for estimating how many people were missed by the Census, based on socioeconomic factors: How many people in the region are immigrants? How many are illegal aliens? How many are non-English speakers? How many are below the poverty level? The Bureau attempts to estimate the answers to these questions, and also to estimate how likely people in each group are to be missed in the census. Of course, the same things that make some people hard to count in the census itself make them hard to survey to determine the answers to these questions. Thus, many statisticians think that there is no reliable way to estimate how many people the Census misses.

10.     The IRS in fact conducts random audits to try to estimate the incidence of tax cheating. Most audits are triggered by suspicious details of tax returns. A certain number, however, are done on randomly selected returns, and are extremely thorough to uncover any forms of fraud or evasion. Note that this method is available only to the IRS, which has access to tax returns and a wide array of other information. Asking people whether they cheat would be a poor survey technique; few respondents would tell the truth.

14.     Blood sugar levels are being compared; they can be measured precisely. 'Strict, low-fat diet' is somewhat vague, but can also be made precise. What, however, was the group eating before going on that diet?

16.     Degrees of whiteness are being compared. These can't be measured precisely. Also, what is new, improved Whitewash being compared with? Old Whitewash? Other brands?

20.     Pitching and baseball are being compared. But the terms of the comparison are so vaguely specified that the statistic seems meaningless.

22.     This argument relies on a survey of "voters" before and after the 1988 presidential election. Those who did not vote preferred Bush by a wider margin than those who did vote. The reliability of this argument depends almost completely on (i) what is meant by 'voters', and (ii) the adequacy of the original sample in representing that group. If 'voters' here means 'registered voters', this doesn't really respond to the point of argument 21, which spoke of the "eligible electorate" (presumably, those who could register to vote). If it means 'those who could register to vote', then it

does respond. But devising a representative sample of those who do not register to vote, some of whom are at extreme ends of the socioeconomic spectrum, is very difficult.

## 14.5 ANALOGIES

8.   a. The city is related to a person; the beauty of the morning to a garment. b. The respects are not specified. c. A garment is a physical object; the morning's beuaty is not.

10.   a. Keats is related to an astronomer and to Cortez. b. All look upon something new and unexpected with amazement. c. Keats's experience is literary; those of the astronomer and Cortez are visual.

14.   a. Browning is related to "men"; qualities of her love are related to striving for right and turning from praise. b. Freedom and purity. c. Browning's love is directed toward an individual person; striving for right and turning from praise have no such obvious object.

16.   a. Rossetti's heart is related to a singing bird, an apple tree, and a rainbow shell. b. All are full and happy. c. The heart, neither a plant nor an animal, is even gladder then they.

20.   a. The task force is related to mosquitoes; high interest rates, to malaria. b. Mosquitoes spread the disease of malaria; the Senate Banking Committee spreads the disease of high interest rates. c. Malaria is a physical illness; high interest rates are an economic malady.

22.   a. Working writers are related to lampposts; critics, to dogs. b. Writers and lampposts are routinely abused by critics and dogs, respectively. c. Critics do not literally urinate on writers.

26.   a. The universe of ideas is related to clothes; the nature of our experiences, to the form of the human body. b. In each case, the former is tailored to fit, and takes its shape from, the latter. c. Clothes and the human body are physical; ideas and the nature of our experience are not.

28.   a. The budget is related to a supertanker. b. Both have tremendous momentum coming from several sources and can't be redirected quickly. c. The budget's momentum is not physical but political.

32.   a. A clock is related to society. b. Both are human constructions that can be reconstructed. c. There are people who understand clocks.

34.   a. The celestial machine is related to a divine organism and a clockwork. b. The heavens and a clockwork both operate predictably according to the laws of mechanics. c. The celestial machine is larger than a clock and operates on different physical principles.

38.   a. Mistletoe is related to fighting animals, and its attraction of birds to a struggle. b. Mistletoe and fighting animals are engaged in competition for survival. c. Mistletoe competes with other species; individual animals fight other individual animals.

40.   a. Light waves are related to waves of water and pulses of sound. b. All can be described as having a certain frequency, and all are subject to certain familiar effects. c. Light is a different form of energy from that of water or sound waves. Light travels faster than sound or water.

44.   a. The relation of parts of the body to the body as a whole is related to the relation of individual people to society. b. Both relations are of a part to a whole; in both cases the whole defines the purposes of the parts. c. Parts of the body do not have independent wills; members of society are not physically linked together; parts of the body cannot switch functions as people in society can switch roles.

46.   a. Contracting muscles around the eyes while crying is related to animals' drawing back their ears to fight. b. In both cases, something begun as a voluntary movement has become involuntary. c. Animals draw back their ears when they feel threatened; people contract their eye muscles when they cry.

50. a. More reliable--an additional similarity.
    b. Less reliable--an additional dissimilarity.
    c. More reliable--an increased number of analogous objects.
    d. Neither--this similarity is probably irrelevant.
    e. Less reliable--an additional dissimilarity.

# CHAPTER
## 15

# CAUSES

This chapter presents a unified analysis of causation as a context-dependent notion. It discusses Mill's methods in connection with an actual medical case study.

## 1.   KEY DEFINITIONS

A condition is *necessary* for an event if and only if the event can't occur when the condition doesn't hold.  A condition is *sufficient* for an event if and only if the event must occur when the condition holds.  An event A *causes* an event B *relative to* a context C if and only if A, together with C, is a sufficient condition for B.

The method of *agreement*: To find the cause of a kind of event, see what the antecedent circumstances have in common.  To find the effect of a given event, see what the subsequent circumstances have in common.

The method of *difference*: If one case shows a certain effect, and another, in most ways similar, doesn't, look for other differences which can account for the presence of the effect in only one case.  Similarly, if a cause is operating in one case but not in another very similar case, find the effect by comparing the two and seeing what other differences follow.

The *joint method of agreement and difference*: "If two or more instances in which the phenomenon occurs have only one circumstance in common, while two or more instances in which it does not occur have nothing in common save the absence of that circumstance; the circumstance in which alone the two sets of instances differ, is the effect, or the cause, or an indispensable part of the cause, of the phenomenon."

The method of *residues*: If we "subtract out" all effects of known causes, the remainder or residue must be the effect of some other cause or causes.

The method of *concomitant variation*: When variations in the antecedent circumstances correlate with variations in effects, we can infer some causal connection between these variations.

Causal fallacies: (1) *post hoc ergo propter hoc*-- "after this, therefore because of this"-- involves drawing a causal conclusion simply from the temporal ordering of events. The forms of the argument are

|  |  |
|---|---|
| E preceded F | Events of kind E precede events of kind F |
| ∴ E caused F | ∴ Events of kind E cause events of kind F. |

(2) The method of concomitant variation allows inferring the existence of some causal connection, but yields no information about its exact form or nature.  If one quantity varies with another, changes in the former may cause changes in the latter, or changes in the latter may cause changes in the former, or changes in both quantities may result from some other causal mechanism.  Finally, of course, the correlation may be just a coincidence.  The fallacy consists in drawing a straightforward causal conclusion from a correlation, bypassing Mill's caution.

# 2. ANSWERS TO UNANSWERED EVEN PROBLEMS

## 15.1 KINDS OF CAUSES

8.  a. No. (It could be hotwired.) b. No. (There could be something wrong with the engine.) c. Proper functioning of the other components of the car. d. Remote.
10. a. No. (We could put the drink in the refrigerator.) b. No. (We could put the drink on top of the stove.) c. There are no significant heat sources warming the drink. d. Proximate.
14. a. No. (Many things could have made her angry.) b. No. (She might have been asleep, or had very different attitudes.) c. Deborah heard what Fran said and was disposed to react angrily. d. Remote.
16. a. No. (Charley's nose might have bled for other reasons.) b. No. (Charley could have been wearing an iron mask.) c. Charley's nose was unprotected and physiologically normal. d. Remote.
20. a, b, c, d. Depends on the chemical properties of the mixture.
22. a. No. (Other things could have led them to change their minds.) b. No. (The jurors might have been asleep, or inattentive, or might have responded differently. c. The jury heard what Nora said and was disposed to change its mind in response. d. Remote.
26. a, b, c.     Neither necessary nor sufficient.
    In the proper context, the leak in the fuel line and the engine failure could count as causing the deaths.
28. a, b, c, d.     Neither necessary nor sufficient.
    In appropriate contexts, the scandal, the electoral defeat, and the change in leadership could each be said to have caused widespread turmoil.
34. Pablo's sister has a baby boy; Pablo's sister has a baby girl; Pablo's sister-in-law has a baby boy; Pablo's sister-in-law has a baby girl; Pablo's brother adopts a child; and so on.
38. Yolanda jumps. She is pushed by terrorists. She slips and falls accidentally. She tries hang gliding.
40. John hits the cue ball, which hits the 8-ball. Beth hits the cue ball, which hits the 8-ball. Carl hits the cue ball, which hits the 4-ball, which hits the 8-ball. Dawn hits the 6-ball, which hits the 2-ball, which hits the 3-ball, which hits the 8-ball. Earl picks up one side of the table.

## 15.2 AGREEMENT AND DIFFERENCE

6.  By the joint method of agreement and difference: Students with GPAs of 3.8 or above are admitted.  Students with at least a 3.9 and 750 GRE-V receive fellowships. Students with at least a 3.5 and a 670 GRE-M make the waiting list. Students with a 3.5 or lower and less than a 680 GRE-V have no chance at financial aid.
8.  A fine example of the method of difference.
10. By the method of agreement, the disease is linked to handling, or being near, birds, though not specifically ducks.
12. (a) By the joint method of agreement and difference, we can attribute the difference to wearing a tie--assuming that there are no other relevant differences.  (b) Probably, the results would be similar, or even more striking, for a jacket, shirt, shoes, pants, or grooming. This would suggest that none is itself the cause of being treated with trust and respect, but that each is a part of the cause, and that failing to wear such an item, or failing to groom one's hair, and so on, causes one to be treated with a lack of trust and respect.

## 15.3 RESIDUES AND CONCOMITANT VARIATION

8. By the method of difference and the method of concomitant variation, this suggests that some difference between the United States and the other countries mentioned causes increased killings by means of handguns in the U.S. Being in the United States is causally linked to an increased chance of dying from a handgun wound.

10. By the method of difference, and the method of residues, having a helmet on is causally linked to avoiding injury.

14. Augustine uses the method of agreement to argue against astrology: Jacob and Esau agreed in their astrological properties, but differed in virtually every important respect.

16. This relies on the methods of agreement and concomitant variation. Note, however, that nothing in the argument supports the conclusion that both alphabets descended from the Phoenician; at most, we can conclude that they have some causal connection.

20. This argument uses the joint method of agreement and difference, which implies that, since the two cases are similar in having furloughs granted to murderers, who then committed crimes, and in the effect of having produced outrage--but are very different racially--the outrage results from crime committed by furloughed murderers, not from racial attitudes.

22. Agreement:  Compare societies excelling in ideas to see whether all have become great.
Difference:  Compare a society similar in other respects but differing in ideas.
Residues:  Compare a society similar in other respects but differing in ideas.
Concomitant variation:  See whether variations in ideas correlate with variations in greatness.

26. Agreement:  See whether people always give handouts first to those whose misfortunes they understand.
Difference and Residues:  Compare people similar to beggars, but who are not blind and lame, to see whether they still get handouts before philosophers.
Concomitant variation:  See whether willingness to give handouts correlates with the intelligibility of a misfortune.

28. Agreement:  See whether situations of shielding people from folly agree in producing fools.
Difference:  Compare a situation in which men are shielded from the effects of folly from a similar situation in which they are not, and see whether only the former produces fools.
Concomitant variation:  See whether variations in shielding men from folly correlate with variations in fool production.

32. Agreement:  See whether people with good judgment all have experience, which in turn has come from previous bad judgment.
Difference:  Examine people with good judgment and otherwise similar people without it to see whether only the former have experience stemming from prior bad judgment.
Concomitant variation:  See whether variations in prior bad judgment correlate with variations in experience, and whether variations in experience correlate with variations in good judgment.

## 15.4 CAUSAL FALLACIES

4. By the methods of agreement and concomitant variation, we can conclude that there is a causal link between eating oat bran and reducing cholesterol levels, provided that the cases agree in all other respects.

# EXPLANATIONS

## 1. KEY DEFINITIONS

A *covering law* explanation explains a particular occurrence by relating it to a general law:
>Covering law
>Particular circumstances
>∴ Particular event or state

Covering law explanations of general truths have the form:
>Covering law
>Universal affirmative relating general truth to covering law
>∴ General truth

This sort of explanation *subsumes* a generalization under the covering law.

Explanations can thus explain a complex of conditions or events in terms of several laws and conditions:
>Laws
>Conditions
>∴ Conditions or Events

Covering laws and explanations involving them arise by a process called *hypothetical reasoning*. *Hypotheses* are sentences tentatively proposed as laws or explanations. Hypothetical reasoning is the process of proposing hypotheses, testing them, and accepting, rejecting, or modifying them in light of evidence. The stages of hypothetical reasoning:

1. Formulate a hypothesis to be explain the phenomena in question.
2. Determine what the hypothesis implies or predicts about the phenomena.
3. Test these implications or predictions.
4. Accept, reject, or modify the hypothesis.

Often, the hypothesis alone will not imply anything we can test. To derive something testable, we need to bring in other assumptions, items of knowledge, hypotheses, principles and facts. These are called *auxiliary assumptions*.

If we discover, through testing, that the implications are true, our test *confirms* the hypothesis (together with any auxiliary assumptions we used). If we discover that at least one implication is false, our test *disconfirms* or *infirms* our hypothesis (assuming that all auxiliary assumptions hold).

Conditions a good explanation should fulfill:

1. *Evidence.* The conclusion should offer evidence for the covering law. So, the conclusion should be more evident than at least one premise.
2. *Relevance.* The explanation should be relevant to the issue at hand.
3. *Grounding.* The explanation should use only those auxiliary assumptions that occupy the common ground between speaker and audience.
4. *Truth.* The premises should be true.
5. *Reliability.* The forms of inference used in the explanation should be reliable.
6. *Confirmation.* An explanation should be confirmed from both above and below.
7. *Power.* An explanation should lead to conclusions or predictions about more than the case at hand.

8.  *Simplicity.* An explanation should be uniform and economical.

# 2. ANSWERS TO UNANSWERED EVEN PROBLEMS

## 16.1 EXPLANATIONS AND HYPOTHETICAL REASONING

8.  Suppose some of the particles of water were heavier than others. (Hypothesis)
    If a parcel of the liquid on any occasion were constituted principally of these heavier particles, it must be supposed to affect the specific gravity of the mass. (Covering law)
    This circumstance is not known. (Disconfirming evidence)
    Similar observations may be made on other substances.
    Therefore, we may conclude that the ultimate particles of all homogeneous bodies are perfectly alike in weight, figure, etc. In other words, every particle of water is like every other particle of water; every particle of hydrogen is like every other particle of hydrogen; etc. (Conclusion)

10. Rays of light are very small bodies emitted from shining substances. (Conclusion)
    For such bodies will pass through uniform mediums in right lines without bending into the shadow. (Covering law)
    This is the nature of the rays of light.
    They will also be capable of several properties and be able to conserve their properties unchanged in passing through several mediums. (Covering law)
    This is another condition of the rays of light.

14. Eye color is determined by a pair of genes. (Covering law)
    Having blue eyes is a recessive trait.
    So, if the parents have blue eyes, both genes of each must be for blue eyes. (Subordinate conclusion)
    The child gets one eye color gene from each parent. (Covering law)
    The child, therefore, must end up with two blue-eye genes, making his or her eyes blue. Children of blue-eyed parents invariably have blue eyes. (Conclusion)

## 16.2 SCIENTIFIC THEORIES

4.  Evidence that the moon revolves around the earth: The phases of the moon repeat roughly every twenty-eight days; the phases of the moon appear alike at any point on the earth's surface; the tides have regular patterns; lunar space travel, based on the premise that the moon orbits the earth, has succeeded.

8.  Hypothesis: There are infinitely many "fixed" stars that seem not to change position, relative to each other, in the sky. Covering law: They exert gravitational attraction for each other. Disconfirming evidence: They do not move closer and eventually collapse.

10. Hypothesis: The general theory of relativity. Prediction 1: Light should bend, or be deflected, in the vicinity of massive objects like the sun, to a greater extent than Newtonian physics allows. Confirming evidence: A British expedition in Principe confirmed this experimentally by photographing a solar eclipse. Prediction 2: Mercury's orbit should turn, its perihelion advancing very slightly with each trip around the sun. Confirming evidence: Observations have indicated that this prediction is correct. Prediction 3: A reddening of light from strong gravitational fields. Confirming evidence: Observations of "white dwarfs," small, very dense stars, have borne out the theory's prediction.

14. Hypothesis: The market will react in the traditional fashion to hemlines. Disconfirming evidence: Miniskirts have been coming back into style, but the market has declined.

## 16.3 EVALUATING EXPLANATIONS

4. B's explanation seems to meet the conditions of a good explanation, assuming that what B says is true. A complains, in effect, that the explanation leads to a dilemma: any loan is either unnecessary or inadvisable. Of course, it is open to B to say that a good loan is unnecessary; it benefits both parties, but isn't absolutely required by either party.

6. This is Aristotle's explanation for objects' falling toward the earth. It seems to run afoul of the evidence condition. What evidence do we have that an object's natural place is on the earth, except that it falls there? This appears to be, in other words, a "dormitive virtue" explanation.

8. This is a joke because it violates the condition of relevance: It does not tell us what we wanted to know and, so, addresses the wrong issue.

# DEDUCTION:
## STYLE TWO

## A: SENTENTIAL LOGIC

This appendix presents a deduction system that differs from that of Chapters 8 and 13. It has two complex rules-- conditional and indirect proof-- that emerge as central to proof strategy. Akin to systems found in Copi's *Symbolic Logic*, as well as in works by Lemmon and others, this system is extremely straightforward and efficient.

## 1. KEY DEFINITIONS

A *natural deduction system* is a set of rules: specifically, *rules of inference*, which allow the deduction of formulas from other formulas. *Proofs* are extended arguments. *Hypothetical* proofs begin with *assumptions* (or *hypotheses*). *Categorical* proofs use no assumptions. A *proof* in a natural deduction system is a series of *lines*. On each line appears a formula. Each formula in a proof (a) is an assumption or (b) derives from formulas on previously established lines by a rule of inference. In the system of this appendix, the last line of a proof is its conclusion; the proof *proves* that formula *from* the assumptions. Formulas proved from no assumptions at all are *theorems* of the system.

Rules of inference are either *simple* or *complex*. Simple rules allow us to derive formulas of certain kinds in a proof if other formulas of certain kinds occupy already-established lines there. Complex rules allow us to derive a formula of a certain kind in a proof if we've completed some other proof. A proof appearing within another is *subordinate* to it. The larger, *superordinate* proof uses the subordinate proof's information by means of a complex rule.

Any line we can use in a proof at a given point *free* at that point. In sentential logic, every line is free, except lines imprisoned within a bracket.

# 2. Summary of Rules

*Rules Applying Only to Entire Formulas*

*Basic Rules*

Assumption (A)

| n. | $\mathcal{A}$ | A |
|----|----|----|

Indirect Proof (IP)

| n. | ⌐ | $\mathcal{A}$ | AIP |
|----|----|----|----|
| . |  | . | . |
| . |  | . | . |
| . |  | . | . |
| n+p. |  | $\mathcal{B}$ & $\neg\mathcal{B}$ | |
| n+r. | ⌐ | $\neg\mathcal{A}$ | IP, n-n+p |

Simplification (S)

| n. | $\underline{\mathcal{A}\ \&\ \mathcal{B}}$ | |
|----|----|----|
| n+m. | $\mathcal{A}$  (or $\mathcal{B}$) | S, n |

Conjunction (C)

| n. | $\mathcal{A}$ | |
|----|----|----|
| m. | $\underline{\mathcal{B}}$ | |
| p. | $\mathcal{A}$ & $\mathcal{B}$ | C, n, m |

Modus Ponens (MP)

| n. | $\mathcal{A} \rightarrow \mathcal{B}$ | |
|----|----|----|
| m. | $\underline{\mathcal{A}}$ | |
| p. | $\mathcal{B}$ | MP, n, m |

Modus Both-ends (E)

| n. | $\mathcal{A} \leftrightarrow \mathcal{B}$ | |
|----|----|----|
| m. | $\underline{\mathcal{A}}$   (or $\mathcal{B}$) | |
| p. | $\mathcal{B}$   (or $\mathcal{A}$) | MB, n, m |

Conditional Proof (CP)

| n. | ⌐ | $\mathcal{A}$ | ACP |
|----|----|----|----|
| . |  | . | . |
| . |  | . | . |
| . |  | . | . |
| n+p. |  | $\mathcal{B}$ | |
| n+q. | ⌐ | $\mathcal{A} \rightarrow \mathcal{B}$ | CP, n - n+p |

Addition (Ad)

| n. | $\underline{\mathcal{A}}$   (or $\mathcal{B}$) | |
|----|----|----|
| n+p. | $\mathcal{A} \vee \mathcal{B}$ | Ad, n |

Biconditional (B)

| n. | $\mathcal{A} \rightarrow \mathcal{B}$ | |
|----|----|----|
| m. | $\underline{\mathcal{B} \rightarrow \mathcal{A}}$ | |
| p. | $\mathcal{A} \leftrightarrow \mathcal{B}$ | B, n, m |

Disjunctive Syllogism (DS)

| n. | $\mathcal{A} \vee \mathcal{B}$ | |
|----|----|----|
| m. | $\underline{\neg\mathcal{A}}$   (or $\neg\mathcal{B}$) | |
| p. | $\mathcal{B}$   (or $\mathcal{A}$)   DS, n, m | |

*Derived Rules*

Indirect proof (extended)

| n. | ⌐ | $\neg\mathcal{A}$ | AIP |
|----|----|----|----|
| . |  | . | . |
| . |  | . | . |
| . |  | . | . |
| n+p. |  | $\mathcal{B}$ & $\neg\mathcal{B}$ | |
| n+q. | ⌐ | $\mathcal{A}$ | IP, n - n+p |

Biconditional-Conditional (BC)

| n. | $\underline{\mathcal{A} \leftrightarrow \mathcal{B}}$ | |
|----|----|----|

Modus Tollens (MT)

| n. | $\mathcal{A} \rightarrow \mathcal{B}$ | |
|----|----|----|
| m. | $\underline{\neg\mathcal{B}}$ | |
| p. | $\neg\mathcal{A}$ | MT, n, m |

Modus Both-Ends, expanded (MB)

| n. | $\mathcal{A} \leftrightarrow \mathcal{B}$ | |
|----|----|----|
| m. | $\underline{\neg\mathcal{A}}$   (or $\neg\mathcal{B}$) | |
| p. | $\neg\mathcal{B}$   (or $\neg\mathcal{A}$)  MB, n, m | |

| | | | | |
|---|---|---|---|---|
| m. | $\mathcal{A} \to \mathcal{B}$ (or $\mathcal{B} \to \mathcal{A}$) | BC, n | | Constructive Dilemma (CD) |

**Contradiction (!)**

Constructive Dilemma (CD)

| | | | | | |
|---|---|---|---|---|---|
| | | | n. | $\mathcal{A} \vee \mathcal{B}$ | |
| | | | m. | $\mathcal{A} \to C$ | |
| n. | $\mathcal{A}$ | | p. | $\mathcal{B} \to C$ | |
| m. | $\neg\mathcal{A}$ | | q. | $C$ | CD, n, m, p |
| p. | $\mathcal{B}$ | !, n, m | | | |

### Rules Applying to Parts of Formulas as well as Entire Formulas

#### Basic Rules

**Double Negation (DN)**

| | | |
|---|---|---|
| n. | $\mathcal{A}$ | DN, m |
| m. | $\neg\neg\mathcal{A}$ | DN, n |

#### Derived Rules

**DeMorgan's Law #1 (DM)**     **DeMorgan's Law #2 (DM)**

| | | | | | |
|---|---|---|---|---|---|
| n. | $\neg(\mathcal{A} \& \mathcal{B})$ | DM, m | n. | $\neg(\mathcal{A} \vee \mathcal{B})$ | DM, m |
| m. | $\neg\mathcal{A} \vee \neg\mathcal{B}$ | DM, n | m. | $\neg\mathcal{A} \& \neg\mathcal{B}$ | DM, n |

**Negated Conditional (NC)**     **Negated Biconditional (NB)**

| | | | | | |
|---|---|---|---|---|---|
| n. | $\neg(\mathcal{A} \to \mathcal{B})$ | NC, m | n. | $\neg(\mathcal{A} \leftrightarrow \mathcal{B})$ | NB, m |
| m. | $\mathcal{A} \& \neg\mathcal{B}$ | NC, n | m. | $\neg\mathcal{A} \leftrightarrow \mathcal{B}$ (or $\mathcal{A} \leftrightarrow \neg\mathcal{B}$) NB, n | |

**Commutativity of Conjunction (Cm)**     **Associativity of Conjunction (As)**

| | | | | | |
|---|---|---|---|---|---|
| n. | $\mathcal{A} \& \mathcal{B}$ | Cm, m | n. | $(\mathcal{A} \& \mathcal{B}) \& C$ | As, m |
| m. | $\mathcal{B} \& \mathcal{A}$ | Cm, n | m. | $\mathcal{A} \& (\mathcal{B} \& C)$ | As, n |

**Commutativity of Disjunction (Cm)**     **Associativity of Disjunction (As)**

| | | | | | |
|---|---|---|---|---|---|
| n. | $\mathcal{A} \vee \mathcal{B}$ | Cm, m | n. | $(\mathcal{A} \vee \mathcal{B}) \vee C$ | As, m |
| m. | $\mathcal{B} \vee \mathcal{A}$ | Cm, n | m. | $\mathcal{A} \vee (\mathcal{B} \vee C)$ | As, n |

**Material Conditional (MC)**

| | | |
|---|---|---|
| n. | $\mathcal{A} \to \mathcal{B}$ | MC, m |
| m. | $\neg\mathcal{A} \vee \mathcal{B}$ | MC, n |

# 3. STRATEGY

| *To get* | *Try to* |
|---|---|
| ¬𝒜 | use indirect proof. |
| 𝒜 & ℬ | prove 𝒜 and ℬ separately. |
| 𝒜 ∨ ℬ | use indirect proof, |
| | or prove 𝒜 or ℬ separately. |
| 𝒜 → ℬ | use conditional proof. |
| 𝒜 ↔ ℬ | prove the two conditionals 𝒜 → ℬ and ℬ → 𝒜. |

| *To exploit* | *Try to* |
|---|---|
| ¬𝒜 | use it with other lines that have 𝒜 as a part, or use a derivable rule. |
| 𝒜 & ℬ | use S to get 𝒜 and ℬ individually. |
| 𝒜 ∨ ℬ | get the negation of one disjunct, and use DS to get the other, |
| | or use CS by taking each case separately. |
| 𝒜 → ℬ | get 𝒜 and then reach ℬ by MP, |
| | or get ¬ℬ and then reach ¬𝒜 by MT. |
| 𝒜 ↔ ℬ | get either component and then reach the other by MB, |
| | or get the negation of either component and then the negation of the other by our expanded MB. |

# 4. ANSWERS TO UNANSWERED EVEN PROBLEMS

## A.2 NEGATION AND CONJUNCTION RULES

### from 8.2

| 8. | 1. | ¬p & ¬q | A |
|---|---|---|---|
| | 2. | r & ¬s | A |
| | 3. | ¬¬r & ¬s | DN, 2 |

## A.3 CONDITIONAL AND BICONDITIONAL RULES

### from 8.3

| 8. | 1. | p → q | A |
|---|---|---|---|
| | 2. | p → r | A |
| | 3. | p | A |
| | 4. | q | MP, 1, 3 |
| | 5. | r | MP, 2, 3 |
| | 6. | q & r | C, 4, 5 |

| 10. | 1. | p ↔ q | A |
|---|---|---|---|
| | 2. | p → r | A |
| | 3. | ⌐p | ACP |
| | 4. | \|q | MB, 1, 3 |
| | 5. | \|r | MP, 2, 3 |
| | 6. | ⌊q & r | C, 4, 5 |
| | 7. | p → (q & r) | CP, 3-6 |

141

| 14. | 1. | p & ¬t | A |
|---|---|---|---|
|  | 2. | p → (r & q) | A |
|  | 3. | r → s | A |
|  | 4. | p | S, 1 |
|  | 5. | r & q | MP, 2, 4 |
|  | 6. | r | S, 5 |
|  | 7. | q | S, 5 |
|  | 8. | s | MP, 3, 6 |
|  | 9. | s & q | C, 8, 7 |

| 16. | 1. | p & q | A |
|---|---|---|---|
|  | 2. | ¬¬p → r | A |
|  | 3. | q → s | A |
|  | 4. | p → t | A |
|  | 5. | p | S, 1 |
|  | 6. | q | S, 1 |
|  | 7. | s | MP, 3, 6 |
|  | 8. | t | MP, 4, 5 |
|  | 9. | ¬¬p | DN, 5 |
|  | 10. | r | MP, 2, 9 |
|  | 11. | r & t | C, 10, 8 |
|  | 12. | (r & t) & s | C, 11, 7 |

| 20. | 1. | p ↔ q | A |
|---|---|---|---|
|  | 2. | p ↔ r | A |
|  | 3. | r → q | A |
|  | 4. | ⌈ p | ACP |
|  | 5. | \| q | MB, 1, 4 |
|  | 6. | \| r | MB, 2, 4 |
|  | 7. | ⌊ q & r | C, 5, 6 |
|  | 8. | p → (q & r) | CP, 4-7 |
|  | 9. | ⌈ r | ACP |
|  | 10. | \| q | MP, 3, 9 |
|  | 11. | \| p | MB, 1, 10 |
|  | 12. | ⌊ p & q | C, 11, 10 |
|  | 13. | r → (p & q) | CP, 9-12 |
|  | 14. | (p → (q & r)) & (r → (p & q)) | C, 8, 13 |

| 22. | 1. | s → (q & t) | A |
|---|---|---|---|
|  | 2. | ¬m → p | A |
|  | 3. | (p → r) & ¬k | A |
|  | 4. | p & s | A |
|  | 5. | (q & r) → ¬m | A |
|  | 6. | p | S, 4 |
|  | 7. | s | S, 4 |
|  | 8. | q & t | MP, 1, 7 |
|  | 9. | q | S, 8 |
|  | 10. | p → r | S, 3 |
|  | 11. | r | MP, 10, 6 |
|  | 12. | q & r | C, 9, 11 |
|  | 13. | ¬m | MP, 5, 12 |
|  | 14. | ¬m & (q & r) | C, 13, 12 |

26.     d: The Democrats obstruct the President's legislative program; m: The market will
        lose confidence; p: The Democrats can gain politically by obstructing.
        1.      d → m                       A
        2.      d → p                       A
        3.      d                           A
        4.      p                           MP, 2, 3
        5.      m                           MP, 1, 3
        6.      p & m                       C, 4, 5

28.     g: Georgia will lose the case; d: The Court decides to base its decision on *Davis*; c:
        The composition of the Court is more conservative than it was a few years ago.
        1.      g ↔ d                       A
        2.      c & d                       A
        3.      d                           S, 2
        4.      g                           MB, 1, 3

## A.4 DISJUNCTION RULES

### from 8.4

8.      1.      p ↔ ¬q                      A
        2.      ¬p ∨ q                      A
        3.      r                           A
        4.   ┌  p                           AIP
        5.   │  ¬q                          MB, 1, 4
        6.   │  ¬¬p                         DN, 4
        7.   │  q                           DS, 2, 6
        8.   └  q & ¬q                      C, 7, 5
        9.      ¬p                          IP, 4-8
        10.     ¬p ∨ (p → s)                Ad, 9

10.     1.      p ↔ s                       A
        2.      q ∨ p                       A
        3.      q → r                       A
        4.   ┌  ¬(s ∨ r)                    AIP
        5.   │┌ s                           AIP
        6.   ││ s ∨ r                       Ad, 5
        7.   │└ (s ∨ r) & ¬(s ∨ r)          C, 6, 4
        8.   │  ¬s                          IP, 5-7
        9.   │┌ p                           AIP
        10.  ││ s                           MB, 1, 9
        11.  │└ s & ¬s                      C, 10, 8
        12.  │  ¬p                          IP, 9-11
        13.  │  q                           DS, 2, 12
        14.  │  r                           MP, 3, 13
        15.  │  s ∨ r                       Ad, 14
        16.  └  (s ∨ r) & ¬(s ∨ r)          C, 15, 4
        17.     ¬¬(s ∨ r)                   IP, 4-16
        18.     s ∨ r                       DN, 17

14.     1.      p ∨ r                       A
        2.      ¬p ∨ ¬q                     A
        3.      p                           A
        4.      ¬r ∨ q                      A

143

|      |      |                       |          |
|------|------|-----------------------|----------|
|      | 5.   | r                     | AIP      |
|      | 6.   | ¬¬r                   | DN, 5    |
|      | 7.   | q                     | DS, 4, 6 |
|      | 8.   | ¬¬q                   | DN, 7    |
|      | 9.   | ¬p                    | DS, 2, 8 |
|      | 10.  | p & ¬p                | C, 3, 9  |
|      | 11.  | ¬r                    | IP, 5-10 |
| 16.  | 1.   | p ∨ q                 | A        |
|      | 2.   | r ∨ s                 | A        |
|      | 3.   | ¬q & ¬s               | A        |
|      | 4.   | ¬q                    | S, 3     |
|      | 5.   | ¬s                    | S, 3     |
|      | 6.   | r                     | DS, 2, 5 |
|      | 7.   | p                     | DS, 1, 4 |
|      | 8.   | p & r                 | C, 7, 6  |
|      | 9.   | (p & r) ∨ t           | Ad, 8    |
| 20.  | 1.   | p & s                 | A        |
|      | 2.   | p → (¬s ∨ r)          | A        |
|      | 3.   | p                     | S, 1     |
|      | 4.   | s                     | S, 1     |
|      | 5.   | ¬s ∨ r                | MP, 2, 3 |
|      | 6.   | ¬¬s                   | DN, 4    |
|      | 7.   | r                     | DS, 5, 6 |
| 22.  | 1.   | p & q                 | A        |
|      | 2.   | r & ¬s                | A        |
|      | 3.   | q → (p → k)           | A        |
|      | 4.   | k → (r → (s ∨ m))     | A        |
|      | 5.   | p                     | S, 1     |
|      | 6.   | q                     | S, 1     |
|      | 7.   | r                     | S, 2     |
|      | 8.   | ¬s                    | S, 2     |
|      | 9.   | p → k                 | MP, 3, 6 |
|      | 10.  | k                     | MP, 9, 5 |
|      | 11.  | r → (s ∨ m)           | MP, 4, 10|
|      | 12.  | s ∨ m                 | MP, 11, 7|
|      | 13.  | m                     | MP, 12, 8|
| 26.  | 1.   | p & q                 | A        |
|      | 2.   | p → ¬¬r               | A        |
|      | 3.   | q → s                 | A        |
|      | 4.   | ¬r ∨ m                | A        |
|      | 5.   | p → t                 | A        |
|      | 6.   | p                     | S, 1     |
|      | 7.   | q                     | S, 1     |
|      | 8.   | ¬¬r                   | MP, 2, 6 |
|      | 9.   | s                     | MP, 3, 7 |
|      | 10.  | m                     | DS, 4, 8 |
|      | 11.  | t                     | MP, 5, 6 |
|      | 12.  | m & s                 | C, 10, 9 |
|      | 13.  | (m & s) & t           | C, 12, 11|

28.

| | | | |
|---|---|---|---|
| 1. | ⌐ | (p ∨ (q ∨ r)) | ACP |
| 2. | │⌐ | ¬((p ∨ q) ∨ r) | AIP |
| 3. | ││⌐ | p | AIP |
| 4. | │││ | p ∨ q | Ad, 3 |
| 5. | │││ | (p ∨ q) ∨ r | Ad, 4 |
| 6. | ││└ | ((p ∨ q) ∨ r) & ¬((p ∨ q) ∨ r) | C, 5, 2 |
| 7. | ││ | ¬p | IP, 3-6 |
| 8. | ││ | q ∨ r | DS, 1, 7 |
| 9. | ││⌐ | q | AIP |
| 10. | │││ | p ∨ q | Ad, 9 |
| 11. | │││ | (p ∨ q) ∨ r | Ad, 10 |
| 12. | ││└ | ((p ∨ q) ∨ r) & ¬((p ∨ q) ∨ r) | C, 11, 2 |
| 13. | ││ | ¬q | IP, 9-12 |
| 14. | ││ | r | DS, 8, 13 |
| 15. | ││ | (p ∨ q) ∨ r | Ad, 14 |
| 16. | │└ | ((p ∨ q) ∨ r) & ¬((p ∨ q) ∨ r) | C, 15, 2 |
| 17. | │ | ¬¬((p ∨ q) ∨ r) | IP, 2-16 |
| 18. | └ | (p ∨ q) ∨ r | DN, 17 |
| 19. | | (p ∨ (q ∨ r)) → ((p ∨ q) ∨ r) | CP, 1-18 |

32.     d: The dollar will fall; s: Foreign banks sterilize their intervention in the currency markets; f: The Fed does nothing to defend it; g: Germany and Japan are eager to keep their currencies strong; i: They'll intervene in the markets.

| | | |
|---|---|---|
| 1. | (s ∨ f) → d | A |
| 2. | g & (d → i) | A |
| 3. | g → s | A |
| 4. | g | S, 2 |
| 5. | s | MP, 3, 4 |
| 6. | s ∨ f | Ad, 5 |
| 7. | d | MP, 1, 6 |
| 8. | d → i | S, 2 |
| 9. | i | MP, 8, 7 |

34.     c: Patricia is clever, but won't w: Patricia will work very hard. If she's clever, b: the boss will like her and either p: promote her or g: give her a bonus. If Patricia is promoted, she'll work hard. Therefore, the boss will give Patricia a bonus.

| | | | |
|---|---|---|---|
| 1. | | c & ¬w | A |
| 2. | | c → (b & (p ∨ g)) | A |
| 3. | | p → w | A |
| 4. | | c | S, 1 |
| 5. | | ¬w | S, 1 |
| 6. | | b & (p ∨ g) | MP, 2, 4 |
| 7. | | p ∨ g | S, 6 |
| 8. | ⌐ | p | AIP |
| 9. | │ | w | MP, 3, 8 |
| 10. | └ | w & ¬w | C, 9, 5 |
| 11. | | ¬p | IP, 8-10 |
| 12. | | g | DS, 7, 11 |

**from 8.5**

14.
1.  $r \to (p \lor q)$                                    A
2.  $\neg((r \to p) \lor q))$                             AIP
3.  $q$                                                   AIP
4.  $(r \to p) \lor q$                                    Ad, 3
5.  $((r \to p) \lor q) \& \neg((r \to p) \lor q)$        C, 4, 2
6.  $\neg q$                                              IP, 3-5
7.  $r$                                                   ACP
8.  $p \lor q$                                            MP, 1, 7
9.  $p$                                                   DS, 8, 6
10. $r \to p$                                             CP, 7-9
11. $(r \to p) \lor q$                                    Ad, 10
12. $((r \to p) \lor q) \& \neg((r \to p) \lor q)$        C, 11, 2
13. $\neg\neg((r \to p) \lor q)$                          IP, 2-12
14. $(r \to p) \lor q$                                    DN, 13

16.
1.  $\neg s \lor (s \& r)$        A
2.  $(s \to r) \to q$             A
3.  $s$                           ACP
4.  $\neg\neg s$                  DN, 3
5.  $s \& r$                      DS, 1, 4
6.  $r$                           S, 5
7.  $s \to r$                     CP, 3-6
8.  $q$                           MP, 2, 7

20.
1.  $r \to \neg p$               A
2.  $q$                          A
3.  $q \to (p \lor \neg s)$      A
4.  $p \lor \neg s$              MP, 3, 2
5.  $s$                          ACP
6.  $\neg\neg s$                 DN, 5
7.  $p$                          DS, 4, 6
8.  $r$                          AIP
9.  $\neg p$                     MP, 1, 8
10. $p \& \neg p$                C, 7, 9
11. $\neg r$                     IP, 8-10
12. $s \to \neg r$               CP, 5-11

22.
1.  $r \to \neg p$                          A
2.  $\neg r \to \neg q$                     A
3.  $q \lor \neg s$                         A
4.  $\neg(\neg p \lor \neg s)$              AIP
5.  $\neg p$                                AIP
6.  $\neg p \lor \neg s$                    Ad, 5
7.  $(\neg p \lor \neg s) \& \neg(\neg p \lor \neg s)$  C, 6, 4
8.  $\neg\neg p$                            IP, 5-7
9.  $r$                                     AIP
10. $\neg p$                                MP, 1, 9
11. $\neg p \& \neg\neg p$                  C, 10, 8
12. $\neg r$                                IP, 9-11
13. $\neg q$                                MP, 2, 12
14. $\neg s$                                DS, 3, 13
15. $\neg p \lor \neg s$                    Ad, 14
16. $\neg\neg(\neg p \lor \neg s)$          IP, 4-15
17. $\neg p \lor \neg s$                    DN, 16

146

26.
| | | |
|---|---|---|
| 1. | r & p | A |
| 2. | r → (s ∨ q) | A |
| 3. | ¬(q & p) | A |
| 4. | r | S, 1 |
| 5. | p | S, 1 |
| 6. | s ∨ q | MP, 2, 4 |
| 7. | ⌈q | AIP |
| 8. | ∣q & p | C, 7, 5 |
| 9. | ⌊(q & p) & ¬(q & p) | C, 8, 3 |
| 10. | ¬q | IP, 7-9 |
| 11. | s | DS, 6, 10 |

28.
| | | |
|---|---|---|
| 1. | s → r | A |
| 2. | (s & r) → p | A |
| 3. | q → t | A |
| 4. | q ∨ s | A |
| 5. | ⌈¬(p ∨ t) | AIP |
| 6. | ∣⌈s | AIP |
| 7. | ∣∣r | MP, 1, 6 |
| 8. | ∣∣s & r | C, 6, 7 |
| 9. | ∣∣p | MP, 2, 8 |
| 10. | ∣∣p ∨ t | Ad, 9 |
| 11. | ∣⌊(p ∨ t) & ¬(p ∨ t) | C, 10, 5 |
| 12. | ∣¬s | IP, 6-11 |
| 13. | ∣q | DS, 4, 12 |
| 14. | ∣t | MP, 3, 13 |
| 15. | ∣p ∨ t | Ad, 14 |
| 16. | ⌊(p ∨ t) & ¬(p ∨ t) | C, 15, 5 |
| 17. | ¬¬(p ∨ t) | IP, 5-16 |
| 18. | p ∨ t | DN, 17 |

32.
| | | |
|---|---|---|
| 1. | r & (¬p & ¬t) | A |
| 2. | r → (s → q) | A |
| 3. | s → (q ↔ (t ∨ p)) | A |
| 4. | r | S, 1 |
| 5. | ¬p & ¬t | S, 1 |
| 6. | s → q | MP, 2, 4 |
| 7. | ⌈s | AIP |
| 8. | ∣q | MP, 6, 7 |
| 9. | ∣q ↔ (t ∨ p) | MP, 3, 7 |
| 10. | ∣t ∨ p | MB, 9, 8 |
| 11. | ∣¬p | S, 5 |
| 12. | ∣t | DS, 10, 11 |
| 13. | ∣¬t | S, 5 |
| 14. | ⌊t & ¬t | C, 12, 13 |
| 15. | ¬s | IP, 7-14 |

34.
| | | |
|---|---|---|
| 1. | ¬(p ∨ ¬s) | A |
| 2. | ¬p → (q ∨ r) | A |
| 3. | ¬r ∨ ¬s | A |
| 4. | (q ∨ t) → (m & (k → ¬s)) | A |

|     |     |     |     |
| --- | --- | --- | --- |
| 5.  | m → k | AIP |
| 6.  | p | AIP |
| 7.  | p ∨ ¬s | Ad, 6 |
| 8.  | (p ∨ ¬s) & ¬(p ∨ ¬s) | C, 7, 1 |
| 9.  | ¬p | IP, 6-8 |
| 10. | q ∨ r | MP, 2, 9 |
| 11. | ¬s | AIP |
| 12. | p ∨ ¬s | Ad, 11 |
| 13. | (p ∨ ¬s) & ¬(p ∨ ¬s) | C, 12, 1 |
| 14. | ¬¬s | IP, 11-13 |
| 15. | ¬r | DS, 3, 14 |
| 16. | q | DS, 10, 15 |
| 17. | q ∨ t | Ad, 16 |
| 18. | m & (k → ¬s) | MP, 4, 17 |
| 19. | m | S, 18 |
| 20. | k → ¬s | S, 18 |
| 21. | k | MP, 5, 19 |
| 22. | ¬s | MP, 20, 21 |
| 23. | ¬s & ¬¬s | C, 22, 14 |
| 24. | ¬(m → k) | IP, 5-23 |

38.

| |     |     |     |
| --- | --- | --- |
| 1. | p | A |
| 2. | ¬p | A |
| 3. | p ∨ q | Ad, 1 |
| 4. | q | DS, 3, 2 |

40.

| |     |     |     |
| --- | --- | --- |
| 1. | p & (q ∨ r) | A |
| 2. | p | S, 1 |
| 3. | q ∨ r | S, 1 |
| 4. | ¬((p & q) ∨ (p & r)) | AIP |
| 5. | q | AIP |
| 6. | p & q | C, 2, 5 |
| 7. | (p & q) ∨ (p & r) | Ad, 7 |
| 8. | ((p & q) ∨ (p & r)) & ¬((p & q) ∨ (p & r)) | C, 7, 4 |
| 9. | ¬q | IP, 5-8 |
| 10. | r | DS, 3, 9 |
| 11. | p & r | C, 2, 10 |
| 12. | (p & q) ∨ (p & r) | Ad, 11 |
| 13. | ((p & q) ∨ (p & r)) & ¬((p & q) ∨ (p & r)) | C, 12, 4 |
| 14. | ¬¬((p & q) ∨ (p & r)) | IP, 4-13 |
| 15. | (p & q) ∨ (p & r) | DN, 14 |

44.

| |     |     |     |
| --- | --- | --- |
| 1. | p ↔ ¬q | A |
| 2. | p ↔ q | AIP |
| 3. | p | AIP |
| 4. | q | MB, 2, 3 |
| 5. | ¬q | MB, 1, 3 |
| 6. | q & ¬q | C, 4, 5 |
| 7. | ¬p | IP, 3-6 |
| 8. | q | AIP |
| 9. | p | MB, 2, 8 |
| 10. | p & ¬p | C, 9, 7 |
| 11. | ¬q | IP, 8-10 |
| 12. | p | MB, 1, 11 |
| 13. | p & ¬p | C, 12, 7 |
| 14. | ¬(p ↔ q) | IP, 2-13 |

46.
| | | |
|---|---|---|
| 1. | $(p \& q) \lor (p \& r)$ | A |
| 2. | $\neg(q \lor r)$ | AIP |
| 3. | $q$ | AIP |
| 4. | $q \lor r$ | Ad, 3 |
| 5. | $(q \lor r) \& \neg(q \lor r)$ | C, 4, 2 |
| 6. | $\neg q$ | IP, 3-5 |
| 7. | $p \& q$ | AIP |
| 8. | $q$ | S, 7 |
| 9. | $q \& \neg q$ | C, 8, 6 |
| 10. | $\neg(p \& q)$ | IP, 7-9 |
| 11. | $p \& r$ | DS, 1, 10 |
| 12. | $r$ | S, 11 |
| 13. | $q \lor r$ | Ad, 12 |
| 14. | $(q \lor r) \& \neg(q \lor r)$ | C, 13, 5 |
| 15. | $\neg\neg(q \lor r)$ | IP, 2-14 |
| 16. | $q \lor r$ | DN, 15 |
| 17. | $\neg p$ | AIP |
| 18. | $p \& q$ | AIP |
| 19. | $p$ | S, 18 |
| 20. | $p \& \neg p$ | C, 19, 17 |
| 21. | $\neg(p \& q)$ | IP, 18-20 |
| 22. | $p \& r$ | DS, 1, 21 |
| 23. | $p$ | S, 22 |
| 24. | $p \& \neg p$ | C, 23, 17 |
| 25. | $\neg\neg p$ | IP, 17-24 |
| 26. | $p$ | DN, 25 |
| 27. | $p \& (q \lor r)$ | C, 26, 16 |

50. r: I'm right; f: I'm a fool.
| | | |
|---|---|---|
| 1. | $r \to f$ | A |
| 2. | $f \to \neg r$ | A |
| 3. | $r$ | AIP |
| 4. | $f$ | MP, 1, 3 |
| 5. | $\neg r$ | MP, 2, 4 |
| 6. | $r \& \neg r$ | C, 3, 5 |
| 7. | $\neg r$ | IP, 3-6 |

52. s: Socrates died; l: He died while he was living; d: He died while he was dead.
| | | |
|---|---|---|
| 1. | $s \to (l \lor d)$ | A |
| 2. | $\neg l$ | A |
| 3. | $\neg d$ | A |
| 4. | $s$ | AIP |
| 5. | $l \lor d$ | MP, 1, 4 |
| 6. | $d$ | DS, 5, 2 |
| 7. | $d \& \neg d$ | C, 6, 3 |
| 8. | $\neg s$ | IP, 4-7 |

56. u: The United States agrees to arms limitation talks; t: Tensions with the Soviets will remain high.
| | | |
|---|---|---|
| 1. | $\neg u \to t$ | A |
| 2. | $u \to t$ | A |
| 3. | $\neg t$ | AIP |
| 4. | $\neg u$ | MT, 2, 3 |
| 5. | $t$ | MP, 1, 4 |
| 6. | $t \& \neg t$ | C, 5, 3 |
| 7. | $\neg\neg t$ | IP, 3-6 |
| 8. | $t$ | DN, 7 |

58.  p: God is all powerful; a: He is able to prevent evil; g: He is all good; w: He is willing to prevent evil; e: Evil exists; x: God exists.

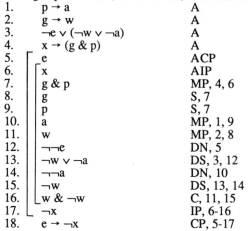

| 1. | p → a | A |
|---|---|---|
| 2. | g → w | A |
| 3. | ¬e ∨ (¬w ∨ ¬a) | A |
| 4. | x → (g & p) | A |
| 5. | e | ACP |
| 6. | x | AIP |
| 7. | g & p | MP, 4, 6 |
| 8. | g | S, 7 |
| 9. | p | S, 7 |
| 10. | a | MP, 1, 9 |
| 11. | w | MP, 2, 8 |
| 12. | ¬¬e | DN, 5 |
| 13. | ¬w ∨ ¬a | DS, 3, 12 |
| 14. | ¬¬a | DN, 10 |
| 15. | ¬w | DS, 13, 14 |
| 16. | w & ¬w | C, 11, 15 |
| 17. | ¬x | IP, 6-16 |
| 18. | e → ¬x | CP, 5-17 |

## A.5  DERIVED RULES

## from 8.6

8.  c: My cat sings opera; l: All the lights are out; i: I am very insistent; h: I howl at the moon.

| 1. | ¬c ∨ l | A |
|---|---|---|
| 2. | i → c | A |
| 3. | (l ∨ h) → i | A |
| 4. | ¬i → h | A |
| 5. | ¬i | AIP |
| 6. | h | MP, 4, 5 |
| 7. | l ∨ h | Ad, 6 |
| 8. | i | MP, 3, 7 |
| 9. | i & ¬i | C, 8, 5 |
| 10. | i | IP, 5-9 |
| 11. | c | MP, 2, 10 |
| 12. | ¬¬c | DN, 11 |
| 13. | l | DS, 1, 12 |
| 14. | (l & i) | C, 13, 10 |
| 15. | (l & i) & c | C, 14, 11 |

10. s: Money serves you; d: Money dominates you; w: You handle it wisely; h: It can help you to attain happiness; g: You will gain much of it; l: You'll be satisfied with your lot.

| | | |
|---|---|---|
| 1. | (s ∨ d) & ¬(s & d) | A |
| 2. | (s & w) → h | A |
| 3. | d → (g & ¬l) | A |
| 4. | l ↔ ¬h | A |
| 5. | s ∨ d | S, 1 |
| 6. | ⌐ w | ACP |
| 7. | ⌐¬h | AIP |
| 8. | l | MB, 4, 7 |
| 9. | ¬¬l | DN, 8 |
| 10. | ¬g ∨ ¬¬l | Ad, 9 |
| 11. | ¬(g & ¬l) | DM, 10 |
| 12. | ¬d | MT, 3, 11 |
| 13. | s | DS, 5, 12 |
| 14. | s & w | C, 13, 6 |
| 15. | h | MP, 2, 14 |
| 16. | ⌊ h & ¬h | C, 15, 7 |
| 17. ⌊ | h | IP, 7-16 |
| 18. | w → h | CP, 6-17 |

14. d: Happiness can be defined; m: There's a way to measure it; s: We can say whether someone is happy; w: We take that person's word for it.; t: We can test the psychological effects of jobs of various kinds.

| | | |
|---|---|---|
| 1. | ¬d → ¬m | A |
| 2. | ¬m → (s → w) | A |
| 3. | t → s | A |
| 4. | ¬w | A |
| 5. | ⌐ ¬d | ACP |
| 6. | ⌐ t | AIP |
| 7. | ¬m | MP, 1, 5 |
| 8. | s → w | MP, 2, 7 |
| 9. | s | MP, 3, 6 |
| 10. | w | MP, 8, 9 |
| 11. | ⌊ w & ¬w | C, 10, 4 |
| 12. ⌊ | ¬t | IP, 6-11 |
| 13. | ¬d → ¬t | CP, 5-12 |

16. s: We maintain high educational standards; a: We accept almost every high school graduate; f: We fail large numbers of students; p: Many students do poorly; l: We will placate the legislature.

| | | |
|---|---|---|
| 1. | ¬(s & a) ∨ (f ↔ p) | A |
| 2. | s | A |
| 3. | l & a | A |
| 4. | ¬(l & f) | A |
| 5. | l | S, 3 |
| 6. | a | S, 3 |
| 7. | s & a | C, 2, 6 |
| 8. | ¬¬(s & a) | DN, 7 |
| 9. | f ↔ p | DS, 1, 8 |
| 10. | ¬l ∨ ¬f | DM, 4 |
| 11. | ¬¬l | DN, 5 |
| 12. | ¬f | DS, 10, 11 |
| 13. | ¬p | MB, 9, 12 |

151

20.    r: The Soviet economy is restructured; d: Decision-making will have to be decentralized; s: Bureaucracies in charge of economic planning will have to become smaller; p: Bureaucracies in charge of economic planning will have to become less powerful; b: Bureaucrats can help it; w: The party hierarchy is willing to cede power to a wide group it can't easily control; c: Central planning will continue to dominate the economy.

| | | |
|---|---|---|
| 1. | r → (d & (s & p)) | A |
| 2. | b → ¬s | A |
| 3. | d → w | A |
| 4. | p ∨ (¬d & c) | A |
| 5. | ┌ ¬w ∨ b | ACP |
| 6. | │ ┌ r | AIP |
| 7. | │ │ d & (s & p) | MP, 1, 6 |
| 8. | │ │ d | S, 7 |
| 9. | │ │ w | MP, 3, 8 |
| 10. | │ │ ¬¬w | DN, 9 |
| 11. | │ │ b | DS, 5, 10 |
| 12. | │ │ ¬s | MP, 2, 11 |
| 13. | │ │ s & p | S, 7 |
| 14. | │ │ s | S, 13 |
| 15. | │ └ s & ¬s | C, 14, 12 |
| 16. | └ ¬r | IP, 6-15 |
| 17. | (¬w ∨ b) → ¬r | CP, 5-16 |

22.    p: The party maintains its current economic policy; f: There will be a flight of capital to other countries; i: The party improves its image abroad; t: It tightens its control over the economy; h: The nation will have to pay large amounts of foreign debt in hard currency.

| | | |
|---|---|---|
| 1. | p → f | A |
| 2. | t → ¬i | A |
| 3. | (p & f) → t | A |
| 4. | (¬i → h) & ¬h | A |
| 5. | ┌ p | DN, 6 |
| 6. | │ ¬i → h | S, 4 |
| 7. | │ ¬h | S, 4 |
| 8. | │ ¬¬i | MT, 6, 7 |
| 9. | │ ¬t | MT, 2, 8 |
| 10. | │ f | MP, 1, 5 |
| 11. | │ p & f | C, 5, 10 |
| 12. | │ t | MP, 3, 11 |
| 13. | └ t & ¬t | C, 12, 9 |
| 14. | ¬p | IP, 5-13 |

26.

| | | |
|---|---|---|
| 1. | p ↔ q | A |
| 2. | ¬(m → q) | A |
| 3. | m & ¬q | NC, 2 |
| 4. | ¬q | S, 3 |
| 5. | ¬p | MB, 1, 4 |

28.

| | | |
|---|---|---|
| 1. | p & q | A |
| 2. | p | S, 1 |
| 3. | q | S, 1 |
| 4. | q ∨ r | Ad, 3 |
| 5. | ¬(¬q & ¬r) | DM, 4 |
| 6. | ¬(¬q & ¬r) & p | C, 5, 2 |

32.  1.    $(p \ \& \ q) \to r$         A
     2.    p                            ACP
     3.    q                            ACP
     4.    p & q                        C, 2, 3
     5.    r                            MP, 1, 4
     6.    q → r                        CP, 3-5
     7.    p → (q → r)                  CP, 2-6

34.  1.    p ↔ q                                        A
     2.    ¬((p & q) ∨ (¬p & ¬q))                       AIP
     3.    ¬(p & q) & ¬(¬p & ¬q)                        DM, 2
     4.    ¬(p & q)                                     S, 3
     5.    ¬(¬p & ¬q)                                   S, 3
     6.    p ∨ q                                        DM, 5
     7.    ¬p                                           AIP
     8.    q                                            DS, 6, 7
     9.    p                                            MB, 1, 8
     10.   p & ¬p                                       C, 9, 7
     11.   p                                            IP, 7-10
     12.   q                                            MB, 1, 11
     13.   p & q                                        C, 11, 12
     14.   (p & q) & ¬(p & q)                           C, 13, 4
     15.   (p & q) ∨ (¬p & ¬q)                          IP, 2-14

38.  1.    p ↔ q                        A
     2.    p                            ACP
     3.    q                            MB, 1, 2
     4.    p → q                        CP, 2-3
     5.    q                            ACP
     6.    p                            MB, 1, 5
     7.    q → p                        CP, 5-6
     8.    q ↔ p                        B, 7, 4

40.  1.    p → q                        A
     2.    p → r                        A
     3.    ¬q ∨ ¬r                      A
     4.    p                            AIP
     5.    q                            MP, 1, 4
     6.    r                            MP, 2, 4
     7.    q & r                        C, 5, 6
     8.    ¬(q & r)                     DM, 3
     9.    (q & r) & ¬(q & r)           C, 7, 8
     10.   ¬p                           IP, 4-9

44. (a) 1.   a → b                  A        (b)  1.   a → b                  A
       2.   c → (a → ¬b)           A             2.   c → (a → ¬b)           A
       3.   c & (a & b)            AIP           3.   ¬(¬a ∨ ¬c)             AIP
       4.   c                      S, 3          4.   ¬¬a & ¬¬c              DM, 3
       5.   a & b                  S, 3          5.   a & c                  DN, 4
       6.   a                      S, 5          6.   a                      S, 5
       7.   b                      S, 5          7.   c                      S, 5
       8.   a → ¬b                 MP, 2, 4      8.   b                      MP, 1, 6
       9.   ¬b                     MP, 8, 6      9.   a → ¬b                 MP, 2, 7
       10.  b & ¬b                 C, 7, 9       10.  ¬b                     MP, 9, 6
       11.  ¬(c & (a & b))         IP, 3-10      11.  b & ¬b                 C, 8, 10
                                                 12.  ¬a ∨ ¬c                IP, 3-11

(a)  1.    a → b                      A
     2.    c → (a → ¬b)               A
     3.  ⌈ ¬b & ¬c                    ACP
     4.  ⌈ a                          AIP
     5.  │ b                          MP, 1, 4
     6.  │ ¬b                         S, 3
     7.  ⌊ b & ¬b                     C, 5, 6
     8.  ⌊ ¬a                         IP, 4-7
     6.    (¬b & ¬c) → ¬a             CP, 3-8

46.  1.    p → (q ∨ r)                A
     2.    (¬q & m) ∨ (s → ¬p)        A
     3.    ¬(¬r → ¬p)                 A
     4.    ¬r & ¬¬p                   NC, 3
     5.    ¬¬p                        S, 4
     6.    p                          DN, 5
     7.    ¬r                         S, 4
     8.    q ∨ r                      MP, 1, 6
     9.    q                          DS, 8, 7
     10.   q ∨ ¬m                     Ad, 9
     11.   ¬¬q ∨ ¬m                   DN, 10
     12.   ¬(¬q & m)                  DM, 11
     13.   s → ¬p                     DS, 2, 12
     14.   ¬s                         MT, 13, 5
     15.   ¬s & q                     C, 14, 9

50.  1.    (p & ¬r) ↔ (s ∨ ¬q)                                A
     2.    t & ((¬s & ¬r) → p)                                A
     3.    (t → q) ∨ (t → r)                                  A
     4.    (p & s) → r                                        A
     5.    t                                                  S, 2
     6.    (¬s & ¬r) → p                                      S, 2
     7.  ⌈ ¬q                                                 AIP
     8.  │ t & ¬q                                             C, 5, 7
     9.  │ ¬(t → q)                                           NC, 8
     10. │ t → r                                              DS, 3, 9
     11. │ r                                                  MP, 10, 5
     12. │ ¬¬r                                                DN, 11
     13. │ ¬p ∨ ¬¬r                                           Ad, 12
     14. │ ¬(p & ¬r)                                          DM, 13
     15. │ ¬(s ∨ ¬q)                                          MB, 1, 14
     16. │ ¬s & ¬¬q                                           DM, 15
     17. │ ¬¬q                                                S, 16
     18. ⌊ ¬q & ¬¬q                                           C, 7, 17
     19.   q                                                  IP, 7-18
     20. ⌈ s                                                  AIP
     21. │ s ∨ ¬q                                             Ad, 20
     22. │ p & ¬r                                             MB, 1, 21
     23. │ p                                                  S, 22
     24. │ p & s                                              C, 23, 20
     25. │ r                                                  MP, 4, 24
     26. │ ¬r                                                 S, 22
     27. ⌊ r & ¬r                                             C, 25, 26
     28.   ¬s                                                 IP, 20-27
     29.   ¬s & q                                             C, 28, 19
     30.   ¬s & ¬¬q                                           DN, 29
     31.   ¬(s ∨ ¬q)                                          DM, 30

154

|     |                          |              |
|-----|--------------------------|--------------|
| 32. | ¬(p & ¬r)                | MB, 1, 31    |
| 33. | ¬p ∨ ¬¬r                 | DM, 32       |
| 34. | ┌ ¬r                     | AIP          |
| 35. | │ ¬p                     | DS, 33, 34   |
| 36. | │ ¬s & ¬r                | C, 28, 34    |
| 37. | │ p                      | MP, 6, 36    |
| 38. | └ p & ¬p                 | C, 37, 35    |
| 39. | r                        | IP, 34-38    |
| 40. | q & r                    | C, 19, 39    |

52.

|    |                  |           |
|----|------------------|-----------|
| 1. | ┌ p              | ACP       |
| 2. | │ ┌ ¬p           | ACP       |
| 3. | │ └ q            | !, 1, 2   |
| 4. | └ ¬p → q         | CP, 2-3   |
| 5. | p → (¬p → q)     | CP, 1-4   |

56.

|    |                                      |          |
|----|--------------------------------------|----------|
| 1. | ┌ p → (q → r)                        | ACP      |
| 2. | │ ┌ p → q                            | ACP      |
| 3. | │ │ ┌ p                              | ACP      |
| 4. | │ │ │ q                              | MP, 2, 3 |
| 5. | │ │ │ q → r                          | MP, 1, 3 |
| 6. | │ │ └ r                              | MP, 5, 4 |
| 7. | │ └ p → r                            | CP, 3-6  |
| 8. | └ (p → q) → (p → r)                  | CP, 2-7  |
| 9. | (p → (q → r)) → ((p → q) → (p → r))  | CP, 1-8  |

58.

|    |                  |          |
|----|------------------|----------|
| 1. | ┌ p ∨ p          | ACP      |
| 2. | │ ┌ ¬p           | AIP      |
| 3. | │ │ p            | DS, 1, 2 |
| 4. | │ └ p & ¬p       | C, 3, 2  |
| 5. | └ p              | IP, 2-4  |
| 6. | (p ∨ p) → p      | CP, 1-5  |

62.

|     |                                     |           |
|-----|-------------------------------------|-----------|
| 1.  | ┌ q → r                             | ACP       |
| 2.  | │ ┌ p ∨ q                           | ACP       |
| 3.  | │ │ ┌ ¬(p ∨ r)                      | AIP       |
| 4.  | │ │ │ ¬p & ¬r                       | DM, 3     |
| 5.  | │ │ │ ¬p                            | S, 4      |
| 6.  | │ │ │ ¬r                            | S, 4      |
| 7.  | │ │ │ q                             | DS, 2, 5  |
| 8.  | │ │ │ r                             | MP, 1, 7  |
| 9.  | │ │ └ r & ¬r                        | C, 8, 6   |
| 10. | │ └ p ∨ r                           | IP, 3-9   |
| 11. | └ (p ∨ q) → (p ∨ r)                 | CP, 2-10  |
| 12. | (q → r) → ((p ∨ q) → (p ∨ r))       | CP, 1-11  |

64.

|    |                                            |          |
|----|--------------------------------------------|----------|
| 1. | ┌ p → q                                    | ACP      |
| 2. | │ ┌ p → r                                  | ACP      |
| 3. | │ │ ┌ p                                    | ACP      |
| 4. | │ │ │ q                                    | MP, 1, 3 |
| 5. | │ │ │ r                                    | MP, 2, 3 |
| 6. | │ │ └ q & r                                | C, 4, 5  |
| 7. | │ └ p → (q & r)                            | CP, 3-6  |
| 8. | └ (p → r) → (p → (q & r))                  | CP, 2-7  |
| 9. | (p → q) → ((p → r) → (p → (q & r)))        | CP, 1-8  |

# B: Adding Quantifiers

This appendix extends the system of Appendix IA to predicate logic. The first two sections present the basic rules for quantifiers. The last two sections extend the system to multiply quantified formulas; instructors who wish to restrict themselves to singly quantified formulas should omit them, with the exception, perhaps, of the quantifier negation rule, discussed near the begging of 13.4. The rules for full predicate logic derive from the system of the first edition of Copi's *Symbolic Logic*, by way of revisions by Kalish and Prawitz. To make the restrictions on rules easy to apply, the method uses Fine's dependency diagrams.

## 1. Key Definitions

$\mathcal{A}[c/v]$ is the result of substituting $c$ for every occurrence of $v$ throughout the formula $\mathcal{A}$. If $\forall v \mathcal{A}$ and $\exists v \mathcal{A}$ are formulas, then $\mathcal{A}[c/v]$ is called an *instance* of them. Conversely, $\forall v \mathcal{A}$ and $\exists v \mathcal{A}$ are *generics* of $\mathcal{A}[c/v]$. If $\mathcal{A}[c/v]$ is an instance of $\forall v \mathcal{A}$ and $\exists v \mathcal{A}$, and those formulas do not contain $c$, then $\mathcal{A}[c/v]$ is a *conservative instance* of $\forall v \mathcal{A}$ and $\exists v \mathcal{A}$.

A proof must never end with a formula containing a constant introduced by ES.

A constant $c$ *immediately depends on* a constant $d$ in a proof if and only if $c$ is introduced into the proof by applying ES to a formula containing $d$. A constant $c$ *depends on* a constant $d$ if and only if there is a chain of constants $c_1, \ldots, c_n$ such that $c$ immediately depends on $c_1$, $c_1$ immediately depends on $c_2$, ..., and $c_n$ immediately depends on $d$. (The chain may be empty; immediate dependence is a kind of dependence.)

*Dependency diagrams* change only when we apply ES: (1) write, horizontally, the constants in $\exists v \mathcal{A}$ not already in the diagram; (2) add the new constant $c$ below the constants in $\exists v \mathcal{A}$, circling it and drawing lines linking it to them. We can use these diagrams to check the fulfillment of the third and fourth restrictions on UG. The third bans the use of the same constant in ES and UG. So, applying UG to a constant circled in the diagram is prohibited. The fourth restriction requires that, in moving from $\mathcal{A}[c/v]$ to $\forall v \mathcal{A}$, no constant in $\forall v \mathcal{A}$ depend on $c$. It is satisfied so long as no constant in $\mathcal{A}[c/v]$ is linked upward to $c$.

## 2. Summary of Rules

*Rules Applying Only to Entire Formulas*
*Basic Rules*

Existential Generalization (EG)

| | | |
|---|---|---|
| n. | $\underline{A[c/v]}$ | |
| n+p. | $\exists v \mathcal{A}$ | EG, n |

Here $c$ may be any constant.

Existential Specification (ES)

| | | |
|---|---|---|
| n. | $\underline{\exists v \mathcal{A}}$ | |
| n+p. | $\mathcal{A}[c/v]$ | ES, n |

Here $c$ must be a constant new to the proof.

Universal Specification (US)

| | | |
|---|---|---|
| n. | $\forall v \mathcal{A}$ | |
| n+p. | $\mathcal{A}[c/v]$ | US, n |

Here $c$ may be any constant.

Universal Generalization (UG)

| | | |
|---|---|---|
| n. | $\mathcal{A}[c/v]$ | |
| n+p. | $\forall v \mathcal{A}$ | UG, n |

Here
(1) $c$ must not occur in $\forall v \mathcal{A}$;
(2) $c$ must not occur in the assumptions or conclusion of the proof;
(3) $c$ must not have been introduced by ES;
(4) no term remaining in $\forall v \mathcal{A}$ may depend on $c$.

*Derived Rule*

Variable Rewrite (VR)

| | | |
|---|---|---|
| n. | $\mathcal{A}$ | |
| m. | $\mathcal{A}[v/u]$ | VR, n |

Here $v$ is foreign to $\mathcal{A}$.

*Rules Applying to Parts of Formulas as Well as Entire Formulas*

Quantifier Negation (QN)

| | | |
|---|---|---|
| n. | $\neg \exists v \mathcal{A}$ | QN, m |
| m. | $\forall v \neg \mathcal{A}$ | QN, n |

| | | |
|---|---|---|
| n. | $\neg \forall v \mathcal{A}$ | QN, m |
| m. | $\exists v \neg \mathcal{A}$ | QN, n |

# 3. ANSWERS TO UNANSWERED EVEN PROBLEMS

## B.1 DEDUCTION RULES FOR QUANTIFIERS

The policy that guided symbolization for this chapter was to introduce (more or less) only as much complexity as is needed to enable the proofs to go through. In those cases in which the meaning of the English is intended to be captured not only through appropriate interpretation of constants but also by circumscribing the universe of discourse, this is indicated.

| 8. | 1. | $\forall x(H_1 x \rightarrow (Lx \;\&\; H_2 x))$ | A | (universe: insects) |
|---|---|---|---|---|
| | 2. | $\exists x(H_1 x \;\&\; Px)$ | A | |
| | 3. | $H_1 a \;\&\; Pa$ | ES, 2 | |
| | 4. | $H_1 a \rightarrow (La \;\&\; H_2 a)$ | US, 1 | |
| | 5. | $H_1 a$ | S, 3 | |
| | 6. | $La \;\&\; H_2 a$ | MP, 4, 5 | |
| | 7. | $Pa$ | S, 3 | |
| | 8. | $(La \;\&\; H_2 a) \;\&\; Pa$ | C, 6, 7 | |
| | 9. | $\exists x((Lx \;\&\; H_2 x) \;\&\; Px)$ | EG, 8 | |

| 10. | 1. | ∀xAxd | A | (universe: people) |
|---|---|---|---|---|
| | 2. | ∀x(Adx → Cxd) | A | |
| | 3. | Add → Cdd | US, 2 | |
| | 4. | Add | US, 1 | |
| | 5. | Cdd | MP, 3, 4 | |

| 14. | 1. | ∃x(Bx & Sx) | A | (universe: people) |
|---|---|---|---|---|
| | 2. | ∀x(Sx → ¬Dx) | A | |
| | 3. | Ba & Sa | ES, 2 | |
| | 4. | Sa → ¬Da | US, 1 | |
| | 5. | Sa | S, 3 | |
| | 6. | ¬Da | MP, 4, 5 | |
| | 7. | Ba | S, 3 | |
| | 8. | Ba & ¬Da | C, 7, 6 | |
| | 9. | ∃x(Bx & ¬Dx) | EG, 8 | |

| 16. | 1. | ∃x(Ax & Bx) & ∃x(Ax & Cx) | A | (universe: people) |
|---|---|---|---|---|
| | 2. | ∀x(Cx → Rx) | A | |
| | 3. | ∀x(Mx → ¬Bx) | A | |
| | 4. | ∃x(Ax & Cx) | S, 1 | |
| | 5. | Aa & Ca | ES, 4 | |
| | 6. | Ca → Ra | US, 2 | |
| | 7. | Ca | S, 5 | |
| | 8. | Ra | MP, 6, 7 | |
| | 9. | Aa | S, 5 | |
| | 10. | Aa & Ra | C, 9, 8 | |
| | 11. | ∃x(Ax & Rx) | EG, 10 | |
| | 12. | ∃x(Ax & Bx) | S, 1 | |
| | 13. | Ab & Bb | ES, 12 | |
| | 14. | Bb | S, 13 | |
| | 15. | Mb → ¬Bb | US, 3 | |
| | 16. | ¬¬Bb | DN, 14 | |
| | 17. | ¬Mb | MT, 15, 16 | |
| | 18. | Ab | S, 13 | |
| | 19. | Ab & ¬Mb | C, 18, 17 | |
| | 20. | ∃x(Ax & ¬Mx) | EG, 19 | |
| | 21. | ∃x(Ax & Rx) & ∃x(Ax & ¬Mx) | C, 11, 20 | |

| 20. | 1. | ∀x(Mx → ¬Lx) | A | |
|---|---|---|---|---|
| | 2. | ∃x(Sx & Mx) | A | |
| | 3. | Sa & Ma | ES, 2 | |
| | 4. | Ma → ¬La | US, 1 | |
| | 5. | Ma | S, 3 | |
| | 6. | ¬La | MP, 4, 5 | |
| | 7. | Sa | S, 3 | |
| | 8. | Sa & ¬La | C, 7, 6 | |
| | 9. | ∃x(Sx & ¬Lx) | EG, 8 | |

| 22. | 1. | ∀x(Lx → Mx) | A | |
|---|---|---|---|---|
| | 2. | ∃x(Sx & ¬Mx) | A | |
| | 3. | Sa & ¬Ma | ES, 2 | |
| | 4. | La → Ma | US, 1 | |
| | 5. | ¬Ma | S, 3 | |
| | 6. | ¬La | MT, 4, 5 | |
| | 7. | Sa | S, 3 | |
| | 8. | Sa & ¬La | C, 7, 6 | |
| | 9. | ∃x(Sx & ¬Lx) | EG, 8 | |

| 26. | 1. | $\forall x(Mx \rightarrow Lx)$ | A |
| | 2. | $\exists x(Mx \,\&\, Sx)$ | A |
| | 3. | Ma & Sa | ES, 2 |
| | 4. | Ma $\rightarrow$ La | US, 1 |
| | 5. | Ma | S, 3 |
| | 6. | La | MP, 4, 5 |
| | 7. | Sa | S, 3 |
| | 8. | Sa & La | C, 7, 6 |
| | 9. | $\exists x(Sx \,\&\, Lx)$ | EG, 8 |

| 28. | 1. | $\forall x(Mx \rightarrow \neg Lx)$ | A |
| | 2. | $\exists x(Mx \,\&\, Sx)$ | A |
| | 3. | Ma & Sa | ES, 2 |
| | 4. | Ma $\rightarrow \neg$La | US, 1 |
| | 5. | Ma | S, 3 |
| | 6. | $\neg$La | MP, 4, 5 |
| | 7. | Sa | S, 3 |
| | 8. | Sa & $\neg$La | C, 7, 6 |
| | 9. | $\exists x(Sx \,\&\, \neg Lx)$ | EG, 8 |

| 32. | 1. | $\forall x(Lx \rightarrow Mx)$ | A |
| | 2. | $\forall x(Sx \rightarrow \neg Mx)$ | A |
| | 3. | $\exists x Sx$ | A |
| | 4. | Sa | ES, 3 |
| | 5. | Sa $\rightarrow \neg$Ma | US, 2 |
| | 6. | $\neg$Ma | MP, 5, 4 |
| | 7. | La $\rightarrow$ Ma | US, 1 |
| | 8. | $\neg$La | MT, 7, 6 |
| | 9. | Sa & $\neg$La | C, 4, 8 |
| | 10. | $\exists x(Sx \,\&\, \neg Lx)$ | EG, 9 |

| 34. | 1. | $\forall x(Mx \rightarrow Lx)$ | A |
| | 2. | $\exists x(Sx \,\&\, Mx)$ | A |
| | 3. | Sa & Ma | ES, 2 |
| | 4. | Ma $\rightarrow$ La | US, 1 |
| | 5. | Ma | S, 3 |
| | 6. | La | MP, 4, 5 |
| | 7. | Sa | S, 3 |
| | 8. | La & Sa | C, 6, 7 |
| | 9. | $\exists x(Lx \,\&\, Sx)$ | EG, 8 |

| 38. | 1. | $\exists x Fx$ | A |
| | 2. | $\forall x Gx$ | A |
| | 3. | Fa | ES, 1 |
| | 4. | Ga | US, 2 |
| | 5. | Fa & Ga | C, 3, 4 |
| | 6. | $\exists x(Fx \,\&\, Gx)$ | EG, 5 |

| 40. | 1. | $\forall x(Gx \rightarrow Hx)$ | A |
| | 2. | $\exists x(Fx \,\&\, Gx)$ | A |
| | 3. | Fa & Ga | ES, 2 |
| | 4. | Ga $\rightarrow$ Ha | US, 1 |
| | 5. | Ga | S, 3 |
| | 6. | Ha | MP, 4, 5 |
| | 7. | Fa | S, 3 |
| | 8. | Fa & Ha | C, 7, 6 |
| | 9. | $\exists x(Fx \,\&\, Hx)$ | EG, 8 |

| 44. | 1. | ∀x(Gx →Hx) | A |
|---|---|---|---|
| | 2. | ∃x(Gx & Fx) | A |
| | 3. | Ga & Fa | ES, 2 |
| | 4. | Ga → Ha | US, 1 |
| | 5. | Ga | S, 3 |
| | 6. | Ha | MP, 4, 5 |
| | 7. | Fa | S, 3 |
| | 8. | Fa & Ha | C, 7, 6 |
| | 9. | ∃x(Fx & Hx) | EG, 8 |

| 46. | 1. | ∃x(Gx & Hx) | A |
|---|---|---|---|
| | 2. | ∀x(Gx →Fx) | A |
| | 3. | Ga & Ha | ES, 1 |
| | 4. | Ga → Fa | US, 2 |
| | 5. | Ga | S, 3 |
| | 6. | Fa | MP, 4, 5 |
| | 7. | Ha | S, 3 |
| | 8. | Fa & Ha | C, 6, 7 |
| | 9. | ∃x(Fx & Hx) | EG, 8 |

| 50. | 1. | ∃x(¬Fx & ¬Gx) | A |
|---|---|---|---|
| | 2. | ∀x(¬Gx → ¬Hx) | A |
| | 3. | ¬Fa & ¬Ga | ES, 1 |
| | 4. | ¬Ga → ¬Ha | US, 2 |
| | 5. | ¬Ga | S, 3 |
| | 6. | ¬Ha | MP, 4, 5 |
| | 7. | ¬Fa | S, 3 |
| | 8. | ¬Ha & ¬Fa | C, 6, 7 |
| | 9. | ∃x(¬Hx & ¬Fx) | EG, 8 |

| 52. | 1. | ∀x(Fx ↔ Gx) | A |
|---|---|---|---|
| | 2. | ∀x(Fx ↔ Hx) | A |
| | 3. | ∃x(¬Hx ∨ Gx) | A |
| | 4. | ⌈ Ha | ACP |
| | 5. | │ Fa ↔ Ha | US, 2 |
| | 6. | │ Fa | MB, 5, 4 |
| | 7. | │ Fa ↔ Ga | US, 1 |
| | 8. | │ Ga | MB, 7, 6 |
| | 9. | ⌊ Ga & Fa | C, 8, 6 |
| | 10. | Ha → (Ga & Fa) | CP, 4-9 |
| | 11. | ¬Ha ∨ (Ga & Fa) | MC, 10 |
| | 12. | ∃x(¬Hx ∨ (Gx & Fx)) | EG, 11 |

| 56. | 1. | ∃yFyy | A |
|---|---|---|---|
| | 2. | ∃x∀zGxz | A |
| | 3. | Faa | ES, 1 |
| | 4. | ∀zGbz | ES, 2 |
| | 5. | Gba | US, 4 |
| | 6. | Gba & Faa | C, 5, 3 |
| | 7. | ∃y(Gya & Faa) | EG, 6 |
| | 8. | ∃x∃y(Gyx & Fxx) | EG, 7 |

58. 1. $\exists xGx$ & $\exists x\neg Gx$     A
    2. $\forall x\forall y(Fxy \leftrightarrow (Gx$ & $\neg Gy))$     A
    3. $\exists xGx$     S, 1
    4. Ga     ES, 3
    5. $\exists x\neg Gx$     S, 1
    6. $\neg Gb$     ES, 5
    7. $\forall y(Fay \leftrightarrow (Ga$ & $\neg Gy))$     US, 2
    8. $Fab \leftrightarrow (Ga$ & $\neg Gb)$     US, 7
    9. Ga & $\neg Gb$     C, 4, 6
    10. Fab     MB, 8, 9
    11. $\exists yFay$     EG, 10
    12. $\exists x\exists yFxy$     EG, 11

62. 1. $\exists x\exists y(Fx$ & $Gyx)$     A
    2. $\forall x\forall y((Fx$ & $Hy) \rightarrow \neg Jxy)$     A
    3. $\exists y(Fa$ & $Gya)$     ES, 1
    4. Fa & Gba     ES, 3
    5. Hb & Jab     AIP
    6. $\forall y((Fa$ & $Hy) \rightarrow \neg Jay)$     US, 2
    7. $(Fa$ & $Hb) \rightarrow \neg Jab$     US, 6
    8. Fa     S, 4
    9. Hb     S, 5
    10. Fa & Hb     C, 8, 9
    11. $\neg Jab$     MP, 7, 10
    12. Jab     S, 5
    13. Jab & $\neg Jab$     C, 12, 11
    14. $\neg(Hb$ & $Jab)$     IP, 5-13
    15. Gba     S, 4
    16. Gba & $\neg(Hb$ & $Jab)$     C, 15, 14
    17. $\exists y(Gby$ & $\neg(Hb$ & $Jyb))$     EG, 16
    18. $\exists x\exists y(Gxy$ & $\neg(Hx$ & $Jyx))$     EG, 17

64. 1. $\forall z\forall x(\neg Hz \leftrightarrow (Fx$ & $Gz))$     A
    2. $\forall x\exists y(Gy$ & $Fx)$     A
    3. $\exists y(Gy$ & $Fa)$     US, 2
    4. Gb & Fa     ES, 3
    5. $\forall x(\neg Hb \leftrightarrow (Fx$ & $Gb))$     US, 1
    6. $\neg Hb \leftrightarrow (Fa$ & $Gb)$     US, 5
    7. Fa     S, 4
    8. Gb     S, 4
    9. Fa & Gb     C, 7, 8
    10. $\neg Hb$     MB, 6, 9
    11. $\exists x\neg Hx$     EG, 10

## B.2 UNIVERSAL GENERALIZATION

8. 1. $\forall x(Gx \rightarrow Hx)$     A
   2. $\forall x(\neg Gx \rightarrow \neg Sx)$     A
   3. $\neg Ha$     ACP
   4. $Ga \rightarrow Ha$     US, 1
   5. $\neg Ga$     MT, 4, 3
   6. $\neg Ga \rightarrow \neg Sa$     US, 2
   7. $\neg Sa$     MP, 6, 5
   8. $\neg Ha \rightarrow \neg Sa$     CP, 3-7
   9. $\forall x(\neg Hx \rightarrow \neg Sx)$     UG, 8

161

| 10. | 1. | ∀x(Ix → ¬Px) | A | (universe: businesses) |
|---|---|---|---|---|
| | 2. | ∀x(Ux → Ix) | A | |
| | 3. | ⎡ Ua | ACP | |
| | 4. | ⎢ Ua → Ia | US, 2 | |
| | 5. | ⎢ Ia | MP, 4, 3 | |
| | 6. | ⎢ Ia → ¬Pa | US, 1 | |
| | 7. | ⎣ ¬Pa | MP, 6, 5 | |
| | 8. | Ua → ¬Pa | CP, 3-7 | |
| | 9. | ∀x(Ux → ¬Px) | UG, 8 | |

| 14. | 1. | ∀x(Sx → ¬¬Hx) | A | (universe: men) |
|---|---|---|---|---|
| | 2. | ∀x(Hx → Rx) | A | |
| | 3. | ⎡ Sa | ACP | |
| | 4. | ⎢ Sa → ¬¬Ha | US, 1 | |
| | 5. | ⎢ ¬¬Ha | MP, 4, 3 | |
| | 6. | ⎢ Ha → Ra | US, 2 | |
| | 7. | ⎢ ¬¬Ha → ¬¬Ra | DN, 6 | |
| | 8. | ⎣ ¬¬Ra | MP, 7, 5 | |
| | 9. | Sa → ¬¬Ra | CP, 3-8 | |
| | 10. | ∀x(Sx → ¬¬Rx) | UG, 9 | |

| 16. | 1. | ∀x((Yx & Lx) → Jx) | A | (universe: animals) |
|---|---|---|---|---|
| | 2. | ∀x((Yx & Jx) → ¬¬Hx) | A | |
| | 3. | ⎡ Ya & La | ACP | |
| | 4. | ⎢ (Ya & La) → Ja | US, 1 | |
| | 5. | ⎢ Ja | MP, 4, 3 | |
| | 6. | ⎢ Ya | S, 3 | |
| | 7. | ⎢ Ya & Ja | C, 6, 5 | |
| | 8. | ⎢ (Ya & Ja) → ¬¬Ha | US, 2 | |
| | 9. | ⎢ ¬¬Ha | MP, 8, 7 | |
| | 10. | ⎣ Ha | DN, 9 | |
| | 11. | (Ya & La) → Ha | CP, 3-10 | |
| | 12. | ∀x((Yx & Lx) → Hx) | UG, 11 | |

| 20. | 1. | ∀x(Wx → Fx) | A | (universe: men) |
|---|---|---|---|---|
| | 2. | ∀x(¬Wx → Hx) | A | |
| | 3. | ⎡ ¬Ha | ACP | |
| | 4. | ⎢ ¬Wa → Ha | US, 2 | |
| | 5. | ⎢ ¬¬Wa | MT, 4, 3 | |
| | 6. | ⎢ Wa → Fa | US, 1 | |
| | 7. | ⎢ Wa | DN, 5 | |
| | 8. | ⎣ Fa | MP, 6, 7 | |
| | 9. | ¬Ha → Fa | CP, 3-8 | |
| | 10. | ¬¬Ha ∨ Fa | DC, 9 | |
| | 11. | Ha ∨ Fa | DN, 10 | |
| | 12. | ∀x(Hx ∨ Fx) | UG, 11 | |

| 22. | 1. | ∀x(Jx → ¬Ox) | A | |
|---|---|---|---|---|
| | 2. | ∀x(Px → ¬¬Ox) | A | |
| | 3. | ⎡ Ja & Pa | AIP | |
| | 4. | ⎢ Ja → ¬Oa | US, 1 | |
| | 5. | ⎢ Ja | S, 3 | |
| | 6. | ⎢ ¬Oa | MP, 4, 5 | |
| | 7. | ⎢ Pa → ¬¬Oa | US, 2 | |
| | 8. | ⎢ Pa | S, 3 | |
| | 9. | ⎢ ¬¬Oa | MP, 7, 8 | |
| | 10. | ⎣ ¬Oa & ¬¬Oa | C, 6, 9 | |

| | 11. | ¬(Ja & Pa) | IP, 3-10 |
|---|---|---|---|
| | 12. | ∀x¬(Jx & Px) | UG, 11 |

| 26. | 1. | ∀x(Tx → ¬Wx) | A |
|---|---|---|---|
| | 2. | ∀x(¬Wx → ¬Cx) | A |
| | 3. | ∀x(¬Tx → ¬Hx) | A |
| | 4. | ⎡ Ca | ACP |
| | 5. | ⎢ ¬Wa → ¬Ca | US, 2 |
| | 6. | ⎢ ¬¬Ca | DN, 4 |
| | 7. | ⎢ ¬¬Wa | MT, 5, 6 |
| | 8. | ⎢ Ta → ¬Wa | US, 1 |
| | 9. | ⎢ ¬Ta | MT, 8, 7 |
| | 10. | ⎢ ¬Ta → ¬Ha | US, 3 |
| | 11. | ⎣ ¬Ha | MP, 10, 9 |
| | 12. | Ca → ¬Ha | CP, 4-11 |
| | 13. | ∀x(Cx → ¬Hx) | UG, 12 |

| 28. | 1. | ∀x(Sx → Tx) | A | (universe: people) |
|---|---|---|---|---|
| | 2. | ∀x(Wx → ¬¬Gx) | A | |
| | 3. | ∀x(Tx → ¬Gx) | A | |
| | 4. | ⎡ Sa | ACP | |
| | 5. | ⎢ Sa → Ta | US, 1 | |
| | 6. | ⎢ Ta | MP, 5, 4 | |
| | 7. | ⎢ Ta → ¬Ga | US, 3 | |
| | 8. | ⎢ ¬Ga | MP, 7, 6 | |
| | 9. | ⎢ Wa → ¬¬Ga | US, 2 | |
| | 10. | ⎢ Wa → Ga | DN, 9 | |
| | 11. | ⎣ ¬Wa | MT, 10, 8 | |
| | 12. | Sa → ¬Wa | CP, 4-11 | |
| | 13. | ∀x(Sx → ¬Wx) | UG, 12 | |

| 32. | 1. | ∀x(¬Sx → Rx) | A | (universe: my ideas) |
|---|---|---|---|---|
| | 2. | ∀x(Bx → ¬Wx) | A | |
| | 3. | ∀x(¬Tx → ¬Sx) | A | |
| | 4. | ∀x(Rx → ¬¬Lx) | A | |
| | 5. | ∀x(Dx → Bx) | A | |
| | 6. | ⎡ ∀x(¬Lx ∨ Wx) | A | |
| | 7. | ⎢ Da | ACP | |
| | 8. | ⎢ Da → Ba | US, 5 | |
| | 9. | ⎢ Ba | MP, 8, 7 | |
| | 10. | ⎢ Ba → ¬Wa | US, 2 | |
| | 11. | ⎢ ¬Wa | MP, 10, 9 | |
| | 12. | ⎢ ¬La ∨ Wa | US, 6 | |
| | 13. | ⎢ ¬La | DS, 12, 11 | |
| | 14. | ⎢ Ra → ¬¬La | US, 4 | |
| | 15. | ⎢ Ra → La | DN, 14 | |
| | 16. | ⎢ ¬Ra | MT, 15, 13 | |
| | 17. | ⎢ ¬Sa → Ra | US, 1 | |
| | 18. | ⎢ ¬¬Sa | MT, 17, 16 | |
| | 19. | ⎢ ¬Ta → ¬Sa | US, 3 | |
| | 20. | ⎢ ¬¬Ta | MT, 19, 18 | |
| | 21. | ⎣ Ta | DN, 20 | |
| | 22. | Da → Ta | CP, 7-21 | |
| | 23. | ∀x(Dx → Tx) | UG, 22 | |

| 34. | 1. | $\forall x(Sx \rightarrow Cx)$ | A | (universe: students) |
|---|---|---|---|---|
| | 2. | $\forall x(Cx \rightarrow Lx)$ | A | |
| | 3. | $\lceil$ Sa | ACP | |
| | 4. | Sa $\rightarrow$ Ca | US, 1 | |
| | 5. | Ca | MP, 4, 3 | |
| | 6. | Ca $\rightarrow$ La | US, 2 | |
| | 7. | $\lfloor$ La | MP, 6, 5 | |
| | 8. | Sa $\rightarrow$ La | CP, 3-7 | |
| | 9. | $\forall x(Sx \rightarrow Lx)$ | UG, 8 | |

| 38. | 1. | $\forall x(\neg Fx \rightarrow Cx)$ | A | (universe: people) |
|---|---|---|---|---|
| | 2. | $\forall x(Cx \rightarrow Dx)$ | A | |
| | 3. | $\lceil$ $\neg$Da | ACP | |
| | 4. | Ca $\rightarrow$ Da | US, 2 | |
| | 5. | $\neg$Ca | MT, 4, 3 | |
| | 6. | $\neg$Fa $\rightarrow$ Ca | US, 1 | |
| | 7. | $\neg\neg$Fa | MT, 6, 5 | |
| | 8. | $\lfloor$ Fa | DN, 7 | |
| | 9. | $\neg$Da $\rightarrow$ Fa | CP, 3-8 | |
| | 10. | $\forall x(\neg Dx \rightarrow Fx)$ | UG, 9 | |

| 40. | 1. | $\forall x((Ix \lor Fx) \rightarrow Dx)$ | A | (universe: people) |
|---|---|---|---|---|
| | 2. | $\forall x(Dx \rightarrow (Bx \& \neg Ox))$ | A | |
| | 3. | $\forall x(Tx \rightarrow Fx)$ | A | |
| | 4. | $\forall x(\neg Cx \rightarrow Ix)$ | A | |
| | 5. | $\lceil$ $\neg$Ba $\lor$ Oa | ACP | |
| | 6. | $\neg$Ba $\lor$ $\neg\neg$Oa | DN, 5 | |
| | 7. | $\neg$(Ba & $\neg$Oa) | DM, 6 | |
| | 8. | Da $\rightarrow$ (Ba & $\neg$Oa) | US, 2 | |
| | 9. | $\neg$Da | MT, 8, 7 | |
| | 10. | (Ia $\lor$ Fa) $\rightarrow$ Da | US, 1 | |
| | 11. | $\neg$(Ia $\lor$ Fa) | MT, 10, 9 | |
| | 12. | $\neg$Ia & $\neg$Fa | DM, 11 | |
| | 13. | $\neg$Ca $\rightarrow$ Ia | US, 4 | |
| | 14. | $\neg$Ia | S, 12 | |
| | 15. | $\neg\neg$Ca | MT, 13, 14 | |
| | 16. | Ca | DN, 15 | |
| | 17. | Ta $\rightarrow$ Fa | US, 3 | |
| | 18. | $\neg$Fa | S, 12 | |
| | 19. | $\neg$Ta | MT, 17, 18 | |
| | 20. | $\lfloor$ Ca & $\neg$Ta | C, 16, 19 | |
| | 21. | ($\neg$Ba $\lor$ Oa) $\rightarrow$ (Ca & $\neg$Ta) | CP, 5-20 | |
| | 22. | $\forall x((\neg Bx \lor Ox) \rightarrow (Cx \& \neg Tx))$ | UG, 21 | |

| 44. | 1. | $\forall x(Fx \leftrightarrow (Gx \& Hx))$ | A | |
|---|---|---|---|---|
| | 2. | Fa $\leftrightarrow$ (Ga & Ha) | US, 1 | |
| | 3. | $\lceil$ Fa | ACP | |
| | 4. | Ga & Ha | MB, 2, 3 | |
| | 5. | $\lfloor$ Ga | S, 4 | |
| | 6. | Fa $\rightarrow$ Ga | CP, 3-5 | |
| | 7. | $\forall x(Fx \rightarrow Gx)$ | UG, 6 | |
| | 8. | $\lceil$ Fa | ACP | |
| | 9. | Ga & Ha | MB, 2, 8 | |
| | 10. | $\lfloor$ Ha | S, 9 | |
| | 11. | Fa $\rightarrow$ Ha | CP, 8-10 | |
| | 12. | $\forall x(Fx \rightarrow Hx)$ | UG, 11 | |
| | 13. | $\forall x(Fx \rightarrow Gx)$ & $\forall x(Fx \rightarrow Hx)$ | C, 7, 12 | |

| | | | |
|---|---|---|---|
| 46. | 1. | ∀x(Fx → Hx) | A |
| | 2. | ∀x(Gx → Hx) | A |
| | 3. | ⌐ Fa ∨ Ga | ACP |
| | 4. | │ Fa → Ha | US, 1 |
| | 5. | │ Ga → Ha | US, 2 |
| | 6. | └ Ha | CD, 3, 4, 5 |
| | 7. | (Fa ∨ Ga) → Ha | CP, 3-6 |
| | 8. | ∀x((Fx ∨ Gx) → Hx) | UG, 7 |

| | | | |
|---|---|---|---|
| 50. | 1. | ∀x(Fx ↔ (¬Gx ↔ ¬Fx)) | A |
| | 2. | Fa ↔ (¬Ga ↔ ¬Fa) | US, 1 |
| | 3. | ⌐ ¬Ga | AIP |
| | 4. | │⌐ ¬Fa | AIP |
| | 5. | ││ ¬(¬Ga ↔ ¬Fa) | MB, 2, 4 |
| | 6. | ││ ¬Ga ↔ ¬¬Fa | NB, 5 |
| | 7. | ││ ¬¬Fa | MB, 6, 3 |
| | 8. | │└ ¬Fa & ¬¬Fa | C, 4, 7 |
| | 9. | │ Fa | IP, 4-8 |
| | 10. | │ ¬Ga ↔ ¬Fa | MB, 2, 9 |
| | 11. | │ ¬Fa | MB, 10, 3 |
| | 12. | └ Fa & ¬Fa | C, 9, 11 |
| | 13. | Ga | IP, 3-12 |
| | 14. | ∀xGx | UG, 13 |

| | | | |
|---|---|---|---|
| 52. | 1. | ∀x((Fx & Gx) → Hx) | A |
| | 2. | ∀xGx & ∀xFx | A |
| | 3. | ∀xFx | S, 2 |
| | 4. | Fa | US, 3 |
| | 5. | ∀xGx | S, 2 |
| | 6. | Ga | US, 5 |
| | 7. | (Fa & Ga) → Ha | US, 1 |
| | 8. | Fa & Ga | C, 4, 6 |
| | 9. | Ha | MP, 7, 8 |
| | 10. | Fa & Ha | C, 4, 9 |
| | 11. | ∀x(Fx & Hx) | UG, 10 |

| | | | |
|---|---|---|---|
| 56. | 1. | ∀x∀y(Fxy → Fyx) | A |
| | 2. | ∀y(Fay → Fya) | US, 1 |
| | 3. | Fab → Fba | US, 2 |
| | 4. | ∀y(Fby → Fyb) | US, 1 |
| | 5. | Fba → Fab | US, 4 |
| | 6. | Fab ↔ Fba | B, 3, 5 |
| | 7. | ∀y(Fay ↔ Fya) | UG, 6 |
| | 8. | ∀x∀y(Fxy ↔ Fyx) | UG, 7 |

| | | | |
|---|---|---|---|
| 58. | 1. | ∀x∀y(Fxy ∨ Fyx) | A |
| | 2. | ∀x∀y(Fxy → Fyx) | A |
| | 3. | ∀y(Fay ∨ Fya) | US, 1 |
| | 4. | Fab ∨ Fba | US, 3 |
| | 5. | ∀y(Fay → Fya) | US, 2 |
| | 6. | Fab → Fba | US, 5 |
| | 7. | ⌐ Fba | ACP |
| | 8. | Fba → Fba | CP, 7 |
| | 9. | Fba | CD, 4, 6, 8 |
| | 10. | ∀yFby | UG, 9 |
| | 11. | ∀x∀yFxy | UG, 10 |

| 62. | 1. | $\forall x \forall y \forall z((Fxy \ \& \ Fyz) \rightarrow Fxz)$ | A |
| | 2. | $\forall x \forall y(Fxy \rightarrow Fyx)$ | A |
| | 3. | $\exists x \exists y Fxy$ | A |
| | 4. | $\exists y Fay$ | ES, 3 |
| | 5. | Fab | ES, 4 |
| | 6. | $\forall y(Fay \rightarrow Fya)$ | US, 2 |
| | 7. | $Fab \rightarrow Fba$ | US, 6 |
| | 8. | Fba | MP, 7, 5 |
| | 9. | $\forall y \forall z((Fay \ \& \ Fyz) \rightarrow Faz)$ | US, 1 |
| | 10. | $\forall z((Fab \ \& \ Fbz) \rightarrow Faz)$ | US, 9 |
| | 11. | $(Fab \ \& \ Fba) \rightarrow Faa$ | US, 10 |
| | 12. | Fab & Fba | C, 5, 8 |
| | 13. | Faa | MP, 11, 12 |
| | 14. | $\exists x Fxx$ | EG, 13 |

| 64. | 1. | $\forall x \forall y \forall z((Fxy \ \& \ Fxz) \rightarrow Fyz)$ | A |
| | 2. | $\forall x \forall y(Fxy \rightarrow Fyx)$ | A |
| | 3. | $\forall x Fxx$ | A |
| | 4. | ⌈ Fab & Fbc | ACP |
| | 5. | │ $\forall y(Fay \rightarrow Fya)$ | US, 2 |
| | 6. | │ $Fab \rightarrow Fba$ | US, 5 |
| | 7. | │ Fab | S, 4 |
| | 8. | │ Fba | MP, 6, 7 |
| | 9. | │ Fbc | S, 4 |
| | 10. | │ Fba & Fbc | C, 8, 9 |
| | 11. | │ $\forall y \forall z((Fby \ \& \ Fbz) \rightarrow Fyz)$ | US, 1 |
| | 12. | │ $\forall z((Fba \ \& \ Fbz) \rightarrow Faz)$ | US, 11 |
| | 13. | │ $(Fba \ \& \ Fbc) \rightarrow Fac$ | US, 12 |
| | 14. | ⌊ Fac | MP, 13, 10 |
| | 15. | $(Fab \ \& \ Fbc) \rightarrow Fac$ | CP, 4-14 |
| | 16. | $\forall z((Fab \ \& \ Fbz) \rightarrow Faz)$ | UG, 15 |
| | 17. | $\forall y \forall z((Fay \ \& \ Fyz) \rightarrow Faz)$ | UG, 16 |
| | 18. | $\forall x \forall y \forall z((Fxy \ \& \ Fyz) \rightarrow Fxz)$ | UG, 17 |

## B.3 FORMULAS WITH OVERLAPPING QUANTIFIERS

| 6. | 1. | $\forall x \forall y \exists z(Fxz \ \& \ Fzy)$ | A |
| | 2. | $\forall x \forall y(Fxy \rightarrow Gyx)$ | A |
| | 3. | $\forall y \exists z(Faz \ \& \ Fzy)$ | US, 1 |
| | 4. | $\exists z(Faz \ \& \ Fzb)$ | US, 3 |
| | 5. | Fac & Fcb | ES, 4 |
| | 6. | $\forall y(Fay \rightarrow Gya)$ | US, 2 |
| | 7. | $Fac \rightarrow Gca$ | US, 6 |
| | 8. | Fac | S, 5 |
| | 9. | Gca | MP, 7, 8 |
| | 10. | $\forall y(Fcy \rightarrow Gyc)$ | US, 2 |
| | 11. | $Fcb \rightarrow Gbc$ | US, 10 |
| | 12. | Fcb | S, 5 |
| | 13. | Gbc | MP, 11, 12 |
| | 14. | Gca & Gbc | C, 9, 13 |
| | 15. | $\forall z(Gca \ \& \ Gzc)$ | UG, 14 (Wrong!) |
| | 16. | $\forall y \forall z(Gcy \ \& \ Gzc)$ | UG, 15 (Wrong!) |
| | 17. | $\exists x \forall y \forall z(Gxy \ \& \ Gzx)$ | EG, 16 |

| | | | | |
|---|---|---|---|---|
| 8. | 1. | $\forall x(Fx \rightarrow \forall y(Gy \rightarrow Hxy))$ | A | |
| | 2. | $\exists x(Fx \ \& \ \exists y\neg Hxy)$ | A | |
| | 3. | Fa & $\exists y\neg$Hay | ES, 2 | (a) |
| | 4. | $\exists y\neg$Hay | S, 3 | \| |
| | 5. | $\neg$Hab | ES, 4 | (b) |
| | 6. | Fa $\rightarrow \forall y(Gy \rightarrow$ Hay) | US, 1 | |
| | 7. | Fa | S, 3 | |
| | 8. | $\forall y(Gy \rightarrow$ Hay) | MP, 6, 7 | |
| | 9. | Gb $\rightarrow$ Hab | US, 8 | |
| | 10. | $\neg$Gb | MT, 9, 5 | |
| | 11. | $\exists x\neg Gx$ | EG, 10 | |

| | | | | |
|---|---|---|---|---|
| 10. | 1. | $\forall x(\exists y Fxy \rightarrow \exists y\neg Gy)$ | A | |
| | 2. | $\exists x\exists y Fxy$ | A | |
| | 3. | $\forall x(Gx \leftrightarrow \neg Hx)$ | A | |
| | 4. | $\exists y Fay$ | ES, 2 | (a) |
| | 5. | $\exists y Fay \rightarrow \exists y\neg Gy$ | US, 1 | |
| | 6. | $\exists y\neg Gy$ | MP, 5, 4 | |
| | 7. | $\neg$Gb | ES, 6 | |
| | 8. | Gb $\leftrightarrow \neg$Hb | US, 3 | |
| | 9. | $\neg\neg$Hb | MB, 8, 7 | |
| | 10. | Hb | DN, 9 | |
| | 11. | $\exists x Hx$ | EG, 10 | |

| | | | | |
|---|---|---|---|---|
| 14. | 1. | $\exists x\forall y\neg Fxy$ | A | |
| | 2. | $\forall y\neg$Fay | ES, 1 | (a) |
| | 3. | $\neg$Fab | US, 2 | |
| | 4. | $\neg$Fab $\vee$ Fbc | Ad, 3 | |
| | 5. | Fab $\rightarrow$ Fbc | DC, 4 | |
| | 6. | $\forall z(Faz \rightarrow Fzc)$ | UG, 5 | |
| | 7. | $\forall y\forall z(Faz \rightarrow Fzy)$ | UG, 6 | |
| | 8. | $\exists x\forall y\forall z(Fxz \rightarrow Fzy)$ | EG, 7 | |

| | | | | |
|---|---|---|---|---|
| 16. | 1. | $\forall x(\exists y(Ay \ \& \ Bxy) \rightarrow Cx)$ | A | |
| | 2. | $\exists y(Dy \ \& \ \exists x((Fx \ \& \ Gx) \ \& \ Byx))$ | A | |
| | 3. | $\forall x(Fx \rightarrow Ax)$ | A | |
| | 4. | $\exists x(Cx \ \& \ Dx) \rightarrow (\exists y(Dy \ \& \ \exists z Byz) \rightarrow \forall x Fx)$ | A | |
| | 5. | Da & $\exists x((Fx \ \& \ Gx) \ \& \ Bax)$ | ES, 2 | (a) |
| | 6. | $\exists x((Fx \ \& \ Gx) \ \& \ Bax)$ | S, 5 | \| |
| | 7. | (Fb & Gb) & Bab | ES, 6 | (b) |
| | 8. | Fb & Gb | S, 7 | |
| | 9. | Fb $\rightarrow$ Ab | US, 3 | |
| | 10. | Fb | S, 8 | |
| | 11. | Ab | MP, 9, 10 | |
| | 12. | Bab | S, 7 | |
| | 13. | Ab & Bab | C, 11, 12 | |
| | 14. | $\exists y(Ay \ \& \ Bay) \rightarrow$ Ca | US, 1 | |
| | 15. | $\exists y(Ay \ \& \ Bay)$ | EG, 13 | |
| | 16. | Ca | MP, 14, 15 | |
| | 17. | Da | S, 5 | |
| | 18. | Ca & Da | C, 16, 17 | |
| | 19. | $\exists x(Cx \ \& \ Dx)$ | EG, 18 | |
| | 20. | $\exists y(Dy \ \& \ \exists z Byz) \rightarrow \forall x Fx$ | MP, 4, 19 | |
| | 21. | $\exists z Baz$ | EG, 12 | |
| | 22. | Da & $\exists z Baz$ | C, 17, 21 | |
| | 23. | $\exists y(Dy \ \& \ \exists z Byz)$ | EG, 22 | |
| | 24. | $\forall x Fx$ | MP, 20, 23 | |

| 25. | Fc → Ac | US, 3 |
| 26. | Fc | US, 24 |
| 27. | Ac | MP, 25, 26 |
| 28. | ∀xAx | UG, 27 |

## B.4  Derived Rules for Quantifiers

8.
| | 1. | ∀x(Ax → ∀y(Ty → Oxy)) | A | (universe: people) |
| | 2. | ¬∃x(Tx & Oxx) | A | |
| | 3. | ∃x(Tx & Ax) | AIP | |
| | 4. | Ta & Aa | ES, 3 | ⓐ |
| | 5. | ∀x¬(Tx & Oxx) | QN, 2 | |
| | 6. | ¬(Ta & Oaa) | US, 5 | |
| | 7. | Aa → ∀y(Ty → Oay) | US, 1 | |
| | 8. | Aa | S, 4 | |
| | 9. | ∀y(Ty → Oay) | MP, 7, 8 | |
| | 10. | Ta → Oaa | US, 9 | |
| | 11. | Ta | S, 4 | |
| | 12. | Oaa | MP, 10, 11 | |
| | 13. | Ta & Oaa | C, 11, 12 | |
| | 14. | (Ta & Oaa) & ¬(Ta & Oaa) | C, 13, 6 | |
| | 15. | ¬∃x(Tx & Ax) | IP, 3-14 | |

10.
| | 1. | ∀x(Ax ↔ (∃yPy → Px) | A | |
| | 2. | ¬∃xAx | AIP | |
| | 3. | ∀x¬Ax | QN, 2 | |
| | 4. | Aa ↔ (∃yPy → Pa) | US, 1 | |
| | 5. | ¬Aa | US, 3 | |
| | 6. | ¬(∃yPy → Pa) | MB, 4, 5 | |
| | 7. | ∃yPy & ¬Pa | NC, 6 | |
| | 8. | ∃yPy | S, 7 | |
| | 9. | Pb | ES, 8 | ⓑ |
| | 10. | ¬∃yPy ∨ Pb | Ad, 9 | |
| | 11. | Ab ↔ (∃yPy → Pb) | US, 1 | |
| | 12. | ∃yPy → Pb | DC, 10 | |
| | 13. | Ab | MB, 11, 12 | |
| | 14. | ¬Ab | US, 3 | |
| | 15. | Ab & ¬Ab | C, 13, 14 | |
| | 16. | ∃xAx | IP, 2-15 | |

14.
| | 1. | ∀x∃y(Fx → Gy) | A | |
| | 2. | ¬∃y∀x(Fx → Gy) | AIP | |
| | 3. | ∀y∃x¬(Fx → Gy) | QN², 2 | a |
| | 4. | ∃x¬(Fx → Ga) | US, 3 | | |
| | 5. | ¬(Fb → Ga) | ES, 4 | b |
| | 6. | Fb & ¬Ga | NC, 5 | | |
| | 7. | ∃y(Fb → Gy) | US, 1 | | |
| | 8. | Fb → Gc | ES, 7 | c |
| | 9. | Fb | S, 6 | | |
| | 10. | Gc | MP, 8, 9 | | |
| | 11. | ∃x¬(Fx → Gc) | US, 3 | | |
| | 12. | ¬(Fd → Gc) | ES, 11 | d |
| | 13. | Fd & ¬Gc | NC, 12 | |
| | 14. | ¬Gc | S, 13 | |
| | 15. | Gc & ¬Gc | C, 10, 14 | |
| | 16. | ∃y∀x(Fx → Gy) | IP, 2-15 | |

168

16. 
| | | | |
|---|---|---|---|
| 1. | ∃xFx → ∃xGx | A | |
| 2. | ⌐¬∃x(Fx → Gx) | AIP | |
| 3. | ∀x¬(Fx → Gx) | QN, 2 | |
| 4. | ¬(Fa → Ga) | US, 3 | |
| 5. | Fa & ¬Ga | NC, 4 | |
| 6. | Fa | S, 5 | |
| 7. | ∃xFx | EG, 6 | |
| 8. | ∃xGx | MP, 1, 7 | |
| 9. | Gb | ES, 8 | ⓑ |
| 10. | ¬Fb ∨ Gb | Ad, 9 | |
| 11. | Fb → Gb | DC, 10 | |
| 12. | ∃x(Fx → Gx) | EG, 11 | |
| 13. | ∟∃x(Fx → Gx) & ¬∃x(Fx → Gx) | C, 12, 2 | |
| 14. | ∃x(Fx → Gx) | IP, 2-13 | |

20.
| | | | |
|---|---|---|---|
| 1. | ∃xFx → ∀y(Gy → Hy) | A | |
| 2. | ∃xJx → ∃xGx | A | |
| 3. | ⌐∃x(Fx & Jx) | ACP | |
| 4. | Fa & Ja | ES, 3 | ⓐ |
| 5. | Ja | S, 4 | |
| 6. | ∃xJx | EG, 5 | |
| 7. | ∃xGx | MP, 2, 6 | |
| 8. | Gb | ES, 7 | ⓑ |
| 9. | Fa | S, 4 | |
| 10. | ∃xFx | EG, 9 | |
| 11. | ∀y(Gy → Hy) | MP, 1, 10 | |
| 12. | Gb → Hb | US, 11 | |
| 13. | Hb | MP, 12, 8 | |
| 14. | ∟∃zHz | EG, 13 | |
| 15. | ∃x(Fx & Jx) → ∃zHz | CP, 3-14 | |

22.
| | | |
|---|---|---|
| 1. | ∀x(∃yFyx → ∀zFxz) | A |
| 2. | ⌐Fba | ACP |
| 3. | ∃yFya → ∀zFaz | US, 1 |
| 4. | ∃yFya | EG, 2 |
| 5. | ∀zFaz | MP, 3, 4 |
| 6. | ∟Fab | US, 5 |
| 7. | Fba → Fab | CP, 2-6 |
| 8. | ∀x(Fbx → Fxb) | UG, 7 |
| 9. | ∀y∀x(Fyx → Fxy) | UG, 8 |

26.
| | | | |
|---|---|---|---|
| 1. | ∀x(Fx → ∀y(Gy → Hxy)) | A | |
| 2. | ∀x(Dx → ∀y(Hxy → Cy)) | A | |
| 3. | ⌐ ∃x(Fx & Dx) | ACP | |
| 4. | ⌐Ga | ACP | |
| 5. | Fb & Db | ES, 3 | ⓑ |
| 6. | Fb → ∀y(Gy → Hby) | US, 1 | |
| 7. | Fb | S, 5 | |
| 8. | ∀y(Gy → Hby) | MP, 6, 7 | |
| 9. | Ga → Hba | US, 8 | |
| 10. | Hba | MP, 9, 4 | |
| 11. | Db → ∀y(Hby → Cy) | US, 2 | |
| 12. | Db | S, 5 | |
| 13. | ∀y(Hby → Cy) | MP, 11, 12 | |
| 14. | Hba → Ca | US, 13 | |
| 15. | ∟Ca | MP, 14, 10 | |

|  |  |  |  |
|---|---|---|---|
| 16. | Ga → Ca | CP, 4-15 | |
| 17. | ∀y(Gy → Cy) | UG, 16 | |
| 18. | ∃x(Fx & Dx) → ∀y(Gy → Cy) | CP, 3-17 | |

28.
| 1. | ∀x∀y(Gxy ↔ (Fy → Hx)) | A | |
|---|---|---|---|
| 2. | ∀zGaz | A | |
| 3. | ∃xFx | ACP | |
| 4. | Fb | ES, 3 | (b) |
| 5. | ∀y(Gay ↔ (Fy → Ha)) | US, 1 | |
| 6. | Gab ↔ (Fb → Ha) | US, 5 | |
| 7. | Gab | US, 2 | |
| 8. | Fb → Ha | MB, 6, 7 | |
| 9. | Ha | MP, 8, 4 | |
| 10. | ∃xHx | EG, 9 | |
| 11. | ∃xFx → ∃xHx | CP, 3-10 | |

32.
| 1. | ∃x(Fx & ∀y(Gy → Hy)) | A | |
|---|---|---|---|
| 2. | ∀x(Fx → (¬Lx → ¬∃z(Kz & Hz))) | A | |
| 3. | ∃x(Kx & Gx) | ACP | |
| 4. | Ka & Ga | ES, 3 | (a) |
| 5. | Fb & ∀y(Gy → Hy) | ES, 1 | (b) |
| 6. | Fb → (¬Lb → ¬∃z(Kz & Hz)) | US, 2 | |
| 7. | Fb | S, 5 | |
| 8. | ¬Lb → ¬∃z(Kz & Hz) | MP, 6, 7 | |
| 9. | ∀y(Gy → Hy) | S, 5 | |
| 10. | Ga → Ha | US, 9 | |
| 11. | Ga | S, 4 | |
| 12. | Ha | MP, 10, 11 | |
| 13. | Ka | S, 4 | |
| 14. | Ka & Ha | C, 13, 12 | |
| 15. | ∃z(Kz & Hz) | EG, 14 | |
| 16. | ¬¬∃z(Kz & Hz) | DN, 15 | |
| 17. | ¬¬Lb | MT, 8, 16 | |
| 18. | Lb | DN, 17 | |
| 19. | ∃xLx | EG, 18 | |
| 20. | ∃x(Kx & Gx) → ∃xLx | CP, 3-19 | |

34.
| 1. | ¬∀x(Hx ∨ Kx) | A | |
|---|---|---|---|
| 2. | ∀x((Fx ∨ ¬Kx) → Gxx) | A | |
| 3. | ∃x¬(Hx ∨ Kx) | QN, 1 | |
| 4. | ¬(Ha ∨ Ka) | ES, 3 | (a) |
| 5. | ¬Ha & ¬Ka | DM, 4 | |
| 6. | ¬Ka | S, 5 | |
| 7. | (Fa ∨ ¬Ka) → Gaa | US, 2 | |
| 8. | Fa ∨ ¬Ka | Ad, 6 | |
| 9. | Gaa | MP, 7, 8 | |
| 10. | ∃xGxx | EG, 9 | |

38.
| 1. | ∀x∀y∀z((Fxy & Fyz) → Fxz) | A | |
|---|---|---|---|
| 2. | ¬∃xFxx | A | |
| 3. | ∀y∀z((Fay & Fyz) → Faz) | US, 1 | |
| 4. | ∀z((Fab & Fbz) → Faz) | US, 3 | |
| 5. | (Fab & Fba) → Faa | US, 4 | |
| 6. | ∀x¬Fxx | QN, 2 | |
| 7. | ¬Faa | US, 6 | |
| 8. | ¬(Fab & Fba) | MT, 5, 7 | |
| 9. | ¬Fab ∨ ¬Fba | DM, 8 | |

| | | | |
|---|---|---|---|
| | 10. | Fab → ¬Fba | DC, 9 |
| | 11. | ∀y(Fay → ¬Fya) | UG, 10 |
| | 12. | ∀x∀y(Fxy → ¬Fyx) | UG, 11 |

| | | | |
|---|---|---|---|
| 40. | 1. | Fa → (∃xGx → Gb) | A |
| | 2. | ∀x(Gx → Hx) | A |
| | 3. | ∀x(¬Jx → ¬Hx) | A |
| | 4. | ¬Jb | ACP |
| | 5. | Fa | ACP |
| | 6. | ¬Jb → ¬Hb | US, 3 |
| | 7. | ¬Hb | MP, 6, 4 |
| | 8. | Gb → Hb | US, 2 |
| | 9. | ¬Gb | MT, 8, 7 |
| | 10. | ∃xGx → Gb | MP, 1, 5 |
| | 11. | ¬∃xGx | MT, 10, 9 |
| | 13. | ∀x¬Gx | QN, 11 |
| | 14. | Fa → ∀x¬Gx | CP, 5-13 |
| | 15. | ¬Fa v ∀x¬Gx | DC, 14 |
| | 16. | ¬Jb → (¬Fa v ∀x¬Gx) | CP, 4-15 |

| | | | |
|---|---|---|---|
| 44. | 1. | ∀x¬Fxc → ∃xGxb | A |
| | 2. | ¬∃x(¬Fxc → Gxb) | AIP |
| | 3. | ∀x¬(¬Fxc → Gxb) | QN, 2 |
| | 4. | ¬(¬Fac → Gab) | US, 3 |
| | 5. | ¬Fac & ¬Gab | NC, 4 |
| | 6. | ¬Fac | S, 5 |
| | 7. | ∀x¬Fxc | UG, 6 |
| | 8. | ∃xGxb | MP, 1, 7 |
| | 9. | ¬Gab | S, 5 |
| | 10. | ∀x¬Gxb | UG, 9 |
| | 11. | ¬∃xGxb | QN, 10 |
| | 12. | ∃xGxb & ¬∃xGxb | C, 8, 11 |
| | 13. | ∃x(¬Fxc → Gxb) | IP, 2-12 |

| | | | |
|---|---|---|---|
| 46. | 1. | ∃x(Px & ¬Mx) → ∀y(Py → Ly) | A |
| | 2. | ∃x(Px & Nx) | A |
| | 3. | ∀x(Px → ¬Lx) | A |
| | 4. | Pa & Na | ES, 2 (a) |
| | 5. | Pa → ¬La | US, 3 |
| | 6. | Pa | S, 4 |
| | 7. | ¬La | MP, 5, 6 |
| | 8. | Pa & ¬La | C, 6, 7 |
| | 9. | ¬(Pa → La) | NC, 8 |
| | 10. | ∃y¬(Py → Ly) | EG, 9 |
| | 11. | ¬∀y(Py → Ly) | QN, 10 |
| | 12. | ¬∃x(Px & ¬Mx) | MT, 1, 11 |
| | 13. | ∀x¬(Px & ¬Mx) | QN, 12 |
| | 14. | ¬(Pa & ¬Ma) | US, 13 |
| | 15. | ¬Pa v ¬¬Ma | DM, 14 |
| | 16. | ¬Pa v Ma | DN, 15 |
| | 17. | ¬¬Pa | DN, 6 |
| | 18. | Ma | DS, 16, 17 |
| | 19. | Na | S, 4 |
| | 20. | Na & Ma | C, 19, 18 |
| | 21. | ∃x(Nx & Mx) | EG, 20 |

| 50. | 1. | $\forall x(Cx \rightarrow Fx)$ | A |
|-----|-----|---------------------------------|---|
|     | 2. | ⌐Pa & $\exists y(Cy \& Day)$ | ACP |
|     | 3. | $\exists y(Cy \& Day)$ | S, 2 |
|     | 4. | Cb & Dab | ES, 3 |
|     | 5. | Cb $\rightarrow$ Fb | US, 1 |
|     | 6. | Cb | S, 4 |
|     | 7. | Fb | MP, 5, 6 |
|     | 8. | Dab | S, 4 |
|     | 9. | Fb & Dab | C, 7, 8 |
|     | 10. | ⌊$\exists y(Fy \& Day)$ | EG, 9 |
|     | 11. | $(Pa \& \exists y(Cy \& Day)) \rightarrow \exists y(Fy \& Day)$ | CP, 2-10 |
|     | 12. | $\forall x((Px \& \exists y(Cy \& Dxy)) \rightarrow \exists z(Fz \& Dxz))$ | UG, 11 |

| 52. | 1. | Pmj | A | (universe: people) |
|-----|-----|-----|---|---|
|     | 2. | $\exists x(Pxm \& Tx)$ | A | |
|     | 3. | $\neg Tj$ | A | |
|     | 4. | ⌐$\forall x(\exists y(Pyx \& Ty) \rightarrow Tx)$ | AIP | |
|     | 5. | $\exists y(Pym \& Ty) \rightarrow Tm$ | US, 4 | |
|     | 6. | $\exists y(Pym \& Ty)$ | VR, 2 | |
|     | 7. | Tm | MP, 5, 6 | |
|     | 8. | Pmj & Tm | C, 1, 7 | |
|     | 9. | $\exists y(Pyj \& Ty) \rightarrow Tj$ | US, 4 | |
|     | 10. | $\exists y(Pyj \& Ty)$ | EG, 8 | |
|     | 11. | Tj | MP, 9, 10 | |
|     | 12. | ⌊Tj & $\neg Tj$ | C, 11, 3 | |
|     | 13. | $\neg \forall x(\exists y(Pyx \& Ty) \rightarrow Tx)$ | IP, 4-12 | |

| 54. | 1. | $\forall x(\forall y(Oay \rightarrow Oxy) \rightarrow Oax)$ | A | (universe: people) |
|-----|-----|-----|---|---|
|     | 2. | $\forall y(Oay \rightarrow Oay) \rightarrow Oaa$ | US, 1 | |
|     | 3. | ⌐Oab | ACP | |
|     | 4. | Oab $\rightarrow$ Oab | CP, 3 | |
|     | 5. | $\forall y(Oay \rightarrow Oay)$ | UG, 4 | |
|     | 6. | Oaa | MP, 2, 5 | |

| 56. | 1. | $\forall x(Fx \rightarrow \forall y(Sy \rightarrow Axy))$ | A | (universe: people) |
|-----|-----|-----|---|---|
|     | 2. | $\forall x \forall y((Sx \& Axy) \rightarrow Cy)$ | A | |
|     | 3. | ⌐Fa & Sa | ACP | |
|     | 4. | Fa $\rightarrow \forall y(Sy \rightarrow Aay)$ | US, 1 | |
|     | 5. | Fa | S, 3 | |
|     | 6. | $\forall y(Sy \rightarrow Aay)$ | MP, 4, 5 | |
|     | 7. | Sa $\rightarrow$ Aaa | US, 6 | |
|     | 8. | Sa | S, 3 | |
|     | 9. | Aaa | MP, 7, 8 | |
|     | 10. | $\forall y((Sa \& Aay) \rightarrow Cy)$ | US, 2 | |
|     | 11. | $(Sa \& Aaa) \rightarrow Ca$ | US, 10 | |
|     | 12. | Sa & Aaa | C, 8, 9 | |
|     | 13. | ⌊Ca | MP, 11, 12 | |
|     | 14. | (Fa & Sa) $\rightarrow$ Ca | CP, 3-13 | |
|     | 15. | $\forall x((Fx \& Sx) \rightarrow Cx)$ | UG, 14 | |

| 58. | 1. | $\forall x \forall y (Lyx \rightarrow Lxy)$ | A | (universe: people) |
|     | 2. | $\forall x (Wx \leftrightarrow \forall yLxy)$ | A | |
|     | 3. | $\forall x (Wx \rightarrow \exists yTyx)$ | A | |
|     | 4. | $\exists x \forall y \neg Tyx$ | A | |
|     | 5. | $\forall y \neg Tya$ | ES, 4 | |
|     | 6. | $Wa \rightarrow \exists yTya$ | US, 3 | |
|     | 7. | $\neg \exists yTya$ | QN, 5 | |
|     | 8. | $\neg Wa$ | MT, 6, 7 | |
|     | 9. | $Wa \leftrightarrow \forall yLay$ | US, 2 | |
|     | 10. | $\neg \forall yLay$ | MB, 9, 8 | |
|     | 11. | $\exists y \neg Lay$ | QN, 10 | |
|     | 12. | $\exists x \exists y \neg Lxy$ | EG, 11 | |

| 60. | 1. | $\forall xKax$ | A | (universe: people) |
|     | 2. | $\forall x (Dxl \leftrightarrow Cx)$ | A | |
|     | 3. | $\forall x (\neg Cx \rightarrow \neg Kxx)$ | A | |
|     | 4. | $Kaa$ | US, 1 | |
|     | 5. | $\neg Ca \rightarrow \neg Kaa$ | US, 3 | |
|     | 6. | $\neg \neg Kaa$ | DN, 4 | |
|     | 7. | $\neg \neg Ca$ | MT, 5, 6 | |
|     | 8. | $Dal \leftrightarrow Ca$ | US, 2 | |
|     | 9. | $Ca$ | DN, 7 | |
|     | 10. | $Dal$ | MB, 8, 9 | |

173

# DEDUCTION:
## STYLE THREE

# A: SENTENTIAL LOGIC

This appendix presents a deduction system that differs from those of Chapters 8, 13, and Appendix I. It has two complex rules--conditional and indirect proof--that emerge as important proof methods. The system's most unusual feature is its use of *Show* lines. First developed by Kalish and Montague, the technique simplifies deduction rules and strategies considerably. It yields proofs that are easy to read, construct, and understand, and that approximate closely the structure of real mathematical arguments.

## 1. KEY DEFINITIONS

A *natural deduction system* is a set of rules: specifically, *rules of inference*, which allow us to derive formulas from other formulas. *Proofs* are extended arguments. There are two kinds of proofs. *Hypothetical* proofs begin with *assumptions* (or *hypotheses*). *Categorical* proofs use no assumptions. A *proof* in a natural deduction system is a series of *lines*. On each line appears a formula. Each formula in a proof (a) is an assumption, (b) occurs on a *Show* line, or (c) derives from formulas on previously established lines by a rule of inference. In the system of this chapter, the formula on the topmost *Show* line of a proof is its conclusion; the proof *proves* that formula *from* the assumptions. Formulas proved from no assumptions at all are *theorems* of the system.

**Hypothetical Proof**
Assumptions
~~Show~~ Conclusion

$$\left[ \begin{array}{c} \cdot \\ \cdot \\ \cdot \end{array} \right.$$

**Categorical Proof**
~~Show~~ Conclusion (Theorem)

$$\left[ \begin{array}{c} \cdot \\ \cdot \\ \cdot \end{array} \right.$$

Rules of inference are either *simple* or *complex*. Simple rules allow us to derive formulas of certain kinds in a proof if other formulas of certain kinds occupy already-established lines there. Complex rules allow us to derive a formula of a certain kind in a proof if we've completed some other proof. A proof appearing within another is *subordinate* to it. The larger, *superordinate* proof uses the subordinate proof's information by means of a complex rule.

Any line we can use in a proof at a given point is *free* at that point. In sentential logic, every line is free, except (1) lines beginning with an uncanceled *Show*; and (2) lines imprisoned within a bracket.

# 2. SUMMARY OF RULES

*Proof Methods*

Direct Proof

n.          ~~Show~~ $\mathcal{A}$

$\begin{array}{ll} \text{n.} & \\ \cdot & \\ \cdot & \\ \cdot & \\ \text{n+m.} & \mathcal{A} \end{array}$

Indirect Proof

$\begin{array}{lll} \text{n.} & \text{~~Show~~} \neg\mathcal{A} & \\ \text{n+1.} & \mathcal{A} & \text{AIP} \\ \cdot & \cdot & \cdot \\ \cdot & \cdot & \cdot \\ \text{n+p.} & \mathcal{B} & \\ \text{n+q.} & \neg\mathcal{B} & \end{array}$

Indirect proof (extended)

$\begin{array}{lll} \text{n.} & \text{~~Show~~} \mathcal{A} & \\ \text{n+1.} & \neg\mathcal{A} & \text{AIP} \\ \cdot & \cdot & \cdot \\ \cdot & \cdot & \cdot \\ \text{p.} & \mathcal{B} & \\ \text{q.} & \neg\mathcal{B} & \end{array}$

Conditional Proof

$\begin{array}{lll} \text{n.} & \text{~~Show~~} \mathcal{A} \rightarrow \mathcal{B} & \\ \text{n+1.} & \mathcal{A} & \text{ACP} \\ \cdot & \cdot & \cdot \\ \cdot & \cdot & \cdot \\ \text{n+p.} & \mathcal{B} & \end{array}$

*Basic Rules, Applying Only to Entire Formulas*

Assumption (A)

n.          $\mathcal{A}$          A

Here line <u>n</u> must precede the first *Show* line in the proof.

Conjunction Exploitation (&E)

$\begin{array}{lll} \text{n.} & \underline{\mathcal{A} \,\&\, \mathcal{B}} & \\ \text{n+m.} & \mathcal{A} \quad \text{(or } \mathcal{B}) & \&\text{E, n} \end{array}$

Reiteration (R)

$\begin{array}{lll} \text{n.} & \mathcal{A} & \\ \text{n+p.} & \mathcal{A} & \text{R, n} \end{array}$

Conjunction Introduction (&I)

$\begin{array}{lll} \text{n.} & \mathcal{A} & \\ \text{m.} & \underline{\mathcal{B}} & \\ \text{p.} & \mathcal{A} \,\&\, \mathcal{B} & \&\text{I, n, m} \end{array}$

Conditional Exploitation (→E)

$\begin{array}{lll} \text{n.} & \mathcal{A} \rightarrow \mathcal{B} & \\ \text{m.} & \underline{\mathcal{A}} & \\ \text{p.} & \mathcal{B} & \rightarrow\text{E, n, m} \end{array}$

Biconditional Introduction (↔I)

$\begin{array}{lll} \text{n.} & \mathcal{A} \rightarrow \mathcal{B} & \\ \text{m.} & \underline{\mathcal{B} \rightarrow \mathcal{A}} & \\ \text{p.} & \mathcal{A} \leftrightarrow \mathcal{B} & \leftrightarrow\text{I, n, m} \end{array}$

Biconditional Exploitation (↔E)

$\begin{array}{lll} \text{n.} & \mathcal{A} \leftrightarrow \mathcal{B} & \\ \text{m.} & \underline{\mathcal{A}} \quad \text{(or } \mathcal{B}) & \\ \text{p.} & \mathcal{B} \quad \text{(or } \mathcal{A}) & \leftrightarrow\text{E, n, m} \end{array}$

Disjunction Introduction (∨I)

| n. | $\mathcal{A}$ (or $\mathcal{B}$) |
|---|---|
| n +p. | $\mathcal{A} \lor \mathcal{B}$   ∨I, n |

Disjunction Exploitation (∨E)

| n. | $\mathcal{A} \lor \mathcal{B}$ |
|---|---|
| m. | $\mathcal{A} \to C$ |
| p. | $\mathcal{B} \to C$ |
| q. | $C$   ∨E, n, m, p |

*Basic Rules, Applying to Parts of Formulas as well as Entire Formulas*

Negation Introduction/Exploitation (¬¬)

| n. | $\mathcal{A}$ | ¬¬, m |
|---|---|---|
| m. | $\neg\neg\mathcal{A}$ | ¬¬, n |

*Derived Rules, Applying Only to Entire Formulas*

Conditional-Biconditional (→↔)

| n. | $\mathcal{A} \leftrightarrow \mathcal{B}$ | |
|---|---|---|
| m. | $\mathcal{A} \to \mathcal{B}$ (or $\mathcal{B} \to \mathcal{A}$) | →↔, n |

Conditional Exploitation * (→E*)

| n. | $\mathcal{A} \to \mathcal{B}$ | |
|---|---|---|
| m. | $\neg\mathcal{B}$ | |
| p. | $\neg\mathcal{A}$ | →E*, n, m |

Biconditional Exploitation * (↔E*)

| n. | $\mathcal{A} \leftrightarrow \mathcal{B}$ | |
|---|---|---|
| m. | $\neg\mathcal{A}$ (or $\neg\mathcal{B}$) | |
| p. | $\neg\mathcal{B}$ (or $\neg\mathcal{A}$) ↔E*, n, m |

Disjunction Exploitation * (∨E*)

| n. | $\mathcal{A} \lor \mathcal{B}$ | |
|---|---|---|
| m. | $\neg\mathcal{A}$ (or $\neg\mathcal{B}$) | |
| p. | $\mathcal{B}$ (or $\mathcal{A}$) ∨E*, n, m |

Contradiction (!)

| n. | $\mathcal{A}$ | |
|---|---|---|
| m. | $\neg\mathcal{A}$ | |
| p. | $\mathcal{B}$ | !, n, m |

*Derived Rules, Applying to Parts of Formulas as well as Entire Formulas*

Negation-Conjunction (¬&)

| n. | $\neg(\mathcal{A} \,\&\, \mathcal{B})$ | ¬&, m |
|---|---|---|
| m. | $\neg\mathcal{A} \lor \neg\mathcal{B}$ | ¬&, n |

Negation-Disjunction (¬∨)

| n. | $\neg(\mathcal{A} \lor \mathcal{B})$ | ¬∨, m |
|---|---|---|
| m. | $\neg\mathcal{A} \,\&\, \neg\mathcal{B}$ | ¬∨, n |

Negation-Conditional (¬→)

| n. | $\neg(\mathcal{A} \to \mathcal{B})$ | ¬→, m |
|---|---|---|
| m. | $\mathcal{A} \,\&\, \neg\mathcal{B}$ | ¬→, n |

Negation-Biconditional (¬↔)

| n. | $\neg(\mathcal{A} \leftrightarrow \mathcal{B})$ | ¬↔, m |
|---|---|---|
| m. | $\neg\mathcal{A} \leftrightarrow \mathcal{B}$ (or $\mathcal{A} \leftrightarrow \neg\mathcal{B}$) ¬↔, n |

Conditional-Disjunction (→∨)

| n. | $\mathcal{A} \to \mathcal{B}$ | →∨, m |
|---|---|---|
| m. | $\neg\mathcal{A} \lor \mathcal{B}$ | →∨, n |

| Commutativity of Conjunction (&C) | | | Commutativity of Disjunction (∨C) | | |
|---|---|---|---|---|---|
| n. | $\underline{\mathcal{A} \,\&\, \mathcal{B}}$ | &C, m | n. | $\underline{\mathcal{A} \vee \mathcal{B}}$ | ∨C, m |
| m. | $\mathcal{B} \,\&\, \mathcal{A}$ | &C, n | m. | $\mathcal{B} \vee \mathcal{A}$ | ∨C, n |

| Associativity of Conjunction (&A) | | | Associativity of Disjunction (∨A) | | |
|---|---|---|---|---|---|
| n. | $\underline{(\mathcal{A} \,\&\, \mathcal{B}) \,\&\, \mathcal{C}}$ | &A, m | n. | $\underline{(\mathcal{A} \vee \mathcal{B}) \vee \mathcal{C}}$ | ∨A, m |
| m. | $\mathcal{A} \,\&\, (\mathcal{B} \,\&\, \mathcal{C})$ | &A, n | m. | $\mathcal{A} \vee (\mathcal{B} \vee \mathcal{C})$ | ∨A, n |

# 3.  STRATEGY

| *To get* | *Try to* |
|---|---|
| $\neg \mathcal{A}$ | use indirect proof. |
| $\mathcal{A} \,\&\, \mathcal{B}$ | prove $\mathcal{A}$ and $\mathcal{B}$ separately. |
| $\mathcal{A} \vee \mathcal{B}$ | use indirect proof, |
| | or prove $\mathcal{A}$ or $\mathcal{B}$ separately. |
| $\mathcal{A} \to \mathcal{B}$ | use conditional proof. |
| $\mathcal{A} \leftrightarrow \mathcal{B}$ | prove the two conditionals $\mathcal{A} \to \mathcal{B}$ and $\mathcal{B} \to \mathcal{A}$. |

| *To exploit* | *Try to* |
|---|---|
| $\neg \mathcal{A}$ | use it with other lines that have $\mathcal{A}$ as a part, |
| | or use a derivable rule. |
| $\mathcal{A} \,\&\, \mathcal{B}$ | use &E to get $\mathcal{A}$ and $\mathcal{B}$ individually. |
| $\mathcal{A} \vee \mathcal{B}$ | get the negation of one disjunct, and use ∨E* to get the other, |
| | or use ∨E by taking each case separately. |
| $\mathcal{A} \to \mathcal{B}$ | get $\mathcal{A}$ and then reach $\mathcal{B}$ by $\to$E, |
| | or get $\neg \mathcal{B}$ and then reach $\neg \mathcal{A}$ by $\to$E*. |
| $\mathcal{A} \leftrightarrow \mathcal{B}$ | get either component and then reach the other by $\leftrightarrow$E, |
| | or get the negation of either component and then the negation |
| | of the other by $\leftrightarrow$E*, or get one or both conditionals by $\leftrightarrow\to$. |

# 4.  ANSWERS TO UNANSWERED EVEN PROBLEMS

## A.2  NEGATION AND CONJUNCTION RULES

### from  8.2

| 8. | 1. | $\neg p \,\&\, \neg q$ | A |
|---|---|---|---|
| | 2. | $r \,\&\, \neg s$ | A |
| | 3. | Show $\neg\neg r \,\&\, \neg s$ | |
| | 4. | $\lceil \neg\neg r \,\&\, \neg s$ | $\neg\neg$, 2 |

## A.3  Conditional and Biconditional Rules

**from 8.3**

8.  1.  p → q                    A
    2.  p → r                    A
    3.  p                        A
    4.  Show q & r
    5.  q                        →E, 1, 3
    6.  r                        →E, 2, 3
    7.  q & r                    &I, 5, 6

10. 1.  p ↔ q                    A
    2.  p → r                    A
    3.  Show p → (q & r)
    4.  p                        ACP
    5.  q                        ↔E, 1, 4
    6.  r                        →E, 2, 4
    7.  q & r                    &I, 5, 6

14. 1.  p & ¬t                   A
    2.  p → (r & q)              A
    3.  r → s                    A
    4.  Show s & q
    5.  p                        &E, 1
    6.  r & q                    →E, 2, 5
    7.  r                        &E, 6
    8.  q                        &E, 6
    9.  s                        →E, 3, 7
    10. s & q                    &I, 9, 8

16. 1.  p & q                    A
    2.  ¬¬p → r                  A
    3.  q → s                    A
    4.  p → t                    A
    5.  Show (r & t) & s
    6.  p                        &E, 1
    7.  q                        &E, 1
    8.  s                        →E, 3, 7
    9.  t                        →E, 4, 6
    10. ¬¬p                      ¬¬, 6
    11. r                        →E, 2, 10
    12. r & t                    &I, 11, 8
    13. (r & t) & s              &I, 12, 7

20. 
```
1.    p ↔ q                              A
2.    p ↔ r                              A
3.    r → q                              A
4.    Show (p → (q & r)) & (r → (p & q))
5.  ┌   Show p → (q & r)
6.  │ ┌  p                               ACP
7.  │ │  q                               ↔E, 1, 6
8.  │ │  r                               ↔E, 2, 6
9.  │ └  q & r                           &I, 7, 8
10. │   Show r → (p & q)
11. │ ┌  r                               ACP
12. │ │  q                               →E, 3, 11
13. │ │  p                               ↔E, 1, 12
14. │ └  p & q                           &I, 13, 12
15. └   (p → (q & r)) & (r → (p & q))    &I, 5, 10
```

22. 
```
1.    s → (q & t)                        A
2.    ¬m → p                             A
3.    (p → r) & ¬k                       A
4.    p & s                              A
5.    (q & r) → ¬m                       A
6.    Show ¬m & (q & r)
7.  ┌  p                                 &E, 4
8.  │  s                                 &E, 4
9.  │  q & t                             →E, 1, 8
10. │  q                                 &E, 9
11. │  p → r                             &E, 3
12. │  r                                 →E, 11, 7
13. │  q & r                             &I, 10, 12
14. │  ¬m                                →E, 6, 13
15. └  ¬m & (q & r)                      &I, 14, 13
```

26.    d: The Democrats obstruct the President's legislative program; m: The market will lose confidence; p: The Democrats can gain politically by obstructing.
```
1.    d → m                              A
2.    d → p                              A
3.    d                                  A
4.    Show p & m
5.  ┌  p                                 →E, 2, 3
6.  │  m                                 →E, 1, 3
7.  └  p & m                             &I, 5, 6
```

28.    g: Georgia will lose the case; d: The Court decides to base its decision on *Davis*; c: The composition of the Court is more conservative than it was a few years ago.
```
1.    g ↔ d                              A
2.    c & d                              A
3.    Show g
4.  ┌  d                                 &E, 2
5.  └  g                                 ↔E, 1, 4
```

## A.4 DISJUNCTION RULES

### from 8.4

8. 
```
1.    p ↔ ¬q                             A
2.    ¬p ∨ q                             A
3.    r                                  A
```

|     |     |                                      |              |
|-----|-----|--------------------------------------|--------------|
|     | 4.  | Show ¬p ∨ (p → s)                    |              |
|     | 5.  | Show q → (¬p ∨ (p → s))              |              |
|     | 6.  | q                                    | ACP          |
|     | 7.  | Show p → s                           |              |
|     | 8.  | p                                    | ACP          |
|     | 9.  | Show ¬¬s                             |              |
|     | 10. | ¬s                                   | AIP          |
|     | 11. | ¬q                                   | ↔E, 1, 8     |
|     | 12. | q                                    | R, 6         |
|     | 13. | s                                    | ¬¬, 9        |
|     | 14. | ¬p ∨ (p → s)                         | ∨I, 7        |
|     | 15. | Show ¬p → (¬p ∨ (p → s))             |              |
|     | 16. | ¬p                                   | ACP          |
|     | 17. | ¬p ∨ (p → s)                         | ∨I, 16       |
|     | 18. | ¬p ∨ (p → s)                         | ∨E, 2, 15, 5 |

|     |     |                 |              |
|-----|-----|-----------------|--------------|
| 10. | 1.  | p ↔ s           | A            |
|     | 2.  | q ∨ p           | A            |
|     | 3.  | q → r           | A            |
|     | 4.  | Show s ∨ r      |              |
|     | 5.  | Show q → (s ∨ r)|              |
|     | 6.  | q               | ACP          |
|     | 7.  | r               | →E, 3, 6     |
|     | 8.  | s ∨ r           | ∨I, 7        |
|     | 9.  | Show p → (s ∨ r)|              |
|     | 10. | p               | ACP          |
|     | 11. | s               | ↔E, 1, 10    |
|     | 12. | s ∨ r           | ∨I, 11       |
|     | 13. | s ∨ r           | ∨E, 2, 5, 9  |

|     |     |                       |                |
|-----|-----|-----------------------|----------------|
| 14. | 1.  | p ∨ r                 | A              |
|     | 2.  | ¬p ∨ ¬q               | A              |
|     | 3.  | p                     | A              |
|     | 4.  | ¬r ∨ q                | A              |
|     | 5.  | Show ¬r               |                |
|     | 6.  | Show ¬r → ¬r          |                |
|     | 7.  | ¬r                    | ACP            |
|     | 8.  | Show q → ¬r           |                |
|     | 9.  | q                     | ACP            |
|     | 10. | Show ¬p → ¬r          |                |
|     | 11. | ¬p                    | ACP            |
|     | 12. | Show ¬r               |                |
|     | 13. | r                     | AIP            |
|     | 14. | p                     | R, 3           |
|     | 15. | ¬p                    | R, 11          |
|     | 16. | Show ¬q → ¬r          |                |
|     | 17. | ¬q                    | ACP            |
|     | 18. | Show ¬r               |                |
|     | 19. | r                     | AIP            |
|     | 20. | p                     | R, 3           |
|     | 21. | ¬p                    | R, 11          |
|     | 22. | ¬r                    | ∨E, 2, 10, 16  |
|     | 23. | ¬r                    | ∨E, 4, 6, 8    |

| 16. | 1. | p ∨ q | A |
|---|---|---|---|
| | 2. | r ∨ s | A |
| | 3. | ¬q & ¬s | A |
| | 4. | Show (p & r) ∨ t | |
| | 5. | ¬q | &E, 3 |
| | 6. | ¬s | &E, 3 |
| | 7. | Show p → (p & r) | |
| | 8. | p | ACP |
| | 9. | Show r → r | |
| | 10. | r | ACP |
| | 11. | Show s → r | |
| | 12. | s | ACP |
| | 13. | Show ¬¬r | |
| | 14. | ¬r | AIP |
| | 15. | s | R, 12 |
| | 16. | ¬s | R, 6 |
| | 17. | r | ¬¬, 13 |
| | 18. | r | ∨E, 2, 9, 11 |
| | 19. | p & r | &E, 8, 18 |
| | 20. | Show q → (p & r) | |
| | 21. | q | ACP |
| | 22. | Show ¬¬(p & r) | |
| | 23. | ¬(p & r) | AIP |
| | 24. | q | R, 21 |
| | 25. | ¬q | R, 5 |
| | 26. | p & r | ¬¬, 22 |
| | 27. | p & r | ∨E, 1, 7, 20 |
| | 28. | (p & r) ∨ t | ∨I, 27 |

| 20. | 1. | p & s | A |
|---|---|---|---|
| | 2. | p → (¬s ∨ r) | A |
| | 3. | Show r | |
| | 4. | p | &E, 1 |
| | 5. | s | &E, 1 |
| | 6. | ¬s ∨ r | →E, 2, 3 |
| | 7. | Show r → r | |
| | 8. | r | ACP |
| | 9. | Show ¬s → r | |
| | 10. | ¬s | ACP |
| | 11. | Show ¬¬r | |
| | 12. | ¬r | AIP |
| | 13. | ¬s | R, 10 |
| | 14. | s | R, 5 |
| | 15. | r | ¬¬, 11 |
| | 16. | r | ∨E, 6, 9, 7 |

| 22. | 1. | p & q | A |
|---|---|---|---|
| | 2. | r & ¬s | A |
| | 3. | q → (p → k) | A |
| | 4. | k → (r → (s ∨ m)) | A |
| | 5. | Show m | |
| | 6. | p | &E, 1 |
| | 7. | q | &E, 1 |
| | 8. | r | &E, 2 |
| | 9. | ¬s | &E, 2 |
| | 10. | p → k | →E, 3, 7 |
| | 11. | k | →E, 10, 6 |

181

| 12. | $r \to (s \lor m)$ | $\to$E, 4, 11 |
|---|---|---|
| 13. | $s \lor m$ | $\to$E, 12, 8 |
| 14. | $m$ | $\to$E, 13, 9 |

26.
| 1. | $p \& q$ | A |
|---|---|---|
| 2. | $p \to \neg\neg r$ | A |
| 3. | $q \to s$ | A |
| 4. | $\neg r \lor m$ | A |
| 5. | $p \to t$ | A |
| 6. | ~~Show~~ $(m \& s) \& t$ | |
| 7. | $p$ | &E, 1 |
| 8. | $q$ | &E, 1 |
| 9. | $\neg\neg r$ | $\to$E, 2, 7 |
| 10. | $s$ | $\to$E, 3, 8 |
| 11. | ~~Show~~ $m \to m$ | |
| 12. | $m$ | ACP |
| 13. | ~~Show~~ $\neg r \to m$ | |
| 14. | $\neg r$ | ACP |
| 15. | ~~Show~~ $\neg\neg m$ | |
| 16. | $\neg m$ | AIP |
| 17. | $\neg r$ | R, 14 |
| 18. | $\neg\neg r$ | R, 9 |
| 19. | $m$ | $\neg\neg$, 15 |
| 20. | $m$ | $\lor$E, 4, 13, 11 |
| 21. | $t$ | $\to$E, 5, 7 |
| 22. | $m \& s$ | &I, 20, 10 |
| 23. | $(m \& s) \& t$ | &I, 22, 21 |

28.
| 1. | ~~Show~~ $(p \lor (q \lor r)) \to ((p \lor q) \lor r)$ | |
|---|---|---|
| 2. | $(p \lor (q \lor r))$ | ACP |
| 3. | ~~Show~~ $p \to ((p \lor q) \lor r)$ | |
| 4. | $p$ | ACP |
| 5. | $p \lor q$ | $\lor$I, 4 |
| 6. | $(p \lor q) \lor r$ | $\lor$I, 5 |
| 7. | ~~Show~~ $(q \lor r) \to ((p \lor q) \lor r)$ | |
| 8. | $q \lor r$ | ACP |
| 9. | ~~Show~~ $q \to ((p \lor q) \lor r)$ | |
| 10. | $q$ | ACP |
| 11. | $p \lor q$ | $\lor$I, 10 |
| 12. | $(p \lor q) \lor r$ | $\lor$I, 11 |
| 13. | ~~Show~~ $r \to ((p \lor q) \lor r)$ | |
| 14. | $r$ | ACP |
| 15. | $(p \lor q) \lor r$ | $\lor$I, 14 |
| 16. | $(p \lor q) \lor r$ | $\lor$E, 8, 9, 13 |
| 17. | $(p \lor q) \lor r$ | $\lor$E, 2, 3, 7 |

32.  d: The dollar will fall; s: Foreign banks sterilize their intervention in the currency markets; f: The Fed does nothing to defend it; g: Germany and Japan are eager to keep their currencies strong; i: They'll intervene in the markets.

| 1. | $(s \lor f) \to d$ | A |
|---|---|---|
| 2. | $g \& (d \to i)$ | A |
| 3. | $g \to s$ | A |

| | | |
|---|---|---|
| 4. | Show̶ i | |
| 5. | g | &E, 2 |
| 6. | s | →E, 3, 5 |
| 7. | s ∨ f | ∨I, 6 |
| 8. | d | →E, 1, 7 |
| 9. | d → i | &E, 2 |
| 10. | i | →E, 9, 8 |

34.  c: Patricia is clever, but won't w: Patricia will work very hard. If she's clever, b: the boss will like her and either p: promote her or g: give her a bonus. If Patricia is promoted, she'll work hard. Therefore, the boss will give Patricia a bonus.

| | | |
|---|---|---|
| 1. | c & ¬w | A |
| 2. | c → (b & (p ∨ g)) | A |
| 3. | p → w | A |
| 4. | Show̶ g | |
| 5. | c | &E, 1 |
| 6. | ¬w | &E, 1 |
| 7. | b & (p ∨ g) | →E, 2, 5 |
| 8. | p ∨ g | &E, 7 |
| 9. | Show̶ p → g | |
| 10. | p | ACP |
| 11. | Show̶ ¬¬g | |
| 12. | ¬g | AIP |
| 13. | w | →E, 3, 10 |
| 14. | ¬w | R, 6 |
| 15. | g | ¬¬, 11 |
| 16. | Show̶ g → g | |
| 17. | g | ACP |
| 18. | g | ∨E, 8, 9, 16 |

**from 8.5**

14.
| | | |
|---|---|---|
| 1. | r → (p ∨ q) | A |
| 2. | Show̶ (r → p) ∨ q | |
| 3. | Show̶ ¬¬((r → p) ∨ q) | |
| 4. | ¬((r → p) ∨ q)) | AIP |
| 5. | Show̶ ¬q | |
| 6. | q | AIP |
| 7. | (r → p) ∨ q | ∨I, 6 |
| 8. | ¬((r → p) ∨ q) | R, 4 |
| 9. | Show̶ r → p | |
| 10. | r | ACP |
| 11. | p ∨ q | →E, 1, 10 |
| 12. | Show̶ q → p | |
| 13. | q | ACP |
| 14. | Show̶ ¬¬p | |
| 15. | ¬p | AIP |
| 16. | q | R, 13 |
| 17. | ¬q | R, 5 |
| 18. | p | ¬¬, 14 |
| 19. | Show̶ p → p | |
| 20. | p | ACP |
| 21. | p | ∨E, 11, 19, 12 |
| 22. | (r → p) ∨ q | ∨I, 9 |
| 23. | (r → p) ∨ q | ¬¬, 3 |

16.
1. $\neg s \lor (s \& r)$      A
2. $(s \to r) \to q$      A
3. Show $q$
4.     Show $s \to r$
5.       $s$        ACP
6.       Show $\neg s \to r$
7.         $\neg s$       ACP
8.         Show $\neg\neg r$
9.           $\neg r$       AIP
10.           $s$        R, 5
11.           $\neg s$       R, 7
12.         $r$        $\neg\neg$, 8
13.       Show $(s \& r) \to r$
14.         $s \& r$       ACP
15.         $r$        &E, 14
16.       $r$        $\lor$E, 1, 6, 13
17. $q$        $\to$E, 2, 4

20.
1. $r \to \neg p$      A
2. $q$      A
3. $q \to (p \lor \neg s)$      A
4. Show $s \to \neg r$
5.       $s$        ACP
6.       $p \lor \neg s$       $\to$E, 3, 2
7.       Show $p \to \neg r$
8.         $p$       ACP
9.         Show $\neg r$
10.           $r$       AIP
11.           $\neg p$       $\to$E, 1, 10
12.           $p$       R, 8
13.       Show $\neg s \to \neg r$
14.         $\neg s$       ACP
15.         Show $\neg r$
16.           $r$       AIP
17.           $\neg s$       R, 14
18.           $s$       R, 5
19.       $\neg r$       $\lor$E, 6, 7, 13

22.
| | | | |
|---|---|---|---|
| | 1. | r → ¬p | A |
| | 2. | ¬r → ¬q | A |
| | 3. | q ∨ ¬s | A |
| | 4. | Show ¬p ∨ ¬s | |
| | 5. | Show ¬¬(¬p ∨ ¬s) | |
| | 6. | ¬(¬p ∨ ¬s) | AIP |
| | 7. | Show ¬¬p | |
| | 8. | ¬p | AIP |
| | 9. | ¬p ∨ ¬s | ∨I, 8 |
| | 10. | ¬(¬p ∨ ¬s) | R, 6 |
| | 11. | Show ¬r | |
| | 12. | r | AIP |
| | 13. | ¬p | →E, 1, 12 |
| | 14. | ¬¬p | R, 7 |
| | 15. | ¬q | →E, 2, 11 |
| | 16. | Show ¬s → (¬p ∨ ¬s) | |
| | 17. | ¬s | ACP |
| | 18. | ¬p ∨ ¬s | ∨I, 17 |
| | 19. | Show q → (¬p ∨ ¬s) | |
| | 20. | q | ACP |
| | 21. | Show ¬¬(¬p ∨ ¬s) | |
| | 22. | ¬(¬p ∨ ¬s) | AIP |
| | 23. | q | R, 20 |
| | 24. | ¬q | R, 15 |
| | 25. | ¬p ∨ ¬s | ¬¬, 21 |
| | 26. | ¬p ∨ ¬s | VE, 3, 19, 16 |
| | 27. | ¬p ∨ ¬s | ¬¬, 5 |

26.
| | | | |
|---|---|---|---|
| | 1. | r & p | A |
| | 2. | r → (s ∨ q) | A |
| | 3. | ¬(q & p) | A |
| | 4. | Show s | |
| | 5. | r | &E, 1 |
| | 6. | p | &E, 1 |
| | 7. | s ∨ q | →E, 2, 5 |
| | 8. | Show q → s | |
| | 9. | q | AIP |
| | 10. | Show ¬¬s | |
| | 11. | ¬s | AIP |
| | 12. | q & p | &I, 9, 6 |
| | 13. | ¬(q & p) | R, 3 |
| | 14. | s | ¬¬, 10 |
| | 15. | Show s → s | |
| | 16. | s | ACP |
| | 17. | s | ∨E, 7, 15, 8 |

**185**

28.
1. $s \rightarrow r$      A
2. $(s \& r) \rightarrow p$      A
3. $q \rightarrow t$      A
4. $q \vee s$      A
5. Show $p \vee t$
6.    Show $q \rightarrow (p \vee t)$
7.      q      ACP
8.      t      $\rightarrow$E, 3, 7
9.      $p \vee t$      $\vee$I, 8
10.    Show $s \rightarrow (p \vee t)$
11.      s      ACP
12.      r      $\rightarrow$E, 1, 11
13.      s & r      &I, 11, 12
14.      p      $\rightarrow$E, 2, 13
15.      $p \vee t$      $\vee$I, 14
16.    $p \vee t$      $\vee$E, 4, 6, 10

32.
1. $r \& (\neg p \& \neg t)$      A
2. $r \rightarrow (s \rightarrow q)$      A
3. $s \rightarrow (q \leftrightarrow (t \vee p))$      A
4. Show $\neg s$
5.    s      AIP
6.    $q \leftrightarrow (t \vee p)$      $\rightarrow$E, 3, 5
7.    r      &E, 1
8.    $\neg p \& \neg t$      &E, 1
9.    $s \rightarrow q$      $\rightarrow$E, 2, 7
10.    q      $\rightarrow$E, 9, 5
11.    $t \vee p$      $\leftrightarrow$E, 6, 10
12.    Show $t \rightarrow \neg s$
13.      t      ACP
14.      Show $\neg s$
15.        s      AIP
16.        t      R, 13
17.        $\neg t$      &E, 8
18.    Show $p \rightarrow \neg s$
19.      p      ACP
20.      Show $\neg s$
21.        s      AIP
22.        p      R, 19
23.        $\neg p$      &E, 8
24.    $\neg s$      $\vee$E, 11, 12, 18

34.
1. $\neg(p \vee \neg s)$      A
2. $\neg p \rightarrow (q \vee r)$      A
3. $\neg r \vee \neg s$      A
4. $(q \vee t) \rightarrow (m \& (k \rightarrow \neg s))$      A
5. Show $\neg(m \rightarrow k)$
6.    $m \rightarrow k$      AIP
7.    Show $\neg p$
8.      p      AIP
9.      $p \vee \neg s$      $\vee$I, 8
10.      $\neg(p \vee \neg s)$      R, 1
11.    $q \vee r$      $\rightarrow$E, 2, 7

|     |     |        |
|-----|-----|--------|
| 12. | Show ¬¬s | |
| 13. | ¬s | AIP |
| 14. | p ∨ ¬s | ∨I, 13 |
| 15. | ¬(p ∨ ¬s) | R, 1 |
| 16. | Show ¬s → ¬s | |
| 17. | ¬s | ACP |
| 18. | Show ¬r → ¬s | |
| 19. | ¬r | ACP |
| 20. | Show q → ¬s | |
| 21. | q | ACP |
| 22. | q ∨ t | ∨I, 21 |
| 23. | m & (k → ¬s) | →E, 3, 22 |
| 24. | m | &E, 23 |
| 25. | k → ¬s | &E, 23 |
| 26. | k | →E, 6, 24 |
| 27. | ¬s | →E, 25, 26 |
| 28. | Show r → ¬s | |
| 29. | r | ACP |
| 30. | Show ¬s | |
| 31. | s | AIP |
| 32. | r | R, 29 |
| 33. | ¬r | R, 19 |
| 34. | ¬s | ∨E, 11, 20, 28 |
| 35. | ¬s | ∨E, 3, 18, 16 |

38.

| | | |
|---|---|---|
| 1. | p | A |
| 2. | ¬p | A |
| 3. | Show q | |
| 4. | Show ¬¬q | |
| 5. | ¬q | AIP |
| 6. | p | R, 1 |
| 7. | ¬p | R, 2 |
| 8. | q | ¬¬, 4 |

40.

| | | |
|---|---|---|
| 1. | p & (q ∨ r) | A |
| 2. | Show (p & q) ∨ (p & r) | |
| 3. | Show ¬¬((p & q) ∨ (p & r)) | |
| 4. | ¬((p & q) ∨ (p & r)) | AIP |
| 5. | p | &E, 1 |
| 6. | q ∨ r | &E, 1 |
| 7. | Show q → ((p & q) ∨ (p & r)) | |
| 8. | q | ACP |
| 9. | p & q | &I, 5, 8 |
| 10. | (p & q) ∨ (p & r) | ∨I, 9 |
| 11. | Show r → ((p & q) ∨ (p & r)) | |
| 12. | r | ACP |
| 13. | p & r | &I, 5, 12 |
| 14. | (p & q) ∨ (p & r) | ∨I, 13 |
| 15. | (p & q) ∨ (p & r) | ∨E, 6, 7, 11 |
| 16. | (p & q) ∨ (p & r) | ¬¬, 3 |

44.
1. $p \leftrightarrow \neg q$            A
2. Show $\neg(p \leftrightarrow q)$
3.    $p \leftrightarrow q$         AIP
4.    Show $\neg p$
5.      $p$            AIP
6.      $q$            $\leftrightarrow$E, 3, 5
7.      $\neg q$          $\leftrightarrow$E, 1, 5
8.    Show $\neg q$
9.      $q$            AIP
10.     $p$            $\leftrightarrow$E, 3, 9
11.     $\neg p$          R, 4
12.    $p$            $\leftrightarrow$E, 1, 8

46.
1. $(p \& q) \vee (p \& r)$      A
2. Show $p \& (q \vee r)$
3.    Show $(p \& q) \to (p \& (q \vee r))$
4.      $p \& q$          ACP
5.      $p$            &E, 4
6.      $q$            &E, 4
7.      $q \vee r$         $\vee$I, 6
8.      $p \& (q \vee r)$    &I, 5, 7
9.    Show $(p \& r) \to (p \& (q \vee r))$
10.     $p \& r$          ACP
11.     $p$            &E, 10
12.     $r$            &E, 10
13.     $q \vee r$         $\vee$I, 12
14.     $p \& (q \vee r)$    &I, 11, 13
15.    $p \& (q \vee r)$    $\vee$E, 1, 3, 9

50. r: I'm right; f: I'm a fool.
1. $r \to f$            A
2. $f \to \neg r$         A
3. Show $\neg r$
4.    $r$            AIP
5.    $f$            $\to$E, 1, 4
6.    $\neg r$          $\to$E, 2, 5

52. s: Socrates died; l: He died while he was living; d: He died while he was dead.
1. $s \to (l \vee d)$     A
2. $\neg l$            A
3. $\neg d$           A
4. Show $\neg s$
5.    $s$            AIP
6.    $l \vee d$         $\to$E, 1, 4
7.    Show $d \to d$
8.      $d$            ACP
9.    Show $l \to d$
10.     $l$            ACP
11.     Show $\neg\neg d$
12.      $\neg d$
13.      $l$            R, 10
14.      $\neg l$          R, 2
15.     $d$            $\neg\neg$, 11
16.    $d$            $\vee$E, 6, 9, 7
17.    $\neg d$          R, 3

56. u: The United States agrees to arms limitation talks; t: Tensions with the Soviets will remain high.

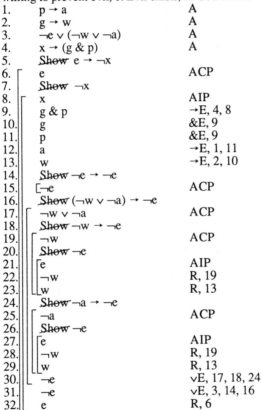

1.  ¬u → t                 A
2.  u → t                  A
3.  Show ¬¬t
4.  ⌐¬t                    AIP
5.  │ ¬u                   →E*, 2, 4
6.  │ t                    →E, 1, 5
7.  └ t                    ¬¬, 3

58. p: God is all powerful; a: He is able to prevent evil; g: He is all good; w: He is willing to prevent evil; e: Evil exists; x: God exists.

1.  p → a                          A
2.  g → w                          A
3.  ¬e ∨ (¬w ∨ ¬a)                 A
4.  x → (g & p)                    A
5.  Show e → ¬x
6.  ⌐ e                            ACP
7.  │ Show ¬x
8.  │ ⌐ x                          AIP
9.  │ │ g & p                      →E, 4, 8
10. │ │ g                          &E, 9
11. │ │ p                          &E, 9
12. │ │ a                          →E, 1, 11
13. │ │ w                          →E, 2, 10
14. │ │ Show ¬e → ¬e
15. │ │ ⌐¬e                        ACP
16. │ │ Show (¬w ∨ ¬a) → ¬e
17. │ │ ⌐ ¬w ∨ ¬a                  ACP
18. │ │ │ Show ¬w → ¬e
19. │ │ │ ⌐ ¬w                     ACP
20. │ │ │ │ Show ¬e
21. │ │ │ │ ⌐ e                    AIP
22. │ │ │ │ │ ¬w                   R, 19
23. │ │ │ │ └ w                    R, 13
24. │ │ │ Show ¬a → ¬e
25. │ │ │ ⌐ ¬a                     ACP
26. │ │ │ │ Show ¬e
27. │ │ │ │ ⌐ e                    AIP
28. │ │ │ │ │ ¬w                   R, 19
29. │ │ │ │ └ w                    R, 13
30. │ │ │ └ ¬e                     ∨E, 17, 18, 24
31. │ │ ¬e                         ∨E, 3, 14, 16
32. └ e                            R, 6

## A.5 DERIVED RULES

## from 8.6

8.  c: My cat sings opera; l: All the lights are out; i: I am very insistent; h: I howl at the moon.

1.  ¬c ∨ l             A
2.  i → c              A
3.  (l ∨ h) → i        A
4.  ¬i → h             A

189

| 5. | $\underline{\text{Show}}$ (l & i) & c | |
|---|---|---|
| 6. | $\underline{\text{Show}}$ i | |
| 7. | ¬i | AIP |
| 8. | h | →E, 4, 7 |
| 9. | l ∨ h | ∨I, 8 |
| 10. | i | →E, 3, 9 |
| 11. | c | →E, 2, 10 |
| 12. | ¬¬c | ¬¬, 11 |
| 13. | l | ∨E*, 1, 12 |
| 14. | (l & i) | &I, 13, 10 |
| 15. | (l & i) & c | &I, 14, 11 |

10. s: Money serves you; d: Money dominates you; w: You handle it wisely; h: It can help you to attain happiness; g: You will gain much of it; l: You'll be satisfied with your lot.

| 1. | (s ∨ d) & ¬(s & d) | A |
|---|---|---|
| 2. | (s & w) → h | A |
| 3. | d → (g & ¬l) | A |
| 4. | l ↔ ¬h | A |
| 5. | $\underline{\text{Show}}$ w → h | |
| 6. | w | ACP |
| 7. | s ∨ d | &E, 1 |
| 8. | $\underline{\text{Show}}$ h | |
| 9. | ¬h | AIP |
| 10. | l | ↔E, 4, 9 |
| 11. | ¬¬l | ¬¬, 10 |
| 12. | ¬g ∨ ¬¬l | ∨I, 11 |
| 13. | ¬(g & ¬l) | ¬&, 12 |
| 14. | ¬d | →E*, 3, 13 |
| 15. | s | ∨E*, 7, 14 |
| 16. | s & w | &I, 15, 6 |
| 17. | h | →E, 2, 16 |

14. d: Happiness can be defined; m: There's a way to measure it; s: We can say whether someone is happy; w: We take that person's word for it.; t: We can test the psychological effects of jobs of various kinds.

| 1. | ¬d → ¬m | A |
|---|---|---|
| 2. | ¬m → (s → w) | A |
| 3. | t → s | A |
| 4. | ¬w | A |
| 5. | $\underline{\text{Show}}$ ¬d → ¬t | |
| 6. | ¬d | ACP |
| 7. | $\underline{\text{Show}}$ ¬t | |
| 8. | t | AIP |
| 9. | ¬m | →E, 1, 6 |
| 10. | s → w | →E, 2, 9 |
| 11. | s | →E, 3, 8 |
| 12. | w | →E, 10, 11 |
| 13. | ¬w | R, 4 |

16. s: We maintain high educational standards; a: We accept almost every high school graduate; f: We fail large numbers of students; p: Many students do poorly; l: We will placate the legislature.

190

| 1. | $\neg(s \mathbin{\&} a) \vee (f \leftrightarrow p)$ | A |
|---|---|---|
| 2. | $s$ | A |
| 3. | $l \mathbin{\&} a$ | A |
| 4. | $\neg(l \mathbin{\&} f)$ | A |
| 5. | Show $\neg p$ | |

| 6. | $\lceil$ $l$ | &E, 3 |
|---|---|---|
| 7. | $a$ | &E, 3 |
| 8. | $s \mathbin{\&} a$ | &I, 2, 7 |
| 9. | $\neg\neg(s \mathbin{\&} a)$ | $\neg\neg$, 8 |
| 10. | $f \leftrightarrow p$ | vE*, 1, 9 |
| 11. | $\neg l \vee \neg f$ | $\neg\&$, 4 |
| 12. | $\neg\neg l$ | $\neg\neg$, 6 |
| 13. | $\neg f$ | vE*, 11, 12 |
| 14. | $\lfloor$ $\neg p$ | $\leftrightarrow$E, 10, 13 |

20. r: The Soviet economy is restructured; d: Decision-making will have to be decentralized; s: Bureaucracies in charge of economic planning will have to become smaller; p: Bureaucracies in charge of economic planning will have to become less powerful; b: Bureaucrats can help it; w: The party hierarchy is willing to cede power to a wide group it can't easily control;  c: Central planning will continue to dominate the economy.

| 1. | $r \rightarrow (d \mathbin{\&} (s \mathbin{\&} p))$ | A |
|---|---|---|
| 2. | $b \rightarrow \neg s$ | A |
| 3. | $d \rightarrow w$ | A |
| 4. | $p \vee (\neg d \mathbin{\&} c)$ | A |
| 5. | Show $(\neg w \vee b) \rightarrow \neg r$ | |
| 6. | $\lceil$ $\neg w \vee b$ | ACP |
| 7. | Show $\neg r$ | |
| 8. | $\lceil$ $r$ | AIP |
| 9. | $d \mathbin{\&} (s \mathbin{\&} p)$ | $\rightarrow$E, 1, 8 |
| 10. | $d$ | &E, 9 |
| 11. | $w$ | $\rightarrow$E, 3, 10 |
| 12. | $\neg\neg w$ | $\neg\neg$, 11 |
| 13. | $b$ | vE*, 6, 12 |
| 14. | $\neg s$ | $\rightarrow$E, 2, 13 |
| 15. | $s \mathbin{\&} p$ | &E, 9 |
| 16. | $\lfloor\lfloor$ $s$ | &E, 15 |

22. p: The party maintains its current economic policy; f: There will be a flight of capital to other countries; i: The party improves its image abroad; t: It tightens its control over the economy; h: The nation will have to pay large amounts of foreign debt in hard currency.

| 1. | $p \rightarrow f$ | A |
|---|---|---|
| 2. | $t \rightarrow \neg i$ | A |
| 3. | $(p \mathbin{\&} f) \rightarrow t$ | A |
| 4. | $(\neg i \rightarrow h) \mathbin{\&} \neg h$ | A |
| 5. | Show $\neg p$ | |
| 6. | $\lceil$ $p$ | AIP |
| 7. | $\neg i \rightarrow h$ | &E, 4 |
| 8. | $\neg h$ | &E, 4 |
| 9. | $\neg\neg i$ | $\rightarrow$E*, 7, 8 |
| 10. | $\neg t$ | $\rightarrow$E*, 2, 9 |
| 11. | $f$ | $\rightarrow$E, 1, 6 |
| 12. | $p \mathbin{\&} f$ | &I, 6, 11 |
| 13. | $\lfloor$ $t$ | $\rightarrow$E, 3, 12 |

26.  1.   p ↔ q                          A
     2.   ¬(m → q)                       A
     3.   Show ¬p
     4.   ⌈ m & ¬q                       ¬→, 2
     5.   | ¬q                           &E, 4
     6.   ⌊ ¬p                           ↔E, 1, 5

28.  1.   p & q                          A
     2.   Show ¬(¬q & ¬r) & p
     3.   ⌈ p                            &E, 1
     4.   | q                            &E, 1
     5.   | q ∨ r                        ∨I, 4
     6.   | ¬(¬q & ¬r)                   ¬&, 5
     7.   ⌊ ¬(¬q & ¬r) & p               &I, 6, 2

32.  1.   (p & q) → r                    A
     2.   Show p → (q → r)
     3.   ⌈ p                            ACP
     4.   | Show q → r
     5.   | ⌈ q                          ACP
     6.   | | p & q                      &I, 3, 5
     7.   ⌊ ⌊ r                          →E, 1, 6

34.  1.   p ↔ q                                              A
     2.   Show (p & q) ∨ (¬p & ¬q)
     3.   ⌈ ¬((p & q) ∨ (¬p & ¬q))                           AIP
     4.   | ¬(p & q) & ¬(¬p & ¬q)                            ¬∨, 3
     5.   | ¬(p & q)                                         &E, 4
     6.   | ¬(¬p & ¬q)                                       &E, 4
     7.   | p ∨ q                                            ¬&, 6
     8.   | Show p
     9.   | ⌈ ¬p                                             AIP
     10.  | | q                                              ∨E*, 7, 9
     11.  | ⌊ p                                              ↔E, 1, 10
     12.  | q                                                ↔E, 1, 8
     13.  | p & q                                            &I, 8, 12
     14.  ⌊ ¬(p & q)                                         R, 5

38.  1.   p ↔ q                          A
     2.   Show q ↔ p
     3.   ⌈ p → q                        ↔→, 1
     4.   | q → p                        ↔→, 1
     5.   ⌊ q ↔ p                        ↔I, 4, 3

40.  1.   p → q                          A
     2.   p → r                          A
     3.   ¬q ∨ ¬r                        A
     4.   Show ¬p
     5.   ⌈ p                            AIP
     6.   | q                            →E, 1, 5
     7.   | r                            →E, 2, 5
     8.   | q & r                        &I, 6, 7
     9.   ⌊ ¬(q & r)                     ¬&, 3

192

44. (a)
| | | | | (b) | | | |
|---|---|---|---|---|---|---|---|
| 1. | a → b | A | | | 1. | a → b | A |
| 2. | c → (a → ¬b) | A | | | 2. | c → (a → ¬b) | A |
| 3. | Show ¬(c & (a & b)) | | | | 3. | Show ¬a ∨ ¬c | |
| 4. | c & (a & b) | AIP | | | 4. | ¬(¬a ∨ ¬c) | AIP |
| 5. | c | &E, 4 | | | 5. | ¬¬a & ¬¬c | ¬∨, 4 |
| 6. | a & b | &E, 4 | | | 6. | a & c | ¬¬, 5 |
| 7. | a | &E, 6 | | | 7. | a | &E, 6 |
| 8. | b | &E, 6 | | | 8. | c | &E, 6 |
| 9. | a → ¬b | →E, 2, 6 | | | 9. | b | →E, 1, 7 |
| 10. | ¬b | →E, 9, 7 | | | 10. | a → ¬b | →E, 2, 8 |
| | | | | | 11. | ¬b | →E, 10, 7 |

(a)
| | | |
|---|---|---|
| 1. | a → b | A |
| 2. | c → (a → ¬b) | A |
| 3. | Show (¬b & ¬c) → ¬a | |
| 4. | ¬b & ¬c | ACP |
| 5. | Show ¬a | |
| 6. | a | AIP |
| 7. | b | →E, 1, 6 |
| 8. | ¬b | &E, 4 |

46.
| | | |
|---|---|---|
| 1. | p → (q ∨ r) | A |
| 2. | (¬q & m) ∨ (s → ¬p) | A |
| 3. | ¬(¬r → ¬p) | A |
| 4. | Show ¬s & q | |
| 5. | ¬r & ¬¬p | ¬→, 3 |
| 6. | ¬¬p | &E, 5 |
| 7. | p | ¬¬, 6 |
| 8. | ¬r | &E, 5 |
| 9. | q ∨ r | →E, 1, 7 |
| 10. | q | ∨E*, 9, 8 |
| 11. | q ∨ ¬m | ∨I, 10 |
| 12. | ¬¬q ∨ ¬m | ¬¬, 11 |
| 13. | ¬(¬q & m) | ¬&, 12 |
| 14. | s → ¬p | ∨E*, 2, 13 |
| 15. | ¬s | →E*, 14, 6 |
| 16. | ¬s & q | &I, 15, 10 |

50.
| | | |
|---|---|---|
| 1. | (p & ¬r) ↔ (s ∨ ¬q) | A |
| 2. | t & ((¬s & ¬r) → p) | A |
| 3. | (t → q) ∨ (t → r) | A |
| 4. | (p & s) → r | A |
| 5. | Show q & r | |
| 6. | t | &E, 2 |
| 7. | (¬s & ¬r) → p | &E, 2 |
| 8. | Show q | |
| 9. | ¬q | AIP |
| 10. | t & ¬q | &I, 6, 9 |
| 11. | ¬(t → q) | ¬→, 10 |
| 12. | t → r | ∨E*, 3, 11 |
| 13. | r | →E, 12, 6 |
| 14. | ¬¬r | ¬¬, 13 |
| 15. | ¬p ∨ ¬¬r | ∨I, 14 |
| 16. | ¬(p & ¬r) | ¬&, 15 |
| 17. | ¬(s ∨ ¬q) | ↔E, 1, 16 |
| 18. | ¬s & ¬¬q | ¬∨, 17 |
| 19. | ¬¬q | &E, 18 |

| | | | |
|---|---|---|---|
| 20. | | Show ¬s | |
| 21. | | ⌐ s | AIP |
| 22. | | s ∨ ¬q | ∨I, 21 |
| 23. | | p & ¬r | ↔E, 1, 22 |
| 24. | | p | &E, 23 |
| 25. | | p & s | &I, 24, 21 |
| 26. | | r | →E, 4, 25 |
| 27. | | ⌐ ¬r | &E, 23 |
| 28. | | ¬s & q | &I, 20, 8 |
| 29. | | ¬s & ¬¬q | ¬¬, 28 |
| 30. | | ¬(s ∨ ¬q) | ¬∨, 29 |
| 31. | | ¬(p & ¬r) | ↔E, 1, 30 |
| 32. | | ¬p ∨ ¬¬r | ¬&, 31 |
| 33. | | Show r | |
| 34. | | ⌐ ¬r | AIP |
| 35. | | ¬p | ∨E*, 32, 34 |
| 36. | | ¬s & ¬r | &I, 20, 34 |
| 37. | | ⌐ p | →E, 6, 36 |
| 38. | | q & r | &I, 8, 33 |

52.

| | | | |
|---|---|---|---|
| 1. | | Show p → (¬p → q) | |
| 2. | ⌐ | p | ACP |
| 3. | | Show ¬p → q | |
| 4. | | ⌐ ¬p | ACP |
| 5. | | q | !, 2, 4 |

56.

| | | | |
|---|---|---|---|
| 1. | ⌐ | Show (p → (q → r)) → ((p → q) → (p → r)) | |
| 2. | | p → (q → r) | ACP |
| 3. | | Show (p → q) → (p → r) | |
| 4. | | ⌐ p → q | ACP |
| 5. | | Show p → r | |
| 6. | | ⌐ p | ACP |
| 7. | | q | →E, 4, 6 |
| 8. | | q → r | →E, 2, 6 |
| 9. | | r | →E, 8, 7 |

58.

| | | | |
|---|---|---|---|
| 1. | ⌐ | Show (p ∨ p) → p | |
| 2. | | p ∨ p | ACP |
| 3. | | Show p | |
| 4. | | ⌐ ¬p | AIP |
| 5. | | p | ∨E*, 2, 4 |

62.

| | | | |
|---|---|---|---|
| 1. | ⌐ | Show (q → r) → ((p ∨ q) → (p ∨ r)) | |
| 2. | | q → r | ACP |
| 3. | | Show (p ∨ q) → (p ∨ r) | |
| 4. | | ⌐ p ∨ q | ACP |
| 5. | | Show p ∨ r | |
| 6. | | ⌐ ¬(p ∨ r) | AIP |
| 7. | | ¬p & ¬r | ¬∨, 6 |
| 8. | | ¬p | &E, 7 |
| 9. | | ¬r | &E, 7 |
| 10. | | q | ∨E*, 4, 8 |
| 11. | | r | →E, 2, 10 |

64.
1.     Show $(p \rightarrow q) \rightarrow ((p \rightarrow r) \rightarrow (p \rightarrow (q \,\&\, r)))$
2.     $p \rightarrow q$                                    ACP
3.     Show $(p \rightarrow r) \rightarrow (p \rightarrow (q \,\&\, r))$
4.     $p \rightarrow r$                                    ACP
5.     Show $p \rightarrow (q \,\&\, r)$
6.     $p$                                                  ACP
7.     $q$                                                  $\rightarrow$E, 2, 6
8.     $r$                                                  $\rightarrow$E, 4, 6
9.     $q \,\&\, r$                                         &I, 7, 8

# B: ADDING QUANTIFIERS

This appendix extends the system of Appendix IIA to predicate logic. The use of *Show* lines pays off handsomely here. A simple formulation of basic quantifier rules suffices as a system for full predicate logic. Proof strategies are readily apparent and relate directly to proof structure.

## 1. KEY DEFINITIONS

The deduction rules needed for quantificational logic are very straightforward. Say that $\mathcal{A}[c/v]$ is the result of substituting $c$ for every occurrence of $v$ throughout the formula $\mathcal{A}$. If $\forall v\mathcal{A}$ and $\exists v\mathcal{A}$ are formulas, then $\mathcal{A}[c/v]$ is called an *instance* of them. Conversely, $\forall v\mathcal{A}$ and $\exists v\mathcal{A}$ are *generics* of $\mathcal{A}[c/v]$.

## 2. SUMMARY OF RULES

*Basic Rules, Applying Only to Entire Formulas*

Existential Introduction ($\exists$I)

| | | |
|---|---|---|
| n. | $\underline{A[c/v]}$ | |
| n+p. | $\exists v\mathcal{A}$ | $\exists$I, n |

Here $c$ may be any constant.

Existential Exploitation ($\exists$E)

| | | |
|---|---|---|
| n. | $\underline{\exists v\mathcal{A}}$ | |
| n+p. | $\mathcal{A}[c/v]$ | $\exists$E, n |

Here $c$ must be a constant new to the proof.

Universal Exploitation ($\forall$E)

| | | |
|---|---|---|
| n. | $\underline{\forall v\mathcal{A}}$ | |
| n+p. | $\mathcal{A}[c/v]$ | $\forall$E, n |

Here $c$ may be any constant.

Universal Proof

| | |
|---|---|
| n. | Show $\forall v\mathcal{A}$ |
| n+1. | Show $\mathcal{A}[c/v]$ |

Here $c$ must be a constant new to the proof.

*Derived Rule, Applying Only to Entire Formulas*

Variable Rewrite (VR)

| | | |
|---|---|---|
| n. | $\underline{\mathcal{A}}$ | |
| m. | $\mathcal{A}[v/u]$ | VR, n |

Here $v$ must be foreign to $\mathcal{A}$.

Quantifier Negation (QN)

| n. | $\neg \exists v \mathcal{A}$ | QN, m |
|---|---|---|
| m. | $\forall v \neg \mathcal{A}$ | QN, n |

| n. | $\neg \forall v \mathcal{A}$ | QN, m |
|---|---|---|
| m. | $\exists v \neg \mathcal{A}$ | QN, n |

# 3. ANSWERS TO UNANSWERED EVEN PROBLEMS

## B.1 DEDUCTION RULES FOR QUANTIFIERS

The policy that guided symbolization for this chapter was to introduce (more or less) only as much complexity as is needed to enable the proofs to go through. In those cases in which the meaning of the English is intended to be captured not only through appropriate interpretation of constants but also by circumscribing the universe of discourse, this is indicated.

| 8. | 1. | $\forall x(H_1 x \rightarrow (Lx \,\&\, H_2 x))$ | A | (universe: insects) |
|---|---|---|---|---|
| | 2. | $\exists x(H_1 x \,\&\, Px)$ | A | |
| | 3. | Show $\exists x((Lx \,\&\, H_2 x) \,\&\, Px)$ | | |
| | 4. | $H_1 a \,\&\, Pa$ | $\exists E, 2$ | |
| | 5. | $H_1 a \rightarrow (La \,\&\, H_2 a)$ | $\forall E, 1$ | |
| | 6. | $H_1 a$ | $\&E, 4$ | |
| | 7. | $La \,\&\, H_2 a$ | $\rightarrow E, 5, 6$ | |
| | 8. | $Pa$ | $\&E, 4$ | |
| | 9. | $(La \,\&\, H_2 a) \,\&\, Pa$ | $\&I, 7, 8$ | |
| | 10. | $\exists x((Lx \,\&\, H_2 x) \,\&\, Px)$ | $\exists I, 9$ | |

| 10. | 1. | $\forall x Axd$ | A | (universe: people) |
|---|---|---|---|---|
| | 2. | $\forall x(Adx \rightarrow Cxd)$ | A | |
| | 3. | Show $Cdd$ | | |
| | 4. | $Add \rightarrow Cdd$ | $\forall E, 2$ | |
| | 5. | $Add$ | $\forall E, 1$ | |
| | 6. | $Cdd$ | $\rightarrow E, 4, 5$ | |

| 14. | 1. | $\exists x(Bx \,\&\, Sx)$ | A | (universe: people) |
|---|---|---|---|---|
| | 2. | $\forall x(Sx \rightarrow \neg Dx)$ | A | |
| | 3. | Show $\exists x(Bx \,\&\, \neg Dx)$ | | |
| | 4. | $Ba \,\&\, Sa$ | $\exists E, 2$ | |
| | 5. | $Sa \rightarrow \neg Da$ | $\forall E, 1$ | |
| | 6. | $Sa$ | $\&E, 4$ | |
| | 7. | $\neg Da$ | $\rightarrow E, 5, 6$ | |
| | 8. | $Ba$ | $\&E, 4$ | |
| | 9. | $Ba \,\&\, \neg Da$ | $\&I, 8, 7$ | |
| | 10. | $\exists x(Bx \,\&\, \neg Dx)$ | $\exists I, 9$ | |

| 16. | 1. | ∃x(Ax & Bx) & ∃x(Ax & Cx) | | A | (universe: people) |
|---|---|---|---|---|---|
| | 2. | ∀x(Cx → Rx) | | A | |
| | 3. | ∀x(Mx → ¬Bx) | | A | |
| | 4. | ~~Show~~ ∃x(Ax & Rx) & ∃x(Ax & ¬Mx) | | | |
| | 5. | ∃x(Ax & Cx) | | &E, 1 | |
| | 6. | Aa & Ca | | ∃E, 5 | |
| | 7. | Ca → Ra | | ∀E, 2 | |
| | 8. | Ca | | &E, 6 | |
| | 9. | Ra | | →E, 7, 8 | |
| | 10. | Aa | | &E, 6 | |
| | 11. | Aa & Ra | | &I, 10, 9 | |
| | 12. | ∃x(Ax & Rx) | | ∃I, 11 | |
| | 13. | ∃x(Ax & Bx) | | &E, 1 | |
| | 14. | Ab & Bb | | ∃E, 13 | |
| | 15. | Bb | | &E, 14 | |
| | 16. | Mb → ¬Bb | | ∀E, 3 | |
| | 17. | ¬¬Bb | | ¬¬, 15 | |
| | 18. | ¬Mb | | →E*, 16, 17 | |
| | 19. | Ab | | &E, 14 | |
| | 20. | Ab & ¬Mb | | &I, 19, 18 | |
| | 21. | ∃x(Ax & ¬Mx) | | ∃I, 20 | |
| | 22. | ∃x(Ax & Rx) & ∃x(Ax & ¬Mx) | | &I, 12, 21 | |

| 20. | 1. | ∀x(Mx → ¬Lx) | A |
|---|---|---|---|
| | 2. | ∃x(Sx & Mx) | A |
| | 3. | ~~Show~~ ∃x(Sx & ¬Lx) | |
| | 4. | Sa & Ma | ∃E, 2 |
| | 5. | Ma → ¬La | ∀E, 1 |
| | 6. | Ma | &E, 4 |
| | 7. | ¬La | →E, 5, 6 |
| | 8. | Sa | &E, 4 |
| | 9. | Sa & ¬La | &I, 8, 7 |
| | 10. | ∃x(Sx & ¬Lx) | ∃I, 9 |

| 22. | 1. | ∀x(Lx → Mx) | A |
|---|---|---|---|
| | 2. | ∃x(Sx & ¬Mx) | A |
| | 3. | ~~Show~~ ∃x(Sx & ¬Lx) | |
| | 4. | Sa & ¬Ma | ∃E, 2 |
| | 5. | La → Ma | ∀E, 1 |
| | 6. | ¬Ma | &E, 4 |
| | 7. | ¬La | →E*, 5, 6 |
| | 8. | Sa | &E, 4 |
| | 9. | Sa & ¬La | &I, 8, 7 |
| | 10. | ∃x(Sx & ¬Lx) | ∃I, 9 |

| 26. | 1. | ∀x(Mx → Lx) | A |
|---|---|---|---|
| | 2. | ∃x(Mx & Sx) | A |
| | 3. | ~~Show~~ ∃x(Sx & Lx) | |
| | 4. | Ma & Sa | ∃E, 2 |
| | 5. | Ma → La | ∀E, 1 |
| | 6. | Ma | &E, 4 |
| | 7. | La | →E, 5, 6 |
| | 8. | Sa | &E, 4 |
| | 9. | Sa & La | &I, 8, 7 |
| | 10. | ∃x(Sx & Lx) | ∃I, 9 |

| | | | |
|---|---|---|---|
| 28. | 1. | ∀x(Mx → ¬Lx) | A |
| | 2. | ∃x(Mx & Sx) | A |
| | 3. | ~~Show~~ ∃x(Sx & ¬Lx) | |
| | 4. | ⌈ Ma & Sa | ∃E, 2 |
| | 5. | | Ma → ¬La | ∀E, 1 |
| | 6. | | Ma | &E, 4 |
| | 7. | | ¬La | →E, 5, 6 |
| | 8. | | Sa | &E, 4 |
| | 9. | | Sa & ¬La | &I, 8, 7 |
| | 10. | ⌊ ∃x(Sx & ¬Lx) | ∃I, 9 |

| | | | |
|---|---|---|---|
| 32. | 1. | ∀x(Lx → Mx) | A |
| | 2. | ∀x(Sx → ¬Mx) | A |
| | 3. | ∃xSx | A |
| | 4. | ~~Show~~ ∃x(Sx & ¬Lx) | |
| | 5. | ⌈ Sa | ∃E, 3 |
| | 6. | | Sa → ¬Ma | ∀E, 2 |
| | 7. | | ¬Ma | →E, 6, 5 |
| | 8. | | La → Ma | ∀E, 1 |
| | 9. | | ¬La | →E*, 8, 7 |
| | 10. | | Sa & ¬La | &I, 5, 9 |
| | 11. | ⌊ ∃x(Sx & ¬Lx) | ∃I, 10 |

| | | | |
|---|---|---|---|
| 34. | 1. | ∀x(Mx → Lx) | A |
| | 2. | ∃x(Sx & Mx) | A |
| | 3. | ~~Show~~ ∃x(Lx & Sx) | |
| | 4. | ⌈ Sa & Ma | ∃E, 2 |
| | 5. | | Ma → La | ∀E, 1 |
| | 6. | | Ma | &E, 4 |
| | 7. | | La | →E, 5, 6 |
| | 8. | | Sa | &E, 4 |
| | 9. | | La & Sa | &I, 7, 8 |
| | 10. | ⌊ ∃x(Lx & Sx) | ∃I, 9 |

| | | | |
|---|---|---|---|
| 38. | 1. | ∃xFx | A |
| | 2. | ∀xGx | A |
| | 3. | ~~Show~~ ∃x(Fx & Gx) | |
| | 4. | ⌈ Fa | ∃E, 1 |
| | 5. | | Ga | ∀E, 2 |
| | 6. | | Fa & Ga | &I, 4, 5 |
| | 7. | ⌊ ∃x(Fx & Gx) | ∃I, 6 |

| | | | |
|---|---|---|---|
| 40. | 1. | ∀x(Gx →Hx) | A |
| | 2. | ∃x(Fx & Gx) | A |
| | 3. | ~~Show~~ ∃x(Fx & Hx) | |
| | 4. | ⌈ Fa & Ga | ∃E, 2 |
| | 5. | | Ga → Ha | ∀E, 1 |
| | 6. | | Ga | &E, 4 |
| | 7. | | Ha | →E, 5, 6 |
| | 8. | | Fa | &E, 4 |
| | 9. | | Fa & Ha | &I, 8, 7 |
| | 10. | ⌊ ∃x(Fx & Hx) | ∃I, 9 |

| 44. | 1. | ∀x(Gx →Hx) | A |
| | 2. | ∃x(Gx & Fx) | A |
| | 3. | Show ∃x(Fx & Hx) | |
| | 4. | Ga & Fa | ∃E, 2 |
| | 5. | Ga → Ha | ∀E, 1 |
| | 6. | Ga | &E, 4 |
| | 7. | Ha | →E, 5, 6 |
| | 8. | Fa | &E, 4 |
| | 9. | Fa & Ha | &I, 8, 7 |
| | 10. | ∃x(Fx & Hx) | ∃I, 9 |

| 46. | 1. | ∃x(Gx & Hx) | A |
| | 2. | ∀x(Gx →Fx) | A |
| | 3. | Show ∃x(Fx & Hx) | |
| | 4. | Ga & Ha | ∃E, 1 |
| | 5. | Ga → Fa | ∀E, 2 |
| | 6. | Ga | &E, 4 |
| | 7. | Fa | →E, 5, 6 |
| | 8. | Ha | &E, 4 |
| | 9. | Fa & Ha | &I, 7, 8 |
| | 10. | ∃x(Fx & Hx) | ∃I, 9 |

| 50. | 1. | ∃x(¬Fx & ¬Gx) | A |
| | 2. | ∀x(¬Gx → ¬Hx) | A |
| | 3. | Show ∃x(¬Hx & ¬Fx) | |
| | 4. | ¬Fa & ¬Ga | ∃E, 1 |
| | 5. | ¬Ga → ¬Ha | ∀E, 2 |
| | 6. | ¬Ga | &E, 4 |
| | 7. | ¬Ha | →E, 5, 6 |
| | 8. | ¬Fa | &E, 4 |
| | 9. | ¬Ha & ¬Fa | &I, 7, 8 |
| | 10. | ∃x(¬Hx & ¬Fx) | ∃I, 9 |

| 52. | 1. | ∀x(Fx ↔ Gx) | A |
| | 2. | ∀x(Fx ↔ Hx) | A |
| | 3. | ∃x(¬Hx ∨ Gx) | A |
| | 4. | Show ∃x(¬Hx ∨ (Gx & Fx)) | |
| | 5. | Show Ha → (Ga & Fa) | |
| | 6. | Ha | ACP |
| | 7. | Fa ↔ Ha | ∀E, 2 |
| | 8. | Fa | ↔E, 7, 6 |
| | 9. | Fa ↔ Ga | ∀E, 1 |
| | 10. | Ga | ↔E, 9, 8 |
| | 11. | Ga & Fa | &I, 10, 8 |
| | 12. | ¬Ha ∨ (Ga & Fa) | ↔∨, 5 |
| | 13. | ∃x(¬Hx ∨ (Gx & Fx)) | ∃I, 12 |

| 56. | 1. | ∃yFyy | A |
| | 2. | ∃x∀zGxz | A |
| | 3. | Show ∃x∃y(Gyx & Fxx) | |
| | 4. | Faa | ∃E, 1 |
| | 5. | ∀zGbz | ∃E, 2 |
| | 6. | Gba | ∀E, 5 |
| | 7. | Gba & Faa | &I, 6, 4 |
| | 8. | ∃y(Gya & Faa) | ∃I, 7 |
| | 9. | ∃x∃y(Gyx & Fxx) | ∃I, 8 |

| 58. | 1. | ∃xGx & ∃x¬Gx | A |
| | 2. | ∀x∀y(Fxy ↔ (Gx & ¬Gy)) | A |
| | 3. | Show ∃x∃yFxy | |
| | 4. | ⌐ ∃xGx | &E, 1 |
| | 5. | Ga | ∃E, 4 |
| | 6. | ∃x¬Gx | &E, 1 |
| | 7. | ¬Gb | ∃E, 6 |
| | 8. | ∀y(Fay ↔ (Ga & ¬Gy)) | ∀E, 2 |
| | 9. | Fab ↔ (Ga & ¬Gb) | ∀E, 8 |
| | 10. | Ga & ¬Gb | &I, 5, 7 |
| | 11. | Fab | ↔E, 9, 10 |
| | 12. | ∃yFay | ∃I, 11 |
| | 13. | ⌊ ∃x∃yFxy | ∃I, 12 |

| 62. | 1. | ∃x∃y(Fx & Gyx) | A |
| | 2. | ∀x∀y((Fx & Hy) → ¬Jxy) | A |
| | 3. | Show ∃x∃y(Gxy & ¬(Hx & Jyx)) | |
| | 4. | ⌐ ∃y(Fa & Gya) | ∃E, 1 |
| | 5. | Fa & Gba | ∃E, 4 |
| | 6. | Show ¬(Hb & Jab) | |
| | 7. | Hb & Jab | AIP |
| | 8. | ∀y((Fa & Hy) → ¬Jay) | ∀E, 2 |
| | 9. | (Fa & Hb) → ¬Jab | ∀E, 8 |
| | 10. | Fa | &E, 5 |
| | 11. | Hb | &E, 7 |
| | 12. | Fa & Hb | &I, 10, 11 |
| | 13. | Jab | &E, 7 |
| | 14. | ⌊¬Jab | →E, 9, 12 |
| | 15. | Gba | &E, 5 |
| | 16. | Gba & ¬(Hb & Jab) | &I, 15, 6 |
| | 17. | ∃y(Gby & ¬(Hb & Jyb) | ∃I, 16 |
| | 18. | ⌊ ∃x∃y(Gxy & ¬(Hx & Jyx)) | ∃I, 17 |

| 64. | 1. | ∀z∀x(¬Hz ↔ (Fx & Gz)) | A |
| | 2. | ∀x∃y(Gy & Fx) | A |
| | 3. | Show ∃x¬Hx | |
| | 4. | ⌐ ∃y(Gy & Fa) | ∀E, 2 |
| | 5. | Gb & Fa | ∃E, 4 |
| | 6. | ∀x(¬Hb ↔ (Fx & Gb)) | ∀E, 1 |
| | 7. | ¬Hb ↔ (Fa & Gb) | ∀E, 6 |
| | 8. | Fa | &E, 5 |
| | 9. | Gb | &E, 5 |
| | 10. | Fa & Gb | &I, 8, 9 |
| | 11. | ¬Hb | ↔E, 7, 10 |
| | 12. | ⌊∃x¬Hx | ∃I, 11 |

## B.2 Universal Proof

### from 13.2

8.
| 1. | $\forall x(Gx \rightarrow Hx)$ | A |
|---|---|---|
| 2. | $\forall x(\neg Gx \rightarrow \neg Sx)$ | A |
| 3. | Show $\forall x(\neg Hx \rightarrow \neg Sx)$ | |
| 4. | Show $\neg Ha \rightarrow \neg Sa$ | |
| 5. | $\neg Ha$ | ACP |
| 6. | $Ga \rightarrow Ha$ | $\forall E, 1$ |
| 7. | $\neg Ga$ | $\rightarrow E^*, 6, 5$ |
| 8. | $\neg Ga \rightarrow \neg Sa$ | $\forall E, 2$ |
| 9. | $\neg Sa$ | $\rightarrow E, 8, 7$ |

10.
| 1. | $\forall x(Ix \rightarrow \neg Px)$ | A | (universe: businesses) |
|---|---|---|---|
| 2. | $\forall x(Ux \rightarrow Ix)$ | A | |
| 3. | Show $\forall x(Ux \rightarrow \neg Px)$ | | |
| 4. | Show $Ua \rightarrow \neg Pa$ | | |
| 5. | $Ua$ | ACP | |
| 6. | $Ua \rightarrow Ia$ | $\forall E, 2$ | |
| 7. | $Ia$ | $\rightarrow E, 6, 5$ | |
| 8. | $Ia \rightarrow \neg Pa$ | $\forall E, 1$ | |
| 9. | $\neg Pa$ | $\rightarrow E, 8, 7$ | |

14.
| 1. | $\forall x(Sx \rightarrow \neg\neg Hx)$ | A | (universe: men) |
|---|---|---|---|
| 2. | $\forall x(Hx \rightarrow Rx)$ | A | |
| 3. | Show $\forall x(Sx \rightarrow \neg\neg Rx)$ | | |
| 4. | Show $Sa \rightarrow \neg\neg Ra$ | | |
| 5. | $Sa$ | ACP | |
| 6. | $Sa \rightarrow \neg\neg Ha$ | $\forall E, 1$ | |
| 7. | $\neg\neg Ha$ | $\rightarrow E, 6, 5$ | |
| 8. | $Ha \rightarrow Ra$ | $\forall E, 2$ | |
| 9. | $\neg\neg Ha \rightarrow \neg\neg Ra$ | $\neg\neg, 8$ | |
| 10. | $\neg\neg Ra$ | $\rightarrow E, 9, 7$ | |

16.
| 1. | $\forall x((Yx \ \& \ Lx) \rightarrow Jx)$ | A | (universe: animals) |
|---|---|---|---|
| 2. | $\forall x((Yx \ \& \ Jx) \rightarrow \neg\neg Hx)$ | A | |
| 3. | Show $\forall x((Yx \ \& \ Lx) \rightarrow Hx)$ | | |
| 4. | Show $(Ya \ \& \ La) \rightarrow Ha$ | | |
| 5. | $Ya \ \& \ La$ | ACP | |
| 6. | $(Ya \ \& \ La) \rightarrow Ja$ | $\forall E, 1$ | |
| 7. | $Ja$ | $\rightarrow E, 6, 5$ | |
| 8. | $Ya$ | $\& E, 5$ | |
| 9. | $Ya \ \& \ Ja$ | $\& I, 8, 7$ | |
| 10. | $(Ya \ \& \ Ja) \rightarrow \neg\neg Ha$ | $\forall E, 2$ | |
| 11. | $\neg\neg Ha$ | $\rightarrow E, 10, 9$ | |
| 12. | $Ha$ | $\neg\neg, 11$ | |

| 20. | 1. | $\forall x(Wx \to Fx)$ | A | (universe: men) |
|---|---|---|---|---|
|  | 2. | $\forall x(\neg Wx \to Hx)$ | A |  |
|  | 3. | Show $\forall x(Hx \lor Fx)$ |  |  |
|  | 4. | Show $Ha \lor Fa$ |  |  |
|  | 5. | Show $\neg Ha \to Fa$ |  |  |
|  | 6. | $\neg Ha$ | ACP |  |
|  | 7. | $\neg Wa \to Ha$ | $\forall E$, 2 |  |
|  | 8. | $\neg\neg Wa$ | $\to E^*$, 7, 6 |  |
|  | 9. | $Wa \to Fa$ | $\forall E$, 1 |  |
|  | 10. | $Wa$ | $\neg\neg$, 8 |  |
|  | 11. | $Fa$ | $\to E$, 9, 10 |  |
|  | 12. | $\neg\neg Ha \lor Fa$ | $\to \lor$, 5 |  |
|  | 13. | $Ha \lor Fa$ | $\neg\neg$, 12 |  |

| 22. | 1. | $\forall x(Jx \to \neg Ox)$ | A |
|---|---|---|---|
|  | 2. | $\forall x(Px \to \neg\neg Ox)$ | A |
|  | 3. | Show $\forall x\neg(Jx \& Px)$ |  |
|  | 4. | Show $\neg(Ja \& Pa)$ |  |
|  | 5. | $Ja \& Pa$ | AIP |
|  | 6. | $Ja \to \neg Oa$ | $\forall E$, 1 |
|  | 7. | $Ja$ | $\&E$, 5 |
|  | 8. | $Pa \to \neg\neg Oa$ | $\forall E$, 2 |
|  | 9. | $Pa$ | $\&E$, 5 |
|  | 10. | $\neg Oa$ | $\to E$, 6, 7 |
|  | 11. | $\neg\neg Oa$ | $\to E$, 8, 9 |

| 26. | 1. | $\forall x(Tx \to \neg Wx)$ | A |
|---|---|---|---|
|  | 2. | $\forall x(\neg Wx \to \neg Cx)$ | A |
|  | 3. | $\forall x(\neg Tx \to \neg Hx)$ | A |
|  | 4. | Show $\forall x(Cx \to \neg Hx)$ |  |
|  | 5. | Show $Ca \to \neg Ha$ |  |
|  | 6. | $Ca$ | ACP |
|  | 7. | $\neg Wa \to \neg Ca$ | $\forall E$, 2 |
|  | 8. | $\neg\neg Ca$ | $\neg\neg$, 6 |
|  | 9. | $\neg\neg Wa$ | $\to E^*$, 7, 8 |
|  | 10. | $Ta \to \neg Wa$ | $\forall E$, 1 |
|  | 11. | $\neg Ta$ | $\to E^*$, 10, 9 |
|  | 12. | $\neg Ta \to \neg Ha$ | $\forall E$, 3 |
|  | 13. | $\neg Ha$ | $\to E$, 12, 11 |

| 28. | 1. | $\forall x(Sx \to Tx)$ | A | (universe: people) |
|---|---|---|---|---|
|  | 2. | $\forall x(Wx \to \neg\neg Gx)$ | A |  |
|  | 3. | $\forall x(Tx \to \neg Gx)$ | A |  |
|  | 4. | Show $\forall x(Sx \to \neg Wx)$ |  |  |
|  | 5. | Show $Sa \to \neg Wa$ |  |  |
|  | 6. | $Sa$ | ACP |  |
|  | 7. | $Sa \to Ta$ | $\forall E$, 1 |  |
|  | 8. | $Ta$ | $\to E$, 7, 6 |  |
|  | 9. | $Ta \to \neg Ga$ | $\forall E$, 3 |  |
|  | 10. | $\neg Ga$ | $\to E$, 9, 8 |  |
|  | 11. | $Wa \to \neg\neg Ga$ | $\forall E$, 2 |  |
|  | 12. | $Wa \to Ga$ | $\neg\neg$, 11 |  |
|  | 13. | $\neg Wa$ | $\to E^*$, 12, 10 |  |

32.    1.   $\forall x(\neg Sx \rightarrow Rx)$           A     (universe: my ideas)
       2.   $\forall x(Bx \rightarrow \neg Wx)$          A
       3.   $\forall x(\neg Tx \rightarrow \neg Sx)$     A
       4.   $\forall x(Rx \rightarrow \neg\neg Lx)$      A
       5.   $\forall x(Dx \rightarrow Bx)$               A
       6.   $\forall x(\neg Lx \vee Wx)$                 A
       7.   ~~Show~~ $\forall x(Dx \rightarrow Tx)$
       8.   ⌐ ~~Show~~ $Da \rightarrow Ta$
       9.   │ Da                                          ACP
      10.   │ $Da \rightarrow Ba$                         $\forall$E, 5
      11.   │ Ba                                          $\rightarrow$E, 10, 9
      12.   │ $Ba \rightarrow \neg Wa$                    $\forall$E, 2
      13.   │ $\neg Wa$                                   $\rightarrow$E, 12, 11
      14.   │ $\neg La \vee Wa$                           $\forall$E, 6
      15.   │ $\neg La$                                   $\vee$E*, 14, 13
      16.   │ $Ra \rightarrow \neg\neg La$                $\forall$E, 4
      17.   │ $Ra \rightarrow La$                         $\neg\neg$, 16
      18.   │ $\neg Ra$                                   $\rightarrow$E*, 17, 15
      19.   │ $\neg Sa \rightarrow Ra$                    $\forall$E, 1
      20.   │ $\neg\neg Sa$                               $\rightarrow$E*, 19, 18
      21.   │ $\neg Ta \rightarrow \neg Sa$               $\forall$E, 3
      22.   │ $\neg\neg Ta$                               $\rightarrow$E*, 21, 20
      23.   └ Ta                                          $\neg\neg$, 22

34.    1.   $\forall x(Sx \rightarrow Cx)$               A     (universe: students)
       2.   $\forall x(Cx \rightarrow Lx)$               A
       3.   ~~Show~~ $\forall x(Sx \rightarrow Lx)$
       4.   ⌐ ~~Show~~ $Sa \rightarrow La$
       5.   │ ⌐ Sa                                        ACP
       6.   │ │ $Sa \rightarrow Ca$                       $\forall$E, 1
       7.   │ │ Ca                                        $\rightarrow$E, 6, 5
       8.   │ │ $Ca \rightarrow La$                       $\forall$E, 2
       9.   └ └ La                                        $\rightarrow$E, 8, 7

38.    1.   $\forall x(\neg Fx \rightarrow Cx)$          A     (universe: people)
       2.   $\forall x(Cx \rightarrow Dx)$               A
       3.   ~~Show~~ $\forall x(\neg Dx \rightarrow Fx)$
       4.   ⌐ ~~Show~~ $\neg Da \rightarrow Fa$
       5.   │ ⌐ $\neg Da$                                 ACP
       6.   │ │ $Ca \rightarrow Da$                       $\forall$E, 2
       7.   │ │ $\neg Ca$                                 $\rightarrow$E*, 6, 5
       8.   │ │ $\neg Fa \rightarrow Ca$                  $\forall$E, 1
       9.   │ │ $\neg\neg Fa$                             $\rightarrow$E*, 8, 7
      10.   └ └ Fa                                        $\neg\neg$, 9

204

| 40. | 1. | $\forall x((Ix \lor Fx) \to Dx)$ | A | (universe: people) |
|---|---|---|---|---|
| | 2. | $\forall x(Dx \to (Bx \& \neg Ox))$ | A | |
| | 3. | $\forall x(Tx \to Fx)$ | A | |
| | 4. | $\forall x(\neg Cx \to Ix)$ | A | |
| | 5. | Show $\forall x((\neg Bx \lor Ox) \to (Cx \& \neg Tx))$ | | |
| | 6. | Show $(\neg Ba \lor Oa) \to (Ca \& \neg Ta)$ | | |
| | 7. | $\neg Ba \lor Oa$ | ACP | |
| | 8. | $\neg Ba \lor \neg\neg Oa$ | $\neg\neg$, 7 | |
| | 9. | $\neg(Ba \& \neg Oa)$ | $\neg\&$, 8 | |
| | 10. | $Da \to (Ba \& \neg Oa)$ | $\forall E$, 2 | |
| | 11. | $\neg Da$ | $\to E^*$, 10, 9 | |
| | 12. | $(Ia \lor Fa) \to Da$ | $\forall E$, 1 | |
| | 13. | $\neg(Ia \lor Fa)$ | $\to E^*$, 12, 11 | |
| | 14. | $\neg Ia \& \neg Fa$ | $\neg\lor$, 13 | |
| | 15. | $\neg Ca \to Ia$ | $\forall E$, 4 | |
| | 16. | $\neg Ia$ | $\& E$, 14 | |
| | 17. | $\neg\neg Ca$ | $\to E^*$, 15, 16 | |
| | 18. | $Ca$ | $\neg\neg$, 17 | |
| | 19. | $Ta \to Fa$ | $\forall E$, 3 | |
| | 20. | $\neg Fa$ | $\& E$, 14 | |
| | 21. | $\neg Ta$ | $\to E^*$, 19, 20 | |
| | 22. | $Ca \& \neg Ta$ | $\& I$, 18, 21 | |

| 44. | 1. | $\forall x(Fx \leftrightarrow (Gx \& Hx))$ | A |
|---|---|---|---|
| | 2. | Show $\forall x(Fx \to Gx) \& \forall x(Fx \to Hx)$ | |
| | 3. | Show $\forall x(Fx \to Gx)$ | |
| | 4. | Show $Fa \to Ga$ | |
| | 5. | $Fa$ | ACP |
| | 6. | $Fa \leftrightarrow (Ga \& Ha)$ | $\forall E$, 1 |
| | 7. | $Ga \& Ha$ | $\leftrightarrow E$, 6, 5 |
| | 8. | $Ga$ | $\& E$, 7 |
| | 9. | Show $\forall x(Fx \to Hx)$ | |
| | 10. | Show $Fb \to Hb$ | |
| | 11. | $Fb$ | ACP |
| | 12. | $Fb \leftrightarrow (Gb \& Hb)$ | $\forall E$, 1 |
| | 13. | $Gb \& Hb$ | $\leftrightarrow E$, 12, 11 |
| | 14. | $Hb$ | $\& E$, 13 |
| | 15. | $\forall x(Fx \to Gx) \& \forall x(Fx \to Hx)$ | $\& I$, 3, 9 |

| 46. | 1. | $\forall x(Fx \to Hx)$ | A |
|---|---|---|---|
| | 2. | $\forall x(Gx \to Hx)$ | A |
| | 3. | Show $\forall x((Fx \lor Gx) \to Hx)$ | |
| | 4. | Show $(Fa \lor Ga) \to Ha$ | |
| | 5. | $Fa \lor Ga$ | ACP |
| | 6. | $Fa \to Ha$ | $\forall E$, 1 |
| | 7. | $Ga \to Ha$ | $\forall E$, 2 |
| | 8. | $Ha$ | $\lor E$, 5, 6, 7 |

50.
1. $\forall x(Fx \leftrightarrow (\neg Gx \leftrightarrow \neg Fx))$  A
2. Show $\forall xGx$
3. ⌐ Show $Ga$
4. │ $\neg Ga$  AIP
5. │ $Fa \leftrightarrow (\neg Ga \leftrightarrow \neg Fa)$  $\forall$E, 1
6. │ Show $Fa$
7. │⌐ $\neg Fa$  AIP
8. ││ $\neg(\neg Ga \leftrightarrow \neg Fa)$  $\leftrightarrow$E*, 5, 7
9. ││ $\neg Ga \leftrightarrow \neg\neg Fa$  $\neg\leftrightarrow$, 8
10. │└ $\neg\neg Fa$  $\leftrightarrow$E, 9, 4
11. │ $\neg\neg\neg Fa$  $\neg\neg$, 7
12. │ $\neg Ga \leftrightarrow \neg Fa$  $\leftrightarrow$E, 5, 6
13. │ $\neg Fa$  $\rightarrow$E, 12, 4
14. └└ $\neg\neg Fa$  $\neg\neg$, 6

52.
1. $\forall x((Fx \,\&\, Gx) \rightarrow Hx)$  A
2. $\forall xGx \,\&\, \forall xFx$  A
3. ⌐ Show $\forall x(Fx \,\&\, Hx)$
4. │ Show $Fa \,\&\, Ha$
5. │⌐ $\forall xFx$  &E, 2
6. ││ $Fa$  $\forall$E, 5
7. ││ $\forall xGx$  &E, 2
8. ││ $Ga$  $\forall$E, 7
9. ││ $(Fa \,\&\, Ga) \rightarrow Ha$  $\forall$E, 1
10. ││ $Fa \,\&\, Ga$  &I, 6, 8
11. ││ $Ha$  $\rightarrow$E, 9, 10
12. └└ $Fa \,\&\, Ha$  &I, 6, 11

56.
1. $\forall x\forall y(Fxy \rightarrow Fyx)$  A
2. Show $\forall x\forall y(Fxy \leftrightarrow Fyx)$
3. ⌐ Show $\forall y(Fay \leftrightarrow Fya)$
4. │ Show $Fab \leftrightarrow Fba$
5. │⌐ $\forall y(Fay \rightarrow Fya)$  $\forall$E, 1
6. ││ $Fab \rightarrow Fba$  $\forall$E, 5
7. ││ $\forall y(Fby \rightarrow Fyb)$  $\forall$E, 1
8. ││ $Fba \rightarrow Fab$  $\forall$E, 7
9. └└ $Fab \leftrightarrow Fba$  $\leftrightarrow$I, 6, 8

58.
1. $\forall x\forall y(Fxy \lor Fyx)$  A
2. $\forall x\forall y(Fxy \rightarrow Fyx)$  A
3. ⌐ Show $\forall x\forall yFxy$
4. │ Show $\forall yFby$
5. │ Show $Fba$
6. │⌐ $\forall y(Fay \lor Fya)$  $\forall$E, 1
7. ││ $Fab \lor Fba$  $\forall$E, 6
8. ││ $\forall y(Fay \rightarrow Fya)$  $\forall$E, 2
9. ││ $Fab \rightarrow Fba$  $\forall$E, 8
10. ││ Show $Fba \rightarrow Fba$
11. ││ $Fba$  ACP
12. └└ $Fba$  $\lor$E, 7, 9, 10

206

62.  1. $\forall x\forall y\forall z((Fxy \ \& \ Fyz) \rightarrow Fxz)$     A
    2. $\forall x\forall y(Fxy \rightarrow Fyx)$     A
    3. $\exists x\exists yFxy$     A
    4. ~~Show~~ $\exists xFxx$
    5. $\quad\lceil\ \exists yFay$     $\exists$E, 3
    6. $\quad\mid\ Fab$     $\exists$E, 5
    7. $\quad\mid\ \forall y(Fay \rightarrow Fya)$     $\forall$E, 2
    8. $\quad\mid\ Fab \rightarrow Fba$     $\forall$E, 7
    9. $\quad\mid\ Fba$     $\rightarrow$E, 8, 6
   10. $\quad\mid\ \forall y\forall z((Fay \ \& \ Fyz) \rightarrow Faz)$     $\forall$E, 1
   11. $\quad\mid\ \forall z((Fab \ \& \ Fbz) \rightarrow Faz)$     $\forall$E, 10
   12. $\quad\mid\ (Fab \ \& \ Fba) \rightarrow Faa$     $\forall$E, 11
   13. $\quad\mid\ Fab \ \& \ Fba$     &I, 6, 9
   14. $\quad\mid\ Faa$     $\rightarrow$E, 12, 13
   15. $\quad\lfloor\ \exists xFxx$     $\exists$I, 14

64.  1. $\forall x\forall y\forall z((Fxy \ \& \ Fxz) \rightarrow Fyz)$     A
    2. $\forall x\forall y(Fxy \rightarrow Fyx)$     A
    3. $\forall xFxx$     A
    4. ~~Show~~ $\forall x\forall y\forall z((Fxy \ \& \ Fyz) \rightarrow Fxz)$
    5. ~~Show~~ $\forall y\forall z((Fay \ \& \ Fyz) \rightarrow Faz)$
    6. ~~Show~~ $\forall z((Fab \ \& \ Fbz) \rightarrow Faz)$
    7. ~~Show~~ $(Fab \ \& \ Fbc) \rightarrow Fac$
    8. $Fab \ \& \ Fbc$     ACP
    9. $\forall y(Fay \rightarrow Fya)$     $\forall$E, 2
   10. $Fab \rightarrow Fba$     $\forall$E, 9
   11. $Fab$     &E, 8
   12. $Fba$     $\rightarrow$E, 10, 11
   13. $Fbc$     &E, 8
   14. $Fba \ \& \ Fbc$     &I, 12, 13
   15. $\forall y\forall z((Fby \ \& \ Fbz) \rightarrow Fyz)$     $\forall$E, 1
   16. $\forall z((Fba \ \& \ Fbz) \rightarrow Faz)$     $\forall$E, 15
   17. $(Fba \ \& \ Fbc) \rightarrow Fac$     $\forall$E, 16
   18. $Fac$     $\rightarrow$E, 17, 14

from 13.3

8.  1. $\forall x(Fx \rightarrow \forall y(Gy \rightarrow Hxy))$     A
    2. $\exists x(Fx \ \& \ \exists y\neg Hxy)$     A
    3. ~~Show~~ $\exists x\neg Gx$
    4. $\quad\lceil\ Fa \ \& \ \exists y\neg Hay$     $\exists$E, 2
    5. $\quad\mid\ \exists y\neg Hay$     &E, 4
    6. $\quad\mid\ \neg Hab$     $\exists$E, 5
    7. $\quad\mid\ Fa \rightarrow \forall y(Gy \rightarrow Hay)$     $\forall$E, 1
    8. $\quad\mid\ Fa$     &E, 4
    9. $\quad\mid\ \forall y(Gy \rightarrow Hay)$     $\rightarrow$E, 7, 8
   10. $\quad\mid\ Gb \rightarrow Hab$     $\forall$E, 9
   11. $\quad\mid\ \neg Gb$     $\rightarrow$E*, 10, 6
   12. $\quad\lfloor\ \exists x\neg Gx$     $\exists$I, 11

10.
1. $\forall x(\exists yFxy \rightarrow \exists y\neg Gy)$    A
2. $\exists x\exists yFxy$    A
3. $\forall x(Gx \leftrightarrow \neg Hx)$    A
4. ~~Show~~ $\exists xHx$
5.    $\exists yFay$    $\exists E, 2$
6.    $\exists yFay \rightarrow \exists y\neg Gy$    $\forall E, 1$
7.    $\exists y\neg Gy$    $\rightarrow E, 6, 5$
8.    $\neg Gb$    $\exists E, 7$
9.    $Gb \leftrightarrow \neg Hb$    $\forall E, 3$
10.    $\neg\neg Hb$    $\leftrightarrow E^*, 9, 8$
11.    $Hb$    $\neg\neg, 10$
12.    $\exists xHx$    $\exists I, 11$

14.
1. $\exists x\forall y\neg Fxy$    A
2. ~~Show~~ $\exists x\forall y\forall z(Fxz \rightarrow Fzy)$
3.    $\forall y\neg Fay$    $\exists E, 1$
4.    ~~Show~~ $\forall y\forall z(Faz \rightarrow Fzy)$
5.      ~~Show~~ $\forall z(Faz \rightarrow Fzb)$
6.        ~~Show~~ $Fac \rightarrow Fcb$
7.        $\neg Fac$    $\forall E, 3$
8.        $\neg Fac \vee Fcb$    $\vee I, 7$
9.        $Fac \rightarrow Fcb$    $\rightarrow\vee, 8$
10.    $\exists x\forall y\forall z(Fxz \rightarrow Fzy)$    $\exists I, 4$

16.
1. $\forall x(\exists y(Ay \& Bxy) \rightarrow Cx)$    A
2. $\exists y(Dy \& \exists x((Fx \& Gx) \& Byx))$    A
3. $\forall x(Fx \rightarrow Ax)$    A
4. $\exists x(Cx \& Dx) \rightarrow (\exists y(Dy \& \exists zByz) \rightarrow \forall xFx)$    A
5. ~~Show~~ $\forall xAx$
6.    ~~Show~~ $Aa$
7.    $Db \& \exists x((Fx \& Gx) \& Bbx)$    $\exists E, 2$
8.    $\exists x((Fx \& Gx) \& Bbx)$    $\&E, 7$
9.    $(Fc \& Gc) \& Bbc$    $\exists E, 8$
10.    $Fc \& Gc$    $\&E, 9$
11.    $Fc \rightarrow Ac$    $\forall E, 3$
12.    $Fc$    $\&E, 10$
13.    $Ac$    $\rightarrow E, 11, 12$
14.    $Bbc$    $\&E, 9$
15.    $Ac \& Bbc$    $\&I, 13, 14$
16.    $\exists y(Ay \& Bby) \rightarrow Cb$    $\forall E, 1$
17.    $\exists y(Ay \& Bby)$    $\exists I, 15$
18.    $Cb$    $\rightarrow E, 16, 17$
19.    $Db$    $\&E, 7$
20.    $Cb \& Db$    $\&I, 18, 19$
21.    $\exists x(Cx \& Dx)$    $\exists I, 20$
22.    $\exists y(Dy \& \exists zByz) \rightarrow \forall xFx$    $\rightarrow E, 4, 21$
23.    $\exists zBbz$    $\exists I, 14$
24.    $Db \& \exists zBbz$    $\&I, 19, 23$
25.    $\exists y(Dy \& \exists zByz)$    $\exists I, 24$
26.    $\forall xFx$    $\rightarrow E, 22, 25$
27.    $Fa \rightarrow Aa$    $\forall E, 3$
28.    $Fa$    $\forall E, 26$
29.    $Aa$    $\rightarrow E, 27, 28$

## B.3 Derived Rules for Quantifiers

8.  1.  $\forall x(Ax \to \forall y(Ty \to Oxy))$      A     (universe: people)
    2.  $\neg\exists x(Tx \,\&\, Oxx)$      A
    3.  ~~Show~~ $\neg\exists x(Tx \,\&\, Ax)$
    4.  $\exists x(Tx \,\&\, Ax)$      AIP
    5.  $\forall x\neg(Tx \,\&\, Oxx)$      QN, 2
    6.  $Ta \,\&\, Aa$      $\exists$E, 4
    7.  $Aa \to \forall y(Ty \to Oay)$      $\forall$E, 1
    8.  $Aa$      &E, 6
    9.  $\forall y(Ty \to Oay)$      $\to$E, 7, 8
    10. $Ta \to Oaa$      $\forall$E, 9
    11. $Ta$      &E, 6
    12. $Oaa$      $\to$E, 10, 11
    13. $Ta \,\&\, Oaa$      &I, 11, 12
    14. $\neg(Ta \,\&\, Oaa)$      $\forall$E, 5

10. 1.  $\forall x(Ax \leftrightarrow (\exists yPy \to Px)$      A
    2.  ~~Show~~ $\exists xAx$
    3.  $\neg\exists xAx$      AIP
    4.  $\forall x\neg Ax$      QN, 3
    5.  $Aa \leftrightarrow (\exists yPy \to Pa)$      $\forall$E, 1
    6.  $\neg Aa$      $\forall$E, 4
    7.  $\neg(\exists yPy \to Pa)$      $\leftrightarrow$E*, 5, 6
    8.  $\exists yPy \,\&\, \neg Pa$      $\neg\to$, 7
    9.  $\exists yPy$      &E, 8
    10. $Pb$      $\exists$E, 9
    11. $\neg\exists yPy \lor Pb$      $\lor$I, 10
    12. $Ab \leftrightarrow (\exists yPy \to Pb)$      $\forall$E, 1
    13. $\exists yPy \to Pb$      $\to\lor$, 11
    14. $Ab$      $\leftrightarrow$E, 12, 13
    15. $\neg Ab$      $\forall$E, 4

14. 1.  $\forall x\exists y(Fx \to Gy)$      A
    2.  ~~Show~~ $\exists y\forall x(Fx \to Gy)$
    3.  $\neg\exists y\forall x(Fx \to Gy)$      AIP
    4.  $\forall y\exists x\neg(Fx \to Gy)$      $QN^2$, 3
    5.  $\exists x\neg(Fx \to Ga)$      $\forall$E, 4
    6.  $\neg(Fb \to Ga)$      $\exists$E, 5
    7.  $Fb \,\&\, \neg Ga$      $\neg\to$, 6
    8.  $\exists y(Fb \to Gy)$      $\forall$E, 1
    9.  $Fb \to Gc$      $\exists$E, 8
    10. $Fb$      &E, 7
    11. $Gc$      $\to$E, 9, 10
    12. $\exists x\neg(Fx \to Gc)$      $\forall$E, 4
    13. $\neg(Fd \to Gc)$      $\exists$E, 12
    14. $Fd \,\&\, \neg Gc$      $\neg\to$, 13
    15. $\neg Gc$      &E, 14
    16. $\neg\neg Gc$      $\neg\neg$, 11

16. 1.  $\exists xFx \to \exists xGx$      A
    2.  ~~Show~~ $\exists x(Fx \to Gx)$
    3.  $\neg\exists x(Fx \to Gx)$      AIP
    4.  $\forall x\neg(Fx \to Gx)$      QN, 3
    5.  $\neg(Fa \to Ga)$      $\forall$E, 4
    6.  $Fa \,\&\, \neg Ga$      $\neg\to$, 5
    7.  $Fa$      &E, 6

| | | | |
|---|---|---|---|
| 8. | | ∃xFx | ∃I, 7 |
| 9. | | ∃xGx | →E, 1, 8 |
| 10. | | Gb | ∃E, 9 |
| 11. | | ¬Fb ∨ Gb | ∨I, 10 |
| 12. | | Fb → Gb | →∨, 11 |
| 13. | | ∃x(Fx → Gx) | ∃I, 12 |
| 14. | | ¬∃x(Fx → Gx) | R, 3 |

20.

| | | | |
|---|---|---|---|
| 1. | | ∃xFx → ∀y(Gy → Hy) | A |
| 2. | | ∃xJx → ∃xGx | A |
| 3. | | Show ∃x(Fx & Jx) → ∃zHz | |
| 4. | | ∃x(Fx & Jx) | ACP |
| 5. | | Fa & Ja | ∃E, 4 |
| 6. | | Ja | &E, 5 |
| 7. | | ∃xJx | ∃I, 6 |
| 8. | | ∃xGx | →E, 2, 7 |
| 9. | | Gb | ∃E, 8 |
| 10. | | Fa | &E, 5 |
| 11. | | ∃xFx | ∃I, 10 |
| 12. | | ∀y(Gy → Hy) | →E, 1, 11 |
| 13. | | Gb → Hb | ∀E, 12 |
| 14. | | Hb | →E, 13, 9 |
| 15. | | ∃zHz | ∃I, 14 |

22.

| | | | |
|---|---|---|---|
| 1. | | ∀x(∃yFyx → ∀zFxz) | A |
| 2. | | Show ∀y∀x(Fyx → Fxy) | |
| 3. | | Show ∀x(Fbx → Fxb) | |
| 4. | | Show Fba → Fab | |
| 5. | | Fba | ACP |
| 6. | | ∃yFya → ∀zFaz | ∀E, 1 |
| 7. | | ∃yFya | ∃I, 5 |
| 8. | | ∀zFaz | →E, 6, 7 |
| 9. | | Fab | ∀E, 8 |

26.

| | | | |
|---|---|---|---|
| 1. | | ∀x(Fx → ∀y(Gy → Hxy)) | A |
| 2. | | ∀x(Dx → ∀y(Hxy → Cy)) | A |
| 3. | | Show ∃x(Fx & Dx) → ∀y(Gy → Cy) | |
| 4. | | ∃x(Fx & Dx) | ACP |
| 5. | | Show ∀y(Gy → Cy) | |
| 6. | | Show Ga → Ca | |
| 7. | | Ga | ACP |
| 8. | | Fb & Db | ∃E, 4 |
| 9. | | Fb → ∀y(Gy → Hby) | ∀E, 1 |
| 10. | | Fb | &E, 8 |
| 11. | | ∀y(Gy → Hby) | →E, 9, 10 |
| 12. | | Ga → Hba | ∀E, 11 |
| 13. | | Hba | →E, 12, 7 |
| 14. | | Db → ∀y(Hby → Cy) | ∀E, 2 |
| 15. | | Db | &E, 8 |
| 16. | | ∀y(Hby → Cy) | →E, 14, 15 |
| 17. | | Hba → Ca | ∀E, 16 |
| 18. | | Ca | →E, 17, 13 |

28.

| | | | |
|---|---|---|---|
| 1. | | ∀x∀y(Gxy ↔ (Fy → Hx)) | A |
| 2. | | ∀zGaz | A |

|     | 3.  | ~~Show~~ $\exists xFx \to \exists xHx$ |                  |
|     | 4.  | $\exists xFx$                           | ACP              |
|     | 5.  | Fb                                       | $\exists$E, 4    |
|     | 6.  | $\forall y(Gay \leftrightarrow (Fy \to Ha))$ | $\forall$E, 1 |
|     | 7.  | $Gab \leftrightarrow (Fb \to Ha)$        | $\forall$E, 6    |
|     | 8.  | Gab                                      | $\forall$E, 2    |
|     | 9.  | $Fb \to Ha$                              | $\leftrightarrow$E, 7, 8 |
|     | 10. | Ha                                       | $\to$E, 9, 5     |
|     | 11. | $\exists xHx$                            | $\exists$I, 10   |

32.
| 1.  | $\exists x(Fx \ \& \ \forall y(Gy \to Hy))$               | A              |
| 2.  | $\forall x(Fx \to (\neg Lx \to \neg \exists z(Kz \ \& \ Hz)))$ | A         |
| 3.  | ~~Show~~ $\exists x(Kx \ \& \ Gx) \to \exists xLx$        |                |
| 4.  | $\exists x(Kx \ \& \ Gx)$                                 | ACP            |
| 5.  | Ka & Ga                                                    | $\exists$E, 4  |
| 6.  | $Fb \ \& \ \forall y(Gy \to Hy)$                          | $\exists$E, 1  |
| 7.  | $Fb \to (\neg Lb \to \neg \exists z(Kz \ \& \ Hz))$       | $\forall$E, 2  |
| 8.  | Fb                                                         | &E, 6          |
| 9.  | $\neg Lb \to \neg \exists z(Kz \ \& \ Hz)$                | $\to$E, 7, 8   |
| 10. | $\forall y(Gy \to Hy)$                                    | &E, 6          |
| 11. | $Ga \to Ha$                                               | $\forall$E, 10 |
| 12. | Ga                                                         | &E, 5          |
| 13. | Ha                                                         | $\to$E, 11, 12 |
| 14. | Ka                                                         | &E, 5          |
| 15. | Ka & Ha                                                    | &I, 14, 13     |
| 16. | $\exists z(Kz \ \& \ Hz)$                                 | EI, 15         |
| 17. | $\neg\neg\exists z(Kz \ \& \ Hz)$                         | $\neg\neg$, 16 |
| 18. | $\neg\neg Lb$                                             | $\to$E*, 9, 17 |
| 19. | Lb                                                         | $\neg\neg$, 18 |
| 20. | $\exists xLx$                                             | $\exists$I, 19 |

34.
| 1.  | $\neg\forall x(Hx \lor Kx)$                | A              |
| 2.  | $\forall x((Fx \lor \neg Kx) \to Gxx)$     | A              |
| 3.  | ~~Show~~ $\exists xGxx$                     |                |
| 4.  | $\exists x\neg(Hx \lor Kx)$                | QN, 1          |
| 5.  | $\neg(Ha \lor Ka)$                         | $\exists$E, 4  |
| 6.  | $\neg Ha \ \& \ \neg Ka$                   | $\neg\lor$, 5  |
| 7.  | $\neg Ka$                                  | &E, 6          |
| 8.  | $(Fa \lor \neg Ka) \to Gaa$                | $\forall$E, 2  |
| 9.  | $Fa \lor \neg Ka$                          | $\lor$I, 7     |
| 10. | Gaa                                        | $\to$E, 8, 9   |
| 11. | $\exists xGxx$                             | $\exists$I, 10 |

38.
| 1.  | $\forall x\forall y\forall z((Fxy \ \& \ Fyz) \to Fxz)$ | A              |
| 2.  | $\neg\exists xFxx$                                       | A              |
| 3.  | ~~Show~~ $\forall x\forall y(Fxy \to \neg Fyx)$         |                |
| 4.  | ~~Show~~ $\forall y(Fay \to \neg Fya)$                  |                |
| 5.  | ~~Show~~ $Fab \to \neg Fba$                             |                |
| 6.  | $\forall y\forall z((Fay \ \& \ Fyz) \to Faz)$          | $\forall$E, 1  |
| 7.  | $\forall z((Fab \ \& \ Fbz) \to Faz)$                   | $\forall$E, 6  |
| 8.  | $(Fab \ \& \ Fba) \to Faa$                              | $\forall$E, 7  |
| 9.  | $\forall x\neg Fxx$                                      | QN, 2          |
| 10. | $\neg Faa$                                               | $\forall$E, 9  |
| 11. | $\neg(Fab \ \& \ Fba)$                                   | $\to$E*, 8, 10 |
| 12. | $\neg Fab \lor \neg Fba$                                 | $\neg$&, 11    |
| 13. | $Fab \to \neg Fba$                                       | $\to\lor$, 12  |

211

| 40. | 1. | Fa → (∃xGx → Gb) | A |
|  | 2. | ∀x(Gx → Hx) | A |
|  | 3. | ∀x(¬Jx → ¬Hx) | A |
|  | 4. | Show ¬Jb → (¬Fa ∨ ∀x¬Gx) | |
|  | 5. | ¬Jb | ACP |
|  | 6. | Show Fa → ∀x¬Gx | |
|  | 7. | Fa | ACP |
|  | 8. | ¬Jb → ¬Hb | ∀E, 3 |
|  | 9. | ¬Hb | →E, 8, 5 |
|  | 10. | Gb → Hb | ∀E, 2 |
|  | 11. | ¬Gb | →E*, 10, 9 |
|  | 13. | ∃xGx → Gb | →E, 1, 7 |
|  | 14. | ¬∃xGx | →E*, 13, 11 |
|  | 15. | ∀x¬Gx | QN, 14 |
|  | 16. | ¬Fa ∨ ∀x¬Gx | →∨, 6 |

| 44. | 1. | ∀x¬Fxc → ∃xGxb | A |
|  | 2. | Show ∃x(¬Fxc → Gxb) | |
|  | 3. | ¬∃x(¬Fxc → Gxb) | AIP |
|  | 4. | ∀x¬(¬Fxc → Gxb) | QN, 3 |
|  | 5. | Show ∀x¬Fxc | |
|  | 6. | Show ¬Fac | |
|  | 7. | ¬(¬Fac → Gab) | ∀E, 4 |
|  | 8. | ¬Fac & ¬Gab | ¬→, 7 |
|  | 9. | ¬Fac | &E, 8 |
|  | 10. | ∃xGxb | →E, 1, 5 |
|  | 11. | Gdb | ∃E, 10 |
|  | 12. | ¬(¬Fdc → Gdb) | ∀E, 4 |
|  | 13. | ¬Fdc & ¬Gdb | ¬→, 12 |
|  | 14. | ¬Gdb | &E, 13 |
|  | 15. | ¬¬Gdb | ¬¬, 11 |

| 46. | 1. | ∃x(Px & ¬Mx) → ∀y(Py → Ly) | A |
|  | 2. | ∃x(Px & Nx) | A |
|  | 3. | ∀x(Px → ¬Lx) | A |
|  | 4. | Show ∃x(Nx & Mx) | |
|  | 5. | Pa & Na | ∃E, 2 |
|  | 6. | Pa → ¬La | ∀E, 3 |
|  | 7. | Pa | &E, 5 |
|  | 8. | ¬La | →E, 6, 7 |
|  | 9. | Pa & ¬La | &I, 7, 8 |
|  | 10. | ¬(Pa → La) | ¬→, 9 |
|  | 11. | ∃y¬(Py → Ly) | ∃I, 10 |
|  | 12. | ¬∀y(Py → Ly) | QN, 11 |
|  | 13. | ¬∃x(Px & ¬Mx) | →E*, 1, 12 |
|  | 14. | ∀x¬(Px & ¬Mx) | QN, 13 |
|  | 15. | ¬(Pa & ¬Ma) | ∀E, 14 |
|  | 16. | ¬Pa ∨ ¬¬Ma | ¬&, 15 |
|  | 17. | ¬Pa ∨ Ma | ¬¬, 16 |
|  | 18. | ¬¬Pa | ¬¬, 7 |
|  | 19. | Ma | ∨E*, 17, 18 |
|  | 20. | Na | &E, 5 |
|  | 21. | Na & Ma | &I, 20, 19 |
|  | 22. | ∃x(Nx & Mx) | ∃I, 21 |

| 50. | 1. | ∀x(Cx → Fx) | A |
|---|---|---|---|
| | 2. | ~~Show~~ ∀x((Px & ∃y(Cy & Dxy)) → ∃z(Fz & Dxz)) | |
| | 3. | ⎡ ~~Show~~ (Pa & ∃y(Cy & Day)) → ∃y(Fy & Day) | |
| | 4. | ⎢ ⎡ Pa & ∃y(Cy & Day) | ACP |
| | 5. | ⎢ ⎢ ∃y(Cy & Day) | &E, 4 |
| | 6. | ⎢ ⎢ Cb & Dab | ∃E, 5 |
| | 7. | ⎢ ⎢ Cb → Fb | ∀E, 1 |
| | 8. | ⎢ ⎢ Cb | &E, 6 |
| | 9. | ⎢ ⎢ Fb | →E, 7, 8 |
| | 10. | ⎢ ⎢ Dab | &E, 6 |
| | 11. | ⎢ ⎢ Fb & Dab | &I, 9, 10 |
| | 12. | ⎣ ⎣ ∃y(Fy & Day) | ∃I, 11 |

| 52. | 1. | Pmj | A | (universe: people) |
|---|---|---|---|---|
| | 2. | ∃x(Pxm & Tx) | A | |
| | 3. | ¬Tj | A | |
| | 4. | ~~Show~~ ¬∀x(∃y(Pyx & Ty) → Tx) | | |
| | 5. | ⎡ ∀x(∃y(Pyx & Ty) → Tx) | AIP | |
| | 6. | ⎢ ∃y(Pym & Ty) → Tm | ∀E, 5 | |
| | 7. | ⎢ ∃y(Pym & Ty) | VR, 2 | |
| | 8. | ⎢ Tm | →E, 6, 7 | |
| | 9. | ⎢ Pmj & Tm | &I, 1, 8 | |
| | 10. | ⎢ ∃y(Pyj & Ty) → Tj | ∀E, 5 | |
| | 11. | ⎢ ∃y(Pyj & Ty) | ∃I, 9 | |
| | 12. | ⎢ Tj | →E, 10, 11 | |
| | 13. | ⎣ ¬Tj | R, 3 | |

| 54. | 1. | ∀x(∀y(Oay → Oxy) → Oax) | A | (universe: people) |
|---|---|---|---|---|
| | 2. | ~~Show~~ Oaa | | |
| | 3. | ⎡ ∀y(Oay → Oay) → Oaa | ∀E, 1 | |
| | 4. | ⎢ ~~Show~~ ∀y(Oay → Oay) | | |
| | 5. | ⎢ ⎡ ~~Show~~ Oab → Oab | | |
| | 6. | ⎣ ⎣ ⎡ Oab | ACP | |
| | 7. | ⎣ Oaa | →E, 3, 4 | |

| 56. | 1. | ∀x(Fx → ∀y(Sy → Axy)) | A | (universe: people) |
|---|---|---|---|---|
| | 2. | ∀x∀y((Sx & Axy) → Cy) | A | |
| | 3. | ~~Show~~ ∀x((Fx & Sx) → Cx) | | |
| | 4. | ⎡ ~~Show~~ (Fa & Sa) → Ca | | |
| | 5. | ⎢ ⎡ Fa & Sa | ACP | |
| | 6. | ⎢ ⎢ Fa → ∀y(Sy → Aay) | ∀E, 1 | |
| | 7. | ⎢ ⎢ Fa | &E, 5 | |
| | 8. | ⎢ ⎢ ∀y(Sy → Aay) | →E, 6, 7 | |
| | 9. | ⎢ ⎢ Sa → Aaa | ∀E, 8 | |
| | 10. | ⎢ ⎢ Sa | &E, 5 | |
| | 11. | ⎢ ⎢ Aaa | →E, 9, 10 | |
| | 12. | ⎢ ⎢ ∀y((Sa & Aay) → Cy) | ∀E, 2 | |
| | 13. | ⎢ ⎢ (Sa & Aaa) → Ca | ∀E, 12 | |
| | 14. | ⎢ ⎢ Sa & Aaa | &I, 10, 11 | |
| | 15. | ⎣ ⎣ Ca | →E, 13, 14 | |

58.  1.    $\forall x \forall y(Lyx \rightarrow Lxy)$           A         (universe: people)
     2.    $\forall x(Wx \leftrightarrow \forall yLxy)$        A
     3.    $\forall x(Wx \rightarrow \exists yTyx)$            A
     4.    $\exists x \forall y \neg Tyx$                      A
     5.    Show $\exists x \exists y \neg Lxy$
     6.    ⎡ $\forall y \neg Tya$                              $\exists$E, 4
     7.    ⎢ $Wa \rightarrow \exists yTya$                     $\forall$E, 3
     8.    ⎢ $\neg \exists yTya$                               QN, 6
     9.    ⎢ $\neg Wa$                                         $\rightarrow$E*, 7, 8
     10.   ⎢ $Wa \leftrightarrow \forall yLay$                 $\forall$E, 2
     11.   ⎢ $\neg \forall yLay$                               $\leftrightarrow$E*, 10, 9
     12.   ⎢ $\exists y \neg Lay$                              QN, 11
     13.   ⎣ $\exists x \exists y \neg Lxy$                    $\exists$I, 12

60.  1.    $\forall xKax$                                      A         (universe: people)
     2.    $\forall x(Dxl \leftrightarrow Cx)$                 A
     3.    $\forall x(\neg Cx \rightarrow \neg Kxx)$           A
     4.    Show $Dal$
     5.    ⎡ $Kaa$                                             $\forall$E, 1
     6.    ⎢ $\neg Ca \rightarrow \neg Kaa$                    $\forall$E, 3
     7.    ⎢ $\neg \neg Kaa$                                   $\neg\neg$, 5
     8.    ⎢ $\neg \neg Ca$                                    $\rightarrow$E*, 6, 7
     9.    ⎢ $Dal \leftrightarrow Ca$                          $\forall$E, 2
     10.   ⎢ $Ca$                                              $\neg\neg$, 8
     11.   ⎣ $Dal$                                             $\leftrightarrow$E, 9, 10